I0820751

The Last Cavalryman

CAMPAIGNS & COMMANDERS
GREGORY J. W. URWIN, SERIES EDITOR

The Last Cavalryman

The Life of General Lucian K. Truscott, Jr.

Harvey Ferguson

University of Oklahoma Press | Norman

Library of Congress Cataloging-in-Publication Data

Ferguson, Harvey, 1945–
The last cavalryman : the life of General Lucian K. Truscott, Jr. /
Harvey Ferguson. — First edition.
pages cm. — (Campaigns & commanders ; volume 48)
Includes bibliographical references and index.
ISBN 978-0-8061-4664-5 (hardcover : alk. paper)
1. Truscott, Lucian King, 1895–1965. 2. Generals—United States—Biography.
3. United States. Army—Cavalry—Biography. 4. United States. Army—Officers—Biography. 5. World War, 1939–1945—Campaigns—Africa, North. 6. World War, 1939–1945—Campaigns—Italy. 7. United States. Central Intelligence Agency—Officials and employees—Biography. I. Title. II. Title: Life of General Lucian K. Truscott, Jr.
E745.T78F47 2015
355.0092—dc23
[B]

2014025316

The Last Cavalryman: The Life of General Lucian K. Truscott, Jr., is Volume 48 in the Campaigns and Commanders series.

The paper in this book meets the guidelines for permanence and durability of the Committee on Production Guidelines for Book Longevity of the Council on Library Resources, Inc. ∞

2 3 4 5 6 7 8 9 10

Interior layout and composition: Alcorn Publication Design

In memory of
Chief Warrant Officer 4
Robert Michael "Robbie" Johnson, 1968–2009,
160th Special Operations Aviation Regiment (Airborne),
"Night Stalkers Don't Quit," U.S. Army.

And for Margie, a gift in my life.

Truscott was one of the really tough generals. . . . [H]e could have eaten a ham like Patton for breakfast any morning and picked his teeth with the man's pearl-handled pistols. . . . Truscott spent half his time at the front—the real front—with nobody in attendance but a nervous Jeep driver and a worried aide.

—*Bill Mauldin*

Contents

Illustrations

Figures

Maps

Preface

In 1965, as a nineteen-year-old U.S. Army infantryman, I reported to Wildflecken Sub-Post in West Germany, then very near the Cold War five-kilometer zone that bordered East Germany. My new unit was the 15th Infantry Regiment, 3rd Infantry Division. I knew the division's shoulder patch—a square with blue and white diagonal stripes—as the one that Audie Murphy had worn during World War II. I had known about Murphy for some time, having read his book, *To Hell and Back,* and watched the movie of the same name. I would soon see it again thanks to the 3rd Infantry Division. Each year sergeants marched their soldiers—at that time mostly teenagers who had enlisted as well as young men in their early twenties who had been drafted—down the hill to the small theater. To a full house, the movie demonstrated once again how Murphy had become the most decorated soldier of World War II.

At the time I did not know that General Lucian K. Truscott, Jr., had once commanded the 3rd Infantry Division. In fact, I had never heard of General Truscott. Coincidentally, he passed away the same year that I arrived in West Germany. Much later I learned that following Truscott's death, the commanding general of the division—my boss too many levels up to count—had sent a telegram to his widow. It read: "The passing of the Marne Division's most illustrious commander has left us all with a great sense of personal loss. His guidance and leadership in combat established a brand of professionalism among his soldiers that remains a hallmark of his beloved 3d division to this day." Since no one shared this telegram with me, I still knew nothing about General Truscott. Only later in life was I introduced to him. That was in the late 1990s, with the resurgence in interest about World War II. Thanks to the exceptional histories and biographies by Stephen Ambrose and Carlo D'Este, my interest in that era revived. D'Este, in particular, made a point of discussing General Truscott and his contributions in the Mediterranean theater of operations.

More than thirty years later, long after my discharge from the army, I retired as chief of operations of the Seattle Police Department, having served in a wide variety of its units. For the next several years, I taught and consulted on criminal-justice issues and then traveled a good deal. After that, searching for a new challenge, I considered writing a book. Years before, the GI Bill had allowed me to complete a bachelor's in English literature and a master's in public administration, but thus far my writing had been limited to perhaps thousands of investigative reports and memos as well as several professional articles published in law-enforcement journals. Now, thinking of writing a book, I needed the right topic.

In 2001 I had learned that Susan Truscott, my wife's friend of many years, was General Truscott's granddaughter. From D'Este I had learned that Lucian Truscott had once commanded the 3rd Infantry Division. I contemplated writing the general's biography, but other activities consumed several years. Then in late 2006 I set about collecting resource materials. I learned that General Truscott was a poor boy from Oklahoma who had *not* attended West Point. He began as a cavalry officer back when members of that branch actually rode horses. Truscott had had some very interesting units under his command—the American-Canadian 1st Special Service Force, the Japanese American 442nd Regimental Combat Team, the 10th Mountain Division, and the 92nd Infantry Division, consisting primarily of African Americans—and had also founded the U.S. Army Rangers. He had fought all over Italy during World War II. That was particularly good news because my wife, Margie, and I had studied Italian in Perugia, Italy, and loved to visit that country. What also intrigued me was that Truscott had worked for the Central Intelligence Agency in its early Cold War years. As I gauged his seemingly interesting life and the absence of any biography, I could only conclude that the bright light that had shone on Eisenhower, Bradley, and Patton for so long had relegated the next tier of generals to the shadows. I had found my topic.

Only later did I learn that at that very moment, two other writers were then in the midst of drafting biographies of Truscott. It took a few days for the rain on my parade to drain off. The upside of the situation, I reasoned, suggested that the general must have been an interesting person if three people, albeit belatedly, were writing his biography. Deciding to continue my research, I felt certain that each book, like each biographer, would differ substantially from the other two and that undertaking this effort would be a worthwhile endeavor. I would just have to present Truscott's life more fully, not only as an army officer but also as a son, brother, husband, father, and friend—warts and all.

Susan Truscott was kind enough to provide me with various family papers. She also put me in touch with other members of her family, including James Truscott, the general's last surviving offspring. Subsequently, other family members graciously permitted the use of papers in their possession and shared with me their recollections of General Truscott. I was always caught off guard when they referred to him simply as "Dad" or "Grandpa."

As I began writing, Margie became my co-conspirator (so much so that I would have listed her as coauthor if she had permitted it). She served as my primary editor, no doubt depleting a couple of red pens in the process. At one point she brought me a copy of Erik Larson's book *The Devil in the White City* and said, "Here, write like this." I got the point. Over the next few years, she and I visited places where General Truscott had grown up or later served in the army. One of our early stops was the George C. Marshall Foundation Research Library in Lexington, Virginia, where Truscott's collected papers reside. Margie and I also explored the National Archives and the Library of Congress in Washington, D.C., as well as various museums in Arizona, New Mexico, Texas, Oklahoma, France, and Italy; she dubbed this process "following the Truscott Trail." Later, especially enjoying our journeys to Italy and southern France, we were thankful that the general had not fought instead on New Guinea or Guadalcanal.

Two individuals read some of my early manuscript material and encouraged me to continue. One is my good friend Janice O'Mahony; the other is also a good friend—and former boss—Norm Stamper. The Truscott family, James, Helen, Lucian IV, Susan, Mary, and Debbie, were exceedingly helpful. My editor, Greg McNamee, kept me on the right track even when I wanted to veer off on tangents. Paul B. Barron, retired U.S. Marine helicopter pilot and Vietnam veteran, now director of library and archives at the Marshall Foundation Research Library, was both friendly and helpful. Bill, Virginia, and Vicky Phillippi, along with Bill Hanrahan, were willing to share their recollections. I also wish to thank Graeme Bruce of Cambridge, United Kingdom; Jim Willinger at Wide World of Maps in Phoenix; Jeremy Frey at the University of Arizona; Theresa Roy at the National Archives; and Lia Apodaca at the Library of Congress. Finally, I am especially grateful to Charles Rankin and the other professionals at the University of Oklahoma Press who helped this book see the light of day.

Introduction

The odds were so stacked against him that the worst gambler in America would not have bet that he would one day wear the three stars of an army lieutenant general.

Lucian King Truscott, Jr., was born in Texas and grew up in hardscrabble Oklahoma. His father was a country doctor with a drug addiction who found it necessary to move his family from settlement to settlement to keep ahead of his reputation. His mother, a college graduate, filled in the educational gaps for young Lucian and his three sisters as the family moved about. Lucian was smart, but he wanted to succeed. The only way for that to happen, he concluded, was to work harder than anyone else. He was honest but on occasion bent the truth when it seemed the right thing to do; looking older than his sixteen years, he lied about his age to become a teacher in rural Oklahoma schools.

As a young boy, Truscott had dreamed of one day becoming an army officer. He might have applied to the U.S. Military Academy but likely concluded that West Point would never admit him. In truth he would have had great difficulty competing with the other young men seeking appointment, almost all of whom had impressive high-school records and perhaps some college experience. His eventual entry into the U.S. cavalry was almost accidental, spurred by the actions of the Mexican outlaw Pancho Villa, whose *bandidos* raided a small town on the American side of the border. Truscott earned a backdoor provisional commission in the army by attending a forerunner of officer-candidate school. He chose to serve in the cavalry branch, which even then had an uncertain future. Though he wanted to take part in the Great War, the army needed him for border duty. Other officers, his competitors for future promotion, went to Europe and earned medals of valor, whereas while serving in Arizona, Truscott nearly died of pneumonia. He recovered but soon faced a disciplinary review board and possible discharge for his involvement in the horsewhipping of a fellow officer.

Truscott became a standout polo player, which brought him accolades in the cavalry but not from the rest of the army. Its key decision makers of the future, Generals George Marshall, Dwight Eisenhower, Omar Bradley, and Mark Clark, served in other branches and likely regarded the cavalry as moribund. As a captain Truscott served at the 1932 Bonus Army March, in which General Douglas MacArthur unleashed infantry soldiers and cavalry troopers—bayonets and sabers—to drive the Great War veterans out of Washington, D.C.; the country saw it as a shameful day for the army. During the 1920s and 1930s, Truscott otherwise built a reputation as an outstanding instructor in prestigious army schools at Fort Riley and Fort Leavenworth, Kansas.

Early on the young officer fortunately met fellow cavalryman George S. Patton, Jr., who steered him toward the nascent armored force at the right time. Their relationship was not without tension, however; his relationship with Mark Clark, his superior during much of World War II, was worse. Truscott was also fortunate to meet Dwight D. Eisenhower, who recognized his strengths. But the Oklahoman's first meeting with General George C. Marshall, the U.S. Army's chief of staff, left the latter unimpressed. Truscott might have found himself in the "do not promote" section of Marshall's legendary little black book had Eisenhower not advocated for him.

At the onset of World War II, Truscott went to England on a special mission, which allowed him to be one of the first to gauge the immense gulf between the Americans and the British on how to conduct the war. As part of his task, he created the U.S. Army Rangers and later elevated a standard infantry division to near-ranger/commando standards. In 1944 at Anzio, Italy, he sent nearly eight hundred rangers on a high-risk mission—six came back.

To his immense credit, Truscott engineered and led the breakout from Anzio, where the Germans had immobilized Allied forces for four months. His invasion of southern France (in coordination with the Normandy invasion) was a masterpiece. The general finished the war in northern Italy, but there his oversight of one of his divisions, the 92nd Infantry Division, consisting primarily of African Americans, was not a high point of his life (nor was his romantic affair with a very famous woman). After the war he became President Eisenhower's eyes and ears within the fledgling CIA, spying on the spies so that Eisenhower would not be blindsided by bad headlines.

Though childhood had been tough, Truscott had been blessed with substantial mental capacity, which he used to develop an intellect that allowed him to be self-confident anywhere life led him. Along the way he developed and maintained a level of character that permitted him to master any situation, from being amid battle to advising the president of the United States. Even so, from the first day he pinned crossed sabers to his uniform collar until his burial at Arlington National Cemetery, he was always a cavalryman.

The Last Cavalryman

PROLOGUE

On May 30, 1945, General Lucian K. Truscott, Jr., U.S. Army, spoke at a Memorial Day ceremony held at the as yet undedicated Sicily-Rome American Cemetery and Memorial at Anzio-Nettuno, Italy. The nearly 20,000 fresh graves held the remains of soldiers who had died in Sicily, Anzio, or during the struggle for Rome; many of these men had been under Truscott's command. In attendance at the ceremony were members of Congress, various senior officers, and a multitude of other VIPs. The general, without speaking notes, walked to the microphone, acknowledged those seated before him, and turned his back. He faced the graves before him and spoke only to his fallen soldiers. In his distinctive gravelly voice, Truscott apologized that they were there and asked their forgiveness if any mistake by him had caused their deaths. He promised that he would never speak of the glorious dead because he saw no glory in having to die while still in your late teens or early twenties.[1]

History has a surprising way of connecting the dots. In 1916 Mexican bandit Pancho Villa raided Columbus, New Mexico, prompting a U.S. invasion of Mexico. In 1944 Major General Truscott and his 3rd Infantry Division were stalled on the beachhead at Anzio, Italy, resisting an all-out effort by the Germans to shove them back into the Mediterranean. The first event led by circuitous path to the second. At Anzio, one of the most debated invasions of World War II, Lieutenant General Mark Clark ordered Truscott to assume command from his superior, Major General John P. Lucas, whom Clark had just relieved. Truscott and Lucas were old friends, each having served in the horse cavalry years earlier. In a twist of history, Lucas, in 1916 a young lieutenant assigned to a temporary post at Columbus, New Mexico, came close to death when Villa attacked the town, the same raid that would initiate Truscott's military career.[2]

Before his service in the army, Truscott had been a schoolteacher. At age sixteen he had "stretched" his age to eighteen so that he could take an examination to become an educator in Oklahoma. He passed and quickly found himself teaching in the same school system where just months before he had been a student. He presumed that education would be his career. All that changed when Pancho Villa, previously known only for his banditry, became a popular leader in the Mexican Revolution.[3]

In November 1915, midway through the uprising, Villa's army suffered a stinging defeat by forces of his primary opponent, Venustiano Carranza. The pivotal battle occurred at Agua Prieta, a small village on the Mexico side of the border opposite Douglas, Arizona. As gun battles raged to the south, citizens of Douglas used binoculars to watch the happenings from the tops of railway boxcars and buildings. Even before that engagement, however, the United States and various Latin American countries had already recognized Carranza's administration as the legitimate government of Mexico. Villa, now declared an outlaw and on the run with fewer than five hundred soldiers, had little choice but to raid villages and towns for necessary supplies and horses as well as for loot to pay his men. Before long, he turned an eye north to the United States.[4]

For Americans living on the border, it was an uncertain time. Villa's raids were now occurring close to home. A concern shared by most Americans elevated to alarm in those living in the Southwest. The governor of Texas sent his own state troops to protect his portion of the border. It was not long before Washington, D.C., heard the loud demands for protection. The U.S. Army already had more than 20,000 troops in the region, where they endeavored to protect a boundary stretching 2,000 miles, most of which passed through hostile desert. The army had set up camps at the larger towns but necessarily relied on mobile patrols—departing from these posts—to discourage raids on the smaller villages. But Villa's deadly raid on Columbus demonstrated that a defensive force averaging ten soldiers per mile was not going to be enough.[5]

One border outpost established by the U.S. Cavalry was Camp Furlong, consisting of temporary barracks and stables hastily built at the edge of that New Mexico town. Assigned there was 1st Lieutenant Lucas, the twenty-six-year-old commander of the 13th Cavalry Regiment's machine-gun troop. Lucas had likely heard the buzzing rumors that Villa and his men might be in the area, knowing that just two months earlier, the Villistas had killed and mutilated the bodies of sixteen Americans riding a train near Santa

Isabel, Mexico. The *El Paso Times* had recently suggested that the next raid was likely to come at Palomas, Mexico, six miles south of the border. Villa, however, saw Columbus as an even better target. His men wanted money and other booty, and he was angry that U.S. president Woodrow Wilson had formally recognized and supported Carranza.[6]

Situated just three miles north of Mexico, Columbus was little more than a dusty border town of 350 residents; its population had doubled when the U.S. Army dispatched a similar number of cavalry troopers there. The town consisted of a number of rustic one- and two-story structures, including the Border Gate, the two-story railway depot, a couple dozen small adobe houses, and various commercial buildings, including a bank, the Commercial Hotel, Sam Ravel's General Merchandise Store, Frost Furniture and Hardware, Miller's Drug Store, a livery-and-feed store, and a two-story school building. It was the merchandise store and the availability of horses that enticed Villa. He planned his attack for the early morning darkness of March 9, 1916.[7]

Lieutenant Lucas, sleeping in the small adobe hut that served as his quarters, awoke about 4:30 A.M. to the sounds of galloping horses. Immediately suspecting a raid by Villa, he raced out and hurriedly drafted two troopers to accompany him to the arms room to retrieve the machine guns. On the way one of Villa's men confronted them and fired a rifle at the officer. That bullet missed, but Lucas's revolver shot blasted at close range struck its target, killing the man. The dusty, smoky battle raged in the early morning light for two hours. Lucas and his men, now armed with Benet-Mercie machine guns, coordinated with Lieutenant James C. Castleman, officer of the day, and his men to defend the town and camp. The other officers of the 13th Cavalry quartered in the town could see that the Mexican marauders were between them and the camp. Thus, Lucas and Castleman, later joined by Captain Hamilton Bowie, were the only officers in the fight. Villa's men, misinformed by their scout that only about thirty cavalrymen were at the camp, found themselves in a shootout with more than ten times that number. About 6:30 A.M. the Villistas remounted and galloped south, leaving behind the bodies of eight troopers and nine civilians. The Mexicans had stolen a number of horses, looted and burned the store, and broken into several other businesses. As the dust settled, a political storm began to gather.[8]

General John J. Pershing, Pancho Villa, Alvaro Obregón, and others at the International Bridge between El Paso, Texas, and Juàrez, Mexico, in 1914, two years before Villa's raid on Columbus, New Mexico. Courtesy of the Aultman Collection, El Paso Public Library, El Paso, Texas (image inadvertently reversed).

As the desert sun began its rise, Major Frank Tomkins and thirty-two cavalry troopers were already pursuing the Villistas illegally into Mexico. Other soldiers and townspeople gathered in the morning glow to see what remained of the town. In the sandy streets now moistened with blood, they found a number of dead Villistas. Soldiers hauled the bodies to the desert and burned them.

Following the raid, disbelief and anger raged across the United States. Pressured to act, President Wilson ordered the Punitive Expedition into Mexico. General John J. "Black Jack" Pershing dispatched three brigades of what would become a force of nearly 7,000 cavalry and infantry personnel. For a month, Pershing personally led his men more than five hundred miles into Mexico, but the bandits had disappeared. Villa and his men, natives in their own harsh, desert climate, evaded capture by the Americans. Other Mexicans had an eye out for Villa, however, and in 1923 his political enemies assassinated him.[9]

Villa's raid not only spurred the Punitive Expedition but also emphasized the need for greater border security. Since the United States would likely dispatch a large military force to participate in the war in Europe, a crisis was at hand. The pathetically small U.S. Army had not done well in protecting the border; most certainly it was in no condition to undertake a major role in France. Unable to ignore this reality, Congress passed the National Defense Act of 1916.

With Villa still on the run but unlikely to be killed or captured, President Wilson withdrew the Punitive Expedition from Mexico so that General Pershing could lead the American Expeditionary Force in Europe. Nevertheless, the army still needed to guard the Mexican border. Since the cavalry was an essential part of that effort, Congress authorized ten new cavalry regiments. Another portion of the National Defense Act addressed the need for more officers. Even with the usual number of Reserve Officer Training Corps graduates from colleges and universities, an accelerated officer-training curriculum at West Point, the activation of National Guard and Army Reserve officers, and the commissioning of capable enlisted soldiers, there would still be too few officers to lead an expanded army. Senior commanders recognized the need for a faster way of commissioning officers. In response, the National Defense Act authorized the Officer Training Camp program. A forerunner of officer-candidate school, it recruited bright young men who could master competitive examinations and undergo rigorous training. If they succeeded, the army would grant them "provisional" reserve commissions as second lieutenants. If they proved their leadership abilities over the course of two years, their provisional commissions would become regular commissions. That was good news for a schoolteacher in Oklahoma.[10]

CHAPTER 1

On the Border with the Horse Cavalry

For Lucian Truscott, a twenty-two-year-old unmarried schoolteacher in rural Oklahoma, a few years in the cavalry, the branch he preferred, sounded like quite an adventure in 1917. He had once wanted to attend West Point, but without hesitation he submitted an application for the recently advertised Officer Training Camp, sending along several letters of reference. The president of Oklahoma State Bank wrote that Truscott was "one of the most honorable and cleanest men in our city." The superintendent of the McIntosh County Schools described him as "a young man of honor, integrity, and capability" and certified that for two years he had served as principal of Mountain View School. The local judge added that the young man was "well educated and one of the most successful teachers in McIntosh County, Oklahoma." Truscott also submitted a notarized affidavit certifying that he had graduated in 1911 from Stella High School in Newella, Oklahoma, explaining that a fire in his father's house in December 1916 had destroyed his diploma. He added that he had subsequently completed work in "training classes" that amounted to the equivalent of a year of college.[1]

Army candidate-selection officers interviewed Truscott on April 29, 1917, in Muskogee, noting that he was five feet, nine inches tall and weighed 170 pounds. Once the candidate had passed various other examinations, a captain of the 3rd Cavalry instructed him to report for training at Leon Springs, Texas; later the army changed his training assignment to Fort Logan H. Roots, Arkansas. Truscott successfully completed his instruction with the 1st Training Company, 12th Provisional Regiment. Thereafter, the training captain concluded that the Oklahoman was "excellent material for an army officer."[2]

On August 15 the army commissioned Truscott as a second lieutenant in the Officer Reserve Corps. When asked his top three

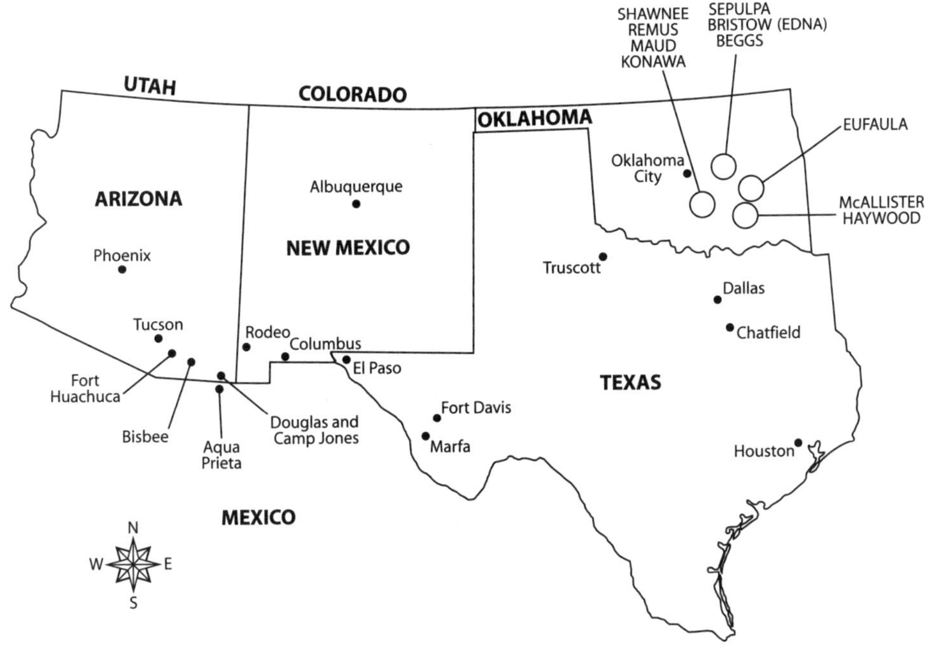

The American Southwest and areas affecting Lucian Truscott. Map by Megan Postell.

choices for branch assignment, the new officer listed cavalry, infantry, and artillery in that order. On August 29, proudly wearing his new lieutenant bars and cavalry branch crossed-sabers insignia, he reported to Camp Harry J. Jones near Douglas, Arizona. Previously called Camp Douglas, the post now had a new name in honor of a young soldier killed while guarding the border during the fighting at Agua Prieta.[3]

In 1917 the United States joined its European allies, which had been fighting the Great War in Europe since 1914. Even so, the border with Mexico was still vulnerable and required continual protection. It was for this reason that Lieutenant Truscott found himself standing in the baking desert at Camp Jones. His immaculate uniform, consisting of tunic with standup collar, riding breeches, and tall boots, all inspection-ready, announced that he was new to the dusty post. He was an imposing young man. His son, Lucian K. Truscott III, later said of his father: "He was a handsome man, attractive to women, but not big, being perhaps five feet-ten and about one hundred and eighty pounds when he was in good physical condition. But he *seemed* like a big man. He had large eyes, a prominent nose, large but not protruding ears, broad shoulders, a big chest, and huge hands, with big, square fingers."[4]

Lieutenant Truscott also had a raspy voice, the result of having accidentally swallowed carbolic acid as a toddler. The burning caused permanent damage to his throat tissue, leaving him with a distinctive voice for the rest of his life. Another son, James J. Truscott, later recalled that his father's voice was one of medium tone, not high or deep and fairly quiet but quite capable of considerable volume when required. Will Lang, a journalist for *Life* magazine, later wrote an article about General Truscott, describing his "rock crusher voice that gives his orders an awesome ferocity."[5]

For the newly arrived officer, Douglas, Arizona, would take some getting used to. For one thing it smelled bad. The tall smokestacks of two copper-mine smelters visible for miles accounted for one—an intense, sulfuric stench. The other odor, just as pungent, was that produced by more than 20,000 horses and mules, the vast majority being prepared for duty in France. The remaining horses at Camp Jones were the regular mounts for the two local regiments. The desert winds always send up more than enough dust, but the three-hour daily drill of 2,000 cavalry troopers and their mounts kicked up much more.[6]

Situated just east of Douglas, Camp Jones looked to the casual observer more like a huge bivouac than an established camp. A few years later, soldiers stationed there would sleep in one-story barracks, but for now the men made do with hundreds of conical squad tents stretched on wooden frames. Sharing the area with the 1st and 17th Cavalry Regiments were the 10th and 11th Field Artillery Regiments. The newly created 17th Cavalry, to which Truscott belonged, was an upstart when compared with the 1st Cavalry. Originally known as the 1st Regiment of Dragoons, it had been the U.S. Army's first permanent mounted unit, rich with a history dating back to the 1832 Black Hawk War.[7]

The 17th Cavalry's portion of the camp consisted of fifteen troop streets, each with about twenty tents, as well as stables and tack rooms. The stables were long and open, each accommodating about a hundred horses facing a center aisle. Along with the many tents for the soldiers, there stood a small number of buildings made of wood or adobe. The main building served as regimental headquarters. Others nearby served as the living quarters of the senior officers. The junior officers, including Truscott and his fellow recently commissioned second lieutenants, made do with their own adobe huts or small tents.

In the horse cavalry, Truscott later recalled, paperwork was an afterthought. The files of the entire regiment, including personnel, pay, property, correspondence, manuals, and regulations, managed to fit inside one small portable field desk, although many records likely made their way to higher headquarters. Clerks made duplicate copies of only the most important paperwork, and as Truscott remembered, "great stress was placed on form in military correspondence and communications, and the use of the third person and the passive voice was habitual."[8]

Of importance to the new lieutenants were the noncommissioned officers (NCOs), most of whom were sergeants with some years of service. The freshly commissioned officers were smart enough to know that they knew little about commanding troopers or conducting mounted drill. The sergeants, of course, had that knowledge and experience but knew that the lieutenants outranked them. More often than not, a new officer and an experienced NCO formed a relationship that worked to the advantage of each. These often resulted in a friendship that lasted many years, long after each had moved on to other assignments. Few senior officers could not recall with fondness the sergeant who had guided him through the early years, and more than a few sergeants could casually drop the name of a successful senior officer that they had mentored years before.

Most of the second lieutenants at Camp Douglas that summer had grown up in the Southwest and were experienced horsemen. Of course, becoming a cavalry officer meant becoming an expert rider. Lieutenant Edward N. "Pink" Hardy, West Point class of 1911, personally handled the task of enhancing the new arrivals' riding skills. One of the toughest officers around, Lieutenant Hardy took his assignment seriously. As Truscott later remembered: "He was a man of rugged appearance, even more rugged character, and a fine horseman. Hour after hour of his suppling exercises at a slow trot without stirrups certainly went a long way toward developing our cavalry seats!"[9]

The saddle on which Truscott and his fellow lieutenants rode during training was the recently adopted Riding Equipment Model 1912.

Shortly after completing their training, they learned that the cavalry was abandoning this newer item to return to the old McClellan saddle, which was an 1858 modification of a Prussian saddle. For some cavalrymen, the Model 1912 had brought substantial improvement, but it never gained lasting acceptance among the many accustomed to the old McClellan. To Truscott, this experience was emblematic of another quality of the U.S. Cavalry: "We young officers drew one important lesson which would stand us in good stead. There is always resistance to change in established habits, to traditional customs, and to familiar equipment. And this resistance is always extremely difficult to overcome." For him this would prove true not only in the cavalry but also for the entire army, not just in 1917 but throughout his career. The McClellan saddle, in fact, remained in use until the demise of the horse cavalry in 1942.[10]

Next in line to take a turn at molding the new officers was the regimental commander, Lieutenant Colonel James J. Hornbrook, West Point class of 1890, having graduated five years before Truscott was born. The Oklahoman's description of his superior is illustrative: "A ruthless disciplinarian, he was strict, abrupt, and treated words as though they were drops of water in a canteen in the desert." Every day at reveille, Colonel Hornbrook rode the length of the regimental street, somehow making sure that each trooper felt certain that he could see him clearly and would spot any defect. Next the colonel rode by the troop kitchens and mess halls, ensuring that everything there was in order. "Woe betide the troop commander at Officers' Call whose area at Reveille was in an improper state of police or whose [troop kitchen] incinerator fires were not blazing away with the swill pans bubbling," Truscott remembered. When it came to the new lieutenants, not much escaped the eyes—or ears—of Hornbrook. On one occasion, overhearing Truscott address his troopers by saying, "Now, boys," the colonel yelled to the lieutenant at the top of his voice: "Mister Truscott, they're men, goddammit! They're men! Every one of them! They're men! Men! MEN!"[11]

Truscott later recalled one of his early days at the camp. He and the other novice officers reported to regimental headquarters straightaway as directed. The colonel's clerk called in each lieutenant while the others waited outside. When his turn came, Truscott entered the office, doing his best to appear calm. Colonel Hornbrook, with no greeting, informed the young man that this coming Sunday all officers, including Hornbrook, would participate in a "Russian ride."

It would include twenty-four jumps over various obstacles, of which Truscott was responsible for building two. The colonel showed him a piece of paper that indicated the locations for the two jumps and some basic measurements as to their design. One was to be a "sandbag" jump three feet high and sixty feet wide, and the other a "brush" jump three and a half feet high and sixty feet wide. Hornbrook asked the lieutenant if he understood. Suspecting it best to answer affirmatively, Truscott did so. The colonel dismissed him and called in the next lieutenant. Puzzlement turned to nervous uncertainty. Truscott had never heard of a Russian ride, had never actually seen either of the jumps specified, and had little information on how to build them. Afterward the lieutenants compared notes and realized that each had the same vague instructions to build two jumps. Some were to be sandbag or brush design, others were to be "ditch," "post-and-rail," or "chicken-coop" jumps. Of greatest concern was that only three days remained before the excursion.

To the immense relief of the young lieutenants, each troop's first sergeant offered advice about materials and possible ways of constructing the jumps. By Sunday, each obstacle was ready, the actual labor provided by troopers. The colonel arrived and led the way, followed by every officer of the regiment. All the riders negotiated the twenty-four jumps without mishap. Since no one complained, the lieutenants assumed that they had successfully completed their assignments. Eventually, some of them were brash enough to suspect that the colonel, sergeant major, and first sergeants had been in cahoots on the project. Along the way, the lieutenants learned how to analyze and solve a problem that required cooperation and oversight as well as, not incidentally, what an assist a first sergeant can be.[12]

Colonel Hornbrook saw to it that his new officers learned everything a cavalry leader needed to know. One class of instruction, seemingly unimportant at the time, would prove useful to Truscott a quarter of a century later in the rugged and nearly impassable mountains of Sicily and mainland Italy, where not even Jeeps or tanks could negotiate the steep and precarious trails.

The class was entitled "Pack Transportation" and taught the officers how to pack a mule. A mule train, the lieutenants learned, consisted of men and animals. The men were the muleteers, sometimes called "muleskinners," and included the pack master, a blacksmith, a stevedore, ten packers, and a cook. The mules consisted of the lead mule, known as the bell mare, fourteen mules for riding, and fifty pack mules to carry the cargo. Each pack mule of the sixty-five-mule train carried more than two hundred pounds on its back and sides, its cargo securely lashed onto a special packsaddle called an "aparejo." Two packers worked together to load a mule, using a sling rope, a diamond hitch, and just five words: "cinch, rope, go, tie, and rope." The bell mare knew what to do, and most of the pack mules were "bell sharp" animals that lined up for packing when they heard the sound of the bell on the mare's neck. Yet some of the newer, untrained mules required close watch. To spot these rookie beasts more easily, the muleteers roached their manes and clipped their tails, leaving only tassels. If not watched, the "shavetail" mules, like the shavetail second lieutenants, were bound to find trouble.[13]

Within a few weeks, Truscott understood the routine and rhythm of the camp. Drills and ceremonies filled the days. Army leadership believed that soldiers had to be ready to fight even if not required to do so, and of course, there was always the possibility of a border flare-up. These duties kept the men prepared for war and, not incidentally, left little time to get into mischief. Commanders believed in something else as well. In those days music was important. A lone bugler—then called a trumpeter—regulated the daily schedule of the entire camp, from the regimental commander to the newest private. Music was also a way to maintain morale, and chorus masters moved from post to post teaching soldiers new songs. "Over There" became a favorite.[14]

In the years before the Great War—its name before it became necessary to count world wars—the essential tactics of the cavalry and the rest of the army still relied on lessons from the Civil War. The army refined its tactics only slightly through their use in the Indian Wars (as the cavalry called them), the Spanish-American War, the Philippine Insurrection, and most recently the Punitive Expedition. Except for those officers and soldiers serving in Europe, exposure to modern tactics remained limited. Stateside officers read about airplanes, tanks, and trench warfare but made no significant changes in their duties as a result. Soldiering at home looked the same as it had for the past fifty years. West Point cadets still studied Gettysburg, not Verdun. There was nothing new or different in the curriculum, nor would there be until some Great War veteran commanders returned home and undertook the arduous and unpopular task of forcing needed changes. Many officers of the cavalry, perhaps the most conservative branch, resisted any real change. For others, including future generals George Patton and Truscott, it was not whether change would come but how best to manage it.[15]

For Truscott and his fellow junior officers and NCOs of the 17th Cavalry, an unanticipated result of the Great War became apparent. Preparing the army for war meant increasing its size significantly and training its many new recruits. Thus in the 17th Cavalry and elsewhere, the army promoted most of the experienced officers to higher rank and commissioned many experienced NCOs. These men moved to other posts to train and lead various units bound for France. Consequently, the previously novice lieutenants found themselves regarded as the experienced cadre and necessarily assumed greater leadership duties sooner than expected.[16]

Armistice Day, November 11, 1918, finally arrived, and not too soon for the vast majority of Americans. For the young, untried, and still-naïve lieutenants looking to make an early mark in the service, however, this meant that service in France was no longer a possibility. Even those officers who had witnessed the horror of trench warfare did not necessarily see Armistice Day as a joyful occasion. The army had given many of them temporary promotions to higher ranks and had commissioned many from enlisted ranks. Both groups would likely lose their temporary promotions and revert to their permanent ranks. It was fortunate for Truscott that on December 10, 1918, his temporary wartime rank of first lieutenant became permanent.[17]

A few months later unexpected news arrived for the 17th Cavalry. The army was transferring the regiment, at least temporarily, to the Territory of Hawaii. Orders stated that it would report to San Francisco to board the transport ship USS *Sherman* on April 5, 1919. The regiment was to bring its mounts, weapons, ammunition, and all varieties of supplies for duty in the islands. Getting all this done would be quite an undertaking, but for the adventurous Lieutenant Truscott, it was an opportunity eagerly anticipated.[18]

CHAPTER 2

The Early Truscotts

At the age of twenty, James Joseph Truscott, son of a Cornish immigrant, met Eliza Jane Kirkland, who was then just seventeen. They were married on October 21, 1852, with Pastor Justus Bulkey officiating. The young couple wasted no time in starting a family. Thomas Isaac was born on August 12, 1853, followed by a succession of siblings. By 1860 James Truscott was working as a farmer in Greene County, Illinois.

In October 1861 the couple's last child was born. They named this son Lucian King Truscott in honor of a close family friend. The original Lucian King, described in family papers as an older neighbor, later served as administrator for the estate of the mother of James Truscott. Unfortunately, the close friendship between Truscott and King faded when they disagreed on the very thing that was about to sever the country. King supported the Union, but Truscott did not. The latter looked south for a new home and chose Texas. Coincidentally, Eliza Jane contracted a serious illness, which was perhaps a second reason for the family's intended move to a drier climate.

When the trek began, little Lucian was just three years old. Family legend holds that at this age his older brother Thomas taught him to read. Thomas, in fact, would go on to become a well-known teacher in later life, and Lucian, despite formidable troubles, remained an avid reader throughout his life, passing this trait on to his own children.

By 1864, as the Confederacy was falling to its knees, the Truscott family rolled and bumped its way southwest by covered wagon. In Arkansas a doctor diagnosed Eliza's illness as tuberculosis. For several years the family remained in Arkansas, where James worked as a teacher. He moved his family on in the early 1870s to Thorpe Springs, Texas, where Eliza passed away. James went on to serve as a lawyer and later the first judge of Knox County, Texas, and still later as mayor of Maud, Oklahoma Territory. The citizens of Truscott, Texas, named the town in his honor.

As soon as he was old enough, Lucian became a Texas cowboy. In 1876 at age fifteen, he helped drive a herd of cattle to Oklahoma. Census records for 1880 report him living in Jack County, Texas, and working as a hired ranch hand for Hillory Bedford, who with his brothers Benjamin and Edward raised livestock. Lucian did not intend to be a cowboy all his life, however, saving his money and dreaming of becoming a doctor. He was an avid reader and always carried books in his saddlebags, reading whenever he could. In a testament to his ability and determination, he applied to and then attended the Missouri Medical College in Saint Louis. In 1891 at thirty years of age, he graduated with high standing. That same year he married Maria Temple Tully, who like him had been born in Carlinville, Illinois, about halfway between Springfield and Saint Louis. She made a fine wife for the young Texas doctor.

The small community of Chatfield, southeast of Dallas, welcomed the Truscotts. There the young couple found a landscape of rolling hills with small ponds in the dales. Oaks and other trees were plentiful, surrounded by scrub undergrowth. The soil was tan and rocky, but enough creeks existed to make it a worthwhile place to graze cattle or raise crops. By January 1893 the Truscotts had their first child, Loretta Estelle Truscott, whose nickname became "Sunny." Two years later, on January 9, 1895, her own birthday, Maria gave birth to a son. They named the infant Lucian King Truscott, Jr., but he acquired the family nickname of "Bud." Another child, Patsy Bryan Truscott, was born in 1896.

By 1900, having served as a country doctor in Chatfield for almost a decade and perhaps in search of a better practice, Truscott moved his family to Maud, Oklahoma Territory, southeast of Oklahoma City. He likely knew of several land rushes that had occurred in the territory during the early 1890s, when land previously granted to American Indians became available to new settlers. Dr. Truscott knew that the recent arrivals would all need medical care. His two brothers, Thomas and George, arrived in Maud at about the same time.[1]

Not long after the family had settled in Maud, Dr. Truscott moved them to nearby Remus. There he practiced medicine and, inexplicably, began a pattern of moving his family to a different small town or settlement every few years.

In the small community of Remus, young Lucian, Jr., began school. His younger sister, Patsy, who later wrote a memoir of her youthful years, wrote that he attended "a one room school where the first four grades were taught at the rear of the room, while the four higher grades were taught at the front at the same time. Mrs. Truscott was the primary teacher, and Mr. S. F. Bailey, later county judge of Pottawatomi County, was the principal." It was during these years that the family began a descent. As Patsy later recalled, her father "dabbled in race horses, and farms, disastrously at Remus, so in the fall of 1903 the family moved [back] to Maud." Many more moves were in store for the family, and more than a little hardship.[2]

Much of the early life of Lucian, Jr., is unknown, but much can be inferred from his sister's memoir. "One night when I was almost eight," she recalled, "my brother and I were sent away from the little brown house for the night. When we returned from the neighbor's next morning we had a little sister whose whole fist was 'no bigger than my thumb' as an older cousin told all over town." Dixie Ozema, the last child born to Dr. and Mrs. Truscott, arrived in 1904.[3]

The family soon moved again, settling in the small town of Stella. "I was unhappy in Stella," Patsy confided. "Dad had been drinking and using drugs since I was seven, that I knew about. . . . Never in my life did anyone mention my father's fault to me. Nor did any of the family ever admit it outside family circles. But at Stella I became conscious of it as never before."[4]

Dr. Truscott's "fault," aside from an affinity for alcohol and gambling, was his growing dependence on laudanum, an opium-based substance widely prescribed and used in the early 1900s. It was the key ingredient in many patent medicines of the time and did wonders for a variety of illnesses—its users certainly thought so and always came back for more. Despite the damage the doctor's drug habit was doing to his family, he endeavored to be a loving husband and father. Both he and Maria attempted to instill good values and habits in their offspring. "We were fortunate children," concluded Patsy, "some of those fortunate few who are exposed to the active and literate minds of their elders, and acquire learning where other children must study for it in a more adult life."[5]

Dr. Truscott, always a reader, ensured that his children had books worth reading. "James Fennimore Cooper, Scott, Carlyle, the [Luise] Mühlbach historical novels, Poe and a host of others were remembered. . . . Dad read everything, and discussed things freely with us," wrote Patsy.[6]

Family finances were always a problem and necessitated that the children help where they could. "I was not too young to go to the cotton patch and chop and pick cotton to help eke out the slender finances of the family," Patsy recalled. "Loretta Estelle stayed at home and did all the house work for us, while mother, Lucian Jr., and I worked in our neighbor's field."[7]

In 1908 at age thirteen, Lucian, Jr., finished grade school and started high school at Stella. By the standards of the day, the Truscotts were poor, but they regarded themselves as somehow different from their neighbors. They had no more money than others, but they came from different backgrounds, especially Maria. "Mama must have felt as I did," Patsy noted, "that people we lived among today must be tolerated; and forgotten tomorrow. She could no more have been one with her neighbors than a butterfly could dig a well. College educated and city bred, she never lost anything of either."[8]

In 1911 at the youthful age of sixteen, Lucian, Jr., quit being a student in rural schools and became a teacher in one of them. Oklahoma had achieved statehood only four years earlier. As a new state with few universities yet founded, those who wished to become teachers often gained their education and teaching credentials through normal schools, which later became known as teachers' colleges. New teachers were required to be at least eighteen years old. With a good test score from a normal school and too little inquiry into his age, Lucian, Jr., earned a certificate, joining his mother in the teaching profession.[9]

Continuing rumors about Dr. Truscott's drug habit proved to be a problem for his wife. One year she and Lucian, Jr., were each assigned schools in which to teach. Instead of an assignment to her previous post in Stella, as she desired, her new assignment was for another school six miles south of the town. Patsy noted that Bill Watson, who was in charge of assigning teachers to various schools, "decided that she shouldn't be so 'hoity toity' since she didn't have anything to be proud of, least of all, her husband."[10]

From November through May, while Maria and Lucian, Jr., taught school at a distant location, Dr. Truscott and Patsy lived alone in Edna. "His practice was very good, and he was, as usual in a new place, on his good behavior," she later wrote. "That was his nature, and perhaps one reason we all stood by him so loyally was that he was neither cross nor mean to his family, regardless of how he neglected them otherwise. . . . Regardless of the mean surroundings, I was completely happy at Edna."[11]

After Maria and Lucian, Jr., finished their school term, they and young Dixie rejoined Dr. Truscott and Patsy. Patsy remembered that summer as one of the best. The family "spent an idyllic summer swimming, fishing, and frog hunting. I ate more frog legs that summer than I've ever seen since."[12]

During the fall term of 1913, Maria and Lucian, Jr., reported to schools in Creek County, northeast of Oklahoma City. At the end of the school term, Dr. Truscott moved his family to Eufaula. It was different from the other communities that he had selected. The land was more open and flat, good for ranching and, in years to come, oil drilling. The heart of the town was the intersection of Main Street and Selmon Road, where multistory buildings lead off in four directions. For the Truscott children, it must have been exciting. One can picture them standing at the town center, looking up at the tall buildings, carefully crossing the streets, keeping an alert eye for the increasing number of horn-tooting motorcars overtaking horse-drawn wagons.[13]

Patsy remembered, "Lucian Jr. was instrumental in construction of the First Christian church, Eufaula, and introduced the idea of leaving the church doors open to the public throughout the week, because the church belonged to the people. . . . He was just a normal healthy specimen of American youth, only different in that he did not drink, smoke, nor swear . . . [and] hadn't had much time for play."[14]

In 1914 another move was in the offing, but Lucian, Jr., declined to go; instead, he would continue teaching in Eufaula. By 1917 he was twenty-two and had been teaching for six years. How he heard about a new army officer-commissioning program is unclear. Records reflect that he had entered the army from Eufaula, Oklahoma, and was already undergoing officer training at Fort Roots, Arkansas, just north of Little Rock, when he first registered in compliance with the military draft. On October 26, 1917, when Lucian Truscott, Jr., graduated from officer training, his permanent rank was second lieutenant, but he pinned on the silver bars of a first lieutenant, his temporary rank. Promotions come fast during wartime, and such was the case for Truscott. That was the good news. The not-so-good news was that his career was most probably already limited. His commission had come through a side door just recently opened, and his chosen branch, the cavalry, would soon become history. His future was anything but certain.[15]

Patsy remained in Oklahoma, caring for her father as her mother continued to teach in sometimes-distant schools. She later wrote:

> So many times I had to hunt him up, to find him sitting in his office or the back of some drug store, soddenly drunk or stupidly drugged. Someone would call and tell me that Dad's horse was loose with the saddle on across town. And I would hunt the horse, and then hunt Dad. That was a horrible summer. It was such a horror to me that one time when he came in stupid, and laid down on a pallet in the back hall way, with a bottle of laudanum beside him, I sat there for hours, when he tried to reach the bottle, and argued with myself about giving it to him and making him drink all of it so to put an end to Mama's worries and mine. It would have been so much better for all of us if I had done it. But I didn't.[16]

CHAPTER 3

HAWAIIAN HOLIDAY

On April 5, 1919, Lieutenant Truscott and more than 1,000 troopers and officers of the 17th Cavalry boarded the *Sherman* bound for the Territory of Hawaii. Traveling with them were a number of military dependents, one of whom was Sarah Nicholas Randolph, who had just recently changed her name to Mrs. Lucian K. Truscott, Jr.[1]

The couple's early courtship managed to involve both pneumonia and army discipline. In the first two decades of the twentieth century, pneumonia ranked high in cause of death among Americans. Army medics at Camp Jones, suspecting that an ailing Lieutenant Truscott had the disease, rushed him to the camp hospital. On June 23, 1918, Medical Corps major A. G. Wilde sent a telegram to the young man's mother in Oklahoma, stating: "Condition of Lieutenant Truscott serious. Advise coming." She replied by telegram: "Reach Douglas 10:50 Tuesday night. Wire condition Lieut Truscott here at once." The next day Major Wilde telegrammed again, this time writing: "Attending surgeon reports Lieut Truscott improved this morning. Outlook for recovery good." He would remain hospitalized until July 17.[2]

Truscott already knew one of the other physicians at the hospital, for he had been dating the daughter of army doctor William Mann Randolph for some time. When the lieutenant was well, the doctor invited him home for dinner. Sarah Randolph had previously attended college in Georgia, but in recent months she had come to live with her parents in Arizona; her grandmother was visiting the family for a while. Truscott arrived at the designated time and, after the usual before-dinner pleasantries, sat with the others at the dining table. While the doctor told amusing stories and his wife and daughter shuttled servings between the kitchen and the dinner table, his mother-in-law noticed something in particular: throughout dinner, the young lieutenant never once took his eyes off Sarah.[3]

Truscott's early courting of Sarah came close to ending his career. A troubling incident took place near Camp Jones involving both Truscott and Dr. Randolph. When Colonel George H. Morgan, Truscott's regimental commander, heard about this, he called for a board of officers to investigate allegations of misconduct by the lieutenant. If the board ruled against Truscott, he would almost certainly lose his provisional commission and probably return to Oklahoma, where, perhaps, he could reclaim his old teaching job.

At the time of the alleged misconduct, March 1918, Truscott and Miss Randolph were dating. One of her sisters was visiting the family, and Sarah introduced her to Captain Robert McCullough, who was both Truscott's superior and a friend. Sometime later the foursome attended a dance held at the Douglas Country Club. During the evening, a lieutenant named Groff somehow insulted Sarah's sister. Both Truscott and McCullough were offended, but the latter demanded "satisfaction" in the matter. Groff reluctantly agreed to meet the captain the next day to discuss the affair. Early the next morning McCullough stopped at Truscott's office and said, "I want you to come with me." He then told his friend that Dr. Randolph was waiting outside in his car. McCullough added, "We are going to get Lieutenant Groff and take him out." When the three men met Groff, the captain took off his coat and demanded that Groff fight. The lieutenant declined, citing that he was recovering from a broken arm. Dr. Randolph, a Virginian of the old school, inserted himself into the conversation and said, "Well, if you don't fight, I'm going to have to horsewhip you." He still refused, whereupon McCullough took the horsewhip from the doctor and gave Groff a lashing.[4]

Soon after Colonel Morgan got wind of the incident, he heard that a general had reportedly "squared off" the whole thing. But this only let Captain McCullough and Dr. Randolph off the hook. Morgan decided to initiate his own action against Truscott. Aside from the horsewhipping incident, the colonel knew of two other instances of alleged poor performance by the lieutenant. He contacted higher headquarters and requested an investigation of Truscott's overall performance, citing as cause, "weak character, no initiative, . . . [and] not a good platoon leader."

Major General W. A. Holbrook, commander of the Southern Department, with headquarters at Fort Sam Houston, Texas, ordered that a board of three lieutenant colonels and two majors convene at Camp Jones to investigate the situation. Lieutenant Colonel J. J.

Boniface, 308th Cavalry, chaired the proceedings, which began on June 12, 1918. An assigned lawyer, Captain J. A. Weeks, represented Truscott. The first witness called was Colonel Morgan. His first complaint was that the lieutenant had failed to bring charges against a trooper found off his guard post. His second complaint was that Truscott had failed to supervise the pickup and delivery of certain government property, which had resulted in some items becoming lost. He also related what he knew of the whipping episode. Morgan's overall conclusion was that Truscott had "a weak character, he had no initiative . . . , he never accomplished anything."

The next witness, Major J. E. Lewis, told the board that Colonel Morgan had been very displeased when he had not been able to locate Truscott in camp and added his own opinion that the lieutenant seemed to be "rather profane." Captain Edwin Hardy, who as a lieutenant had taught Truscott horsemanship, took the stand and described the young officer as "a man with a good deal of vim, a good deal of character . . . , but I was left with the impression that he . . . was with Captain McCullough in spirit in the action he took against Lieutenant Groff and gave him moral support." Another witness, Captain Donald Strogh, supported this, saying, "I believe he was an accessory to the fact."

McCullough then took the stand and testified that he thought Truscott had "excellent character" and was the best troop commander in the regiment. He added: "I went up to him and said, I want you to come along with me. . . . I said that, not exactly as his captain, but I did it because he was with me the night before. . . . I just told him to come with me; I explained right afterwards, as he came, what was going to happen."

Captain Weeks brought forth two witnesses on Truscott's behalf. Captain Phillip Sherwood said he had taken notice of the Oklahoman early on because Truscott had finished first in Officer Training Camp. He added that he thought he was "rather literary . . . , does a good deal of studying . . . , and rides very well." First Lieutenant Henry White testified that he had attended officer training with Truscott, who "made a hundred in nearly every examination except one or two," adding, "I don't know a solitary thing against his character; I never heard anyone say anything against him."

Wecks then called Truscott to the stand. The young officer first addressed not having disciplined the trooper who had left his guard post, explaining that he had concluded that Colonel Morgan intended to file such charges himself. As for the lost supplies, Truscott said that his duty had been to unload the material from train to trucks in Globe, Arizona, and another lieutenant was responsible for unloading the supplies at Camp Jones. As for the horsewhipping incident, he admitted that he had been with Captain McCullough when the insult occurred, and that the next morning McCullough had come to him, saying, "I want you to come with me." Truscott told the board that he had heard Dr. Randolph say, "Well, if you don't fight I am going to have to horsewhip you, and you can take your choice." He finished his testimony by declaring, "Lieutenant Groff chose the whipping and he got it." Truscott denied anything more than being present. Groff did not appear before the board, nor was his full name listed in the court documents, suggesting that he may have wanted the matter dropped. Nor was the general who had informally handled the matter in regards to McCullough and Randolph called to testify.[5]

The board considered the situation and reached its conclusion. Their report stated, "The Board finds that First Lieutenant Lucian K. Truscott, 17th Cavalry, has the capacity, qualifications, character, and efficiency to continue in his present position." Even better for Truscott, on July 18, 1918, Colonel George Dunn, judge advocate, sent a letter to General Holbrook, stating, "The evidence scarcely disclosed sufficient cause for his having been brought before the board." Major General Frank McIntyre, executive assistant to the army's chief of staff, signed the board's recommendation with the comment, "Approved: Retain in the service."[6]

Sarah Randolph had been born in Charlottesville, Virginia in 1896, a year after her future husband was born. She was a fourth-generation descendant of President Thomas Jefferson and Martha Wayles Skelton. Another Jefferson descendant had at one time married Thomas Mann Randolph and thus forever linked two famous Virginia families.[7]

Generations of Randolphs followed before William Mann Randolph, born in 1869, married his cousin Mary Walker Randolph, born in 1866. Debbie Truscott has noted that branches of the Randolphs had intermarried with such regularity that the ladies of the family had once joked that "whole generations passed before anyone needed to change their monograms."[8]

Within eleven years, the couple had eight children, one of whom was Sarah. Her best companions would be her two younger sisters,

Sarah Nicholas Randolph Truscott, circa 1917. Courtesy of Susan Truscott and James Truscott.

Agnes Dillon, two years her junior, and Mary Walker, seven years her junior. Sarah had a characteristic shared by all of the Randolph women, notes Debbie Truscott: "One of the most remarkable things about these Randolph ladies was how they spoke. They had soft, slow, faintly southern voices with broad English A's. . . . Sarah's voice used to waver, which added to its charm. It was a unique accent, local to the area around Charlottesville where they were born and raised."[9]

Sarah's father wanted a private-school education for his children. For decades following the Civil War and Reconstruction, cash was hard to come by in Virginia. Needing money for their tuition, Dr. Randolph moved west and eventually accepted a commission in the U.S. Army Medical Corps as a physician assigned to Camp Jones. Thereafter his daughters spent their summer months in Arizona and their school months at Agnes Scott College in Decatur, Georgia, not far from Atlanta. It was a private, liberal-arts college for women, known for having one of the oldest honor systems in the country. The "Scotties" were famous for earning international scholarships. Each year after spring finals, the Randolph daughters traveled by train back to Arizona, regarding each summer as something of a new adventure. They were all smart and fun-loving, but Sarah was less interested in school than her sisters and left college early to live full time in Arizona.[10]

Now she had met Lucian Truscott, and they had fallen in love. The army, not particularly interested in the young officer's love life, notified him of his impending transfer to Hawaii. The crisis must have spurred the young couple's courtship, for on March 29, 1919, Lucian and Sarah married in Warren (now Bisbee), Arizona, a week before his scheduled departure. Now they would both take part in the sea voyage of the 17th Cavalry. They were excited about the new assignment to the famous islands they knew only from pictures. To their dismay, however, they learned that lack of space on the troopship necessitated that wives sleep apart from their husbands. Thus, Sarah and the other wives of junior officers would have to share the cabins of wives and children of senior officers, sleeping on whatever settee or sofa could be wedged therein. Such arrangements might be disappointing for any couple, but for newlyweds it seemed downright unfair. Such was Sarah's transition from "army brat" to army wife.[11]

After easing away from San Francisco's waterfront, the *Sherman* passed through the Golden Gate. The immense Pacific Ocean lay ahead, and before long the ship began to dip and sway. Once passengers gained their sea legs, the voyage became enjoyable. They formed new friendships, and on most days they or the crew staged some kind of entertainment. Fortunately, the food was good. Truscott captured the spirit of the whole affair when he wrote, "Even though shipboard friendships and romances may not survive the vicissitudes of separation imposed by the prosaic business of living, one can only be better for having experienced the pleasure and satisfaction of an ocean voyage."[12]

A week later those on deck thought they saw Diamond Head in the distance. Word spread quickly and passengers filled the decks. When the *Sherman* approached Honolulu Harbor, all on board shared a collective excitement. As the ship nudged the dock, friends ashore and on board looked intently for one another. Excited voices shouted, "There they are!" as arms shot into the air, waving left and right. Off to the side, Hawaiian boys dove for coins tossed from the deck, and bands onshore played welcoming music. As the passengers disembarked, young Hawaiian women greeted them with the traditional leis. Few would ever forget the cruise or their arrival in Honolulu. "The sea voyage, which was my first, was a pleasure I shall never forget," recalled Sarah. "But the glory of Hawaii! The soft warm damp air, the glorious color, color in things that had always been in dull tints; the many natives and Orientals; the smells good and bad; the entirely new sensation of a foreign country and a first tropical one, swept over us both."[13]

Truscott and the officers and soldiers of the 17th Cavalry would do their soldiering at Castner Station, a portion of the larger Schofield Barracks situated about twenty-five miles north of Honolulu. As the arriving families disembarked, soldiers escorted them to waiting staff cars that would carry them along the two-lane concrete highway to their new quarters on post. NCOs formed the enlisted troopers and marched them to the nearby railway station, where narrow-gauge cars of the Oahu Railroad waited to take them to their new barracks. There was good news for the troopers—their billets were three-story concrete buildings, not the tents they had known so intimately at Camp Jones. Athletes among the ranks, especially boxers, received special attention. As historian Edward Coffman notes: "There they learned a very significant fact about Hawaii. Athletes were highly prized." More than a few jocks received a choice assignment or even a promotion from a commander who found himself in sports competition with fellow commanders. (Author James Jones, who served as a soldier in Hawaii and later on Guadalcanal, captured this aspect of prewar army life in Hawaii in his novel and its subsequent film, *From Here to Eternity.*)[14]

There was a reason for this assignment of cavalry to Hawaii. Just as Congress had created a much larger army at the onset of the Great War, now, with the country at peace, it was time to scale it back. The army deactivated some units entirely. One such command was the Hawaii National Guard; later a new regular-army division, the Hawaiian Division, would replace it. For now, the 17th Cavalry and various support units would fill the gap, joining the sailors and marines at Pearl Harbor in providing security for the islands. In 1919 only a few Americans suspected that before long the Empire of Japan would begin its expansion throughout the Far East.[15]

Feeling comfortable with their new mission, the members and family of the 17th Cavalry settled in. Colonel John K. L. Hartman, West Point class of 1888, was now regimental commander. He had been a temporary brigadier general during the Great War but now reverted to his permanent rank. Hartman was recognizable even at a distance by his impeccable uniform, highly polished boots, and riding crop, which he carried even when no horse was in sight. Despite his lowered rank, he showed no bitterness and was sincere and pleasant. Most who came to know Hartman thought highly of him.[16]

This was Sarah's first experience as an army wife, and she came to her own conclusion about the post and its inhabitants. "The Regiment was a funny mixture. It was almost entirely made up of officers who had come in during the war and enlisted men who had been commissioned. . . . Everybody except one or two field grade officers and the colonels were new and awkward, but we soon became acclimated and found ourselves becoming a part of the regular army." One enlisted man especially endeared himself to her. "There was a sergeant bugler in the Regiment who could make his bugle sound like something inspired from heaven itself. I hope he lives forever."[17]

Sarah found herself getting used to the army and Hawaii at the same time. "I felt too scared and new to do much more than listen and try to learn," she recalled. She felt conflicted about something else. Even though her father was serving as an army doctor, the Randolph family was not pleased that she was an army wife. "When I was married I was determined to try and get Lucian to leave the Army. My family did not feel that it was a profession with a great deal of future. . . . I fell in love with the life. . . . It would have been a sacrilege if I could have so influenced Lucian, because being an Army officer had been his dream since he was a tiny boy." Having resolved her confliction in her husband's favor, she became a dedicated officer's wife.[18]

For the new arrivals, Hawaii proved a delight. The narrow-gauge railroad made for an easy trip to Honolulu, where the white sand of Waikiki, peppered with the tanned bodies of young women in swimsuits, made the trip a delight for the young troopers. The nearby village of Wahiawa was popular for its *okolehao,* a Hawaiian form of moonshine. The usual athletic events found on any army post were available to the soldiers, but at Schofield Barracks one sport was special. "Boxing was one of the most popular spectator sports among the services in Hawaii during this period," remembered Truscott. "Competition was keen between the navy and marines at the great naval base at Pearl Harbor and at the army posts, especially Schofield Barracks. The services had some very able fighters in all classes."[19]

For the officers, soldiers, and families, Hawaii was something of a shock, albeit a pleasant one. The variety of seafood, fruits, and vegetables, many previously unknown to the mainlanders, became popular. The same village that supplied the *okolehau* offered a variety of Japanese foods. Hawaiian mullet was plentiful and delicious. The new arrivals were well acquainted with bananas and pineapples, but mangos, papayas, and guavas were new. They required some getting used to but soon became fully appreciated.[20]

For Sarah, prices were a concern. As she recalled: "I soon found that living on the border was much cheaper than Hawaii. . . . Eggs were never less than a dollar a dozen, and usually a little over that. Oranges, lemons and lettuce were all shipped in from the States, so they were high."[21]

The Officers Club was the center of social activity for the Truscotts and their friends. The food there was usually good. The steward and his staff were of Chinese origin and had had a long history of providing service. Truscott recalled one incident that many found amusing. A new cavalry officer, entertaining and hoping to impress his friends at dinner, found something quite unpleasant on his plate and immediately summoned the waiter. Upon seeing what was on the plate, "the waiter threw up his hands, eyes opened wide, and shrilled in a voice carried over the entire dining room, 'Oooooee! Cockee roach! I get you nudder one.'" Thereafter, whenever anyone encountered something of a surprise, the waiter's comment was repeated, entering the regiment's local lexicon.[22]

Unfortunately, more complaints about the food were forthcoming. As a result the post commander, Brigadier General John Heard, decided that someone should look into the matter. For this he called upon Colonel Charles C. Farmer, a sophisticate who had traveled the world as an attaché officer. Colonel Farmer had money from private sources and a reputation as an engaging storyteller. Upon receiving, but hardly relishing, his new culinary assignment, he called a meeting of the regimental officers.

Farmer began by relating his considerable experience with and appreciation for some of the grand saddle rooms of the world, especially those in Spain and Persia. Next he talked about the great kitchens with which he was familiar. He always found it worthwhile to become acquainted with the managers of the best hotels; doing so usually brought forth an invitation to meet the chef, tour the kitchen, and inspect food preparation. The colonel then described to the assembled officers one such occasion. While visiting the kitchen of a well-known restaurant on the French Riviera, he caught sight of something unusual. A waiter returned to the kitchen from the dining room with a dish of food that a customer had refused. As the officer watched from out of view, the waiter lowered the dish, spat into it, stirred it, and after a minute or two returned it to the customer. When the surprised American brought the incident to the manager's attention, his response was one of resignation. The manager was familiar with the customer, he said. She was a regular who demanded the return of at least one dish per meal, in the process often belittling the waiter, and seldom left a tip. The manager voiced frustration but reminded the officer that waiters who feel mistreated usually find a way to get even. Colonel Farmer ended his story by saying, "Now when we are dining in a restaurant and Mrs. Farmer complains about the food or service, as she sometimes does, I push my plate aside and eat no more."[23]

On July 19, 1919, Truscott moved from provisional status to regular status. He and other formerly new lieutenants successfully completed their oral final examinations in eleven military subjects. The examining board awarded Truscott three "excellents," six "very goods," and two "goods," concluding that he had the "suitability and moral, professional and physical fitness for permanent assignment."[24]

In Hawaii Lieutenant Truscott discovered something that would become a lifelong passion and that would enhance his reputation throughout the cavalry. He had grown up riding horses, but he had never before played polo, which was popular in Hawaii. Fortunately, Sarah grew to like watching the game. As she later reflected: "At the time of our arrival . . . army polo was in a very embryonic state, but interest was being stimulated . . . by some of the older officers. . . . They played on McClellan saddles at first, and the horses were as green as the men. . . . This was Lucian's beginning in polo, and it has always offered him just as much pleasure . . . as it did in the very start."[25]

Truscott and some of his fellow officers bought all the equipment needed for the game. They found and thoroughly studied a book that became their bible, *As to Polo,* by William Cameron Forbes, a former governor-general of the Philippine Islands. Because of polo's steep learning curve, the new players showed little improvement for some time, but they enjoyed the game nonetheless. It was a perfect pastime for cavalry officers; they had the horses, the playfield, and the time to practice. Before long they formed a team and braved entry into a few interisland tournaments against local teams. If being at the bottom of such scores as 15–0 and 23–1 embarrassed the officers, it did not reduce their enthusiasm. They continued to play and rather quickly became not only decent players but also strong proponents of polo for the benefits it brought to their horsemanship. Eventually, the game became very popular among cavalry officers. Major General John K. Herr, destined to serve as the last chief of cavalry, applauded these early players, saying, "Polo was officially approved as a sport which developed the qualities so valuable to combat officers in war, and wisely so, for it graduated such men as Patton, Truscott, Wainwright, Terry Allen, Paddy Flint, and many others who later became outstanding leaders in battle."[26]

By 1920, significant changes were occurring for the Truscotts and for the U.S. Army. In May of that year, the couple's first child, Mary Randolph Truscott, was born. But the child had a rough start. As her yet unborn brother would later recall, "When my sister Mary was born a year before I was, in May of 1920, they didn't make it from Schofield down to Honolulu, because my mother started having her halfway down, so they turned around and went back to Schofield."[27]

The second significant change came on July 1, 1920, when Lucian became a captain and took command of a troop. More importantly for the army as a whole, Congress passed the National Defense Act of 1920. Among other things, the act directed that the army now include not only the regular commands but also the Organized Army Reserve and the National Guard. Instead of the 5,000 officers authorized when Truscott joined the service, now there would be 14,000 as well as 365,000 soldiers. Unfortunately, as happens not infrequently, Congress declined to fully fund its own creation. The act may have authorized an army of 365,000 men, but lawmakers wanted to pay for only 150,000 troops.[28]

There would be cutbacks and reorganization in the existing force as well. The army deactivated three of the newest cavalry regiments, which had been formed by the National Defense Act of

1916. These included the 15th, 16th, and Truscott's unit, the 17th Cavalry. The army attached the 17th Cavalry to the 11th Cavalry, which was then assigned to the Presidio of Monterey in California. Truscott and the others would have to hang in limbo for a while: the transfer would likely occur in 1921.[29]

On October 20, 1920, Mr. Hollins N. Randolph, a lawyer with Randolph & Parker of Atlanta and uncle to Sarah Truscott, sent a personal note to his friend, General P. C. Harris, adjutant general, at the War Department. He asked Harris if the general might be able to assist Captain Truscott, who was interested in attending the Cavalry School at Fort Riley, Kansas. He ended his note by saying, "I need not say to you how deeply I will appreciate whatever you may be able to do." The record is silent as to what extent Truscott was aware of this communication. It seems unlikely that he would not have known about it, thus putting him in a position of going along with the personal favor. As it turned out, the request was for naught. Harris's reply pointed out that the captain was still in Hawaii and was required to complete his tour of duty there before he could apply for the Cavalry School. The general closed by suggesting that Truscott "make application to be sent to the School upon his return from the foreign service." Truscott was likely doubly disappointed. It was one thing to circumvent the chain of command, still another to be unsuccessful at it.[30]

When asked at the end of the year where he desired to be assigned next, Truscott listed Camp Jones or Fort Apache, Arizona; Monterey, California; Fort Oglethorpe, Georgia; Hawaii; Panama; or the Philippines. The army assigned him to Monterey, at least temporarily. By October 1921 Truscott and the entire 17th Cavalry would report for duty at the Presidio. One personal complication was that Sarah was again pregnant and was due right about the time of the planned departure. As she remembered: "By this time I was expecting a second child who was to be our first son and his father's namesake. The transport's departure and the arrival of this little mite did not go well together, and so after a lot of discussion about it we were allowed to wait over and go on the next boat. And so we bade farewell to everybody." Their first son, Lucian King Truscott III, was born on September 17, 1921, in the Territory of Hawaii. The couple had learned their lesson from little Mary's early arrival and took no chances this time. The family nickname for Lucian III would become "Doodie," shortened from "doodlebug." As Doodie later remarked:

"they made sure they got down to Tripler Hospital in time for me the following year. So that's why I was born in Honolulu, rather than in Schofield Barracks where we lived."[31]

The *Sherman* had brought the newlywed couple to Hawaii; the transport *Thomas* now took away the Truscott family of four. In the near future a third army brat, another son, would join the first two. Two of the three siblings would go on in later life to produce military brats of their own. One of those grandchildren, Mary Truscott, would one day write a book, *Brats*, about the singular experience of growing up in the military.[32]

As had happened upon their arrival, the hustle and bustle on the dock at Honolulu took place, but for the Truscotts it was a sad occasion. As Sarah reflected: "The natives [were] selling leis, the band played Aloha, which we had grown to love so. Then as we slipped out into the water, we again saw the little native boys diving for pennies. Their dark figures are like beautiful bronzes in the clear pale green of the water." Lucian shared the feeling: "There was only a sense of sadness and regret. . . . Aloha!" Hawaii would always be special for the couple. "Since Lucian and I left Hawaii we have lived in eleven houses," Sarah later counted. "Each one has had its own place in our hearts, and each one represents a change that has added to our experience and to Lucian's development as an Army Officer, but none of them will ever mean more to us than that first one."[33]

CHAPTER 4

Back to the Mainland

The Truscotts missed Hawaii, but soon enough they realized that Monterey was not a bad alternative. "That beautiful bay in the moonlight I will never forget," Sarah reminisced. "It is almost a perfect semicircle, and the tall pines seem to rise from the water straight up the hill the post is built on." The town was easy to reach by a bus service provided by horse-drawn Dougherty wagons. The close proximity of the sardine-processing plants was a minor irritant as the winds carried their odor up the hill.[1]

Like Hawaii, Monterey's beauty and abundance of outdoor activities made it a tourist destination. Golf and tennis were popular as was horseback riding. The Hotel Del Monte, one of the finest establishments around, and Pebble Beach, already well known to golfers, were close by. Polo was played here as well, increasingly so by cavalry officers; thus Truscott felt certain that he could continue to improve his game. As a temporary assignment at which to await permanent orders, the Presidio of Monterey turned out to be more than acceptable to the young family.[2]

An immediate problem for the Truscotts was that too few family housing units existed on post to accommodate the newcomers. Sarah was not pleased. "Two families were in almost every set of quarters, and so the pleasure of having my two crying babies descend upon her was given an awfully nice captain's wife. I don't see how we did it, but we became warm friends during those weeks."[3]

To the puzzlement of the new arrivals, the members of the 11th Cavalry, permanently assigned at the Presidio, seemed somewhat unfriendly. Perhaps they resented the additional residents, who competed for the various amenities, or perhaps it was because the 17th Cavalry would soon be gone anyway, so making them feel at home seemed unnecessary. Either way there appeared to be little reason to follow a well-known and widely accepted tradition among the officer corps. Under normal circumstances, new officers and their families could expect to be welcomed by officers and families already assigned on post, including the formal exchange of calling cards.

Colonel John M. Jenkins, West Point class of 1887, was commander of the 11th Cavalry. Upon investigating what he suspected to be coolness by his own officers toward the new officers, he inquired and learned that the greeting and card exchange, usually done within three days, had not occurred. A man of the old school, he was not one to procrastinate. At the next officers' call, following completion of routine business, Jenkins dismissed the newly arrived officers but instructed those of the 11th Cavalry to remain. Truscott never found out exactly what the colonel said to those who stayed, but "the officers and wives of the Eleventh Cavalry were out in force that night, and calling cards descended like a snowstorm upon the unsuspecting Seventeenth Cavalrymen and their wives during the calling hours of the next several evenings."[4]

Two months later, in December 1921, permanent orders arrived for Truscott. As he and Sarah had suspected, they were to return to Camp Jones at Douglas, Arizona. For her, previously familiar with the green hills and forests of Virginia and now accustomed to the greenery and oceanfront of both Hawaii and Monterey, a return to the desert was probably a disappointment. The captain had to depart on Thanksgiving Day to report on time, leaving Sarah to follow with the children. Her parents were then living in the mining town of Bisbee, Arizona, about twenty-five miles northeast of Douglas. She and the children visited with them for a while before joining Lucian at his post. Sarah had intended to stay three or four months but found that after a few weeks, she was "so homesick for Lucian, that with no excuses at all to save the family's feelings, I left."[5]

The Truscotts found that Camp Jones had changed some during their absence. Wooden buildings now housed the soldiers, replacing the tents previously dotting the landscape. The frenetic pace of life and duties during the Great War had slackened, and even the town of Douglas seemed quieter. A very big change for all was that the border with Mexico, so closely guarded earlier, was now very much open. The small village of Agua Prieta, with its restaurants and cantinas, became a frequent destination for soldiers and civilians alike. Prohibition, mockingly called the "great noble experiment," was now in force throughout the United States, but Agua Prieta was but a short walk away.[6]

Truscott, now commanding a troop of the 1st Cavalry Regiment, found that duty at Camp Jones had changed little since he had first reported there four years before. What was new was that officers were now playing polo. Before long the Camp Jones players, including Truscott, learned of a junior polo tournament taking place in June 1922 at Fort Bliss, Texas, a distance of about two hundred miles. The players looked forward to testing their skills and were disappointed when told that no money existed to ship their horses by either rail or truck. Undaunted, the twenty team members and their mounts rode the distance over the course of ten days. Their journey proved worthwhile when they defeated the favored team. Several months later they confirmed their status as regional champions by winning a senior polo tournament.[7]

Once at Camp Jones for only a little over a year, the Truscotts groaned when they learned that budget cuts and organizational consolidation necessitated closing Camp Jones. The entire 1st Cavalry would relocate to Camp Marfa, Texas, about two hundred miles southeast of El Paso. Most of those departing Arizona would motor to Marfa, but Captain Truscott and the other members of the regiment would complete the winter journey on horseback, bivouacking and conducting military maneuvers along the way. With a short layover at Fort Bliss, the journey took almost a month.[8]

Camp Marfa was located in high-plateau country—almost 4,700 feet above sea level—with mountains visible in the distance. There were few trees and less water but plenty of dust. Ocotillo, yucca, and creosote bushes, along with short grass, competed for the eight inches of rain that fell each year. As was the case everywhere in the southwestern deserts, when the large raindrops pelted the creosote bushes, the entire area took on a surprisingly pleasant aroma, and the colors of the various desert plants became more pronounced.[9]

A number of small but newly built cottages would serve as quarters for the soon-to-arrive officers and families of the 1st Cavalry. The winter of 1922–23 was one of often subzero weather, which at one point caused the water in the small cottages to freeze. Truscott recalled seeing "mounds of ice three feet high as a result of bursting water pipes and water heaters the morning after the big freeze." Supply sergeants oversaw troop labor in getting the mess cleaned up before most of the families arrived.[10]

The army then made family life a little more comfortable by a common practice not permitted in today's armed forces. In that era most officers ranked captain and above had a soldier who was detailed, in essence, as a personal servant. Called "strikers," the duty of these men was to care for the officer and his family. To Sarah's relief, "we always had a man who was good around the house and who liked children, and so a part of his job of taking care of the Captain was to take care of the Captain's family. It was a life saver, and if it hadn't been for these willing and cheerful soldiers I don't know what we would have done."[11]

Nearby Marfa was mostly a cattle town, although farming along the Alamito River and mining in the region employed some. The town had its own station of the Galveston, Houston, and San Antonio Division of the Southern Pacific Railroad, which seemed to lessen the feeling of isolation. There were also electric lights, telephones, cafes, and a local newspaper. North of Marfa stood the Davis and Barrilla Mountains, with peaks as high as 8,000 feet. The small town of Fort Davis, twenty miles distant, stood at the base of a modest mountain range of exposed boulders and cottonwood trees and had once been on the route of the Butterfield Stagecoach line; not far from it were the ruins of its namesake cavalry post, which had been in use during the Indian Wars. South of Marfa one could see the vast open cattle ranges, canyons, and mountains leading to the Rio Grande, about sixty miles away, and beyond the river, Mexico. The civilian population of about 3,000 got along well with the cavalrymen. Sarah recalled the residents as "the most hospitable of any civilian community we have ever known." Apparently, some of the locals were especially hospitable. As she remembered, "Almost all the girls in town married Army officers, and so the Army was doing its share for Marfa and Marfa never forgot it."[12]

For Truscott's men, it was business as usual. His troopers engaged in "the usual equitation, with its slow trotting and suppling exercises; squad, platoon, and troop drill; and squadron and regimental exercises. . . . In addition, there was always horse exercise, for the cavalryman could not forget his horse, even for a day. This responsibility for something other than himself was one of the features that distinguished the mounted from the dismounted services." The captain also continued playing polo and improving his skill, before long becoming the regimental polo-team manager.[13]

While stationed at Camp Marfa in 1924, Truscott met two individuals from whose acquaintance he would benefit. The first was Brigadier General Ewing E. Booth, commander of the 1st Cavalry

Brigade. Booth had been associated with the establishment of the new and very important advanced-training "school system" within the U.S. Army and was known for his knowledge of staff work and training. He had written a book entitled *Methods of Training,* which was then in use at the prestigious Command and General Staff School. General Booth inculcated in his captains a valuable lesson in how to determine available time for training, what subjects to teach, how to schedule instruction, and how to record its completion. As Truscott later recalled: "General Booth was always quiet and patient, but he knew what he wanted. He persisted until the troop commanders fully understood precisely what he wanted. . . . All of this was one of the most instructive and valuable experiences any group of troop officers could have."[14]

His other beneficial acquaintance was a champion polo player, Major Harry D. Chamberlin, considered "the finest horseman in the army and a distinguished polo player." He was a graduate of West Point as well as both the French and Italian cavalry schools. Truscott described him as "tall, handsome, [with] a magnetic personality—the very beau ideal of a cavalryman."[15]

Chamberlin had seen Truscott play polo at Camp Marfa and later in San Antonio at the Mid-Winter Polo Tournament. The major, stationed at Fort Bliss, was then the coach of the 8th Cavalry Regimental Polo Team, which would compete in a national championship tournament in Philadelphia. Knowing that Truscott would be a fine addition to his roster, Chamberlin engineered his permanent reassignment to Fort Bliss. The captain, of course, was eager for the opportunity. Just one problem existed. The army had already scheduled Truscott to attend the September 1925 troop officers course at the Cavalry School, and the Philadelphia tournament dates conflicted with the start of class. To make it all work, Chamberlin had to pull some strings. He had Truscott write a request to the commanding general of the Cavalry School asking for permission to report a week or two late. The major then added a note to the bottom of Truscott's letter: "I personally spoke to the Chief of Cavalry at the time of his visit to Fort Bliss, in reference to Capt. Truscott's playing in Philadelphia and delaying his reporting at the Cavalry School. He said he thought it would be practicable to delay his reporting until about the end of September. . . . The success of this expedition is largely dependent on Capt. Truscott's playing with the team." With the chief of cavalry approving the delay, Brigadier General Booth, now commandant of the Cavalry School, concurred. As Chamberlin had hoped, his polo team, including Truscott, won the tournament and its prize, a large sterling-silver fruit bowl engraved with the names of the championship squad.[16]

Sarah was pleased as well that Lucian would attend the Cavalry School. By now they both knew that this would be critical for advancement, for "it was becoming obvious that such training was essential to an officer's career." Even so, she would miss Marfa, which she had come to like so much. "When we left our little house in Marfa," she remembered, "I kept turning around and looked back as far as I could see."[17]

When Truscott reported to the Cavalry School in 1925, seemingly minor occurrences elsewhere in the world hinted at major changes ahead. Field Marshal Paul von Hindenburg was the new president of Germany. James W. Gerard, former U.S. ambassador at Berlin, warned that this was a signal that the Germans were returning to monarchism and militarism. British prime minister Neville Chamberlain was more hopeful. Studying a July diplomatic security note sent by the German government relative to a Rhine peace compact, he concluded that its message was one of peace. The French read the same note and interpreted it as a trap. In Rome a mob of Fascists attacked and beat Giovanni Amendola, head of the Aventine Opposition, which had challenged their party in elections.[18]

It was still quiet at the Cavalry School in Kansas, however. In 1852 the army had built Fort Riley near the place where the main immigrant wagon trail from the east divided. One fork worked its way northwest to Oregon, and variations of the other fork headed west to Colorado and Utah and southwest to New Mexico, Arizona, and California. From this fort and others like it, the U.S. Cavalry had fanned out onto the Great Plains to protect the settlers from American Indians. Not surprising, the Indians saw it differently.

Once the conquest of the West was complete, the army closed many of these frontier posts. Fort Riley was one that managed to remain on active duty, however. The likelihood of its survival increased when it became the home of the cavalry. From the Spanish-American War until the Pershing Expedition, it also provided some form of advanced training for the cavalry.[19]

When Captain Truscott arrived at Fort Riley, the Cavalry School was regularly conducting three separate, full-year classes annually.

The Troop Officers' Class was primarily for captains, with more than fifty students a year, and the Advanced Class was for field-grade officers, about twenty-five students per year. The third program, called Advanced Equitation Class, was an instructor class intended to prepare a dozen exceptional participants from the graduating Troop Officers' Class to serve as instructors for the upcoming class. Truscott attended the Troop Officers' Class, which he found very demanding. He underwent instruction eight hours a day and then studied several hours each night. By the time of graduation, he had received more than 1,400 hours of instruction in horsemanship, maps, reconnaissance, tactics, and weapons.[20]

While Lucian trained and studied, Sarah managed the family's home life. Their quarters were in Godfrey Court, originally built as a large hospital complex during the Great War. The campus consisted of ten buildings, each of which was two stories and now contained four apartments. Walkways connected the buildings to a mess hall at the center. Resident families averaged two or three children each, so kids on roller skates, tricycles, and bicycles now plied paths once filled with wheelchairs and gurneys. The army provided mess-hall meals not only for the student officers but for their families as well. As Truscott later recalled, "With more than a hundred children and eighty adults, most with strong personal feelings about food, diet, and taste, mealtime at Godfrey Court often approached a state of pandemonium."[21]

The "school detachment" handled the behind-the-scenes work that made the post function as smoothly as it did. This was the 9th Cavalry Regiment, the earliest members of which had arrived in the West following the Civil War as some of the original Buffalo Soldiers. In 1925 the U.S. Army still segregated African American and white soldiers. Added insult was that the former did largely servile work. Aside from mess duty, Truscott recalled, "these men worked in the various shops and offices, cared for the many animals used in the classes at the school, and performed certain maintenance and janitorial work in the buildings and quarters. Many of the wives and daughters were employed in the officers' messes and in the quarters of the officers of the garrison and the school." The army essentially enforced segregation at night as well. The unmarried soldiers lived in separate barracks, while the married soldiers and sergeants lived in a different section of post housing. Truscott recalled, "Rileyville was a sort of shantytown, a collection of noncommissioned officers' and married soldiers' quarters of temporary construction, to which had been added many others built of salvaged materials."[22]

The social life of the Truscotts and the other families was lively. Apart from various activities supplied by the army, the student-officers and their families found ways to entertain themselves as well. Dances and dinner parties were very popular. The latter, Truscott recalled, "were usually on the formal side, that is, one dressed for dinner, officers either in uniform or tuxedo, their wives in long dresses."[23]

Prohibition was still in force in the nation, but in Kansas, as with most other states, the amount of alcohol consumed changed little. A local farmer supplied the lubricant for social events at Fort Riley. "This potent distillate," Truscott confessed, "he dispensed to a select clientele of customers, mostly officers on the post, for the very reasonable price of six dollars a gallon." A local grocer helped out and "stocked sugar, malt syrup, bottles, bottle caps, capping machines, and would even confide to certain customers the 'receipt' he used. . . . Sunday nights were always a good time for bottling, because the brew would then be ready when classes let out on Friday afternoon."[24]

With June came graduation. Those who had completed their course had the opportunity to compete in various horsemanship events, three of which were the most popular. The first was a competition for the Patton Cup, originally presented to the Cavalry School by George S. Patton, Jr., when he was the saber instructor there. The course was a fast and winding ride over four jumps during which the contestant attacked twenty straw dummies with his saber, all within one and a half minutes. The second event was a six-hour night ride, which consisted of negotiating a dark and difficult course of sixty miles during which contestants had to navigate their way to various stations and arrive within a specified time limit.

The final event was the Standard Stakes, named for the school's newspaper. Any officer on the post could enter the contest, but student officers considered it a "must." The winner was awarded a trophy cup and prize money from contestant fees. It was the most grueling of the three events. In phase one, each contestant ran three hundred yards on foot to a bareback horse, saddled and bridled it, negotiated various kinds of jumps at a gallop, and rode to a saber course. In phase two, each contestant seized a saber while at a full gallop, attacked three straw dummies, and rode to a pistol course. In phase three, each contestant dismounted, fired a pistol a distance of twenty-five yards at a particular bottle, remounted, rode to a river crossing, forded the river, led his horse for a mile, remounted, forded the river a second time, rode to Sherman Heights, dismounted, led his horse up a steep climb, remounted, galloped to a rifle range, dismounted, seized and fired a rifle a distance of one hundred yards at a particular bottle, remounted, and rode to the finish line. Contestants lost points for missed jumps, missed saber attacks, and missed shots.

In his later writings Truscott described the above events in detail, though not how well or poorly he did. Of course, Major Chamberlin had already identified him as one of the army's best polo players, and the Cavalry School was eyeing Truscott as a future instructor. There seems little doubt that he entered all three events and did well in each.[25]

While the Cavalry School itself was highly regarded, things were not good for the cavalry as a whole. The days of the horse-mounted branch were numbered. Most officers saw the end coming, even if they were not happy about it, and most were not. "These were troublesome days for the cavalry branch of the army," lamented Truscott, "for it was becoming evident that there were increasing numbers who opposed the branch and did not wish it well." Major General Herbert B. Crosby, then chief of cavalry, sounded a warning during his address at the school. "There is no use beating about the bush, because there is no doubt that the cavalry is on the defensive at the present time. . . . We are fighting for our lives and we have to keep fighting all the time." Nevertheless, he recommended that the officers regard mechanization not as an enemy, but as something that was likely to create an even greater demand for the cavalry.[26]

By 1930, General Douglas MacArthur served as army chief of staff. Mechanization was destined to become a much bigger part of the army, and as Truscott noted, MacArthur "decided that the missions contemplated for the Mechanized Force were cavalry missions and that it should be a cavalry responsibility." Some cavalrymen agreed. Indeed, most of the instructor cadre at the Cavalry School supported this transformation as did many thoughtful cavalry officers throughout the army. They understood that their mission was still indispensable; it was only the means of transportation that was in need of updating. Others disagreed: for them the horse itself defined the cavalry.[27]

Perhaps the most ardent keeper of this faith was Major General John K. Herr, who in 1953 warned: "One basic and immutable truth stands out through all our wars. Sometimes our commanders have had to learn it the hard way: *There is no substitute for cavalry!*" When Herr wrote this, he was aware, of course, of the mechanization of the branch that had already occurred during World War II as well as helicopter use during the Korean War. One can only imagine what he might have thought when the 1st Cavalry Division became the 1st Cavalry Division (Air Mobile) at the beginning of the Vietnam War. Known informally as "the Air Cav," it ushered in the concept of large-scale troop movement and assault by helicopter.[28]

Truscott graduated from the Troop Officers' Class in 1926. As he had hoped, the army assigned him to the Advanced Equitation Class as one of the exceptional graduates from his group. Upon the captain's graduation, the army next selected him as one of the primary instructors at the Cavalry School. An additional advantage of this was that the Truscotts would now have much better family quarters than they had at Godfrey Court.[29]

By now, the army's professional-school system was in step with its promotional system. Officers were acutely aware that one's career depended on doing well in the important schools; promotion would otherwise be difficult to come by. When his tour of duty at the Cavalry School ended, Truscott's first hope was to attend the all-important Command and General Staff School at Fort Leavenworth, Kansas. His second choice was posting at Fort Myer, Virginia. In 1931, no doubt disappointed, he reported to his next assignment—Fort Myer. Before that, however, he and Sarah—especially Sarah—had to attend to something else. On December 26, 1930, another child was born to the couple. The baby was a source of joy. As Sarah noted: "The Christmas before we left Riley had brought a Christmas present to the whole family, but one day late, another son. We were all more than happy, and he was a darling little mite of humanity." His name was James Joseph Truscott III, and within the family, he acquired the nickname of "Jas" or "Jasbo," later "Jamie." As with his older brother, Doodie, Jamie would one day graduate from West Point. While Captain Truscott must have been disappointed about his transfer to Fort Myer, Sarah could not conceal her excitement. "I was so thrilled over going east, I hardly knew how to contain myself, and the thought of a city like Washington seemed too good to be true."[30]

CHAPTER 5

THE DEAD

In June 1931 Captain Truscott reported for duty at Fort Myer, Virginia, a Civil War–era post situated adjacent to Arlington National Cemetery. It was home to a famous regiment, the 3rd Cavalry, which had distinguished itself during the Mexican War; Truscott would assume command of Troop E. A second unit, the 16th Field Artillery Battalion, also served with the 3rd Cavalry there. The horse-drawn caissons of the 16th, once used to transport artillery ammunition, now transported coffined bodies to gravesites. Together, the soldiers of these two mounted units conducted funeral services for veterans and dignitaries and handled other ceremonial and demonstration duties.[1]

More than 116,000 American soldiers, sailors, and marines had died from injury or illness during the Great War. Burial parties interred the remains at cemeteries in England, France, and Belgium. Following the war, American families were given the opportunity, if they so desired, to have the remains of their loved one returned to the United States for reburial in one of the many national military cemeteries. Many elected to do so, and for Arlington National Cemetery, this accommodation resulted in the U.S. Army conducting scores of funerals each day.[2]

Arlington, the most famous U.S. military cemetery, began as an informal burial ground in 1864. Union soldiers transported many sick or wounded comrades to hospitals in Washington, D.C. Those who died there rapidly filled local cemeteries, necessitating additional grave space.

Mary Anna Custis Lee, a descendant of Martha Washington, owned the land on which the federal government later built Arlington National Cemetery and Fort Myer. When Mary inherited the estate, along with two hundred slaves and other properties, she was married to U.S. Army officer Robert E. Lee, an outstanding graduate of West Point. After Lee resigned his commission and later accepted command of Confederate forces in Virginia, the Union

Captain Lucian K. Truscott, Jr., U.S. Cavalry, 1931. Courtesy of the U.S. Army and the National Archives.

government confiscated the Lee estate, which at the time consisted of 1,100 acres of woods and fields and a mansion, Arlington House. Thereafter, the Union army used parts of the land as an encampment. Situated some two hundred feet higher than Washington, D.C., the site made for an excellent observation post and artillery position and was ideally suited to protect the Executive Mansion, the various bridges over the Potomac River, and boat traffic.

Brigadier General Montgomery C. Meigs, the army's quartermaster general, was aware of the need for more burial space. He was also angered at Lee for defecting to the Confederacy. Meigs concluded that he could locate additional grave space and at the same time frustrate any future attempts by the Lee family to recover the estate by burying Union soldiers and officers in the immediate vicinity of Arlington House and the other buildings constituting the main residence. His plan ultimately proved sound. After the U.S. Supreme Court ruled in 1882 that the federal government had illegally seized the land, the Lee family elected to sell it to the government for $150,000. The family had no interest in disinterring 20,000 graves.[3]

In 1887 Lieutenant General Philip H. Sheridan began to turn Fort Myer into a national attraction. He assigned cavalry troopers and 1,500 fine horses there for funeral and ceremonial duties. The post's proximity to the nation's capitol, coupled with its growing reputation for impressive horsemanship demonstrations, allowed its senior officers to be included in Washington's governmental and social circles.[4]

Well before his arrival, Truscott knew that Fort Myer had a reputation as a "proving ground" for cavalry colonels looking to make general. He was junior to that group, of course, but suspected that it could likely benefit his own career to be in the company of such officers. As Truscott later noted, for ambitious men, "the chance of lightning's striking was perhaps better near the eye of the Washington storm center, where colonels were under the immediate notice of the chief of staff of the army."[5]

Indeed, as it turned out a storm was brewing, one that would hit the nation's capital the following year, 1932. It would involve not only Truscott but also Dwight D. Eisenhower, George Patton, Douglas MacArthur, President Herbert Hoover, and a host of others. And its damage to the U.S. Army would be considerable.

In 1931 Colonel Harry N. Cootes commanded the 3rd Cavalry at Fort Myer. He ensured that its troopers and officers met the ultra-high appearance standards required of the army's most visible unit. Cootes had two special attributes for his assignment at Fort Myer. He was a member of Virginia's old school, and, according to Truscott, had, "ample means and a most attractive wife." Certainly, having sufficient money was essential in maintaining "the pace of the Washington diplomatic social whirl without undue financial embarrassment." Cootes and his successor, Kenyon Joyce, delegated most of the administrative work of running the regiment to its two majors, Alexander D. Surles, squadron commander, and his soon-to-arrive executive officer, Major Patton. Surles was one of the few cavalry officers of the day who preferred golf to polo, and Patton was already in the process of establishing his legendary reputation for actions good and bad.[6]

The noncommissioned officers assigned to Fort Myer were of the highest caliber. The army had commissioned many of them as officers during the Great War but, following Armistice Day, had reduced them to their permanent enlisted ranks. In the future, when the United States entered World War II, those NCOs still on active duty at Fort Myer would once again hold officer commissions.[7]

The primary business of the post was the escort of military funerals, and for each one, the army appointed a funeral officer. Designated by headquarters for an entire month, each assigned officer found himself racing about to get everything accomplished in time. The duties included working with the funeral home and cemetery, adjusting procedures for various religious preferences, determining the specific route for the funeral train, arranging for and supervising the military-escort detail, and addressing whatever problems developed in the process. Written protocol was precise, with each funeral given exacting detail. Tradition dictated many things, including the use of the rumbling caisson to transport the coffin; the presence of a riderless black horse, saddled with highly polished boots reversed in its stirrups; seven soldiers firing volleys of three rifle shots each; and the plaintive bugling of "Taps." Each tradition had its own history, variously dating back to Civil War soldiers, medieval knights, and Roman legionnaires. The expectation was that every service would come off perfectly. As Truscott recalled, "woe betide any firing party that let off a volley that did not sound like a single shot."[8]

A secondary duty at Fort Myer was the performance of expert horsemanship. Continual practice went into frequent exhibitions given in the riding hall, usually to a full house of 1,800 spectators. Each troop had its own particular program involving up to two dozen riders performing "many intricate movements executed with the greatest precision." The acrobatics demonstration was perhaps the most popular, with soldiers in Cossack attire standing on galloping horses, riding through burning hoops, vaulting from one side of the horse to the other, and picking up handkerchiefs with their teeth from the arena floor.[9]

Young, handsome, and usually unmarried lieutenants performed yet another duty at Fort Myer. Washington society was replete with dinners, receptions, and ceremonies, many of which sought a number of young military officers to serve as guides, ushers, and escorts. Not surprising, there was no shortage of volunteers among the lieutenants, who usually found themselves so busy serving Washington's society that they seldom had time for on-post social events. Of course, none failed to notice that there were many attractive young women at the various affairs in the capital. When duty called, it need only to whisper.[10]

The senior officers had their own social duties with the Washington elite. As for those officers in the middle ranks, which included Captain Truscott, they created most of their own social affairs. Since Prohibition was still in effect, these men did what everyone else was doing: "gin of our own manufacture was the most common beverage," as Truscott later explained. Someone managed to supply a name and telephone number to each newly arrived officer. When called, the deliveryman, dressed in suit and tie, arrived in a newer car, walked to the residence, exchanged pleasantries with the customer, and provided, for the price of six dollars a gallon, a quantity of pure alcohol and small vials of special "drops" that produced two gallons of gin.[11]

Funeral duty, horsemanship demonstrations, and social and diplomatic affairs filled the time of the officers and troopers week after week, month after month. Then with little warning, an event happened that drastically changed the routine of those assigned to Fort Myer, at least for a few weeks.

The Great Depression was well into its second year. If prosperity was just around the corner, it must have been at the far end of the block. Into Washington marched thousands of men, most of whom were dirty, smelly, tired, broke, and hungry. They came on a mission. Over the summer of 1931, the men arrived in small and large groups, most jumping off freight trains, others stepping down from trucks, and some thanking car drivers for a lift. More than a few arrived on foot, with pieces of cardboard stuffed between the soles of their feet and the soles of their shoes. A surprising number arrived with wives and children. Having lost hope, it made sense for them to bring their families along.

By summer's end, Truscott and the other officers at Fort Myer knew who these men were and why they had come to Washington. Veterans of the Great War—the one Truscott had regretted missing—now were down and out. Even before this large influx of destitute former servicemen, others had shown up. They had not come seeking a handout but looking for a job—any kind of job. As Truscott later recalled, "The first veterans that came to the notice of the troops at Fort Myer . . . were indigent individual veterans seeking food, shelter, and work." Most all of the soldiers chipped in and hired some of them to keep the kitchen and stables clean. Soldiers made little money themselves, however, and there was only so much work available on post. Nevertheless, the veterans kept coming. Hundreds were soon sleeping in vacant buildings and makeshift campgrounds.[12]

The whole thing had begun brewing at the end of the Great War when W. Bruce Shafer, Jr., a successful Virginia farmer, thought he had a good idea. He believed that the country should give some additional financial compensation—a bonus—to those doughboys who had served in the war, during which many had earned as little as a dollar a day. The country could do little for the more than fifty thousand who had been killed, having caught a bullet or piece of shrapnel in the trenches, or the many others who had succumbed to various illnesses. But perhaps it could do something for the more than four million men who had made it home. Shafer went to Washington to pitch his idea.[13]

He was pleased to find some congressional support for his proposal, but he was disappointed when little economic assistance actually materialized. By 1924, after several years of wrangling, Congress passed the World War Veterans Act, granting "adjusted service compensation" to veterans who had served during the Great War. Known as the "Bonus Bill," lawmakers eventually enacted it despite its veto by President Coolidge. It provided $1.00 or $1.25 for each day a veteran had served, depending on whether service had been at home or overseas. The bonus would amount to an average of $1,000 per veteran, though most of the recipients would have to wait until 1945, more than over twenty years in the future, to collect it.[14]

Following the stock market crash of 1929, the United States plunged into its deepest economic depression to date. Many Great War veterans simply accepted that they would never see their bonus. As they lost their jobs and farms, they joined hundreds of thousands of other Americans who wandered throughout the land, hoping to find work but often settling for a spot in a breadline. By one estimate, as the decade of the 1930s progressed, up to two million men and more than 25,000 families moved about on the roads and rails.[15]

In 1931 Texas representative Wright Patman reintroduced a measure that he had submitted previously. The bill regarding "payments on adjusted compensation certificates" survived long enough to result in hearings before the House Committee on Ways and Means. A key witness addressing the committee on February 4 was a bone-thin veteran named Joseph T. Angelo. He and a comrade had walked from Camden, New Jersey, to Washington to give testimony. Angelo described his service during the war, his two-year search for work to support his family, and his fear that unpaid taxes would take his house, which he had built himself. He also mentioned something that many found interesting. During the Great War, he had served as personal orderly for Major Patton, now serving at Fort Myer. Angelo had saved the officer's life when he "dragged [the wounded Patton] into a shell hole, sheltered him under heavy fire, and had then got him back to the American lines." As a result, Angelo received the Distinguished Service Cross for his actions, second only to the Medal of Honor. To the disappointment of Angelo and millions of other veterans, President Hoover vetoed this bill on February 26. But that did not mean that their fight for the bonus was over. Before long Angelo would have occasion to meet George Patton once again. Captain Truscott would be present to witness the ugly reunion.[16]

CHAPTER 6

THE DOWN AND OUT

On March 15, 1932, an unemployed former army sergeant named Walter W. Waters attended a meeting of several hundred Great War veterans in Portland, Oregon. Waters had seen action as a combat medic with the 146th Field Artillery Regiment at Saint-Mihiel, Château-Thierry, and Meuse-Argonne. After listening to the veterans' complaints about the bonus owed them, he stood up and proposed that they all hop a freight train to Washington, D.C., and demand their bonus. No one joined him. It took Waters two months of delivering the same message before anyone was ready to go. On May 11 he and more than three hundred other veterans gathered at the Union Pacific rail yard to begin their journey. Each man gave what money he had to the group—the total was thirty dollars.[1]

Union Pacific officials soon learned of the plan. The train the veterans were hoping to ride highballed past them at fifty miles per hour. Angry at the company for outwitting them, the men simply waited in the yard for the next train. Unable to reach agreement with Union Pacific, the veterans sat down on the tracks and refused to leave until they could ride a train heading east. With the men not budging and the train engineer refusing to drive his locomotive through them, the railroad officials relented, allowing the veterans to ride in empty stock cars, which still held visible and pungent reminders of their most recent riders.[2]

The men were soon on their way to Washington. By the time they reached Pocatello, Idaho, they were calling themselves the "Bonus Expeditionary Force," or BEF, later the "Bonus Army." Waters, elected "regimental commander" of the BEF, persuaded the men that they were a disciplined army and not a mob. As they rolled into and stopped at various towns, other veterans who had heard about the group hopped on. Waters set up companies of forty men each, appointed captains and military police, and ordered "no drinking, no panhandling, [and] no anti-government talk."[3]

Other railroads along the route followed the Union Pacific lead and reluctantly granted boxcar accommodations to veterans. Some did not, however, occasionally resulting in confrontations. For the most part, the police, many of whom were veterans themselves, did what they could to keep the protesters moving on their way, sometimes arranging to provide them with food. Newspapers picked up the story, which overnight went national. Veterans across the country wondered if they should head to Washington too.[4]

On May 24 the sheriff of Caseyville, Illinois, arranged to have the BEF switched from trains to trucks and cars. Before long the convoy crossed the Wabash River into Indiana. By now each state along the route picked up the veterans and quickly shuttled the problem to the next state. Last in line, the Maryland governor ordered National Guard trucks to meet the men at the state line and carry them deep into the heart of the District of Columbia. The relay handoff of the hot potato from state to state and finally to the national seat of government was complete. The BEF, destined to grow much larger, had become the problem of Pelham D. Glassford, Washington's new superintendent of police. The veterans had no idea that in him they had found their best ally.[5]

Those in the nation's capital, including top officials of the U.S. Army, knew the veterans were coming to Washington to demand their bonus and that things could get nasty. "Press and radio reflected an atmosphere of unrest in the land, and there were occasional clashes with police," recalled Truscott. Early in 1932, as a general precaution relative to ongoing hunger marches, the 3rd Cavalry and other units had begun special training so that soldiers could "assist civil authorities in maintaining or restoring order in riot conditions." Truscott and his fellow officers doubted that they would actually become involved in such duty.[6]

Retired army colonel Pelham Glassford was not a typical police chief, especially during the Great Depression. He had graduated from West Point and later served in the Great War as a regular-army colonel with the 26th "Yankee" Division, a New England National Guard unit. He saw action at Saint-Mihiel, where his personally trained artillerymen fired their guns so quickly that the Germans thought the Americans had automatic cannons. By 1918 Glassford held the (temporary) rank of brigadier general, the youngest in the U.S. Army. After the war, among other things, he was an instructor at West Point, teaching art and painting. While assigned to the

Army War College in the mid-1920s, he became popular with the Washington arts community. Glassford stood six feet three inches tall, had the build of an athlete, and offered everyone a friendly smile, so much so that his nickname was "Happy." In 1930, at age forty-seven, he retired from the army and moved to Arizona to help his father raise horses. He also intended to serve in the Arizona state guard and to paint, mostly watercolors, decorative screens, and murals.[7]

Glassford was nonetheless pleased when, in late September 1931, the Veterans of Foreign Wars asked him to come to Washington to help plan a grand Armistice Day jubilee. Upon arriving in Washington, he began planning the upcoming celebration. While making traffic arrangements at the police building, he encountered Herbert B. Crosby, a retired army major general. Crosby was an old acquaintance, now serving as one of the District of Columbia's three commissioners appointed by Congress to manage the local government. Because of corruption problems within the police department, the district needed a new police chief. The day after their chance meeting, Crosby looked up Glassford and insisted that he take on the position. The former colonel had no police experience and knew little about District of Columbia internecine politics, but he agreed.[8]

By June, Waters and his BEF had arrived, and even more veterans were on their way. As Truscott later recalled, Chief Glassford, "on his own responsibility and against the wishes of the District's commissioners, made valiant efforts to assist these veterans as a measure of preserving public order." The police chief's first task was finding ways to feed and shelter the thousands who had arrived or were on their way. Without permission from his superiors, Glassford took the bold but risky step of visiting some of Hoover's staff and a few members of Congress. Continuing to seek assistance for the destitute men, he called a meeting of veterans' groups and local charities. District Commissioner Crosby attended the meeting and took the occasion to caution his friend. "If you feed and house them, others will come by the thousands." Glassford replied, "It would be far better to have 10,000 orderly veterans under control than 5,000 hungry, desperate men breaking into stores and committing other depredations." Crosby did not push the issue, but the chief had irreversibly devalued his stock with the commissioners.[9]

It did not take long for Waters and Glassford to meet. Their relationship was not one of former sergeant to former general, but of two leaders who shared a problem and knew they needed to work together to solve it. Each had concluded that the small number of avowed communists within the BEF merited close attention, but that the problem was manageable. The U.S. Secret Service would have agreed. It had infiltrated the BEF and later reported that there were only a small number of communists within the Bonus Army, and they seemed to have little influence over the others. Other government officials took a much different view. General MacArthur, serving as U.S. Army chief of staff, viewed communists, wherever they might be, as a serious threat to the nation. Brigadier General George Van Horn Moseley, who oversaw the army's Military Intelligence Division and who would next serve as MacArthur's deputy chief of staff, agreed with that assessment. In his view the presence of both black and white veterans meant that African American and Jewish communists were using them as fuel to ignite a revolution.[10]

Glassford checked the various veteran encampments frequently, riding through on his blue police motorcycle, wearing his police uniform with Sam Browne belt and billed cap, and stopping to chat with veterans along the way. On several occasions he personally arranged for hot meals and medical assistance. What the veterans did not know was that Glassford was paying for much of the food from his own pocket; in fact, he likely spent about $1,000 on their behalf. At the same time, he received only a modicum of cooperation from district and federal officials. They, like Commissioner Crosby, believed that supporting the veterans on hand only encouraged more to come. Glassford saw their point, but for now he was doing his best to finesse a major problem not of his own making. His strategy was simple: if he fed the veterans, perhaps his police officers would not have to fight them.[11]

To house the Bonus Army's increasing numbers, Glassford arranged to use vacant land on the Anacostia Flats across the Anacostia River near the Eleventh Street drawbridge. The camp quickly became a giant "Hooverville," and at its peak housed more than 15,000 people, more than 1,000 of whom were women and children. Most of the veterans and their families were gaunt from months or even years on the road; most recalled having always been hungry—a full stomach was too distant to remember. They were disappointed when the district commissioners announced that city officials would cut off food and shelter on June 9 and that trucks would take the veterans out of town. Food was cut off as threatened,

Washington, D.C., chief of police Pelham D. Glassford inspecting the Bonus Army's Anacostia Camp, June 1932. Underwood and Underwood photograph courtesy of the Prints and Photographs Section, Library of Congress.

but the commissioners put off any eviction, likely unsure of what might result. None of the veterans intended to leave—they would stay as long as it took to get their bonus.[12]

While most news reporters across the country reported favorably on the Bonus Army, the *Washington Post* was not so kind, calling the veterans dupes and urging them to go home. Surprisingly, most reporters failed to capture one of the most visible oddities of camp life. At a time when the entire U.S. military and all schools, buses, restaurants, and theaters in Washington practiced segregation, African American and white veterans lived side by side in the Bonus Army's Hooverville. Some who did notice were John Dos Passos, Thomas Henry of the *Washington Evening Star,* and Roy Wilkins, then a novice reporter with *Crisis* magazine.[13]

The army watched events in Washington closely. Should military intervention become necessary, troops at Fort Myer were the closest and most available to respond. Especially critical to Truscott and the other cavalry officers was that their "horses and men were thoroughly accustomed to the sound and fury and would advance into any crowd, regardless of any action it might take."[14]

On July 8, 1932, Major Patton arrived for duty as the new executive officer of the 3rd Cavalry. A veteran of the Great War, Patton nevertheless held personal feelings about communists similar to those of General MacArthur and General Moseley. Later, he would author a paper entitled "Federal Troops in Domestic Disturbances," written for the training benefit of army officers. In it Patton advised: "If you must fire do a good job—a few casualities become martyrs, a large number an object lesson. . . . When a mob starts to move keep it on the run. . . . If they are running a few good wounds in the buttocks will encourage them. If they resist they must be killed."[15]

While Hoover administration officials were not happy about the Anacostia Flats camp, they considered the ones in downtown Washington as a more immediate problem. Situated not far from the White House and Capitol, the abandoned buildings now occupied and thrown-together shanties were eyesores that belied official statements that the depression was winding down. On July 21 the administration advised the district commissioners that all downtown encampments, then holding about 12,000 occupants, must be cleared as soon as possible. Later they expanded the expulsion to include all BEF camps. The commissioners fully supported the order and directed Glassford to clear the encampments by July 22. The police chief notified Waters of the order and arranged for an airdrop of pamphlets warning of the impending eviction over the two dozen camps. Truscott and the others at Fort Myer moved to high alert.[16]

The eviction date came and went, but by July 26 Waters and Glassford were certain that anything other than a peaceful removal would lead to the use of federal troops, which would likely result in bloodshed. Some veterans and their families departed, but most stayed. Aware that hundreds of women and children were still living in the camps, Waters appealed to the Red Cross. The head of that organization declined to assist directly but did offer to call General MacArthur's office, which resulted in Waters and his associates meeting face to face with the army chief of staff and Secretary of War Patrick J. Hurley.

At the meeting, Waters requested the use of army tents, which he hoped would permit his people to relocate their camps. Former

New Hampshire governor John Bartlett, who was also a former U.S. assistant postmaster general, had offered the veterans the use of his nearby property for this purpose. While MacArthur paced the room, Hurley got to the point: "Waters, the War Department has no tentage available, and if it did have we certainly would not place it at your disposal. . . . We are interested only in getting you out of the District. At the first sign of disorder or bloodshed in the BEF, you will all get out. And we have plenty of troops to put you out." Waters asked if he might march the veterans out of Washington if it appeared that federal troops would clear the camps. MacArthur answered, "Yes, my friend, of course."[17]

On July 28 at 10:00 A.M., upon orders of federal and district officials, Glassford and about one hundred police officers began the evacuation of the downtown encampments. The clearing of one at the old National Guard armory occurred with little trouble. Things even looked promising enough to allow a break for lunch. Then quite suddenly, so it seemed, other veterans riding in trucks flooded in from outlying camps, hoping to reoccupy the building. The officers quickly formed a line to stop them. But the veterans pressed on and began hurling bricks and rocks; the police reacted by using their nightsticks. Glassford, although struck by several missiles, rushed into the center of the fight and somehow got everyone's attention long enough to calm them down. Unfortunately, even more veterans arrived. A police commander summoned available men from the other precincts and rather quickly had five hundred additional officers on the scene.[18]

Complicating matters, Commissioner Crosby had a spy—a police lieutenant—reporting on Glassford's actions. News of the violence almost immediately reached government officials, and with it any hesitancy to use the troops evaporated. Thereafter, matters worsened at the evacuation site. Veterans mobbed two police officers at the Ford Building. One officer fired his revolver, hitting two men, killing one and mortally wounding the other. Glassford shouted orders to stop the shooting, but it was too late. In that instant everyone present sensed that the situation had changed irrevocably. Then a news reporter approached the police chief and told him that army troops were gathering at the Ellipse near the White House. MacArthur had decided to take personal command of these forces. His young personal aide, Major Dwight D. Eisenhower, argued that it was unnecessary for the army chief of staff to become personally involved. The general saw it differently. For him, the violence was the beginning of a communist-led revolutionary movement.[19]

In the early afternoon MacArthur, through Major General Perry L. Miles, commanding local army forces, had ordered the cavalry at Fort Myer and the infantry at Fort Washington to report to the Ellipse. Because Major Surles of the 3rd Cavalry was not immediately available, Major Patton alerted the officers and troopers. By now nothing—not even the veterans marching out of town—could stop what was about to happen. MacArthur had started the military engine and placed it in gear, and he was determined to drive the BEF out of town. As executive officer, Patton was not a field commander and had no troops assigned under him. As his biographer Martin Blumenson notes, "There was no need for Patton . . . to accompany the cavalry contingent . . . , but the excitement and chance of action was too attractive to resist."[20]

Truscott later recalled that once Major Surles arrived and assumed command, the squadron moved out and "pounded down through Arlington National Cemetery, over the recently completed Memorial Bridge, and halted on the Ellipse south of the White House at about half past two o'clock." As it turned out, the full gallop was unnecessary. Boats and trucks transporting the infantrymen would not arrive for nearly two hours.[21]

Glassford sped by motorcycle to the Ellipse. He approached MacArthur and asked what he intended to do. The general made it quite clear that authorities intended to break the BEF, adding that his forces would clear the downtown buildings and other camps by nightfall. Glassford asked for a ten-minute head start, which MacArthur granted. The chief raced back to the camp and ordered his police officers to spread the word among the veterans that everyone, especially women and children, needed to evacuate immediately. Few heeded the warnings, though most were tense but waited calmly. For many of the veterans, it must have seemed similar to their experiences in the Great War, quietly anticipating the whistle that signaled them to climb out of the trenches and trot into no-man's land.[22]

If MacArthur, General Miles, or any other senior army commander present had any tactical plan on how best to remove the Bonus Army from downtown Washington without risking injury to an estimated 10,000 bystanders and spectators, he must have kept it to himself. A frontal assault employing 2,000 teargas canisters, sabers, and bayonets would be the crude solution to a complicated problem. Miles briefed his soldiers about 4:00 P.M., telling them that they would use necessary force and teargas but that they would treat any women and children encountered with tenderness. He referred to the veterans as "the mob" and the onlookers as "the crowd." Within a half hour, the troops were on their way. "The squadron moved out in a column of platoons," Truscott remembered, "followed by the infantry battalion with a few of their old World War tanks. . . . Simultaneously, so it seemed, every office building and business establishment in downtown Washington discharged its occupants onto the streets. This parade was indeed witnessed by thousands, and a tense atmosphere of excitement pervaded the scene." "The crowd" quickly overflowed the sidewalks into the streets. In a matter of moments, army leaders realized that they had woefully underestimated the problem.[23]

The troops began their final advance at 4:30. MacArthur already had his own instructions, which President Hoover had sent to him personally. The orders emphasized that the Washington, D.C., Metropolitan Police Force was in charge; that soldiers would turn all prisoners over to the police; and that soldiers would treat women and children humanely. But the general did not need the president to tell him how to do his job.[24]

The military force included trucks carrying several tanks, four hundred infantrymen, and more than two hundred cavalrymen. The troopers formed with steel helmets, slung carbines, gas masks, and drawn sabers; the foot soldiers formed with steel helmets, gas masks, and rifles with fixed bayonets held at port arms. They moved forward in unison, filling Pennsylvania Avenue from curb to curb many ranks deep. Former governor Bartlett saw and heard the mounted men coming, "a force of cavalry with sabers glistening, making the ominous click of iron feet on the pavement, which sounded so much like war."[25]

The infantry moved into and through the abandoned buildings. Those occupants who refused to leave changed their minds when the soldiers dropped teargas canisters from the tops of the stairwells to the floors below. The cavalry then herded the disgorged veterans, as well as those already outside, along Third and Fourth Streets toward Missouri Avenue. The veterans taunted the troopers, which the cavalrymen ignored, and some threw rocks and bricks. The troopers ignored the verbal and physical insults. Truscott remembered: "Their only action was to apply the flat of a saber whenever individuals tried to slip through the thin lines. Theirs was a magnificent illustration of Regular Army discipline."[26]

From his horse, the Oklahoman could see some veterans picking up objects from rubble piles. "The cavalry troops moved forward with drawn sabers in hand," he later wrote. "There was a hail of bricks and stones. . . . Many veterans sought refuge in shacks they had built along the Mall or in trucks parked along the streets. A few blows with the pommel of a saber on the tin roofs or the thrust of a saber through cracks soon emptied the shacks and trucks." Major Patton later recalled: "Bricks flew, sabers rose and fell with a comforting smack, and the mob ran. We moved on after them, occasionally meeting serious resistance. . . . Two of us charged at a gallop, and had some nice work at close range with the occupants of the truck, most of whom could not sit down for some days."[27]

Onlookers saw the action differently. They described a scene of gas-masked soldiers lobbing teargas without warning, cavalrymen riding into men and women and pushing them aside, and thousands of spectators unexpectedly finding themselves caught in the action. The air thickened with white gas that limited both sight and breath. Most veterans ran. Bartlett described the cavalry attack: "Into the crowds they ruthlessly drove, scattering us like sheep, knocking down many pedestrians. I backed double-quick or a horse would have hit me."[28]

The soldiers next moved against a site at Fourteenth and C Streets S.W., which had a reputation as the communist camp. Soon, some of the shacks there began to burn as the infantry continued to move the veterans. The troops paused at the Eleventh Street Bridge about 6:30 P.M., most of the veterans having crossed the river in flight back to their principal encampment. Alerted earlier to the melee, President Hoover (through Secretary of War Hurley) sent General Moseley with a rushed, verbal order to MacArthur that expressly forbade troops from crossing the bridge to the Anacostia Flats camp. Nevertheless, shortly after 9:00 P.M., MacArthur sent both the cavalry and the infantry across the span.[29]

Two hours later flames engulfed the giant Hooverville. Its hovels were little more than cardboard, plywood, and scraps of lumber, which ignited easily in the hot July evening. The flames leaped and spread quickly from shack to shack. The smoke thickened and the fire became so intense that it lit the sky. Truscott later wrote that the cavalry halted to allow the veterans to vacate the area but the infantry battalion moved in to clear it. "It was soon a mass of flames," he remembered. "By morning, the veterans were gone, and the huge primitive camp was a smoldering mass. No one knew who set off the first fires, but it was the complete answer from both a sanitary and disciplinary point of view."[30]

One reporter recalled that he was very close to General MacArthur and saw him give an order to a sergeant, after which the NCO and his men wadded newspapers near deserted huts and set them ablaze. Another reporter said he saw soldiers torching the shacks. The following day a newspaper photograph showed troops using a torch to burn a shanty. Secretary of War Hurley, when later questioned by reporters, admitted that some soldiers had ignited some of the hovels for sanitary reasons.[31]

The veterans, along with their wives and children, ran into the night not knowing where they were heading except away from the flames. Those walking to Virginia found the bridges blocked by soldiers, and those heading to Maryland found the roads blocked by state troopers. Eventually, Maryland authorities allowed those in flight to pass through—so long as they kept moving. Many veterans simply walked on, not caring that it had started to rain and not knowing for sure where they would end up. Washington had rid itself of the Bonus Army.[32]

As news stories and photographs revealed what had happened, many Americans were angered. Hoover was mad too. He knew that he had expressly forbidden MacArthur from sending troops across the Eleventh Street Bridge. General Moseley reported that he had carried the message to MacArthur and that they had discussed it. He added that the chief of staff was quite annoyed and did not like anyone interfering with the implementation of his plans. General Miles and Major Eisenhower later verified that Mosley had delivered the president's message.[33]

After midnight, while the smell of smoke was still pungent, MacArthur addressed the press. As one might expect, he magnified the threat posed by the veterans to justify the response. The group became, in the general's words, "insurrectionists." "The mob down Pennsylvania Avenue looked bad," he told the assembled reporters. "They were animated by the spirit of revolution. The gentleness and consideration with which they had been treated had been mistaken by them as weakness and they had come to the conclusion that they were about to take over the government in an arbitrary way or by indirect methods." MacArthur doubted that even one in ten was actually a veteran. In an action conveying his political acumen, he next lavished praise on President Hoover. "Had he let it go another week I believe that the institutions of our Government would have been very severely threatened. . . . Had he not acted with the force and vigor which he did, it would have been a bad day for the country tomorrow." When Hoover read the newspapers the next morning, he knew that MacArthur's generous praise had neatly shifted any blame to him.[34]

Sometime later, social workers in Johnstown, Pennsylvania, were interviewing thousands of veterans who had sought refuge there. One reported speaking with seventy-five individuals, all of whom produced papers of honorable discharge. The Veterans Administration later conducted a survey and reported that 94 percent of the men with the Bonus Army were veterans, 67 percent had served overseas, and 20 percent had some disability.[35]

One short, slender veteran did not leave Washington the night of the eviction. The next day in the hazy, still-smoky morning light, the smell of burnt wood and cardboard heavy in the air, he approached a tall sergeant of the 12th Infantry and asked to speak to Major Patton. At the time Captain Truscott and other officers were standing with Patton in the ash remnant of the encampment, sipping morning coffee from a field kitchen. The sergeant brought forth the veteran and told the major that the man claimed to know him. Patton looked at the man and said: "Sergeant, I do not know this man. Take him away, and under no circumstances permit him to return!" As the soldier led away the man, Patton said to Truscott and the others: "That man was my orderly during the war. When I was wounded, he dragged me from a shell hole under fire. I got him a decoration for it. Since the war, my mother and I have more than supported him. . . . Can you imagine the headlines if the papers got wind of our meeting here this morning! . . . Of course, we'll take care of him anyway!" Joe Angelo, a decorated veteran, slipped back into the Great Depression. Patton, who had given money to Angelo several times over the years, did so again in 1939. He sent him twenty-five dollars.[36]

In early 1933 thousands of veterans of the Great War found their way back to Washington, still seeking their bonuses. A new president and a new Congress were now on hand, but neither favored giving the men this money. In actuality, the down-and-out veterans were but a small percentage of the total population living in poverty at the time. By then, however, President Franklin Roosevelt had a program of relief ready, which he quickly implemented. On March 9, having been in office just five days, he sent for advisors to flesh out some thoughts he had about putting 500,000 young men to work doing national conservation projects. By 9:00 that same night, he had a draft of the required legislation, and by March 31 the Civilian Conservation Corps (CCC) was born.

The new president told his assistant Louis Howe to give one group of 3,000 arriving veterans food, shelter, and medical care. Additionally, Eleanor Roosevelt visited them, wading through mud up to her ankles to have coffee with the men. The Roosevelt administration later recruited 2,600 of these men, along with another 25,000 veterans, to become members of the CCC. Granted an age-limit exemption, they joined 2.75 million young men, ages eighteen to twenty-five, and labored for years planting trees, building bridges, and carving roads in the nation's many natural areas, forests, and parks. For their work they earned thirty dollars per month, twenty-two dollars of which they had to send home if they had a dependent family. In the end the CCC provided a lasting legacy that hundreds of thousands of Americans still utilize every year.[37]

American military veterans who subsequently benefited from the Servicemen's Readjustment Act of 1944, better known as the GI Bill of Rights, can trace those benefits directly back to the BEF. In July 1943, midway through World War II, President Roosevelt in a fireside chat warned: "Veterans of this war must not be demobilized into an environment of inflation and unemployment, to a place on a bread line or on a corner selling apples. . . . We must this time, have plans ready." From the more than two million veterans of World War II and Korea who used their GI Bill's education benefit, the United States gained 67,000 doctors, 22,000 dentists, 91,000 scientists, 450,000 engineers, and 238,000 teachers. Nearly eight million veterans benefited in some way from the GI Bill.[38]

CHAPTER 7

STUDENT AND INSTRUCTOR AGAIN

Amid the charred rubble of the Anacostia Flats encampment, the U.S. Army exuded the cockiness of the bully who had just run the new kid out of town. But an even bigger bully was waiting to take a shot at the army. President Roosevelt and his New Deal programs endeavored to get the country back on its feet, but each program came with a price. Although much smaller than it had been during the Great War, the army was still too expensive to maintain, a champion polo pony that played occasionally but needed to be fed daily. Every American needed to help in tightening the country's belt, and that included the soldiers. After a 10 percent cut in pay to help get the nation back on track, military paychecks amounted to what they had been twelve years previous.[1]

Of all the New Deal recovery programs initiated by the Roosevelt administration, just one had a direct effect on the army. Charged with setting up and running the Civilian Conservation Corps, the army had to do it in a very unmilitary way so as not to disturb the postwar isolationist sentiment that had settled over the country like a comfortable quilt. Of course, someone had to set up the CCC, and the officers and NCOs were in the best position to do so. "It fell to the lot of the army," Truscott noted, to "conduct recruiting, provide tools, transportation, and equipment, and, finally, supervise the work. . . . Any form of military drill, semblance of military organization, or military command and discipline was forbidden." The regular service did much of the initial work throughout the spring and summer of 1933, but its role ended in the late fall when it activated reserve officers to assume management of the program.[2]

What the army did was significant. One-quarter of its officer corps and 5,000 soldiers oversaw the work of 250,000 young men in 1,350 separate camps, leaving the remaining officers and NCOs to run the army itself. The cavalry did its share but still managed to remember its priorities, one of which was polo.

Captain Truscott continued to practice and play, and in March 1934—much to his delight—he was selected to play mallet number three on the U.S. Army Polo Team in an international tournament in Mexico City. He, along with team members Major Charles Smith, Captain Chester Davis, 1st Lieutenant Gordon Rogers, and 1st Lieutenant Charles McFarland, later received a memorandum from General MacArthur saying: "Glowing reports have come to me concerning the impression created in Mexico City by the Army Polo Team, of which you were a member. The scores of course speak for themselves and I congratulate you for your important share in the splendid victory."[3]

A few months later there was more good news. Truscott would attend the two-year Command and General Staff School at Fort Leavenworth starting in August 1934. He had wanted the assignment ever since leaving Fort Riley. Although it had come later than he wished, Truscott was relieved as attendance had become almost essential for promotion. He knew it would be difficult, but completion of the course of study there would help prepare him for higher command.[4]

Sarah had mixed feelings. She was committed to helping Lucian's career and assumed that Fort Leavenworth would be just as nice as Fort Riley. Even so, she would miss her family and friends in Virginia and the thrill of living in Washington. She had long ago accepted that an army wife had to subordinate herself and her children to support her husband's career. And there was more to it than many imagined. Lucian K. Truscott IV, West Point graduate and popular novelist, recalled his remarkable grandmother: "My grandfather married the right woman. He was a redneck from nowhere. Without my grandmother at his side, he would never have been a commanding general at Anzio. He might have been captain of the polo team, but not a general. With her Jefferson and Randolph background, she refined him so that he could one day be a general."[5]

Situated just west of the Missouri River and northwest of Kansas City, Missouri, Fort Leavenworth was a small post of only about twelve square miles. Aside from the Command and General Staff School, it included two unlikely neighbors: the Leavenworth Federal Penitentiary, operated by the Department of Justice, and the U.S. Disciplinary Barracks, intended for military prisoners. In 1881 General William Tecumseh Sherman, commanding general of the U.S. Army, realized the need for advanced military education. He directed Philip Sheridan, then commander of the Division of Missouri, to establish at Fort Leavenworth a new school to be called—after several variations—the U.S. Infantry and Cavalry School. Sherman preferred establishing it without the need of federal legislation, otherwise, he warned Sheridan, "like West Point, it will be made political and taken out of our control." Although the school had begun as a two-year program for basic branch training for the cavalry and infantry, by 1922 it had evolved into an armywide program for postgraduate education. Other training provided at Fort Leavenworth moved elsewhere, and the post became home to the Command and General Staff School.[6]

The army intended that the instruction, which focused on "command, leadership, and staff procedures," be demanding. Truscott recalled: "The course was intensely competitive. The school posted class standings regularly. Officers were made to feel that their entire future careers depended on their class standings."[7]

That Truscott did well during the two-year course was no surprise. He had once described himself as "rather serious and studious." Nonetheless, the school intended its classes to be graduate education for those who had attended West Point or other colleges and universities. Fortunately, the army left open a door to admit an officer with abundant intelligence and leadership even if his early education had been nonstandard. It helped that Truscott had done exceptionally well in his basic and advanced branch training and had been an instructor at the Cavalry School. He had also developed a reputation as a fine officer.[8]

By the time Truscott arrived at the school, it was in transition away from teaching the trench-warfare theory that had dominated its instruction after the Great War. Now with developments in aviation, armor, and transport, the army realized that the battlefield had once again become mobile. This pleased Truscott, for mobility was what a cavalry officer knew best.[9]

At a time when army officers faced strong probability that the United States would become involved in another European conflict, it was propitious to be studying new concepts that would determine the outcome of that war. Upon graduation, Truscott would have attended almost 1,000 hours of theory and experienced 350 hours of practical field application of the theories presented. Topics included offensive and defensive operations, collection and use of intelligence information, communications, logistics, mechanization, history, geography, training, and tactics.[10]

Family accommodations at Leavenworth were similar to what the Truscotts had known at Fort Riley—mostly remodels. The Doniphan and Pope Apartments had once been troop barracks. Engineer Hall, which had once been home to a regiment of engineers, was now the Bell Apartments, known affectionately as "The Beehive" because of its teeming population. The apartment provided to the Truscotts was quite nice, however, and included a master suite with bath and study, three additional bedrooms, baths, full kitchen, living room, and dining room. The study, in which Truscott would do several hours of homework each night, was isolated from the other rooms.[11]

The social structure was also much the same. New officers "called on" senior officers and school instructors, and all dinner parties and the majority of cocktail parties required formal dress. Truscott and his fellow student-officers, cocktails in hand, enjoyed their weekly get-togethers, where discussion centered mostly on the new and radical school theories and concepts of warfare. Even though Prohibition had now ended, Kansas remained a dry state. The wet state of Missouri, however, was only thirty miles away. Runs across the state line were frequent enough to keep the cocktail conversations lively. Sarah would later described Lucian as "socially, a very vivid and attractive person, who is always at the center of a group, which is having either a lively and intelligent discussion, or which has in it the most entertaining person in the crowd."[12]

As at the Cavalry School, the army did a commendable job of caring for an officer's family. The philosophy at Leavenworth was the same: the student-officer can better concentrate on his studies if his family is content. Thus, the school attended to "the accommodation, education, recreation, entertainment, and amusement of the wives and children."[13]

The two forts were similar in another respect. At Fort Riley, the African American 9th Cavalry served as "the school detachment" and did wonders behind the scenes. At Fort Leavenworth the 10th Cavalry, also an original Buffalo Soldiers regiment, did similar work as "school troops." As one might suspect, the men of the 10th Cavalry found themselves working as much as servants as soldiers. The employment of African American troopers—especially NCOs—in servant roles would come back to haunt the army. In the future, when the military began ramping up for World War II, numerous African Americans would volunteer or be drafted. Still segregated into "colored" units, these soldiers would need training cadre and supervisors. Under the circumstances of the time, African American NCOs would do such work best; thus the army would draw upon the 9th and 10th Cavalry and the 24th and 25th Infantry Regiments for such duty. What officials later found within these units, as noted by historian Edward Coffman, was that there were "too few [African American] regulars, and most of them had spent much of their time looking after horses and performing service chores."[14]

For those at Fort Leavenworth in that era, perhaps the most memorable member of the 10th Cavalry was "Harris," along with his ponies. Truscott said of the man: "He was a colored soldier of considerable girth and great humor. He was a genius with horses and with children. . . . His cheerful voice and infectious laugh could be heard for a block or so, and both drew children like a magnet. . . . He was a fixture; he was a wonderful part of Fort Leavenworth." The Truscott children never forgot him.[15]

In August 1935, midway through his two-year studies, Truscott earned promotion to major. Under normal circumstances, this advancement would have come earlier. The problem had been "the hump." The National Defense Act of 1920 had commissioned 5,229 additional officers, but various subsequent acts had slimmed down the army. Consequently, promotions all but stopped. General MacArthur calculated in the 1930s that a second lieutenant could expect to wait thirty-six years or more to reach the rank of colonel—if he was lucky. Truscott had made captain ahead of the hump, which was fortunate. Even so, by 1935 he had been a captain for fifteen years. That same year Congress finally passed legislation mandating certain promotions and increasing the number of field-grade officers, which resulted in promotions for about half of those under the rank of colonel. For Truscott, the gold leaves were a relief. In addition to promotions, pay raises were long overdue. Between 1908 and 1928, military pay had gone up only 11 percent but had decreased 15 percent during the Great Depression. The 1935 legislation restored salaries to what they had been before the cut. Still, soldiers found themselves behind. It did not help morale that while new members of the CCC earned thirty dollars a month, new army privates received less than eighteen dollars.[16]

Less than a year later, in June 1936, after two demanding years, Truscott completed his studies at Leavenworth. The Cavalry School had previously asked him to remain as an instructor after graduation there, and now the Command and General Staff School did the same. His educational career, begun as a sixteen-year-old schoolteacher in Oklahoma, now brought him to a four-year stint as an instructor at the U.S. Army's most prestigious school. The army clearly recognized Truscott as one of its premier instructors, undoubtedly destined for higher command. Sarah later said of Lucian, "For the most part he was inclined to be silent but an untiring talker for a principle or ideal and was never happier than when talking to younger officers, helping and guiding them."[17]

The previous year had brought a change to the Command and General Staff School. With war knocking at the door, the army sought to double the number of officers attending its course of study. The school accomplished this by revising the course from two years to one year. Thus, in 1936, when Truscott's two-year class graduated, so did a one-year class.[18]

Serving as an instructor was demanding, but it allowed Truscott more time for his passion—polo. "Horses, horses, horses! In many ways," Truscott remembered, "Leavenworth was almost as much of a cavalry post as Riley." There was considerable interclub competition as well as championship games and, during the winter, even indoor polo. During the summers, the major traveled to Cleveland, Ohio, to coach a private country-club team. But he was not the only cavalry officer who did such outside coaching, nor was he the only one who would later benefit from personal acquaintances made during these excursions. Indeed, these activities also aided the army in general by bringing powerful friends into its corner.[19]

Polo was not a game for lightweights, however. As historian Martin Blumenson notes, "There was nothing genteel about the game—men riding fast horses each weighing 1,000 to 1,300 pounds, running at top speed, just under forty miles an hour, and often colliding with bone-bruising force." Blumenson further notes that the cavalry saw the experience as "ideal for commanders, for the sport demanded speed, split-second decision, teamwork, concentration, judgment, and physical fitness—all in the context of danger." Truscott's older son, Doodie, would one day describe his father's polo playing: "He was absolutely fearless, which gave him an advantage over many opponents who would eventually back off a little when he pushed them too far. And he played to win. For sport and exercise, too, but mainly to *win.*"[20]

Truscott wanted his sons to play the game as well. Younger son Jamie's first horse riding took place on ponies led by Harris at Fort Leavenworth. Doodie recalled that he first began riding—and training for polo—not on a pony, but on a wooden horse. This practice was "in a padded pen with sloping floors, so that one could hit a polo ball time after time and have it roll back so that he could hit it again. "When you get on that [real] horse," his father cautioned him one day, "I want you hitting the ball and not his legs or ankles." When Doodie moved to a real horse, younger brother Jamie mounted the wooden dummy. Truscott taught Doodie the basics of the game of polo after his son turned fourteen. In the beginning he played on his father's team, learning the duties of each position. After two years Truscott announced, "Today I start teaching you polo." From then on he played on the opposing team.[21]

When Doodie was fifteen, his father took him to Fort Riley for a visit. There they joined Captain Edward M. Daniels, 13th Cavalry, one of Truscott's friends from border duty and later at Fort Riley. While reminiscing about their experiences, Truscott and Daniels decided to give the teenager a compressed version of all that they had learned at Fort Riley, though in just three days. Doodie remembered that they took him "on every wild ride they had ever been on in those earlier years: in and out of all the canyons; down all of the slides; fording and then swimming the Republican River, in the water holding on to the horse's tail and being pulled along behind him; over every type of jump known to man." At the end of the day, Truscott and Daniels pronounced the youngster to be the "only man to graduate from the Advanced Equitation Course in three days, but only because of the high quality of the instructors, not the ability of the student." When he attended West Point, Doodie played polo for three years, the last year as team captain.[22]

Later, when Doodie served as an infantry officer and was departing for action in Korea, his father equated polo with war in one respect: "Listen, Son, goddammit . . . you play games to *win,* not lose. And you fight wars to win! . . . They're won by men who can be first-class sonsofbitches when they have to be. . . . No sonofabitch, no commander."[23]

Truscott the husband had a softer side. While at Fort Leavenworth, he and Sarah taught themselves French, which Lucian utilized to translate articles from the *French Cavalry Journal* (published by the Cavalry School at Saumur) for benefit of the Command and General Staff School. Self-teaching had always been one of his best qualities. While he clearly benefited from his army training, in many ways Truscott was a self-educated man—always reading, always learning. In later years his softer side would find expression in flower gardening, cooking, and woodworking, which Doodie remembered as "making beautiful furniture by hand, *never* with a power tool."[24]

Sarah had smoothed Lucian's jagged Oklahoma edges. She taught him about good manners, fine furnishings, appreciation of the best food and wine, and the way to serve formal dinners. When it was their turn to host a cocktail party or dinner, which on occasion might have fifty to one hundred guests, Sarah was the dedicated hostess, orchestrating the event like a bandleader who also played the most difficult instrument. As Doodie later recalled, when it came to her husband, "she helped him become the gentleman who in later years would feel perfectly at ease with both infantry privates in foxholes and royalty in palaces." Nevertheless, she never hesitated to curb his excesses. If at a dinner party he became a little boisterous, she would lean over and say quietly, "Lucian, you're *not* being very attractive." Sarah was five feet, two inches tall and weighed a little over one hundred pounds, but she was a powerhouse well deserving of Lucian's pet name for her—"Powerful Katrinka" (a cartoon and cinema character from the 1920s). To his credit, Truscott accepted the admonitions and was the better for them.[25]

Sometimes the couple's southern roots showed. They grew up on the far sides of the South during an era when the use of racial epithets was so commonplace as to be acceptable in many circles. Race relations as such hardly existed in the 1930s because, for the most part, the races did not relate. African Americans, denied access to any significant education or employment opportunity, were subsequently castigated for their lack of education and employment skills. The Truscott children, whenever possible, attended private schools. As Doodie later related to one of his own children, while at Fort Riley, "I went to Catholic grade school downtown. The reason I went to the Catholic grade school was because they allowed blacks in the public schools . . . , and it was the same when we went to Fort Leavenworth in high school. Practically all of the post kids went to the Catholic high school for basically the same reason."[26]

In 1938 Truscott's seventy-one-year-old mother, Maria Temple, suffered a stroke. He arranged her transportation to Station Hospital at Fort Leavenworth, where she died on August 7 at 3:30 in the morning. As his sister Patsy recalled, "She died . . . without regaining consciousness, and we buried her in Hickory Grove Cemetery in Haywood, Oklahoma, next to Dad." Doodie later recalled: "Although I doubt he would have admitted it, he was an emotional man, and very sentimental. I saw him cry when his mother died."[27]

The children of Marie Temple and Lucian Truscott, Sr., reunited for her funeral: Lucian from Fort Leavenworth; Loretta Estelle from Oklahoma City; Patsy Bryan from Nowata, Oklahoma; and Dixie Ozema from Tidra, Oklahoma. They buried their mother under the largest tree in the cemetery's grove.[28]

Dr. Truscott had died of pneumonia in June 1922 at age sixty. A relative who was a young girl at the time recalled that her own father, a preacher, had taken the Rock Island train from McAlester to Haywood, a distance of fifteen miles, to conduct his funeral. She later recalled: "I believe alcohol contributed to Dr. Truscott's death, but if there was ever drug involvement, I was too naïve to hear of it. I remember him as a quiet man, likable; there, when we needed him. . . . [W]orse than the possible negatives . . . were the hints that perhaps Dr. Truscott didn't believe in God."[29]

Lucian had another family problem at the time. He thought that his daughter, Mary, was simply too attractive to be on an army post. The man who would eventually become her second husband—Graeme Bruce—recalled: "When Mary got to her teens she was very bright, attractive, sexy, and surrounded by men. She was high-spirited and had a very good figure and beautiful legs—not much imagination needed to picture what that did when she walked past a bunch of fit young troopers! Her father adored her and guarded her, and she had no real freedom to date and experiment with boys of her own age." Bruce further speculated that her qualities, which Truscott so admired in his wife and her sisters, were not necessarily the qualities he wanted in his daughter, and that he had probably wanted a son when Mary was born. Bruce recalled Mary saying that her father "made her ride and jump and fall and get up and go on, and a bit he treated her like a trooper who needed breaking in to discipline. . . . Mary loved her father and admired him in many ways, and I suppose she forgave him for wanting her to be a boy, but I think some damage was done."[30]

Lucian the father was as strict with his children as Truscott the officer was with his troops. Doodie once recalled, "He was a stern, always demanding, and frequently ruthless disciplinarian." Yet he was a caring father as well. Lucian interested Mary and younger son Jamie, age nine, in joining him to become members of the Fort Leavenworth Hunt Club, a chartered club of the National Steeplechase and Hunt Association. The Hunt Club expected Jamie to maintain a journal in which for each hunt he noted the date, weather, and temperature; type of hunt; number of miles; and number of hounds. At the end of each outing, he summarized the highlights. On November 19 he jotted: "I got very much mud in the face. And how!" Finally, at one of the club breakfasts, the group formally admitted the Truscotts as members. On December 24 Jamie penciled in his journal: "The hounds rioted [ran out of control] twice on the last run. Dad, Mary, and I got our FLH colors at the hunt breakfast today."[31]

CHAPTER 8

Preparing for War

As June 1940 arrived, Truscott's tour of duty at the Command and General Staff School ended. In August the army promoted him to lieutenant colonel. By now, Truscott was well aware that there was pressure to do away with the cavalry branch, and he was anxious to join other progressive officers, including old friend George Patton, in embracing the concept of mechanized and armored cavalry.

One who refused to do so was Major General John K. Herr, chief of cavalry. He fiercely defended the use of horses from all foes and dismissed the arguments of anyone who saw it as a moribund practice. Truscott, who would always think highly of the general, nonetheless remembered with sadness: "It was a real sorrow to him that so many cavalry officers were seeking . . . experience in the mechanized units and in the burgeoning armored force at Fort Knox. He was especially distressed that among these were many of the best horsemen and polo players in the cavalry." It must have been a startling slap to him that even Patton and Truscott were closing the gate on the horse cavalry. Truscott concluded, "It was General Herr's misfortune that he would not recognize that the missions of mechanized and armored elements were cavalry missions and that the office of the chief of cavalry should have been in the forefront of the organization and development of such units." Instead, Herr minimized the effectiveness of the "untried" machine gun over the "proved and tried horse" and as late as 1938 attempted to get the army to reconsider the combat use of the saber. While sorry to leave Fort Leavenworth and the horse cavalry, Truscott had no choice but to consider a different future. "The old order was changing," he could see. "What the future held was problematical, almost frightening—and challenging!"[1]

Beginning in September 1939, the German army, known as the Wehrmacht, gave the American and other armies a preview of that challenging future. Newsreels showed the German blitzkrieg rolling into Poland, the May 1940 withdrawal of the British from Dunkirk, and the June 1940 defeat of France. When Poland fell, the U.S. Army, like those of Britain and France, was still somewhat mentally mired in the muddy trenches. In the Great War before a major battle, generals positioned hundreds of thousands of tons of war materiel at selected railhead supply dumps, obvious clues as to where an attack would come. Days of artillery bombardments followed, revealing about when the attack would commence. Finally, along a twenty- or thirty-mile-wide front, infantry soldiers left their trenches and trotted toward no-man's land—a frontal assault against an entrenched enemy. Throughout the resulting battle, senior commanders remained in the rear, well out of artillery range.[2]

Long before 1939, the Wehrmacht had dismissed trench warfare, instead focusing on the future and bounding forward in a new direction. Between the wars, other countries dabbled with variations of modernized warfare that involved armor, airplanes, and mechanized mobility, but the Germans were able to put it all together. Major General Oswald Lutz and Lieutenant Colonel Heinz Guderian, his chief of staff, revolutionized the battlefield. Guderian, in particular, essentially created the blitzkrieg. In terms of strategy everything about it was different. Guderian and his commanders stayed close to the front—not the rear—and remained in continual contact among themselves and with their planners, not by Morse code, but by transmitted speech. Their headquarters were kept purposefully small—consisting of a few armored vehicles only—and were highly mobile. Reconnaissance aircraft dropped photographs each day of whatever lay ahead.[3]

Blitzkrieg battles might initiate with German parachute infantry drops, under Luftwaffe command, or silent, precise glider landings often followed by air-transported infantry. (On at least one occasion, German soldiers made a premature landing at an enemy airfield in Oslo; it was fortunate for them that their commanders had drilled them on getting out of the plane and into battle rapidly.) The Luftwaffe assisted ground forces, providing close air support and protecting the exposed flanks of relatively fast-rolling armored spearheads. Instead of preliminary artillery bombardments that alerted the enemy, surprise attacks by dive bombers delivered amazingly accurate strikes. Diving from 10,000 to 3,000 feet at angles of seventy to eighty degrees, the Stuka dive bombers also utilized built-in sirens to deliver a terrifying, high-pitched scream during their attacks.[4]

Ground attacks often began with armored scout cars probing forward, with motorcycle soldiers aiding in reconnaissance. Then a narrow front, perhaps four miles wide and consisting of two or three columns of tanks, followed behind. Usually, they traveled along two or three parallel roads with connecting side roads through an area selected to minimize opportunities for defense or counterattack. Infantry in trucks and half-tracks followed. Assisting the soldiers were German "pioneers," combat engineers who were highly trained can-do experts with a vast assortment of specialized equipment. They could rapidly build, repair, or destroy whatever commanders needed in order to keep the armored spearhead ramming forward.[5]

Instead of attacking the strongest point, armored columns often bypassed it, turning in various directions to keep the enemy guessing as to the columns' destination until a pincer movement caught the defenders by surprise. If called upon, artillery was close behind, though with forward observers directing fire from leapfrogging units so that at least one was always in position to fire. In one city slated for capture, Rotterdam, German floatplanes landed in a river and disgorged infantry troops into rafts, while parachute infantry landed inside the city's sports stadium and commandeered streetcars to take them to their objectives.[6]

The U.S. Army watched the newsreels, read the summaries, and stood stunned in anxious amazement. It was a lesson for Americans on how a forward-thinking military intended to conduct modern warfare. Blitzkrieg tactics so startled General George Marshall that he immediately ordered Major General Adna R. Chaffee to create an armored force. Chaffee, described by Truscott as "a distinguished cavalryman from a distinguished army family," was the right choice. By July 1940 he had organized both the 1st Armored "Old Ironsides" Division at Fort Knox, Kentucky, and the 2nd Armored "Hell on Wheels" Division at Fort Benning, Georgia. There is little doubt that Chaffee would have commanded an army in Europe had cancer not ended his life prematurely.[7]

As the U.S. Army accelerated its preparation for war, whenever and wherever it arrived, competition for scarce resources turned cutthroat. Air and armor commanders had the best argument for a bigger cut of the budget, but infantry and artillery skillfully resisted inroads on their funding. The fat of the horse cavalry had never looked more appetizing, and it was served up quickly. Throughout

1940 and 1941, the army raced to make up for lost time. One of its most intensive efforts was to develop the nascent mechanized and armored units at Fort Knox. The 1st and 13th Cavalry Regiments of the 7th Cavalry Brigade, already assigned there, swiftly added the word "mechanized" to their names.[8]

Patton saw the future as armor, not horses. He encouraged Truscott to do the same, stating in a letter: "I saw [Major] General [Jacob L.] Devers the other day and stated that you had hopes of getting into the Armored Force. He told me that if you would apply for a transfer, he would be more than delighted to approve it. My advice to you is to get here as fast as you can."[9]

The Truscott family arrived at Fort Knox soon thereafter. The post must have seemed like a small town surprised to find itself hosting an immense rock concert. There was little in the way of accommodations for the new arrivals. Shaking their heads in disbelief, even full colonels found themselves—and their families—having to live in large pyramidal tents stretched on wood floors and eating their family meals at the officers' mess. Eventually, many, including the Truscotts, resorted to renting houses in the nearby communities of Louisville or Elizabethtown, almost twenty miles away. Traffic was also a problem. The roads were too few and too narrow in the area, and the armored convoys were too many and too long. Truscott found it necessary to leave early in the morning and stay late at night, paying the price in loss of family time.

Assigned for six months as operations officer for the 13th Armored Regiment, he underwent initial armor indoctrination with all the other officers. They started with the basics: how to drive and do primary maintenance on all the motor and armored transports likely to be under their command someday. Truscott realized that he had traded saddle for throttle and horseshoes for tracks.[10]

Meanwhile, the army's prewar expansion continued in other areas as well, necessitating assignments of staff officers to develop and train the many new units. Having received at least some experience with armor capabilities, many Fort Knox officers, including Truscott, were assigned elsewhere, whether interested in a new assignment or not. In March 1941 the lieutenant colonel reported to Fort Lewis, Washington, assigned as assistant G-3 (operations and training) for the IX Army Corps, which served as training and tactical command for the Fourth Army, headquartered at San Francisco. For Truscott it would be a seminal assignment, bringing him into close contact with Colonel Dwight D. Eisenhower. Although they had both been in Washington, D.C., in 1932, this would be their first meeting.[11]

When Truscott arrived at Fort Lewis, it was home to the 3rd Infantry Division, nicknamed the "Rock of the Marne" from its service during the Great War, when it had held the line near Château-Thierry, protecting Paris as other units gave way to advancing Germans. In 1939 the army had reorganized the command as one of the experimental "triangular" divisions, with three regiments, each of which was expandable into a regimental combat team (RCT) by inclusion of supporting artillery, engineers, and service troops. In the not-so-distant future, Truscott would command the 3rd Infantry Division, and for the rest of his life, it would hold a special place in his heart.[12]

At the time, Colonel Eisenhower served in the 3rd Infantry Division, commanding a battalion of the 15th Infantry "Can Do" Regiment. From 1911 to 1938, the regiment had seen service in Tientsin, China, where its soldiers earned the sobriquet "Old China Hands." Although only a lieutenant colonel at the time, Eisenhower had come to the attention of the division's commander, Major General Kenyon Joyce, who was in need of a chief of staff. Since the 3rd was one of the two primary combat divisions assigned within IX Corps, Truscott had a front-row seat to observe Eisenhower. It was a lesson in how to do staff work. As he noted: "When a command decision or approval of any proposal or contemplated action was required, Colonel Eisenhower . . . invariably had the staff officer who was primarily concerned with the problem make the presentation. . . . Colonel Eisenhower conducted no staff conferences as chief of staff; he preferred to work with the individual staff officers concerned with the staff preparation on problems, and he was always readily accessible for consultation and advice to such officers."[13]

Truscott continued to juggle his professional and family responsibilities, even though he necessarily spent more time away from his family. In June 1941 one of his concerns was that son Doodie, now age nineteen, was anxious to win an appointment to West Point. On June 4 he received a Western Union telegram from his son: "Very important all Ohio friends particularly Cleveland District use influence with Mrs. Bolton either directly or through other senators and representatives to appoint me. Her vacancy my only chance. Have been advised appointment will probably depend on number and degree of pressure from her own district. She is Republican. Time element important."[14]

Truscott garnered whatever political influence he could. The "Ohio friends" were most probably members of the country club where he had coached summer polo years earlier. Doodie would go on to receive an appointment to West Point, but not the easy way. On his first try he received the nomination but had not done well enough on the qualifying tests; the following year he did well enough on the tests but no longer had the nomination. In a testament to his determination, he enlisted in the army, served in a military-police unit for a period, and received an appointment from within the ranks, an opportunity reserved each year for a very small number of active-duty soldiers. Lucian and Sarah were pleased when the U.S. Military Academy finally admitted their son. Doodie would graduate in 1945, with Sarah, though not Lucian, there to see him toss his cadet hat into the air.[15]

One of Truscott's principal staff duties at Fort Lewis was to plan and oversee large-scale war maneuvers. He labored for months, planning and implementing division-against-division contests. Throughout this time, he and Sarah were frequently apart, sharing the emotional cost of separation that is always either present or potential within a military family. In a letter to Sarah dated May 20, 1941, Lucian mentioned reconnoitering a California maneuver area and saying how much he liked the landscape near Fort Ord and the old Monterey Presidio, one of their previous assignments. Perhaps in an effort to offer her a ray of hope, he wrote, "A ranch like this would be my idea of a perfect life." He was pleased with the outcome of the war games. On June 9, in another letter to Sarah, Lucian mentioned that the maneuvers had been "a grand success from every point of view." When Eisenhower moved on to San Antonio for the even bigger job of chief of staff of the Fifth Army, Truscott lamented on the seventeenth, "I certainly am sorry to see him go—my regard for him has grown steadily ever since I came to Lewis."[16]

During the maneuvers, Truscott had occasion to meet Brigadier General Mark W. Clark, recently promoted directly from lieutenant colonel. Clark served as deputy chief of staff to Major General Lesley J. McNair, and he had brought with him a task force of staff officers from General Headquarters in Washington, D.C., to observe the exercises. The immediate critique of the division was positive, but the eventual report was much less so. Truscott found such to be typical of the "fashion of inspectors from time immemorial in the army." The good news, however, was that Clark seemed to take note of Truscott.[17]

In August 1941 Truscott's duties sent him to Camp Polk, Louisiana, to help umpire the largest series of maneuvers in the U.S. Army's history. For the mock armies, General Clark devised a simple scenario that would result in some sort of geographical collision. The rules for the generals were just as simple, something akin to meet and defeat. Just getting hundreds of thousands of appropriately supplied soldiers in place and then keeping them supplied was a tremendous effort. Adding river crossings, withdrawals, and combined operations of infantry, artillery, armor, and air support was exactly the kind of training the commanders needed. At the end of the maneuvers, Eisenhower's planning for what turned out to be the winning army earned him a brigadier's star. His approach of drafting flexible and responsive orders proved to be superior to the planning of his opposition, which had followed the detailed style of instructions used during the Great War.[18]

In November 1941 Truscott received something he had dreamed of—command of a cavalry regiment. The family traveled back to Fort Bliss, where he took command of the 5th Cavalry Regiment, 1st Cavalry Division. It was a return not only to Fort Bliss but also to a cavalry unit—and with it came a chance to play polo again. In actuality, the 1st Cavalry Division was now a hybrid cavalry command. While it still had 6,000 horses, it now also had 178 scout cars, twelve mortar carriers, seventeen combat cars (later called tanks), and 420 motorcycles.

Truscott's time with the regiment would be short-lived, however. On a warm Sunday morning in December, some at Fort Bliss were coming home from church; others were taking part in the weekly drag hunt; and still others, in barracks and homes, were listening to the radio while doing other things. When the music suddenly stopped, most of them looked at their radios. In a few seconds an excited announcer told them that the Japanese had just attacked the U.S. naval base at Pearl Harbor.[19]

CHAPTER 9

CALLED TO WASHINGTON, 1942

Between the wars, the U.S. Army was like an abandoned bicycle—parts not yet stripped away rusted quickly until it was barely usable. No one denied that the country still needed the military, but once the Allies had won the "war to end all wars," what was the sense in having more soldiers than necessary? Americans knew that the Atlantic and Pacific Oceans were the country's real defense east and west, and that neither nation north or south presented a problem.

Still, the blitzkrieg into Poland had been downright alarming. That first day of September 1939, the Germans spearheaded sixty divisions into its eastern neighbor. By June 1940 the Germans also had smashed north and west through Denmark, Norway, the Netherlands, Belgium, Luxembourg, and France.[1]

The shock of these events in Europe prompted Congress to enlarge the U.S. Army to 185,000 soldiers. Even at that, it was still smaller than was the army of Romania. Ostensibly made up of nine divisions, just three were fully organized, and even those were only partially staffed. All of the various National Guard units amounted to just under 200,000 soldiers, but its divisions were skeletonized, its equipment obsolete or nonexistent, and its training poor. Worse was that many senior National Guard officers had been installed through political favor or were simply too old. Poorly trained, equipped, and led, the guard would need a serious overhaul to be of any help to the regular army.[2]

One small hole in the black clouds above America beamed in a little brightness. That was when General Marshall became army chief of staff, coincidently on the same day as the blitzkrieg into Poland. President Roosevelt now had in place the second leader the nation needed. Roosevelt and Marshall were very different men, and they would not have been friends in any other situation. Nonetheless, they formed one of the best political partnerships in American history. What made their partnership even more unusual was that they soon disagreed on one immensely important issue: how best to fight the Germans. What they did agree on, however, was that war was coming, and they needed to get Americans ready for it. During the fall of 1940, Marshall tiptoed his way through a post–Great War isolationist minefield and successfully advocated for a one-year military draft and activation of the Army Reserve and the National Guard. Later he persuaded Congress to extend the call-up, which it achieved by a sliver vote of 203 to 202. Had lawmakers not done so, the original activation would have expired only a few months before the Pearl Harbor attack.[3]

Now that Japanese forces had ravaged American bases in Hawaii, Roosevelt knew that Americans, even members of Congress, were ready to roll up their sleeves and go to work. Never before had the nation achieved such unity of purpose in undertaking an immense mission. Fortunately, Roosevelt had already taken some action to bolster Great Britain. He had accomplished this by pushing Congress to pass and implement the Lend-Lease Act. As historian Charles MacDonald notes, "Even Congressmen had discovered that it would take more than a wave of the magic wand of appropriations to undo the neglect of twenty years." From its beginning in the spring of 1941 through the end of World War II, the equipment "lent" included fifty destroyers, 37,000 tanks, 43,000 airplanes, 800,000 trucks, and two million rifles.[4]

For British prime minister Winston Churchill, the Japanese attack on Pearl Harbor meant that America would go to war and that Britain would not have to fight alone. Still, he was nervous. The previous year he and Roosevelt had secretly agreed that they would fight the war in Europe first, then deal with Japan. Now, Churchill was certain that Americans were lacing up their gloves and getting ready to drive a knockout punch to their opponent. His concern, though, was that they were looking at Japan, not Germany. He needed to talk with Roosevelt in person, and soon. While the spilled blood of American sailors and soldiers was still fresh, Churchill journeyed to Washington, D.C., to meet with the American president. Most pressing during this conference was a reaffirmation of the policy of "Germany First." Meeting privately, neither Churchill nor Roosevelt shied away from their previous commitment that it was essential to defeat the Nazis before dispatching significant forces to the Pacific.[5]

The next discussion centered on how best to organize and command the amalgam of Allied forces. The two readily agreed that Roosevelt's senior military staff and Churchill's senior military staff would become the Combined Chiefs of Staff and as such would develop and guide overall military strategy. The final area of discussion was the most contentious: how should the Allies go about defeating Germany? From the beginning, it was obvious that the Americans and British were far from agreement. Marshall had accepted the necessity of making the lesser effort in the Pacific for the time being. In fact, his staff was already considering some sort of invasion in Europe should it become apparent that the Soviet Union's Red Army was about to collapse. Churchill and his staff looked at one another and shook their collective heads at the American naïveté. The Germans had just jackbooted the English out of Europe, and they had no doubt that Hitler could easily handle any premature Allied invasion. For them, even suggesting any kind of European invasion was recklessly premature.[6]

Churchill hoped to persuade Roosevelt and his generals and admirals that some action in the Mediterranean, which he termed Germany's "soft underbelly," might be the better alternative. Josef Stalin had first suggested the idea to the prime minister, asking, "Why stick your head in the alligator's mouth at Brest [France] when you can go to the Mediterranean and rip his belly." While Roosevelt pondered the possibilities, Marshall argued forcefully that anything in the Mediterranean would be little more than a diversion. Anyway, he added, an invasion there would probably not be enough of a second front to satisfy or benefit the Soviets. Churchill, who took delight in taking his considerable persuasive talent for a power walk now and then, smiled and nodded at the general and then looked to the president, listing the benefits of invading North Africa. He enumerated that it might be possible to trap the German Afrika Korps between a new Allied invasion force and the British Eighth Army, which was already fighting in Egypt. In addition, liberating North Africa could result in the reopening of the Suez Canal, saving time, distance, and shipping. Such a campaign also would give U.S. forces some relatively easy battle experience and might allow Vichy French forces to rejoin the Allies. Finally, he argued, it would be a good-faith second front to assist Stalin. Roosevelt needed time to study the matter, but he was astute enough to see that a North African invasion was particularly important to Churchill because it also protected British interests in the Mediterranean. Still, much to Marshall's discomfort, the president recognized the merits to this strategy.[7]

If anyone had any doubt about the ability of Marshall, it was not Roosevelt. He once said that he would have trouble sleeping at night if the general were out of the country. Roosevelt needed him at home to manage the war in both Europe and the Pacific and to oversee preparations on the home front. Marshall could read between the lines; someone else would have to become combat commander in Europe. Roosevelt saw in Marshall what others perhaps missed: he was not only an able general but also a superb politician and an impressive statesman.[8]

Of Marshall's many skills, the one for which he is often remembered was his ability to identify future commanders. Rumor had it that his "little black book" held the names of many officers he had encountered over the years. In due time some would be promoted early, others would remain in obscurity, and more than a few would be forced into retirement. Some he championed were future stars—Eisenhower, Omar N. Bradley, and Mark Clark—others were troublesome but battle-willing warriors—Patton, Terry de la Mesa Allen, and Joseph W. Stilwell—and a couple turned out to be bad picks—Lloyd R. Fredendall and Edward M. Almond. All were destined to wear general's stars. Others never even made the little black book—one of them being Lucian Truscott.[9]

While much was going on in Washington, D.C., Truscott, back in Texas as commander of the 5th Cavalry, had received a promotion to full colonel (temporary) the day before Christmas 1941. He and many other commanders were busy securing the Southwest—an immense area—from possible invasion or sabotage by the Japanese. While he enjoyed commanding his horse soldiers in the desert country, he thirsted for a taste of action. Most of all, he hoped that he would not miss this war as he had the last. While Truscott was well known within the cavalry, that branch was essentially obsolete and virtually ignored. Few in the infantry, artillery, or other branches of the army knew him. He wondered if he would command in the Pacific or Europe, or if would he languish in an obscure staff or training position. At the dawn of World War II, it was fortunate for him that a few noncavalry commanders knew of his talents. These men were already in Washington, D.C., or on their way, and they would remember him.[10]

The first to arrive in the capital was Mark Clark, whom Truscott had met at Fort Lewis. Clark still served as deputy chief of staff to

Lieutenant General McNair, who had the unenviable job of growing an army of 185,000 to more than 8 million men. Because McNair, a former artilleryman, was hard of hearing, he often relied on his deputy to attend meetings in his stead. This brought Clark to Marshall's attention. The chief of staff had attended the Louisiana maneuvers of 1941, and there he saw two other commanders he considered standouts. The first was Colonel Eisenhower, whose maneuver planning as Fifth Army chief of staff had been masterful. The other was George Patton, now a major general, whose aggressive and unorthodox style appealed to Marshall, who could tolerate a few faults if he could find a fighter looking for a scrap. He saw immediately that Patton could lead a unit through hell or high water but that it would be essential to keep a tight rope around his neck. With Clark, Eisenhower, and Patton running some plays on the field, they might encourage Marshall to pull Truscott from the bench to join them.[11]

Five days after the Pearl Harbor attack, Colonel Walter Bedell "Beetle" Smith of the War Department summoned Eisenhower to Washington, telling him to "hop a plane and get up here right away." Previously, Marshall had asked General Clark for ten names of senior officers to consider for the then-vacant position of deputy chief of war plans, the office responsible for the major planning of America's military effort. Clark replied that he could give Marshall one name and nine dittos, all "Dwight D. Eisenhower." Upon touching down at Washington's airport, Eisenhower lost no time in making his way to the chief of staff's office. Within moments of meeting Marshall, Eisenhower realized that every day in Washington from then on would be an Olympic challenge. Worse, the challenge would continue for the next four years. Long hours, incredible stress, and pack after pack of cigarettes would be his closest companions.[12]

By March 1942 the army had reorganized at the highest level. After an uncertain beginning, the U.S. Joint Chiefs of Staff came into being, consisting of Marshall as chairman and army chief of staff; Admiral Ernest J. "Ernie" King as chief of naval operations; Lieutenant General Henry H. "Hap" Arnold as commanding general of the Army Air Forces; and, as President Roosevelt's personal representative, Fleet Admiral William D. Leahy, previously ambassador to Vichy France. Leahy, although a member of the navy, was not close with King and thought highly of Marshall. Somehow, for the country's sake, Marshall had to pull this group together.

Getting the navy to join with the army and Army Air Forces in accepting the basic concept of a joint-chiefs operating group might not have been so difficult had it not been for Admiral King. He seemed always to be enraged about something. Marshall concluded that he would have to watch his colleague as closely as the Germans and Japanese. One who was not a fan of King was Eisenhower, who confided in his diary that shooting the admiral, whom he considered rude, exceedingly uncooperative, and something of a bully, would be a help to the war effort. King ignored Eisenhower and focused his considerable talents on garnering military resources for the Pacific War, which was where he thought the country should fight. Many disliked him, but few questioned his competence. He knew the navy as few others did, having served as a destroyer flotilla commander, submariner, aviator, and carrier captain.[13]

Regardless of whether their first invasion occurred in Europe or in the Pacific, the Allies needed landing craft, but none seemed to be available. Eisenhower lost all patience attempting to find out who controlled the flow of their production. The answer, as it turned out, was King, whose hand was on that particular spigot. Since the admiral was most interested in the Pacific, he directed shipping production there first, which meant building big ships, not landing craft. Not until Marshall threatened that the army would build its own landing craft and train its own crews did King loosen the valve on production. "The legacy of the Navy's reluctance to develop landing craft," historian Charles MacDonald notes, "would complicate many an Allied decision as the war progressed."[14]

A significant problem surfaced early between the army and the Army Air Forces, a fundamental disagreement about the role of airpower in the war. The air forces viewed its job as wresting control of potentially hostile airspace and then delivering strategic bombing, thus laying waste to the enemy's infrastructure. The best way to assist the ground effort, its leaders reasoned, was to destroy munitions factories, rail yards, and troop concentrations. The army agreed, but it also needed close air support, meaning tactical bombing against ground targets on demand. Seldom were there sufficient resources and the inclination to do both.[15]

In March 1942 Eisenhower's Washington planning staff produced three ultrasecret major war plans. The first was codenamed Operation Sledgehammer, which envisioned an immediate invasion of France should it appear that the Soviet Union was about to collapse. The second was Operation Bolero, the plan for a major buildup and staging of U.S. forces in the British Isles. The third was Operation Roundup, intended as a spring 1943 cross-channel invasion of France. Churchill was not impressed with Sledgehammer. It would fail, he concluded, and a failed invasion was worse than none at all. He fully supported Bolero since it brought the Americans closer to the seat of war. He was most certainly not a fan of Roundup, hoping instead to persuade the Americans that the Mediterranean offered a better portal into Europe.

In June while visiting Washington, the prime minister was introduced to Generals Eisenhower and Clark. He was still cool to Operation Sledgehammer but warmed to the two young generals. "Thus began," Churchill later wrote, "a friendship which across all the ups and downs of war I have preserved with deep satisfaction to this day." He later paid the U.S. Army a mighty compliment: "It remains to me a mystery as yet unexplained how the very small staffs which the United States kept during the years of peace were able not only to build up the armies and air force units, but also to find the leaders and vast staffs capable of handling enormous masses and of moving them faster and farther than masses have ever been moved in war before."[16]

The answer to this "mystery" was the U.S. Army's "school system" developed between the wars. The small officer corps had always been a professional group, but with significant attention given to the various branch schools, the Command and General Staff School, and the Army War College, the army had become, in today's managerial parlance, a learning organization. The decision to couple successful completion of the various educational programs with promotions ensured survival of the school system. Truscott's attendance at the Cavalry School and the Command and General Staff School, and his subsequent teaching positions in each, gave him the foundation he would need to earn general's stars in the future. Marshall would later conclude that the system had been hugely successful. In a later interview with historian Edward Coffman, General J. Lawton "Lightning Joe" Collins would add that the school system had saved the army.[17]

As Marshall, Clark, and Eisenhower designed and implemented the American war plan for Europe, Colonel Truscott continued to help prepare the 1st Cavalry Division to go to war. On one clear April morning at Fort Bliss, before early coolness gave way to warmth, Truscott rode over the mesa to watch his regiment conduct maneuvers below. Unnoticed by the colonel, who focused on the dust-kicking commotion, his regimental messenger had come up with an urgent message from the sergeant major: Washington wanted to talk to Truscott right away. It was the call for which he had been hoping.

One can picture Truscott letting his horse break into a run as he returned to headquarters and, after a quick dismount worthy of a cowboy-movie stuntman, calling Washington and soon finding himself speaking with General Clark. "Take what time you need to get ready," Clark said, "but you ought to be here within the next two or three days. . . . All I can tell you is that you are going overseas. Be prepared for extended field service in a cold, not arctic, climate." Truscott squeezed preparations for what would become a four-year absence into two days. On the third day, before dawn, he sat in a civilian passenger plane flying east into the sunrise. He was a little uneasy since he was still in the dark as far as his future was concerned. His thoughts alternated between the cloaked mission and uncertainty about when—if ever—he would see Sarah, Mary, Doodie, and Jamie again.[18]

In April 1942 Washington, D.C., was already a busy place, though not the hectic wartime machine it was to become. Men in military uniforms seemed to be everywhere. Truscott reported to General Clark's office, located in what previously had been the serene campus of the Army War College at Washington Barracks, now Fort McNair. It was not far from where he and his cavalry troopers had confronted the Bonus Marchers a decade earlier. Now the campus served as headquarters for U.S. Army Ground Forces. Clark greeted him by asking how he might like being a "commando." Truscott had heard of the British commandos, for they had been in the news recently. Somewhat surprised, he said he thought he might like it very much. Clark then revealed Truscott's orders. He would go to London, where the colonel would lead a group of American planning officers whose mission was to work with British planning staff under Lord Louis Mountbatten. Clark then dispatched Truscott to meet with General Eisenhower.[19]

Still feeling uneasy about his future role, Truscott made his way to Eisenhower's office, which prior to completion of the new Pentagon, operated out of the Munitions Building on Twentieth Street. Upon arriving, the colonel realized that he stood at the epicenter of the army's military-planning effort. He could see that at any given moment as many people were entering the building as were leaving. Military police thoroughly checked the identification of all who entered and further ensured that they proceeded directly to their approved destination. Building occupants displayed the uniforms of all U.S. military branches as well as those of Allied forces. Everyone seemed to carry charts, maps, or other papers in overstuffed briefcases. Modifications to the building were in progress, requiring Truscott to navigate through carpenters, plumbers, and electricians attempting to fit yet another office into some corner. He concluded that for whatever was going on in this building, there was no time to waste.[20]

Truscott located the right office. Eisenhower was as friendly as ever and paused to inquire about the colonel's family, mutual friends, and how the Southwest was proceeding in the face of war. After a moment the general got to the point. Marshall was considering an invasion of France, perhaps by the spring of 1943. There was even the possibility of something happening in the fall of 1942 should some exigency materialize. Eisenhower related that Marshall had asked Royal Navy vice admiral Lord Mountbatten if the United States could establish a group of American planners within his Combined Operations Headquarters. Mountbatten was more than willing. Eisenhower also mentioned that it was he who had suggested that Truscott was the right man for the job. He added that the War Department had already selected some key staff members for Truscott and that other Americans officers were already in various British planning groups. Eisenhower noted that the idea was not only to assist the planning effort but also to get to know their British friends better. He explained that what Marshall particularly wanted from him was the creation of opportunities for some American soldiers to gain combat experience, which they would then share with their fellow soldiers and subordinates.

As Truscott understood it, his mission was to ensure that in each assault unit there would be "a few men who had met the Germans in battle and who could be instructors and examples to their comrades and friends." He considered this doable. Commandos were conducting raids from time to time and were, in fact, about the only Allied ground forces in Europe gaining battle experience. Perhaps he could persuade their commanders to allow some Americans to go along, at first as observers, but later as participants.[21]

The U.S. Navy, Eisenhower told him, was not interested in the plan, favoring instead sending resources to the Pacific. Despite the amphibious training being conducted by Mountbatten's staff, Admiral King was doing all he could to enable the Pacific effort. As a result, the navy would assign no personnel—or landing craft—to Truscott's group. Eisenhower mentioned that ground forces was organizing "special Army engineer units to operate and maintain landing craft, establish bases, and the like." As it turned out, the navy managed to accommodate Marshall, but had it not done so, the result might have been better than what actually occurred.[22]

Truscott's later writings reflect his uncertainties at the time about his new mission. "I had no battle experience. . . . My cavalry background had brought limited contact with the Navy, and but little more with the Air Force. . . . But this assignment to a staff of battle-seasoned veterans of naval, ground, and air battles, actively engaged in planning and conducting operations against the Germans, would seem to call for an expert. This I definitely was not." He started to explain this to Eisenhower, who dismissed his concerns, citing the colonel's experience in both cavalry and armor and as an instructor and staff officer. He then added: "Even your experience as a polo player especially fit you for this assignment. You know that Lord Louis [Mountbatten] wrote a book on polo. You can learn, can't you?"[23]

In truth, the army had not recognized Truscott's talent during his early years. His officer-efficiency report of 1919 described him as an "able and efficient officer," while a similar report in 1921 called him an "average officer." Yet by 1925 a superior said of him, "I should be pleased to have Captain Truscott under my command at any time and under any circumstances." His efficiency report for 1929 read: "This officer has a fine, rugged, sturdy character and possesses outstanding characteristics of loyalty, straight forwardness, tenacity of purpose, and dogged determination. He is intense in both his professional work and in athletic competition." In 1932 his report noted that he "possesses unusual force and self-reliance." Moreover, by 1940 General McNair, then commandant at the Command and General Staff School (and now one of General Marshall's top subordinates), said of Truscott: "Keen, energetic, of pleasing personality, dependable and efficient. A deliberate, calm, stable character and an original thinker." Now, thanks to Eisenhower, Truscott would meet General Marshall for a special assignment. Marshall, of course, had reviewed the colonel's personnel file and had seen all the various comments. Even so, he was a man who could instantly see through any fluff and would come to his own conclusions.[24]

A few days later Marshall sent for Truscott. They had not met before. As the colonel entered the chief of staff's office, the general shook his hand and pointed to a chair. Marshall sat back in his own chair, focused on Truscott, and then spoke. "You are an older man than I wanted for this assignment. I looked you up—you are forty-seven. Mountbatten is forty-three. Most of his staff are younger. All of them are battle-experienced." Truscott's throat managed a hard swallow. Marshall continued, "But some of your friends assure me that you are younger than your years, and that your experience especially fits you for this assignment." Truscott recalled that his "mouth was more than dry enough to make speech difficult." Still, he had to say something. He professed his lack of credentials for the assignment, which Marshall easily parried. The meeting was short but illuminating. "General Marshall," Truscott recalled, "had removed any confusion in my mind as to what was expected of me. For the rest, it was up to me—and I could not fail."[25]

While Marshall would come to think very highly of Truscott, such was not the case at their first meeting. For whatever reason, he did not take an immediate liking to the Oklahoman. Not long after the meeting, Marshall spoke with Eisenhower, saying that he was not at all impressed with Truscott. He characterized the colonel as a wild Indian and asked Eisenhower where he had found him. By now, Eisenhower knew Marshall well enough not to back down. He replied that if the general trusted him, he should trust his judgment in selecting men. Marshall thought for a moment and then affirmed that Eisenhower was right. Apparently, despite Sarah's Pygmalion efforts, some of Truscott's Oklahoma rough edges still showed.[26]

Sarah, still at Fort Bliss, would have to represent herself and the absent Lucian at the wedding of their daughter, Mary, to Robert "Bobby" Wilbourn, a cavalry officer who would be sent with the 1st Cavalry Division to the Pacific. After the wedding Sarah packed the house and with young Jamie made her way to Washington, D.C. Because of flight delays, Lucian was still in the capital when they arrived. "Once again," he lamented, "she was to see me off to face an uncertain future. But there were no tears, only pride. Hers was the courage of the Roman matron."[27]

When Colonel Truscott departed for England, he knew nothing of the discussions among the American and British chiefs about North Africa and the Mediterranean. Within six months, however, he would know more about amphibious landings and North Africa than he ever thought possible. His efforts to gain some combat experience for a relatively small number of soldiers would eventually result in one of the finest units ever created in the U.S. Army. First, however, Truscott had a major challenge. He had to get to know the British.

CHAPTER 10

A Truscott Returns to England

On May 10, 1942, *Apache*, the Pan American World Airways Stratoliner carrying Colonel Truscott and a few of his staff, cautiously made its way through uncertain weather to England. Like its namesake, *Apache* moved stealthily through dangerous territory. Of the ten Stratoliners built by Boeing, the military had drafted five for the Army Transport Command. The aircraft flew at 20,000 feet as its four propellers pulled it along at 220 miles per hour for a distance of 2,400 miles. For its full load of five crewmembers and thirty-three passengers, the trip across the Atlantic might be pleasant, but it would not be quick. For Truscott, whose father's family had emigrated from Cornwall, England, it was a chance to return to his familial homeland.[1]

The flight had begun at Bolling Field, a military airfield across the Potomac River from Washington's civilian National Airport. The Stratoliner climbed and nosed its way to Montreal, where British officials placed on board confidential equipment known as "Identification Friend or Foe"; without it, as *Apache* neared England, an anxious Spitfire pilot might mistake it for an enemy aircraft. The route continued through adverse weather to Newfoundland, then on to Iceland, and finally to Prestwick Airfield, about thirty miles from Glasgow, Scotland. The whole trip, with time allowed for equipment installation and an impatient wait for improved weather, took the better part of a week.[2]

By happenstance, Truscott's traveling companion on both the flight and subsequent overnight train ride to London was an Englishman. He listened intently as the man described how the storm of war was buffeting the British people. They had lost many loved ones already in land battles overseas and in the Blitz, and they were doing without things once thought essential. A small percentage of the people had simply lost hope, believing that the war would go on forever and that life would never be the same. Now seated in a sleeping car of the rumbling train snaking its way south, Truscott sipped morning tea and scanned the passing countryside to where it finally morphed into London cityscape. There he saw the ugly bruises of war like the busted and bloodied nose of a boxer, having lost all shape under repeated poundings until it was hardly recognizable. Homes, office buildings, factories, and rail yards had been bombed, battered, and burned. Lucian dashed off a letter to Sarah on May 17, his first opportunity to do so, letting her know that he had arrived safely. By previous arrangement, Sarah and young Jamie would live at her family's home, Wild Acres, in Charlottesville, Virginia, where they would remain until Lucian's homecoming. She was certain that he would return and refused to think otherwise.[3]

Before Truscott had left Washington, Eisenhower had helped prepare him for his new assignment. As a silent observer in a string of high-level meetings, Truscott absorbed as much as he could. For him, the meetings were another chance to watch Eisenhower in action, another opportunity to learn. "Every view was considered," Truscott recalled. "Each problem was carefully analyzed. There was the same extraordinary ability to place his finger at once upon the crucial fact in any problem or the weak point in any proposition. There was the same ability to arrive at quick and confident decisions. And the same charming manner and unfailing good temper." Truscott would emulate the model for the rest of his career. He regarded these hours with Eisenhower as some of the most instructive of his career.[4]

As the train bumped and clacked into London over repeatedly repaired tracks, Truscott once again reviewed his instructions. His mission was to study the combined operations of the British military, especially those that were commando-related; cooperate fully in planning; keep Washington informed; and especially, promote "actual battle experience for as many as practicable of our personnel."[5]

Staff members of Lord Mountbatten's Combined Operations Headquarters welcomed the Truscott party at the train station. From there an American military-police lieutenant showed them to their quarters, which for a short while would be at the plush Grosvenor Hotel on Hyde Park. The following month they would move to breakfast lodgings in the private home of Mrs. Gordon Leith on Manchester Square, where they would remain for as long as they were in England. They took their meals, other than Mrs. Leith's fine breakfast, at a nearby American officers' mess. The menu was a product of American rations, English cuisine, and wartime shortages. A meal both typical and served much too frequently consisted of heavy gray bread, sausages made of mostly potato and cereal, Brussels sprouts or cabbage, and Spam. The last item caused Truscott to marvel that no matter how it was prepared, the result was no "change whatever in identity, or flavor."[6]

The appearance of British women surprised Truscott. For one thing, many wore military uniforms and performed military functions. They drove most of the army vehicles that continually scurried about like olive-drab ants in a giant rubble pile. This was something the arriving Americans had not seen in the United States—not yet, anyway. Those women not in uniform, the ones working in the shops or simply going about their business on the streets, seemed to Truscott to be "drab and untidy." No doubt, they cared for themselves as best they could, but it was clear that the "rough hand of war" had been cuffing them around for some time.[7]

Truscott was more than pleased with his new staff members, each having been carefully selected by Eisenhower's headquarters. They were Lieutenant Colonel H. B. Cleaves of the Army Signal Corps, Lieutenant Colonel Loren B. Hillsinger of the Army Air Forces, and Major Theodore J. Conway of the infantry. Conway, whose most recent assignment had been as a faculty member at West Point, would become one of Truscott's key staff throughout the war. These three officers had come with the colonel from the States, but another staff member, an American lieutenant commander unknown to Truscott, would soon join them in England. Lord Mountbatten had specifically requested and received the addition of a naval officer by suggesting it to U.S. Navy admiral Harry R. Stark, senior navy commander in London. In the fallout from Pearl Harbor, it was necessary to sacrifice a few admirals and generals. Stark, formerly navy chief of staff, was an indirect victim of the air raid, having been relieved from his position for the mistakes of others, though he never complained about it.[8]

On Monday, May 18, at 9:00 A.M., Truscott and his staff reported to Major General James E. Chaney, U.S. Army Air Forces, commanding general of army forces in the British Isles. The reception accorded them was underwhelming. Chaney seemed to have neither knowledge of nor interest in Truscott or his mission. Other senior officers in the general's headquarters subsequently passed on to Truscott their opinions that those in Washington seemed to be trying to run the war from their cozy desks. Two of Chaney's top officers, Brigadier General Charles L. Bolte and Brigadier General John E. Dahlquist, tendered their opinion that American officers had no business working as part of any British staff. As it turned out, Dahlquist would find himself working for Truscott in the future.[9]

The following morning the colonel and his staff reported to the office of Lord Mountbatten, for whom they would be working directly. Mountbatten called a meeting for the occasion and introduced the new arrivals to his principal officers, all of whom seemed pleased at the prospect of American involvement. Truscott, in a letter to Sarah, reported that he found Mountbatten to be friendly, graceful, relaxed, and with "more personality and force apparent than in any other Britishers I have met—and much more appealing to an American."[10]

Learning how the Combined Operations Headquarters worked was the first challenge. Not only was the British military much different in organization and culture from the American armed forces, but members of all four principal branches worked in the various sections. The mixing of Royal Army, Navy, Marines, and Air Force had evolved from the need for one combined unit to plan and lead commando raids on the coast of France, each operation having a definite ground, sea, and air component. The original force of about 20 officers had grown to more than 150, with even more administrative staff. Lord Mountbatten met with the group weekly to provide his personal support and to assess progress.[11]

The next challenge for Truscott was simply understanding the peculiarities of British English. Before coming to England, he had likely heard few Britons speak. Their use of the broad "a" and the frequency of abbreviations made comprehending them difficult. Truscott found that "they gave many words a pronunciation not common in America and used familiar words in unfamiliar ways." It must have been quite a challenge for a man who grew up in Texas and Oklahoma. Of course, he encountered a few puzzled expressions looking back at him when he spoke. He learned to mention early on that he had been born in Texas, which seemed to explain a lot. Once he managed to tune his ears, though, Truscott found himself impressed with how the British conducted their business meetings. Group members gave careful attention to represent differing views and to precision of language. Sincere courtesy seemed to be the rule even when disagreements arose, and meeting minutes carefully and accurately reflected the conversations. "Their staff papers," Truscott conceded, "usually had a literary quality generally superior to staff papers within my own experience in American practice."[12]

The British were also sticklers for maintaining top-level security for all military information, much more so than were the newcomer Americans. When Truscott once unknowingly dropped in a courtyard a paper with some meeting notes he had written, the following morning he received a visitor, a senior British intelligence officer. He advised the colonel that if Mountbatten were to learn of the unfortunate incident, he would have no choice but to ask General Marshall to relieve Truscott of his position. Thankfully, the intelligence officer did not pursue the matter, but from then on Truscott kept all confidential papers in trusted hands or locked in a safe.[13]

Over the next few weeks, the colonel visited various British training sites, witnessed raid rehearsals, toured the U.S. Army Air Forces' Eighth Bomber Command, and watched demonstrations of British parachute drops. On May 26 Marshall promoted Truscott to brigadier general, less than two weeks following his arrival. After work he and his staff repaired to a bar at 8 South Audley. Somehow, one of his staff had come up with a set of brigadier stars and bestowed them on Truscott. The new general was somewhat surprised but pleased when he realized almost immediately that his new rank brought about a greater willingness by others to cooperate.[14]

To Truscott's dismay, he began to suspect that the primary mission given to him personally by General Marshall—that of obtaining combat experience for some American troops—would be much harder to achieve than he had thought. While British troops were indeed fighting in North Africa, little ground combat was taking place in Europe except for the occasional commando raid. Worse, over the course of the coming summer, only a few such expeditions were projected, and just one required more than 400 men. Also queued up and anxious for combat experience were 4,500 fully trained British commandos, whose leaders saw them as the most qualified to handle such raids. Standing by for leftovers were the regular regiments of both the British and Canadian armies. Their involvement seemed unlikely because teams of commandos, specifically selected, organized, and trained for such operations, best handled the small in-and-out strikes.

Last in line were the Americans. It worried Truscott that it might be a long wait before he could squeeze in any of his countrymen.

Yet another complication was that more than a little disagreement existed within the British military regarding the value of the elite commandos. The attention accorded these special-operations soldiers exasperated many officers of the traditional regiments, each of which had its own proud history. It further grated them that some of their best men had volunteered to attend commando training, with many subsequently transferring from their home regiments. Noncommando officers felt their own soldiers slighted, essentially performing guard duty in England while the commandos raced off to France and returned to headlines. Even some American officers voiced similar concerns. Elite units, they warned, had the effect of watering down the regular units.[15]

Truscott's preference was to promote combat experience for soldiers of the only two U.S. Army divisions already in Great Britain. The first to arrive was the 34th Infantry "Red Bull" Division, a National Guard unit from the Dakotas, Minnesota, and Iowa. They had begun arriving in Belfast, Northern Ireland, in January 1942. The other was the 1st Armored "Old Ironsides" Division, which had arrived in May. Neither was yet at full strength, nor did either have soldiers with commando-like skills. Truscott knew the likelihood of filtering any of these traditionally trained American soldiers into British commando operations was remote. Of course, Eisenhower had suggested that some form of American commando unit to operate within the British raiding system might be in order. Then after a number of soldiers had undergone commando training and received some battle experience, they would depart the special unit so that others could take their place. The overall effect would be at least a sprinkling of combat experience among the American units destined to invade Europe. That was the intention, at least.[16]

Truscott submitted a detailed proposal for such a special unit, which the War Department in Washington approved. In early June the general traveled to Northern Ireland and, over the course of two days, met with Major General Russell P. Hartle of the 34th Infantry Division and Major General Orlando Ward of the 1st Armored Division as well as some of their key staff. Hartle supported his request, but Ward saw little value in having "trained tankers" become commandos until being reminded that General Marshall had personally ordered the project. Truscott had in mind a unit consisting of a headquarters company and six line companies totaling twenty-six officers and 447 soldiers. But he still needed a name for this special unit. Eisenhower had previously advised him against calling it "Commandos," for that distinctive British unit rightfully held title to the name. Several names were suggested by staff members, from which Truscott selected "Rangers," seeing it as a name cherished in American military history, when in "colonial days, men so designated had mastered the art of Indian warfare and were guardians of the frontier."[17]

In what would become a momentous moment in U.S. Army history, General Hartle, on advice of his chief of staff, Colonel Edmond H. Leavey, suggested that Truscott might want to consider as commander of the rangers a just-promoted major named William Orlando Darby. Bill Darby was Hartle's aide and, coincidentally, had been Truscott's guide in Northern Ireland. Truscott thought it a great idea and assigned one of his key assistants, Major Conway, to liaise with Darby for the formation of the new unit. All involved in the effort were pleased to discover that recruiting volunteers for the Rangers would be easier than expected.[18]

Darby was a 1933 West Point graduate and an artillery officer who also had cavalry and infantry experience. He was more than happy to give up his desk job for something that sounded more exciting. Especially important to Truscott, Darby had already received amphibious training in the United States and Puerto Rico. His impression of the major was one of "outstanding in appearance, possessed of a most attractive personality, and he was keen, intelligent, and filled with enthusiasm." At West Point Darby had been average academically, but leadership exuded from his every pore. Before long his adoring ranger trainees—behind his back—would call him "El Darbo." Others described him as charismatic, industrious, and enthusiastic. As historian Robert Black notes, Darby's "flair for leadership set the tone from the beginning of the World War II ranger experience."[19]

As the initial commander and thus designer of the rangers, Darby had a blank page before him. He formed his unit in the small town of Carrickfergus on the North Channel coast of Northern Ireland, just north of Belfast. He personally interviewed and selected his new officers and men and organized and equipped them. More than 2,000 soldiers from the 34th Infantry Division, the 1st Armored Division, and associated units volunteered to become rangers. Of that number,

Darby selected 575 to report to Carrickfergus, and of those, 471 made it through the demanding training. Officers, including Darby, who wanted to become rangers went through the same training as their men, but as leaders they faced each challenge ahead of them. Darby, a regular-army officer, appointed a National Guard cavalry officer as his executive officer and gave another key position to an Army Reserve officer, underscoring his belief that an officer's competence was more important than his background.[20]

Most instruction took place at the Achnacarry British Commando Training Depot at Inverness, Scotland. British Special Services Brigade Commando officers and NCOs delivered the instruction, and for them "perfect" was the only acceptable grade. Ranger Robert Slaughter remembered one instructor in particular, a captain with the Scottish Black Watch regiment. He viewed his job as turning soldiers into rangers—but only if they could make the grade. Every day he ordered soldiers to pack their duffle bags and return to their home units. Slaughter arrived weighing 205 pounds and departed at 176 pounds, remembering ranger training as the toughest thing he had ever attempted in his life.[21]

Training began even before an early breakfast, with teams of several students shouldering a telephone pole and lifting it over their heads, tossing and catching it for what seemed like hours. After breakfast came the speed marches, the obstacle course, and the firing range. Hand-to-hand combat drills occurred daily. One particular obstacle course required completion as a squad, the members of which had to run through together, stopping only to shoot at pop-up targets as they appeared along the way. When an instructor declared a team member to be a casualty, his teammates had to carry him through the rest of the course. Students had to scale walls, negotiate rivers, and endure live-fire amphibious training. As another exercise, commando instructors dropped off the students somewhere in the wilds of Scotland with a map and compass but without water or food, their task being to find their own way back to camp. At the heart of ranger training was the speed march. In the field the men would need to get where they were going quickly and still be able to fight when they arrived. Throughout the program, safety took a backseat to realistic combat conditions; indeed, one student drowned while crossing a river and another suffered a hip wound during a live-fire exercise. Truscott visited the instruction camp whenever he could and paid close attention to the frequent reports that Major Conway sent him. The general was already contemplating the possibilities of using ranger training as a way to enhance the combat effectiveness of a standard infantry division.[22]

The commando instructors provided no gift memberships: every man earned his place in the new unit. Evaluation was constant. Typical written comments by the instructors were to the point. "He is not the Commando type and prefers to watch rather than lead." Or, "He is not the Commando type. He carries too much weight and has not enough energy." Officers received special attention. "I do not consider this officer to be suitable for a Company Commander. He tries to drive his men too much and does not take a personal interest in them." Yet the instructors saw Major Darby as "the ideal Commando type. He possesses the energy, keenness, and personality, which produces the best out of those under his command. He has the right idea in Commando Training and during the schemes exercised perfect control and appreciated all situations in a very able manner."[23]

While visiting London to attend a meeting, General Marshall noticed what appeared to be inactivity within the command of General Chaney, the commander who had shown little interest in Truscott's mission. Upon returning to Washington, Marshall sent Eisenhower to investigate. The subsequent report indicated that those in Chaney's organization wore civilian clothes, kept banker's hours, were unclear as to their mission, and seemed lackadaisical about the effectiveness of Operations Bolero and Roundup. By June Chaney was back to the United States and Eisenhower had taken over his command, now reclassified the European theater of operations (ETO). Eisenhower had suggested another officer to replace Chaney, but Marshall overruled him. When Eisenhower returned to London, Truscott recalled, he "was to infuse into the organization in England some of the intensity of purpose and spirit of cooperation which characterized the war effort at home."[24]

Two other events of significance took place that summer. The first, occurring in June, was a consolidation of planning staffs among various separate commands, to be housed at Norfolk House, previously a residence of various British royalty for more than two hundred years. The second event occurred in July, when the Combined Chiefs of Staff appointed Eisenhower as supreme Allied commander for any future invasion of North Africa as a prelude to Operation Roundup, the cross-channel invasion.

Thus far, the Combined Chiefs had not named anyone as supreme Allied commander for Roundup. Most planners in England, American *and* British, favored an American for the job. While surprised at this, Truscott concluded that the reason was the alarming record of recent land defeats by British forces as well as the probability that Americans would not accept a British commander. Regardless of who the commander would be, British leadership from Churchill on down remained nervous about Roundup. They had been in the business of fighting the Germans for two years now and were much less enthusiastic and considerably more cautious than the Americans. "British staff officers had learned in practice," Truscott noted, "to allow wide margins for error between promise and fulfillment, and broad safety factors for errors in calculations and estimates." He came to realize that the American timeline for the invasion—1943—was, by British estimates, wishful thinking. Not long after Eisenhower's arrival, Truscott met with him to share his growing belief that the British had serious misgivings about Roundup. Eisenhower was surprised and found this hesitation disconcerting, knowing that it affected combined operations.[25]

Aware, perhaps for the first time, of the depth of the differences between the British and the Americans on the conduct of the war, Truscott wrote to Sarah. "I have been terribly depressed recently on many accounts," he confided. "There is so much confusion, so much talk, so many grandiose plans, so little action, so much petty jealousy and ambition, that one can't help getting discouraged. It has been a most interesting and educational experience."[26]

On July 18 General Marshall and other senior American military commanders visited London for "high level talks." That afternoon, as directed, Truscott reported to Marshall at his quarters. The general greeted him and insisted that he stay for dinner, which began with a scotch and soda for each. Marshall was full of questions. Truscott recollected that the dinner was quite good but that he could recall little of it because he "was being subjected to the most thorough examination and in the most charming manner that one can imagine . . . ; nothing was overlooked." Marshall was particularly interested in his opinion as to how the British viewed Operation Sledgehammer, the emergency invasion of Europe should the Soviet Union be on the verge of collapse. Truscott reported that some of the "younger planners" thought the plan workable. In their view, seizing and holding the northwest peninsula below

Cherbourg, France, was practicable. It was the middle level of planners who disagreed.[27]

About 10:00 P.M. Generals Eisenhower and Clark arrived. Later Admiral King and others came by. It was the first time that Truscott met the chief of naval operations. The discussion continued until after midnight, with Marshall informing the others of Truscott's comments regarding the "young planners." Having now conferred with his own senior commanders, Marshall would next meet with the British chiefs of staff. He told Truscott to prepare an outline for a revised Operation Sledgehammer. On July 22, a few days after this meeting, Lucian wrote to Sarah saying how impressed he was with Marshall, adding that he "carries a load, and I wonder if history will ever make clear the extent of it."[28]

The next morning, his homework done, Truscott provided Marshall with a written outline of the thoughts of the young planners. "In this plan," he remembered, "the strength of the assault force was determined by the capacity of the landing craft which it was estimated would be available." It envisioned a seaborne invasion by specially trained infantry, assisted by armored and airborne forces, attacking and capturing the seaport and airport of Cherbourg. The force would then hold a defensive line across the base of the peninsula until four additional divisions landed. Once these units were in place, a determined defense would hold the captured territory throughout the coming winter, during which additional supporting forces and supplies would arrive. When good weather returned, the force would launch attacks deeper into France. In the view of the young planners, the critical element of surprise afforded by the bold plan was that the Germans, certain that the Allies could not invade before the spring of 1943, had not yet sufficiently prepared the peninsula for defense. Not surprising, the initial force would be small, for there were too few landing craft available to do anything larger.[29]

Marshall's visit sparked a power surge throughout American planning, which Truscott noted involved "much pushing of pencils, much pounding of typewriters, and much burning of midnight oil." British planners were busy as well, doing their own, somewhat confidential, work. Everyone knew that in the "atmosphere of mystery and of curiosity ill-concealed," change was afoot. The upshot of American planning was a refurbished plan for Operation Sledgehammer, now code-named Operation Wetbob, which might be suitable for a surprise lodgment on continental Europe by the fall of 1942. Yet it would no longer be an invasion plan initiated only if the Soviet Union was about to collapse, but something possible under lesser but still urgent circumstances. The Americans liked the idea; the British winced at the thought. Final approval of the operation stalled because the British lacked confidence in it. In its place they proposed another plan, one that Churchill had sold to Roosevelt. Codenamed Operation Torch, it would be an invasion of French North Africa comprising three or more landings involving twelve divisions. For political reasons, the initial invasion force would consist only of American troops, who the planners thought to be more agreeable to the French. Not incidentally, this operation would necessarily delay the cross-channel invasion for at least twelve months.[30]

Even as Operation Torch became the strategic focus of Allied efforts in Europe, the British continued planning small- and medium-scale raids. Some were approved but never launched, others fizzled during planning, and still more remained on the drawing board. Planners grew frustrated because the tremendous effort they put into their work often proved fruitless when commanders canceled the raids. Exacerbating matters, some British officers disagreed with the entire concept of the small raids. One very senior naval officer was highly critical of these operations, noting, "Circumstances suggest that we are using these raids either to train our own forces or to employ our own forces." He added that pinpointing small weaknesses in the German defenses merely gave the enemy pointers on where to invest its time and resources: "As it is our present intention at some future date to make an attack in force upon the enemy's coast, we are now doing our best to make that attack less likely to achieve success." For Truscott, already frustrated at his inability to get American troops some actual battle experience, this was troubling, for the trickle of raids now occurring might dry up altogether. Amid this, Marshall still anticipated having some seasoned American combat troops by the time of the first invasion. Thus far, however, no freshly minted rangers had made it beyond waiting and shivering in cold, damp, tightly packed landing craft for raids destined to be canceled. Truscott feared that he was failing in the most important part of his mission.[31]

CHAPTER 11

FIRST LOOK AT WAR

With Eisenhower taking over the reins, planning for Operation Torch broke into full stride. Lord Mountbatten reassigned Truscott and his staff to Eisenhower to assist in that effort. They joined the general's planners at Norfolk House.[1]

On August 9, with the Torch plan in its third iteration, General Patton visited from the United States. Marshall had designated him to command one of three invasion forces in the operation. He almost missed the opportunity, however. Following the defeat of the British at Tobruk, Libya, Marshall had summoned Patton, then in charge of armored-warfare training in Indio, California, to Washington. His mission would be to develop a plan to send one U.S. armored division to assist the British Eighth Army, then in North Africa. Marshall cautioned the general not to ask for more than one division, though. The next morning Patton submitted a proposal for *two* American divisions to aid the British, suggesting it as the absolute minimum. A much-irritated Marshall ordered Patton to return to his training duties in California that very morning. To be certain that this happened, he sent a staff member with the brash general to watch him get on the plane and see it fly away. There existed for Patton no worse punishment than the prospect of sitting out the war in a training command. He might have been master of the sword at West Point and a saber instructor at the Cavalry School, but he was outmatched when he crossed blades with Marshall. Eventually, the army chief of staff recalled a more penitent Patton back to Washington. Marshall later quipped to Lieutenant General Joseph T. McNarney, his deputy chief of staff, that that was how you handle a man like Patton.[2]

The innovative cavalryman had now arrived in England to gather all the information he could about the upcoming North African invasion. Truscott briefed him on the plan thus far, noting that Patton's command for Operation Torch was unique in that its troops would sail directly from the United States to North Africa; the other two forces would depart from the British Isles to rendezvous with it somewhere in the Atlantic. Patton was pleased with the briefing and afterward said to his old cavalry friend: "Dammit, Lucian, you don't want to stay on any staff job in London with a war going on. Why don't you come with me? I will give you a command." Truscott replied that he would like nothing better but that he would need Eisenhower's approval. Within a short time, Patton had wrangled that permission. Almost immediately, Truscott and his planning group moved from overall Operation Torch preparations to specific planning for Patton's force.[3]

While Patton was in London, Truscott arranged for him to meet Lord Mountbatten as well as a number of British officers with whom the Oklahoman had worked. That visit led to an invitation the following evening to attend a social gathering with English aristocracy. The general arrived wearing riding britches and spit-polished boots complete with spurs. Patton, whom Truscott labeled as the "master of the art of startling anecdote," later held those gathered spellbound as he rolled forth with stories of chasing Pancho Villa in Mexico, meeting various outlaws and murderers, and what the notches on his revolvers represented. He also mentioned once enjoying a particularly rare vintage of California wine only to learn, when someone cleaned the large oak cask, that it had contained the body of a drowned Mexican.[4]

By mid-August Eisenhower had assigned his good friend Mark Clark as deputy commander in chief for Operation Torch planning. Clark reviewed the current proposal and concurred with it. Although still in outline form, the British plan at that time called for three landings from the Mediterranean Sea at approximately the same time at Oran, Algiers, and Bône, all in Algeria. Air, naval, and ground forces would assist, with a preliminary invasion date of October 15. Once landed, most ground forces would move east from Algeria to occupy Tunisia, while a smaller force went west into French Morocco, a region immediately south of Gibraltar. The latter effort was to ensure continued control of the main passage into the Mediterranean and its surrounding countries.

Patton's invasion force would land at Oran (later changed to Casablanca). Truscott's group was already doing the pick-and-shovel work for the plan. Once finalized, the documents would be personally carried by Patton to his unit commanders in the United States, who would then do more detailed planning. Fortunately, Truscott had found that previously completed British intelligence of the proposed landing area, including aerial photographs, was both thorough and current. His group calculated the desired size and makeup of the assault forces and rates of debarkation to the beach. As he later wrote, when Patton returned to the United States, the general carried a "skeletonized assault plan which would provide a basis for further planning, and outline military, naval, and air plans for all of the assaults."[5]

Concurrent with preparations for North Africa, British raid planning kicked up a notch. For some time Lord Mountbatten's men had eyed Dieppe, France, a port and resort village on the English Channel. Code-named Operation Jubilee (previously Operation Rutter), the raid would be the largest to date. As previously agreed, Mountbatten asked Truscott to furnish fifty U.S. soldiers as well as some American observers, one of whom would be Truscott himself. Within hours the general alerted Darby (now a colonel) that six officers and forty-four soldiers from his 1st Ranger Battalion would join British commandos and Canadian units, with the latter making up the bulk of the strike force. Although Darby had wanted to go along, the raid already had its leadership in place, and senior commanders probably considered Darby too valuable to the fledgling rangers to be killed or injured in its first raid.

Truscott informed Patton, who was about to leave London, about the raid. He not only approved Truscott's role as an observer but also lamented that he himself would not be able to go along. He next informed Mark Clark, who refused permission for Truscott to go, saying his efforts in planning Operation Torch were more important. Going around Clark—a risky move—Truscott presented the situation to Eisenhower, who gave him the okay. If such action perturbed Clark, it would not be the last time it happened.[6]

On August 5 Truscott received a letter from his younger son, Jamie. It hit all the high points. "I hope you are enjoying yourself, Pa 'cause I am except that I miss the horses. I can't think of anything else to say except don't let any Germans kill ya. Your devoted Son, James III."[7]

Truscott was about to witness his first battle. Upon its conclusion, he would pronounce himself a "sadder and wiser man." The raid was primarily a Canadian operation, even though Mountbatten had first asked for battle-experienced commandos and Royal Marines, knowing the mission more suited to them. But the Canadians prevailed, being as eager as the Americans were to get their forces some battle experience. The purpose of the raid was to harass the Germans on a larger scale than previously attempted, gather intelligence about their defenses, and (secondarily) provide combat experience for additional Allied soldiers. There was also the possibility that the Luftwaffe might be enticed to come up and have a go at the Allied flyers.[8]

Truscott would observe from the destroyer HMS *Fernie,* following the action at sea, in the air, and onshore. He assigned two of his original staff from Washington, Major Conway and Lieutenant Colonel Hillsinger, as well as two others to accompany him. The general would alternate between the ship's deck and its operations room below, seeking to take in all that he could.[9]

Dieppe is located where the D'Arques River flows down through steep, chalk cliffs to pour its waters into the English Channel. The town has a ten-mile front with a mile-long beach. It also had an airport, oil dumps, train yards, and power stations. The Germans were using this seaport to supply distant military posts and also as the base from which small, fast torpedo boats, called E-boats, pursued their prey in the channel. Critical for the raid's success was that Dieppe was within range of cover by British Spitfires.[10]

The plan called for No. 3 Commando (about five hundred British commandos with the addition of forty American rangers) and No. 4 Commando (about the same size but with only four rangers) to land northeast and southwest of town, respectively. They would then slip inland to destroy two batteries of coastal-defense guns situated on high ground overlooking the channel. Without elimination of these guns, Royal Navy ships would not be able to get close enough to shore to support the operation. Following naval and air bombardment of the area by these vessels and Allied planes, various units from the 2nd Canadian Division, including six additional rangers, would go ashore.[11]

Two Canadian units, the Royal Hamilton Light Infantry Regiment and the Essex Scottish Regiment, would be the main assault force. They were to storm ashore, clear Dieppe's western and eastern beaches (respectively), and make way for the 14th Canadian Army Tank Battalion (Calgary Regiment) to land and roll into town. West of the main assault, the South Saskatchewan Regiment would capture a radio station, antiaircraft guns, and the town of

Pourville and then assume a defensive position. The Queen's Own Cameron Highlanders Regiment would arrive next, pass through the Saskatchewans, and capture an airfield. East of the main assault, the Royal Regiment of Canada would land at Puits and capture another coastal-defense battery. Planners considered a drop of British paratroopers too but dismissed it because of unfavorable weather.[12]

The raid was not small. It included more than 250 ships and landing craft and would deposit more than 6,000 soldiers onto the beaches. In order to arrive at morning twilight, the force sailed from England on August 18, 1942, at 6:30 P.M. and traveled the seventy miles to the French coast under moonlit skies. Truscott later described standing on the deck of the *Fernie* and watching "flat tank landing craft crawling along like great dark water beetles with white waves now and again splashing against their tall snout-like ramps."[13]

Yet even before the first commando unit landed, the raid turned ugly. Shortly before 4:00 A.M., about seven miles offshore, E-boats detected No. 3 Commando. That unit's men were huddled aboard an English steam gunboat, anticipating landing in about an hour. The E-Boats, escorting a German oil tanker, happened upon the British craft and began firing as flares illuminated the water. At least five E-Boats hammered streams of rounds into the British vessel, putting it out of commission. Rudely awakened but now forewarned, the Germans onshore had ample time to adjust the sights on an impressive array of guns, large and small, to welcome the Allies. Watching from the destroyer's deck, Truscott next saw "intense flashes and streaks of red and white and green crisscrossing in the sky like a great display of fireworks."[14]

Ranger Edwin Furru recalled the detection by the E-boats as something not unlike a July 4th celebration, with rockets and shells igniting and bursting everywhere, seeming to turn the night into day. Many of the other landing craft veered left or right, but Furru's craft headed straight for the beach. It managed to land safely, but the Germans eventually netted Furru and the others who had managed to scramble ashore.[15]

The main Canadian assault force approached the shore, left their landing crafts, and immediately collided with a hail of lead, with the Essex Scottish and the Royal Regiments catching most of it. In the sky the Luftwaffe, apparently up for the challenge, arrived and took on the Allied flyers. Truscott watched the resulting dogfights, seeing aircraft erupt in smoke and flames and then fall, splash, and disappear forever into the choppy English Channel. He studied the shoreline, barely visible through the increasingly thick smoke. He could see flashes of explosions and hear the continual fire of machine guns. Spitfire and Hurricane fighters dove deeply into the smoke, disappeared briefly, and then reappeared, climbing steeply into the clouds. A damaged Spitfire, struggling to keep itself above the water, headed back to England but appeared to be coming directly at the *Fernie.* Antiaircraft crews, mistaking it for a German aircraft, fired but within seconds recognized its markings and relaxed their trigger fingers. The Spitfire zoomed past low, its pilot at last taking a breath.[16]

Ranger sergeant Marcell Swank, crouched low in a landing craft made mostly of plywood, occasionally lifted his head to sneak a peek over the metal bow of the bouncing boat. He was going in with the second wave of Cameron Highlanders and was about a thousand yards off the beach inbound when German shore cannons, mortars, and machine guns fired on them. Aircraft screamed overhead, and the loud drone of numerous landing-craft engines assaulted his ears. Somehow over all the noise, Swank heard something starkly different. Looking about, he saw that the sound was coming from a landing craft to his right. Standing in full view in that craft was Highlander corporal Alex Graham, appearing fearless, playing his bagpipes as loud as he could. Years later Swank reminisced about how he watched as Graham put the Germans on notice that the Camerons were coming.[17]

The captain of the *Fernie* steered the sleek destroyer closer to shore. Those topside, including Truscott, saw burning tanks and destroyed landing craft on the beach and at the water's edge. One disabled tank landing craft, its ramp open, displayed the broken bodies of its final passengers, whose feet had never touched the sand. Entranced by the sight, sound, and smell of the disturbing panorama, something slammed Truscott against the railing and almost pushed him down to the deck. He next felt something strike his boot. A large shell had struck the aft of the *Fernie,* killing or wounding sixteen of its sailors. Truscott checked his foot and found that a large metal nut from part of the ship's structure had hit him. The damaged *Fernie* moved seaward, pumping covering smoke behind it.[18]

News arrived that No. 4 Commando had accomplished its mission, disabling the coastal batteries and killing about two hundred Germans. The Royal Marine Commando (battalion), held in reserve, started toward shore in hopes of assisting the Royal Hamiltons, still struggling on the beach and in the town; the Fusiliers Mont Royal had already gone in to assist the Essex Scottish. Within moments, however, it became clear that other coastal batteries had not been knocked out and were now furiously firing into the invaders. The situation turned desperate.

The Canadian force commander, now certain that the situation was hopeless, ordered a withdrawal under heavy curtain of smoke. Landing craft that had previously deposited soldiers now made an even more dangerous run to pick up survivors, relying on gunboats and destroyers to provide covering fire. Brigadier Mann, Canadian forces chief of staff, aware that the men on shore could hold neither the town nor the beach, turned to Truscott and said, "General, I am afraid that this operation will go down as one of the great failures of history."[19]

Mesmerized, Truscott continued to watch. "It was bloody business," he recalled. "Fire was intense. Craft were hit, yet others ploughed their way forward to the water's edge under withering fire. . . . [Y]et on and on they came, a marvelous display of courage." The *Fernie* moved back in to assist, spreading smoke to conceal what still survived. Truscott and the others soon beheld a beach littered with wrecks and burning hulks. Soon machine-gun bullets were clanking off the *Fernie*'s hull, encouraging its captain to steer back into the darkened sea. Onshore, a Canadian commander, speaking by radio to Brigadier Mann, said he and others were about to be captured and added, "Goodbye, and take a message to—" before the radio went silent.[20]

Lieutenant Colonel Hillsinger of Truscott's staff was observing events from a different ship, the HMS *Berkeley*. Bombs from a German Junkers 88 struck the ship, causing considerable damage and loss of life. One explosion blew off Colonel Hillsinger's foot. He used his handkerchief and necktie as a tourniquet to stem the rush of blood. Rescue boats soon after arrived to take off what was left of those aboard. Sailors helped Hillsinger to a gunboat, but he refused medical attention until the sailors could assist others in need of rescue. He then refused to go below, choosing instead to serve as a spotter for the antiaircraft crews. Truscott would later have the honor of pinning onto Colonel Hillsinger's chest—then hospitalized—the Distinguished Service Cross, second only to the Medal of Honor, along with the Purple Heart.[21]

The *Fernie* began taking on the wounded as well. Bloodied bodies quickly occupied every space available. Medics were in short supply but darted about giving what aid they could. Truscott found his way to a large wardroom, its floor covered with wounded men—some unconscious, some sedated, all bloody; a few remained awake. Staying out of the way but surveying the scene, the general needed a smoke. Pulling his bag of Bull Durham tobacco from his pocket, he rolled and lit a cigarette. Nearby a voice asked, "I say, you wouldna have another un about yuh?" Reflecting on the scene years later, Truscott remembered, "I gave him my cigarette and, then, until my sack was empty, I rolled and lit cigarettes for the others."[22]

German planes chased the *Fernie* almost to the English coast. Trains were already at Portsmouth, standing by to ferry the wounded to hospitals. Truscott said his goodbyes to Brigadier Mann and the others with whom he had shared the sad affair and took a train to London.[23]

Truscott, who personally learned a great deal from the raid, later wrote: "I am not among those who consider the Dieppe Raid a failure. It was an essential though costly lesson in modern warfare." Others disagreed as to the value of the operation. Of the Canadian soldiers who had waded ashore, more than 3,000 were now casualties: 600 dead, 600 wounded, 300 missing, and 1,900 who would suffer the next three years in German prisoner-of-war camps. One regiment suffered 97 percent casualties. The Allies had also lost one destroyer, twenty-eight tanks, many landing craft, and about one hundred aircraft. On the German side, ninety-eight aircraft had gone down, three hundred more were likely damaged, and an unknown number of soldiers were killed or wounded. Criticism lingered about the Dieppe Raid. Historian Carlo D'Este notes, "The raid contributed virtually nothing to the war effort, ruined reputations, [and] left a legacy of bitterness that has endured to this day." It did accomplish one thing, however, presenting bloody proof to Marshall and Eisenhower that what the British had been saying all along—that the Allies were not ready to invade France—was true.[24]

CHAPTER 12

Preparing for Battle

Churchill and Roosevelt, now having agreed to invade North Africa, gave their generals permission to proceed. If all went well, the two leaders hoped to see German and Italian forces there caught in a pickle play between an Allied invasion of French North Africa and British field marshal Bernard Montgomery's Eighth Army, already battling in northeastern Africa.[1]

It was for this reason—hoping to fight the Germans and Italians and not the French—that General Truscott and 9,000 U.S. soldiers under him were on board navy transport ships. Ironically, no one of high rank in the U.S. Army, least of all General Marshall, had any serious interest in these troops participating in this invasion; they were just following Roosevelt's orders. What Marshall wanted most was for the Mediterranean venture to be quick in, quick out.

As a young cavalry officer, Truscott had crossed the Pacific Ocean to Hawaii more than two decades earlier. Now, in the last week of October 1942, he was crossing the Atlantic Ocean, though to a less certain future. The fleet transporting the invasion force had pulled anchor at Hampton Roads, leaving behind the Virginia capes and home. "I was sobered by the thought," he recalled, "that for many of these on board this would be their last view of our native land."[2]

Following the Dieppe debacle, Truscott had remained in England as Patton's deputy, working on the North African invasion plan. At that time there was still significant disagreement between the British and the Americans on where to debark the invasion force. The American Chiefs of Staff thought the troops should land on the Atlantic beaches. Their British counterparts regarded a landing on the Atlantic side during winter as too risky and preferred sites within the confines of the more weather-friendly Mediterranean Sea. The Americans pointed out that the British plan could entrap the entire invasion force, giving it little space to maneuver, if necessary. Should the neutral Spanish government see fit to grant

German forces passage through Spain to seize Gibraltar, they could take control of the mouth of the Mediterranean, effectively choking off Allied reinforcements and supplies. The British still disagreed. Churchill and Roosevelt would need to make the call. They decided that part of the Allied forces would land near Casablanca, a deep-water port on Morocco's Atlantic Coast, and part would land inside the mouth of the Mediterranean on Algerian shores. Thus if the Germans did seize Gibraltar, the Allies could still move reinforcements and supplies by rail and truck from Casablanca to wherever needed in North Africa.[3]

With the strategic arguments settled, Patton's planners fleshed out his portion of Operation Torch. His forces would land on the Atlantic beaches, not within the Mediterranean. Three Atlantic ports existed on the Moroccan coast where landings were possible even in November: Fedala, just north of Casablanca; Safi, 130 miles south of Casablanca; and Port Lyautey, 80 miles north of Casablanca. These areas would work as landing sites, but the bigger question was just what the French would do in response to an Allied invasion. Collaborators with Hitler and the Nazis, the government of Unoccupied France operated out of Vichy, France, northwest of Lyon. From there, its officials administered southern France and French North Africa. By agreement, the German army did not occupy either area, although no one doubted that this could change at any moment. Under such circumstances, the Americans and British could do little more than guess as to what the French military in Africa would do. The general thinking seemed to be that the air force would support the Allies, though the navy would not. Members of the latter were still furious that in 1940 the British had sunk most of the French fleet, killing 1,200 sailors in the process, worried that the ships might fall into German hands. The French army, Allied planners concluded, was likely to be pro-American even if not pro-British.[4]

Considerable diplomatic efforts were then underway aimed at divining which senior French military commander, if any, had the requisite leadership—and courage—necessary to persuade all French forces to acquiesce to the Allied invasion. Eisenhower ordered a high-level Allied covert mission to this end. It involved sending his primary deputy, General Clark, and a shore party by submarine and subsequent small wood-and-canvas boats to the Algerian shore. There they hoped to meet secretly with French military officers in hopes of gaining their pledge of cooperation. The result of Clark's efforts was disappointing, for it became clear that the Allies were feeling in the dark in identifying the right leader. More surprising, perhaps, was that Eisenhower had approved of this mission at all. He knew that Clark was not only familiar with all the plans for Operation Torch but also privy to Ultra, the extremely secret Allied dismantlement of the German communications code by which they transmitted their most secret information. At one point during Clark's mission, Vichy authorities nearly discovered him and his party. The general and his associates hid in a wine cellar until dark, then raced on foot for the beach. From there they paddled in their small boats through crashing breakers to a waiting submarine. Had the French—or their German contacts—captured and tortured Clark, a confession might have revealed not only details of the forthcoming invasion but also that the Allies had broken the German code. Such would have caused incalculable damage to the Allied war effort.[5]

In a smaller but more successful covert operation, two cooperative Frenchmen who had come forward with information were subsequently spirited out of French North Africa. Carl Victor Clopet was familiar with Casablanca and knew much about its beaches, ports, and coastal security. The other man, René Malvergne, was a veteran river pilot in the Port Lyautey area who had equally valuable information about river passage there. Both were willing to do what they could to help the Allies. Upon learning of their arrival in London, Truscott immediately realized their value and ordered them taken to Patton's staff in the United States.[6]

By September 19 Truscott was ready to leave England. He said goodbye to his associates in London who had been his mentors, coworkers, and friends. After a final calling on General Eisenhower, he departed for the United States to become part of Patton's invasion force.[7]

By September 26 Truscott was back at work, reporting at Fort Bragg, North Carolina, to prepare for his part in the invasion. His specific mission would be to capture the airport at Port Lyautey, Morocco. To accomplish this, he would have under his command the 60th Infantry Regiment of the 9th Infantry "Varsity" Division as well as an armored-battalion combat team of the 2nd Armored Division. Also under Truscott's control would be forty smaller units of "infantry, artillery, armor, aviation, antiaircraft artillery, tank destroyers, engineers, signal and medical troops, prisoner of war interrogators, [and] counter-intelligence and military government personnel." A complication was that these soldiers and their equipment were scattered throughout North Carolina, Virginia, New Jersey, and California. Worse, the actual locations of several units, shown on paper to exist, were unknown.[8]

Truscott's invasion command, codenamed Sub–Task Force Goalpost, would be a temporary command and as such would be operational only for the actual invasion and its immediate aftermath; thereafter, its troops would report elsewhere. Truscott understood that because his would be a temporary headquarters, his planning staff would be small. To his dismay, though, he learned that he had no assigned planning staff whatsoever. He spoke with Patton's aides who assured him that his staff would come from the 2nd Armored Division. This was news to the division's commanding general, Major General Ernest "Ernie" Nason Harmon, a former cavalryman turned armor commander. He said he had no senior planning staff to lend Truscott but that he could provide two captains and a lieutenant. Truscott might have pushed the matter to Patton for a decision, but he thought better of it and went about scrounging together his own staff. He and Harmon would go on to become a very good team.

Truscott immediately contacted two American officers who had worked for him in London, Major Conway and Major Pierpont Hamilton. They were now part of Patton's staff in the United States, but he was able to acquire them shortly thereafter. What Truscott needed next was a good chief of staff. For this, he reached back to his old Fort Bliss 5th Cavalry Regiment and wrangled loose a good friend, Colonel Don E. Carleton, who joined him in early October. He also selected for his staff a cavalry lieutenant, Alvin Netterblad. His headquarters complement of eight officers was a small but good beginning. Carleton would become Truscott's primary assistant throughout World War II and one of his closest friends for life. The colonel had served in World War I as a sergeant and later was commissioned in the National Guard. While a second lieutenant attending the Cavalry School, he had met Truscott, who was then an instructor. Like him, Carleton was a fine horseman, enthusiastic polo player, and a graduate of the Command and General Staff School.[9]

Fortunately, Truscott's two line commanders were already in place, Colonel Frederic J. de Rohan, 60th Infantry Regiment, and

Lieutenant Colonel Harry Semmes, 1st Battalion, 66th Armored Regiment. He was pleased with both men and found that their existing organizations were at strength and adequately trained, including having completed amphibious training.[10]

Colonel Carleton went to work getting the general's headquarters organized, staffed, and equipped. Meanwhile, Truscott arranged for naval assistance, which would be essential for getting his men and equipment loaded onto ships and ready to sail with the task force for Africa. Preparing the invasion force would be an around-the-clock effort for both the army and navy, made more difficult since new and inexperienced officers filled most positions in the wartime military. In three weeks, however, Truscott's small headquarters embarked 9,000 soldiers; nearly 1,000 vehicles, including tanks and towed weapons; and 15,000 tons of other equipment and supplies. By October 16 all hands were on board and ready to sail for their first training exercise at Solomons Island in Chesapeake Bay.[11]

Truscott, an experienced instructor, considered an invasion rehearsal to be the final exam for the preparations his soldiers had undergone. Problems with staffing, equipment, planning, and training would become apparent during a rehearsal, especially, as Truscott noted, with "hastily assembled and inexperienced commands." The planned rehearsal at Solomons Island prohibited the use of naval and air live fire but would permit navy personnel to coordinate and practice lowering and operating landing craft. It would also allow army personnel to practice descending nets into landing craft, unloading at the beach, and moving to assigned positions onshore—both day and night. Fortunately, U.S. Navy commodore Augustine H. Gray was equally committed to ensuring that his own officers and sailors were prepared for their roles.[12]

A major problem surfaced early. Instead of permission to use four landing beaches for night training, as had been promised to Truscott, Vice Admiral Henry Kent Hewitt's staff now said that only one beach was available; the other beaches contained underwater obstructions that might damage landing-craft propellers, and replacements were in short supply. Truscott argued that landing his three battalions one after another would not afford soldiers the practice they needed for combat. He concluded that the navy seemed to be more concerned about propellers than soldiers' lives.[13]

Truscott telephoned Patton in Washington to complain, hoping he could make the navy bend a little. Patton was in no mood for yet another problem. "Dammit, Lucian, I've already had enough trouble getting the Navy to agree to undertake this operation. All I want is to get them to sea and to take us to Africa. Don't you do a damn thing that will upset them in any way." He immediately slammed down the telephone receiver.[14]

Then in Norfolk, Patton jotted a note in his diary about the ship-loading operation: "While things were not perfect, they were satisfactory. . . . I am just a little worried about ability of Truscott." Little did he suspect that his bluster had missed its mark. Truscott simply went around Patton. Having worked in the past with Admiral Hewitt, the general found it hard to believe that the admiral would not allow the training to go on as planned. Ignoring Patton's legendary wrath, Truscott contacted Hewitt directly. He lost count of how many telephone exchanges his call went through and what if any security breaches he committed before, finally, Hewitt came on the line. Truscott explained the problem and the importance of rehearsals. The admiral agreed and said that his staff had made the decision in his absence. He told Truscott to use all the beaches he needed.[15]

About 10:00 P.M. that same night, the next problem surfaced. The navy now decided that some ships needed to return to port that very night to be "topped off" with fuel and supplies, which Truscott knew would effectively cancel the night exercises. Knowing he was pushing what little luck he had left, he once again went in search of Admiral Hewitt, this time reaching him by telephone at 3:00 A.M. Truscott explained the problem to Hewitt, who once again said his staff had not consulted him about the matter. As Truscott fondly recalled, the admiral "won my undying gratitude right there by telling me to forget it and go on with the night rehearsal as we had planned. He would see that the ships remained for the necessary time."[16]

The night rehearsals revealed serious shortcomings, but enough time existed for the navy and army to remedy them. In a few days the training was complete and all were set to sail. For Truscott, it was a time for reflection. "I experienced a solemn moment," he remembered. "It was borne in upon me with an awesome finality that, for better or worse, the die was cast. . . . My own mistakes and the mistakes of others in preparing this command for battle would be paid for in the lives of Americans for whom I was responsible. It was a sobering thought." Of one thing he was positive, a principle that he would follow religiously throughout the war. "I had learned that preparation is the first essential for success in war, and that the adequacy of preparation reflects the capacity of a commander and his staff."[17]

Operation Torch, as large as it was, was inadequate in most respects. Too little time existed to perform essential tasks, which resulted in too little planning and too little training. The invasion's overall goal was one of significant magnitude, but ships had to first transport the troops to North Africa. Transportation involved three separate naval task forces, parts of which departed from various locations in the United States and the British Isles. At some specified time and place, more or less, the three fleets would converge in the stormy Atlantic and set a single azimuth for North Africa. The invasion force consisted of 117,000 U.S. and British soldiers, 75 percent of whom were American. General Eisenhower, the overall invasion commander, would exercise command—and scribble worried notes to himself—from his headquarters at Gibraltar. He knew that so much could go wrong: German submarines or spies; possible Spanish cooperation with the Germans; French indecision; bad weather; personnel inexperience. Other than the recent Pacific ramp-down at Guadalcanal, this would be the first large U.S. amphibious landing in well over four decades. To make matters even more disconcerting, Eisenhower was new to his job. In 1940 he had been a lieutenant colonel; now just two years later, he was a lieutenant general. Overall, he estimated that the invasion had a fifty-fifty chance of success.[18]

The fleet designated as Naval Task Force 34 carried Patton's command, protected by a screening escort of three battleships, forty cruisers and destroyers, and air support from accompanying aircraft carriers. Admiral Hewitt commanded the entire task force. He and Patton sailed on the flagship, the USS *Augusta.* Truscott devoted his days crossing the Atlantic to constant troop training. His soldiers were prepared, but they needed to remain sharp. He wanted them mentally and physically ready to race up the beach when the landing-craft ramps splashed down. For Truscott and those coming from the United States, the voyage took more than two weeks, covered 4,500 miles, and included more than one hundred ships cruising in nine columns encompassing a total area of 600 square miles. His troopships were so crowded that each GI shared a hammock with two others on a rotating basis. Seemingly impossible, the huge armada had to sneak across the Atlantic, zigzagging to frustrate ever-watchful U-boat captains. As the ships were also necessarily blacked out at night, those at the helms had to be hyperalert to avoid colliding with any other ship about them.[19]

In discussing the invasion plan with the navy commanders, Truscott was surprised when they reminded him, the landlubber, that finding a particular beach on a shoreline at the time still more than 2,000 miles away and landing at a precise time was essentially impossible. In fact, they warned, the beach landing could be in daylight or it could be at night; it was just too soon to say. For Truscott, this meant that his troops had to be equally prepared to land secretly in the dark—his preference—or during the day, possibly under heavy fire.[20]

During the first week of November, the armada approached the waters off North Africa and gradually disassembled into smaller task forces, representing the three landing forces that would go ashore. The tricky part was sending off the ships in a way that confused the Germans as to their real intentions. The Allies hoped to seize and hold nine seaports and airfields, after which a follow-up land drive across North Africa into Tunisia would allow for the capture of the key ports of Tunis and Bizerte. As it turned out, the Germans *were* confused about what the Allies were doing. They had seen the ships coming through Gibraltar the night of November 5 and watched as more vessels came through the following day. Still, they could not agree as to the final destination. The German Naval High Command concluded that the Allied ships were on their way to Malta to assist British forces under siege there. Hitler scoffed and said that they were on their way to Tripoli or perhaps Benghazi in the eastern Mediterranean to attack the Afrika Korps from the rear. Mussolini thought the Allies intended to invade French North Africa. He guessed right, but his stock was so devalued that the Germans ignored him.[21]

Then, on the early morning of November 8, the three invasion forces landed at various points along 1,000 miles of coastline. The Center Task Force, under Major General Lloyd Fredendall, which had sailed from Scotland, would land its 39,000 soldiers inside the Mediterranean near Oran. His force had many "firsts" associated with it: the 1st Infantry "Big Red One" Division, under the controversial Major General Terry "Terrible Terry" Allen; the 1st Armored Division, under Major General Ward; the 1st Ranger Battalion, under Colonel Darby; and a first-ever American airborne combat drop,

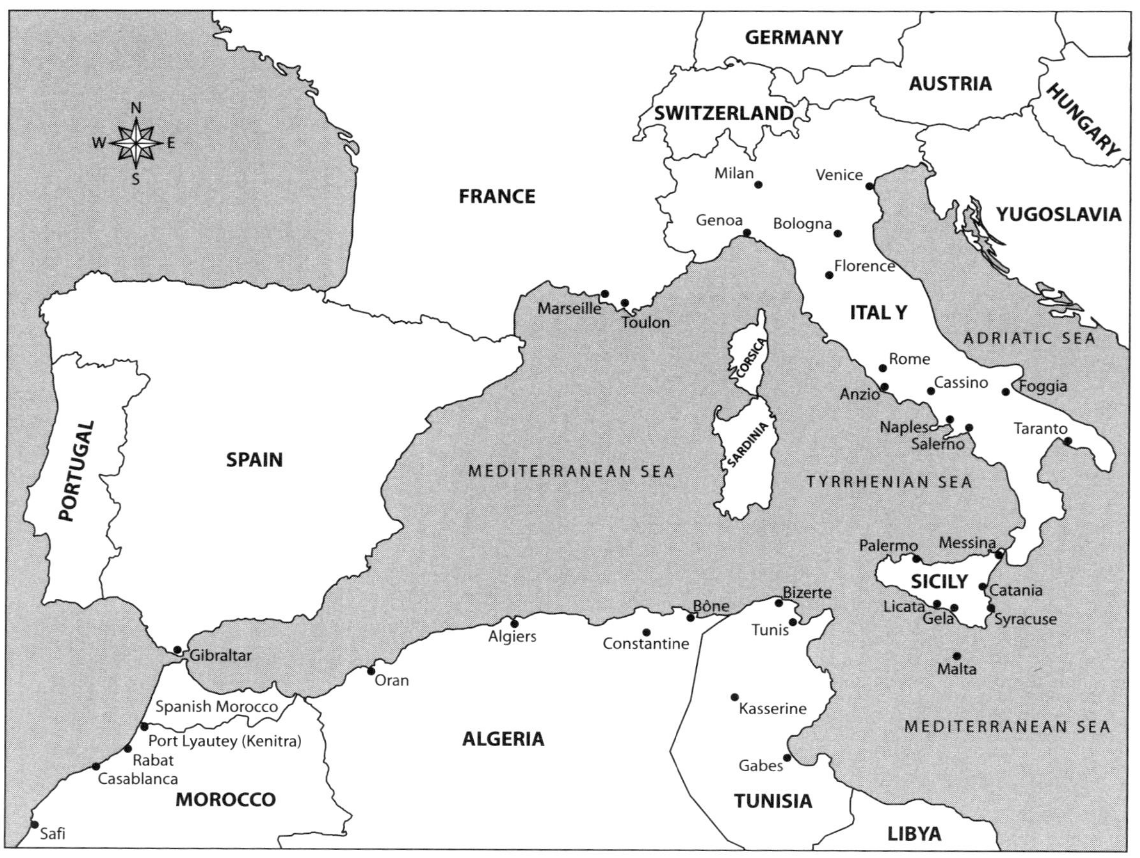

The Mediterranean Sea and surrounding areas constituting the Mediterranean theater of operations. Map by Megan Postell.

made by the 509th Parachute Infantry Battalion under Colonel Edson Raff. In addition, the Army rangers, contrary to Marshall's clearly stated intention of sprinkling combat-experienced veterans throughout infantry divisions, would fight as its own battalion.

The Eastern Task Force, under U.S. major general Charles Ryder, which had come from England and Northern Ireland, would land its 33,000 soldiers inside the Mediterranean near Algiers. It was a mixed force of 23,000 British soldiers and 10,000 American soldiers of the 34th Infantry Division.[22]

The Western Task Force, under General Patton, would land its 35,000 soldiers at three locations in Morocco. This command included units of the 3rd Infantry Division, the 2nd Armored Division, and the 9th Infantry Division. Patton's largest landing force would be the 19,000 soldiers of the 3rd Infantry Division, which would seize Fedala before moving on to nearby Casablanca. The prize at Casablanca was its railroad, which could accommodate future transport of Allied troops and supplies. Major General Harmon's 6,500 soldiers of the 2nd Armored Division would land its armored vehicles at Safi and protect the south flank against any reinforcements coming from Marrakech. Truscott would land his 9,000 soldiers at Port Lyautey. The critical target there was the airport, which could support future Allied air operations. The linear distance among these three landings sites was almost 150 miles, meaning that mutual support, if necessary, would be difficult.

Patton's instructions to his soldiers were simple. "Use steamroller strategy; that is, make up your mind on course and direction of action, and stick to it. But in tactics, do not steamroller. Attack weakness. Hold them by the nose and kick them in the pants." His in-person message to his senior officers was brutally blunt: "If you don't succeed, I don't want to see you alive." He followed with written orders to them that concluded, "I see no point in surviving defeat."[23]

CHAPTER 13

INVADING NORTH AFRICA

While on board the USS *Henry T. Allen,* Truscott had continually considered his mission. To take the airport, his principal objective, his troops first had to take the town of Port Lyautey and its adjacent fortress. Port Lyautey was not a seaport on the Atlantic coast but a river port nine miles inland up the shallow and winding Sebou River. Now looking through his binoculars from the *Allen*'s deck, Truscott could make out sand dunes and cliffs on the shoreline. A report had come in from a British scouting submarine that the mouth of the river had been located. Moments later he overheard something of a tense discussion among the navy officers, which seemed to involve some confusion as to their exact location. More than a little curious, Truscott asked Commodore Gray where he thought they were. In something of a concerned tone, Gray said, "Well, General, to be perfectly honest, I am not right sure exactly where we are." For Truscott, while nervous about the precise location of the fleet, he nonetheless considered the lights onshore to be good news. Apparently, no one was expecting an invasion.[1]

By now, the fleet commander had realized that their position was too close to shore and ordered all ships to move seaward eight miles to a designated transportation area. This resulted in a somewhat confused movement that caused ships to reposition themselves relative to one another, sometimes by miles. In the dark few captains now knew exactly which other ships were anchored in their vicinity. Already behind schedule, the mix-up caused the invasion force to become even more so. Timing was critical because just as the troops were about to land, President Roosevelt would broadcast a message informing the world, and especially the French, that the Allies had just landed in North Africa. Thereafter, Eisenhower would broadcast a similar message. Ideally, the invasion would be just underway as radio stations made the announcements, leaving enough time for the French to comprehend what was happening but too little time to mount stiff resistance. Since Port Lyautey was a rural area, Truscott further speculated that its communications infrastructure might be somewhat basic. He thought it at least possible that the local French commander, when informed of an imminent invasion, might hesitate to act until directed to do so by a higher command in some distant location. If such were the case, Truscott hoped that a friendly and personal message from himself, hand-carried to the local commander and suggesting that the Americans were coming as friends, might prevent resistance and thus unnecessary death and destruction. Sending emissaries would be a risky proposition to be sure, but as Truscott realized, perhaps for the first time, "desperate ventures never want for volunteers."[2]

Among the volunteers for just such a dangerous mission were two who were perfectly suited for it. Both were Army Air Forces officers who spoke French and were familiar with French culture. The first, Major Hamilton, who had served as a pilot in World War I, had previously lived in France for a number of years. The other, Colonel Demas "Nick" Craw, Truscott's air-contingent commander, was a persuasive man who was personally acquainted with a number of foreign officers, including some French. The challenge for Hamilton and Craw was to slip ashore, make contact with the local commander, and deliver to him a carefully prepared message from Truscott, asking the French military to acquiesce to the invasion. It was not just a written note, however, but a carefully prepared "translation engrossed in fine Old English lettering on a scroll . . . bound with ribbons and seals." If all went well, the invasion force would walk ashore and shake hands with the French.[3]

But it might *not* work. Indeed, the French might not take kindly to anyone invading their portion of Africa. If so, Truscott knew that Port Lyautey was well suited for defense. The nine-mile distance up the Sebou River from the Atlantic included a double loop in the river: the first loop was broad and open to the south and closed at the north, the second more narrow and open to the north and closed at the south. The town lay outside and at the bottom of the narrow loop. The airport was north of town, within the broad loop, and rested on high ground, making it suitable for a spirited defense. To complicate matters, the area just beyond the landing beach was a long coastal lagoon and beyond that marshland, all of which lay parallel to the beach. Farther inland was a commanding ridgeline that afforded elevated defensive positions. Near the river and between the beach and Port Lyautey stood a massive fortress, called the Kasbah, previously built by the Portuguese in the sixteenth century. Still in use, its thick stone walls housed a coastal battery ready to prevent unwanted passage up the river or along the rail line or main road into town. Not far from the fortress, the French had also stretched a large cable across the Sebou, effective in preventing unauthorized boats from approaching the airport or the town. The river itself could be hazardous, for at low tide it was only about thirteen feet deep. Additionally, the airport had its own antiaircraft guns, and a detachment of soldiers guarded a key rail-and-vehicle bridge over the Sebou close to town. Of particular concern in Port Lyautey was the French army garrison, which housed an infantry regiment, several artillery battalions, and a cavalry force. Finally, if called upon, the town of Rabat, twenty miles south, could dispatch nearly fifty old but serviceable tanks to aid in a defense. Truscott's attack plan had to take into account all of the above and assume that the French would resist. Of course, bearing in mind that they might not fight, there could be no preinvasion bombardment. Truscott hoped for the best but prepared for the worst.[4]

His plan called for five separate beach landings. Three landings would take place near the mouth of the river, close to the Kasbah and the small beach village of Mehdia. The other two landings included one more distant to the north and one more distant to the south.

The 2nd Battalion, 60th Infantry Regiment, under Major John Dilley, would land on the beach immediately south of the river mouth at 4:00 A.M. Its mission was a surprise capture of the nearby fortress and destruction of its coastal-defense battery by 6:00 A.M. If Dilley's soldiers could not capture the fortress by 6:15 A.M., Allied aircraft would bomb it. Army and navy demolition experts, whose job was to destroy the cable blocking the river, would accompany Dilley's battalion. Once the fortress guns were out of commission and the river open to travel, a World War I–era destroyer, the USS *Dallas,* would steam up the shallow river. At its helm would be René Malvergne, whose knowledgeable hand would guide the old warship upriver while avoiding its various hazards. Aboard the *Dallas* would be a company-size raider detachment from the 60th Regiment, whose men had received special ranger/commando training. Malvergne would transport them close enough to the airport to attack quickly and capture it.

The 3rd Battalion, 60th Regiment, under Major John Toffey, was to land at two locations north of the river, one just north of the mouth and the other more distant. Toffey's mission was more complicated. Part of his force would assist in the capture of the Kasbah by use of machine-gun fire and indirect light-howitzer fire from across the river. The other part of his force would proceed overland to a point near the airport, cross the river in small boats, and assist the raider detachment in capturing the airport. Thereafter, this force would depart to capture the bridge near town.

The 1st Battalion, 60th Regiment, under Major DeWitt McCarley, was to land on the two more distant beaches south of the river. Its mission was to move south around the long lagoon and protect the south flank by setting up roadblocks. McCarley's soldiers would use antitank and machine-gun fire to block any reinforcements that might race up from Rabat. Afterward the battalion would shut off western exits from the town, then help take the airfield.

Once the three battalions had landed, the armored battalion under Lieutenant Colonel Semmes would land south of the river. Its mission was to scout southward, watching for any French reinforcements, then further assist with the capture of the airport. If for some reason Truscott's other troops could not capture that position, Semmes would send his armored vehicles south to seize the airfield at Rabat.[5]

Truscott would remain shipboard, in radio contact with his onshore battalions, until his headquarters, under Colonel de Rohan, could land and establish communications from the beach. Ideally, all units would achieve their initial objectives and then by 11:00 A.M., under Truscott's personal direction, would converge for the final assault on the airport, their primary objective.

Such was the plan. It would be the first battle that Truscott had devised and directed. What he knew well in theory—the old adage that no plan survives first contact with the enemy—he would know from experience. Eisenhower would later explain it another way: "In preparing for battle I have always found that plans are useless, but planning is indispensable." Truscott, already excellent in preparations, would now have a chance to see how well he could think on his feet. His plan was more complex than he preferred. As the war progressed, he would endeavor to keep tactical plans as simple as possible.[6]

Truscott's most immediate problem, though, was that the ships, including those loaded with his troops and equipment, were no longer in their original positions. Landing the right units at the right beach at the right time had now become more difficult. He knew his commanders assigned to his own ship would follow the disembarkation schedule, but he was uneasy about those on the other vessels, the locations of which were something of a mystery. With radios silenced, the general worried that those commanders might hesitate in case new orders arrived.

After midnight the troops on the *Henry T. Allen* began their slow, awkward descent down the surprisingly long landing nets into the landing craft below, which rose and fell with the rhythm of the ocean swells. Timing the final jump was a critical decision for each soldier, each of whom was laden with his weapon and other heavy, bulky equipment. Truscott could see that these men were loading into the boats, but he could not see what was happening on the other ships. Not one to leave an important element to chance, he and his aide descended a landing net and with the aid of a navy coxswain motored in search of the ships he knew carried his troops. Able with some effort to convince the lookouts on other ships that he really was the army commanding general, he boarded each one, talked with his commanders, and ensured that it was offloading his soldiers.

It was nearly 3:30 A.M. when Truscott returned to the *Henry T. Allen.* Colonel Carleton immediately greeted him and ushered him into the communications center. There Truscott recognized the unmistakable voice of Eisenhower on the ship's radio, who was proclaiming to the world that the Allies had just landed in North Africa. Anyone onshore with a radio now knew that an invasion was underway. The other two task forces, which had landed inside the Mediterranean, had beached an hour earlier. Truscott's problem was that his own troops were still bobbing in saltwater, either in landing craft or on ships. Surprise was no longer a possibility.

This was underscored a short time later when the general saw five well-lit French naval vessels leave the river's mouth and steam toward the U.S. fleet. The Americans held their fire, giving the French a temporary benefit of the doubt. Then a signal light onboard one of the French ships blinked a message in English: "Be warned. They are alert on shore. Alert for 0500." With that, they passed silently through the U.S. fleet and headed out into the Atlantic.[7]

Truscott's landing craft began their shoreward journey in the early morning light, their human cargo cold, possibly wet, and certainly worried. For the soldiers, the boat ride was simultaneously much too long and much too short. Each craft approached the beach, lowered its ramp, and spilled forth its anxious men into foreign darkness. Never feeling more exposed, the green troops left what little safety the boats afforded and slogged through the saltwater to the surprisingly soft sand, knowing that any moment could be their last.[8]

Truscott's only hope for a peaceful landing now rested with his two French-speaking officers. As he later recalled, Major Hamilton and Colonel Craw, "clad in their best uniforms, in blouses and caps, brass and leather gleaming, with rows of ribbons and pilot's wings adding a touch of color, were ready for their mission." The two officers, outfitted with a radio-equipped Jeep that flew the U.S. flag, the French tricolor, and a white flag of truce, motored away in a landing craft. From there it was up to them. Trailing the landing craft of the assault battalions, Hamilton and Craw proceeded to shore, armed with little more than good will and French fluency. Once the two hopeful ambassadors departed, things became quiet on the *Allen.* Half of the troops were now on or near the beach, but the other half would not disembark for three hours, once landing craft again became available. How it would go was still a question. Then shortly before 6:00 A.M., the French coastal battery opened fire on the U.S. fleet. The navy responded by unmuzzling its own big guns. Red arcs of light, chased by thunderous sounds, passed in opposite directions, with large shells splashing in water or exploding on land. Hamilton and Craw, having reached the mouth of the river, radioed back that both the French and the navy seemed to be dropping shells on them. Then their radio went silent; their last message had said that their Jeep was stuck on the beach but that "troops landed and moving inland. Proceeding on mission." Truscott would hear nothing more from the officers for two days.[9]

The general walked the deck of the ship, outwardly calm but inwardly irritated and frustrated that so little information came back from the beach. Communication glitches conspired with silent radios onshore to keep him in the dark, which, in turn, kept General Patton in the dark. He waited, hoping news would arrive, but little came. Returning coxswains gave what information they had, but much of it was conflicting. Then lookouts on the *Henry T. Allen* announced that a plane, thought to be German, was coming toward the ship. Every vessel close enough to respond did so. Antiaircraft guns spun around and alternately pumped back and forth, rhythmically sending shells into the air, bursting all around the aircraft.

Then Colonel Carleton yelled—not soon enough—that it was a friendly. The plummeting British plane and crew, now surrendering to the dark water, had been on a mission from Eisenhower to learn how the invasion was going.

Uncomfortable with how little he knew about the activity onshore, Truscott, with his key staff and a dozen soldiers, loaded into landing crafts. They motored to the beach about 3:00 P.M., also taking a command half-track and several Jeeps with them. As his boat chugged forward, Truscott could see that the ocean swells were getting higher and that the surf was building. It was not a good sign, for his other troops were still waiting on their ships.

Truscott slogged through the battering surf and found the beach a mess. Troops intended for a different site had landed at this one, the sand of which turned out nearly to be the texture of powder, making driving difficult. Some craft had broached to the waves, with equipment and weapons now in the seawater. His own Jeep embedded into the soft sand. Transferring to the half-track, the general continued forward. Soon, his landing party encountered a tank destroyer, two tanks, and their crews and took them along. An accidental burst of machine-gun fire from one of the tanks behind them, came within inches of decapitating Truscott. "One of the tank gunners," he chuckled some years later, long after his shock and anger had subsided, "almost ended my career right then and there."[10]

As naval gunfire boomed from behind and machine guns pounded ahead, Truscott's party picked its way along Major McCarley's route, following his telephone line through thick woods. They eventually found him, south of the lagoon where his troops were attempting to eliminate French machine-gun positions to the east. Truscott had hoped that all his battalions would have achieved their objectives by 11:00 A.M., but now, as the afternoon sun edged closer to the horizon, he could see that none had. As darkness approached, he told McCarley to leave one of his companies to protect the south flank and to push forward during the night and link up with Dilley's 2nd Battalion, which was attempting to take the Kasbah. To help protect the south flank, the general assured McCarley that he would dispatch another company of soldiers right away, to be followed by Lieutenant Colonel Semmes's armored battalion.[11]

Truscott returned to his beach command post, the chaos of which had lessened little in his absence. Now it was getting darker and colder. He sat exhausted and apprehensive, anxiously waiting for

Semmes, hopefully somewhere on the beach rounding up his tanks. Feeling chilled and alone, Truscott recalled that "more than anything else right then I wanted a cigarette." He had issued a blackout order, which no one on the beach was violating. Still, the ships offshore had their signal lights flashing constantly, and lookouts had not spotted any enemy aircraft since morning. What harm could a small light on the beach do? Addiction shoving caution aside, he lit a cigarette and inhaled deeply. That was all it took. "In a matter of moments, I was glad when other glows appeared as other lonely and uncertain men sought the comfort of tobacco." Little did they suspect that the first violator of the blackout order was the person who had issued it; tobacco would be a constant but insidious comfort to the old cavalryman as the war progressed. Eventually, the shore-party commander arrived and started organizing the beach, and Semmes drove up with several tanks from his complement. During the night, Truscott learned that Dilley's battalion had not yet been able to take the Kasbah but was still working at it. The arrival of morning light brought a little warmth, which improved spirits if not the situation.[12]

Early on day two, Colonel Semmes, armed with seven tanks, set off to check the south flank. His tankers found their prey within two hours, attacking and driving off a company of French infantry before engaging a group of tanks from Rabat. Semmes's armor knocked out four hostile tanks, causing the rest to retreat; the colonel had personally taken out two of them. When Truscott arrived shortly thereafter, Semmes showed him two defective armor-piercing rounds that had embedded but not exploded in his own tank. About 8:00 A.M. a disappointed Truscott found McCarley not far from where he had been the previous night, the upshot being that the major's patrols had not probed deeply enough to locate and connect with Dilley's battalion. Truscott could hear gunfire about a mile away, which he was certain was from Dilley's men. Truscott took McCarley aside and urged him "to press his advance with the utmost vigor for it was essential to capture the airfield during the day."[13]

By now the surf had become forbidding, necessitating the suspension of any additional landings. As much as he would have preferred otherwise, Truscott came to a realization. "One look at the mounting surf was more than enough to show that we had to take the fort and open the river or we were lost, and we had to do it with what forces we had for there were no more reserves." The battle could still be lost, he knew, and with it, the airport.[14]

Truscott was puzzled when information arrived that Dilley's battalion was still in trouble, having suffered many casualties. The general could see that his troops had captured a sizable number of French soldiers, now confined at the beach. At the same time, he saw that his medical-aid stations were not overwhelmed with American wounded. Suspecting inaccuracy in Dilley's report, Truscott sent Colonel de Rohan forward to investigate. The colonel determined that "straggling" by some soldiers was the problem, a common phenomenon when confusion and disorder reign among green troops. Accompanied by a group of officers and NCOs, de Rohan searched every building and wooded area in the vicinity and rounded up more than two hundred stragglers. The colonel's guiding hand, coupled with the roundup of additional troops, helped reorganize the 2nd Battalion. For the time being, de Rohan would remain at Dilley's side, ensuring that his troops captured the Kasbah. As Dilley focused on the fortress, McCarley continued toward the airport and was soon calling for armor to assist. Luckily, this had made it to shore. At about 4:30 P.M. Truscott dispatched the tanks to McCarley and told him to push on through the night.[15]

That second night on the beach, Truscott ate the first food he had had since coming ashore—K-rations and coffee. If the food was good, the news was not. Two Frenchmen, supportive of the invasion, reported to the general that French forces had greeted Hamilton and Craw with machine-gun fire, killing Craw and taking Hamilton captive.

The news improved at 2:00 A.M. when, while under fire, the army-engineer and navy-demolition team managed to destroy the cable blocking the river. Sometime later the *Dallas* appeared, Malvergne at the helm. Truscott had hoped the fortress would be out of commission before the destroyer headed upriver, but such was not the case. He heard the guns of the *Dallas* firing as it pressed upstream, its engines working as hard as they could, the guns smoking hot as it traded shots with the fortress's artillery and French machine guns somewhere in the hills. The channel was dangerously narrow and the water rough. At one point Malvergne had to power through mucky river bottom and dodge two scuttled steamers. After several miles—which seemed like more—Malvergne watched the seventy-five members of the raider detachment disembark into their rubber boats and paddle to shore.[16]

Major Toffey reported that his troops were now in position across the river from the airport, but communications problems made it impossible for Truscott to know if McCarley's battalion had arrived. Determined to accelerate the action, he told his regimental S-3 officer to gather every available soldier on the beach, regardless of his usual assignment, and get them into action. The result was a "motley crew of seventy or eighty men from along the beach—air force mechanics, cooks, clerks, and chauffeurs." Truscott's orders were to form the men into squads and concentrate on the French snipers between Mehdia and the Kasbah. One airman among the group made a request. Armed with his newly issued submachine gun, he asked, "General, we have never shot these things. Couldn't we try them out to see how they work before we have to fight?" Truscott agreed, watched them practice, and then sent them off into the fracas.[17]

Dilley next reported that his battalion was close to the walls of the Kasbah, but machine-gun and mortar fire had them pinned down and requested air support. A navy aviator on the beach was able to redirect a group of eight dive bombers on their way to another target. With Colonel Carleton describing the appearance of the Kasbah, the aviator directed the bombers to their new target. Meanwhile, Truscott radioed Major Dilley to immediately withdraw three hundred yards and remain there until the last bomb struck.

Truscott went forward and watched. One by one, the dive bombers rolled to the side and aimed their noses at the interior of the old fortress, released their bombs at the last moment, and then screamed up steeply. The images within Truscott's binoculars shook wildly as the ground beneath him shuddered. Dust and smoke shot up from inside the compound. As the last bomber dropped its load and the pilot pulled back hard on his stick, Dilley sent forward his two 105-mm self-propelled guns and, at pointblank range, had the crews slam round after round into the impressive gate and stone walls until an opening appeared. When the gun crews paused, the major's infantry, bayonets affixed, stormed through the breach and into the fortress. Stunned French officers and colonial soldiers, arms raised in capitulation, met them. "It was a beautiful sight for a soldier's eyes," Truscott remembered. If Dilley thought he and his troops could now rest, he was wrong. The general sent them and their 105-mm guns to the airport. There the raider detachment, part of Toffey's battalion, and part of McCarley's battalion, joined by several tanks, captured the airport. Increasingly, French resistance was collapsing.[18]

That afternoon a message arrived from McCarley that the French commander, now captured, wished to surrender his forces. Truscott refused to meet with him until French troops released Major Hamilton. By that evening an unharmed Hamilton was back in U.S. hands at the airport, and arrangements were underway for the surrender of the defending troops the next morning at the Kasbah. General Patton coincidently sent out a radio message that all French forces in North Africa would soon surrender. Truscott reflected some years later, "Our first battle had ended." He notified navy and air forces units standing by that the airport would soon open for business.[19]

The surrender the next day made for an odd ceremony. Truscott and his key staff, still attired in dirty battle dress, met the French commander at the Kasbah. He arrived wearing "blue cape thrown back over one shoulder with its scarlet lining gleaming in the sun, and seven or eight other French officers in trim uniforms with gleaming belts and boots." Truscott as yet had no specific orders from Patton on the conditions of the French surrender. Knowing generally what was acceptable, he cobbled together his own terms: troops not captured in action could retain their weapons but must retire to their barracks, promising not to resist further; all prisoners would be exchanged; American forces would occupy the area; civil servants would continue their normal duties; any supplies requisitioned by the Americans would be paid for in full; and U.S. forces would protect the French as they went about locating their dead.[20]

In Casablanca Patton accepted the surrender of other French forces, but he did Truscott one better. Following the ceremonial surrender, Patton warned French officers that "one disagreeable formality" required their attention. French eyebrows, raised at the comment, lowered when the Amercians carried in bottles of champagne. Once the noise of popping corks subsided, the general offered a toast to the "resumption of the age-old friendship between France and America."[21]

Patton was pleased with Truscott's handling of his part of the invasion. When later it became time to give the general his officer-efficiency report, Patton described him as a "superior organizer and trainer, and a superb fighting leader of men." Of the 183 generals known to Patton, he rated Truscott as number 4. Major Hamilton and Colonel Craw, for their dangerous mission, each received the Medal of Honor, the latter posthumously. Truscott later wrote the difficult letter to the colonel's wife, Victoria Wesson Craw. She replied to him on January 9, 1943, saying how much his letter meant to her and that she would keep it always for their son. René Malvergne, for his piloting expertise and bravery, received the Silver Star, a rare honor for a civilian.[22]

Allied losses in North Africa, when compared with those of future invasions, were light. Nearly 1,200 soldiers were dead or missing, and more than 1,000 wounded. The French paid a higher price for their resistance: 1,600 killed and 900 wounded. Truscott's thorough plan and competent battle decisions limited his casualties to 80 killed and 250 wounded. The Port Lyautey French buried almost 300 of their soldiers. Those defenders who survived the battle became comrades once again and would fight throughout the remainder of the war side by side with American and other Allied troops.

Overall, the North African landings reflected the inexperience of its invaders. While the entire operation could not be termed a success, it was hardly a catastrophe. Without a doubt, it proved to be valuable training for the more serious fighting ahead. Truscott's conclusion for Operation Torch, including his own portion of it, was that there had been some good and bad, but it likely would have been a disaster had the enemy been sufficiently armed and committed to resistance. Indeed, such an enemy was waiting elsewhere in North Africa and in Sicily, and by the time the Allies reached mainland Italy, the enemy would be mostly veteran Germans with honed defensive skills.[23]

CHAPTER 14

Running Ike's Advanced Command Post

New Year's Day 1943 would be more festive in New York than in Berlin or Tokyo. As 1942 queued up to join the list of years gone by, hopeful observers noticed that the path of World War II was undergoing a course correction. Those in Berlin, while concerned about the Allied invasion of North Africa, were alarmed more by events in the Soviet Union. There, in the desperately cold winter snows, six Soviet armies had German forces encircled at Stalingrad. By February, 160,000 German soldiers would be dead and another 90,000 captive and marching to Siberia, a march that would kill thousands more. In Tokyo the focus was on Guadalcanal, an unfamiliar name to most Americans. There U.S. Marines had made significant gains against the entrenched Japanese. After much fighting, the battle-bruised and malaria-riddled 1st Marine Division withdrew, its accomplishments legendary. Even so, more than enough jungle fighting remained for the incoming 2nd Marine Division as well as for the army's 23rd "Americal" and 25th "Tropic Lightning" Infantry Divisions. The fighting would go on for some time, but now the Japanese were on the defensive.[1]

On January 14 Roosevelt, Churchill, and their respective generals and admirals met again, this time at the Hotel Anfa just outside Casablanca. Stalin did not attend, but he renewed his demand for an Allied second front. Ignoring this for the moment, Churchill and Roosevelt agreed to delay the cross-channel invasion and were pleased that the troop buildup in the British Isles was going well. For now, instead of invading France, the Allies would complete their task in North Africa while beginning to focus on Sicily. A successful campaign there would push Italy out of the war and leave the Allies in command of the Mediterranean. Churchill also argued for a follow-up invasion of the Balkans, another "soft underbelly" of Nazi-occupied Europe. General Marshall cursed the thought, but he was pleased when the British proposed appointing Eisenhower as supreme Allied commander of all Mediterranean operations. By doing so, the British privately thought they could elevate the general high enough that he would be out of the way of his subordinate commanders, primarily British, who then could orchestrate the war on land, sea, and air. Had Marshall known their real motive, a wry smile might have appeared on his lips. He knew Eisenhower much better than they did. Interestingly, one topic somehow *not* discussed was just what the Allies would do in Sicily *after* they landed.[2]

A few levels beneath Roosevelt and Churchill, General Truscott was in search of a new job. Patton's command had its full complement of generals, leaving no slot available for him once the North African landings were accomplished. Of course, any available position would need to be one for a two-star general, as on November 21, 1942, the army had promoted Truscott to major general. The general without a command made his way to Allied headquarters in Algiers, hoping Eisenhower might have an assignment for him. Eisenhower was away, but his staff expected the general back in a day or two. As might be expected, Truscott did not want just any job. "I was hopeful that I would remain in the theater, but even more, I wanted an active assignment," he later wrote. "What was left of that cheerless Christmas Eve, Conway and I spent in the Alletti Hotel in Algiers." War correspondents often used this hotel as well, among them John Steinbeck.[3]

Truscott was understandably apprehensive. The army could send him to the Pacific, which was acceptable, but it could also return him to the States, which was not. Without a doubt, Sarah would have loved to have Lucian home, but she knew he would need to be in the thick of the action. His preference, if allowed a voice in the matter, was to remain in Europe; Sarah and the children would just have to understand.

By December 29 Truscott had an assignment; he would be Eisenhower's deputy chief of staff. The Tunisia campaign, then in progress, had many problems, one of which would serve to his benefit. The newly allied French military, still bitter at the Royal Navy for having sunk their fleet, refused to work under a British commander. Necessarily, the Allied commands would all have to report directly to Eisenhower, a huge burden for him. Truscott's job would be to serve as the general's eyes and ears closer to the front. It was a critical moment in the war. As Truscott later recalled, "it was during this period in the deserts and mountains . . . that American forces first crossed swords with veteran German legions and learned of war from them—the hard way." With the new appointment, he immediately sent for Colonel Carleton and his old staff.[4]

Truscott's mission was to set up and operate an advanced command post in the city of Constantine in northeast Algeria, close to the headquarters of the British army, which oversaw Allied operations in nearby Tunisia. His was a staff position, but though he would not command troops, the post would give him an excellent view of the campaign and all of its principal commanders. "Essentially," Truscott remembered, "the purpose was to furnish General Eisenhower with an office closer to the front than AFHQ [Allied Force Headquarters] so that all the information concerning the situation would be available, and where his personal contact with subordinate commanders would be more convenient than in Algiers." As Eisenhower's deputy, Truscott would continually coordinate with three very different Allied commands. While not an easy task in peacetime, it was a much more difficult one during war.[5]

Truscott had no doubt that others would see him as a something of a snoop for Eisenhower. As he knew, "Few subordinates ever look with much favor upon inspectors and observers who represent superior headquarters and most staff officers are inclined to be somewhat jealous of their prerogatives." Truscott was not the only staff officer that Eisenhower inserted somewhere as his eyes and ears. In February he sent Major General Omar N. Bradley as his "personal observer" to II Corps, commanded by Major General Fredendall. A surly Fredendall saw to it that Bradley's quarters were located in a nearby fleabag hotel. Later, when Patton assumed command of II Corps, he would tell Bradley that he did not want "one of Ike's goddamn spies" watching him. Not surprising, Patton found a solution to his problem. He persuaded Eisenhower's chief of staff, Major General Bedell Smith, to have his boss appoint Bradley as Patton's deputy corps commander. Now, instead of reporting *on* Patton, Bradley reported *to* him.[6]

Having only recently arrived from Morocco, Truscott realized that he was not fully aware of all that had gone on in the rest of North Africa during the previous month. What he found in Algeria and Tunisia was disheartening. The original Allied plan had been to capture key seaports and airports, set up communication lines, and trap the Germans. Unfortunately, British, American, and French troops had failed in that effort. Eisenhower's most pressing problem now was his need to regroup and resupply while protecting his 500-mile-long supply line, which stretched across Algeria to Tunisia. The Allied front, 250 miles long, ran from near Bizerte in northern Tunisia through the Atlas Mountains to near Gabes in the south. Staffing was a hodge-podge of intermingled British, American, and French units. Meanwhile, the Germans were anything but idle. Hitler had immediately reinforced North Africa with more than 100,000 German and Italian troops under General Hans-Jürgen von Arnim. Soon, he hoped, they would connect with Lieutenant General Erwin J. E. Rommel's 170,000 troops coming up from the south.[7]

The Atlas Mountains in central Tunisia consist of two north–south ranges that run parallel for a distance and then join in the north like an inverted "Y." The Allies held the western range, the Axis the eastern range, along with the territory and routes in between. Throughout the cold winter, each side did its best to monitor the other, remaining alert for any threat. Thus far the Americans had done reasonably well in their first combat. The Torch landings and subsequent battles had been successful even if not stellar. Of course, that fighting had been against the French, not the Germans.

In many respects, as the Tunisia campaign would show, the Americans were still very inexperienced. British general Sir Harold Alexander, soon to command all Allied ground forces in North Africa, emphasized such in a letter to his superior, Commanding General Sir Alan Brooke, chief of the Imperial General Staff (Marshall's counterpart in England). Undeniably, American soldiers and their leadership—including Eisenhower—*were* green. Unmentioned by Alexander, however, was that the British leadership—now in overall command of ground operations—continued to rely on obsolete methods. Called "penny-packet" tactics, the concept was to use small units, typically reinforced brigades, to fight small, almost individual battles. Worse was that American and French units had been picked apart to plug weak spots in British lines, essentially destroying their unit cohesion. The even more bad news was that American armor, while better than that of the British and French, was still noticeably inferior to that of the Germans. The only good news seemed to be that American artillery was quite good.[8]

Perhaps the most critical part of Allied strategy was something the Allies did not seem to recognize. It was their inability to coordinate air and land forces. German field marshal Albert Kesselring was about to give them a painful lesson in how to do it. He was an artillery officer who had later transferred to the air force. A pilot himself, he had helped build the Luftwaffe between the wars and then had overseen air attacks in Poland, France, and Norway. Now he was the senior commander of all German forces in the Mediterranean. The Allies would find him to be a fierce competitor.[9]

When Truscott took the reins of his new job, he discovered that "the front had literally bogged down in a sea of mud." Eisenhower had previously called a halt in the race to Tunis, and now he had postponed any new attack indefinitely. The pounding rains would likely persist through February, allowing both sides to do little more than reorganize and resupply. Truscott met with his commander and recalled, "He had been terribly disappointed that the Allied drive had been stopped before capturing Tunis." Now winter had arrived, and the rain was wet and cold, the mud deep and sticky, and the supply lines long and difficult to maintain. Mother Nature would punish equally all soldiers—British, French, American, German, and Italian.[10]

Truscott kept his advanced-command-post operation, Eisenhower's front-row seat, purposely small. A handful of staff officers addressed problems of supply—the most pressing—as well as air support, communications, operations, and intelligence. An American orphanage building served as their headquarters. Truscott shared one conclusion about his new assignment in a letter to Sarah: "I'm rather inclined to think that DDE is keeping me around because he feels the need of someone whom he knows is loyal and has no axe to grind. God knows he needs a few like that."[11]

Truscott's personal aide was kind enough to write Mrs. Truscott on February 2 to let her know that her husband was busy but also doing fine. He added: "The general is in good health and has been able to get away from our headquarters for a trip here and there for a few days. It has done him a world of good. . . . [T]his country was old, dirty and worn out when Jesus was a baby and it hasn't improved yet."[12]

Battles continued to rage in the south, where General Rommel's Italo-German Panzerarmee and General Montgomery's Eighth Army "Desert Rats" continually engaged in fighting. "From now on," Truscott noted, "the battle to drive the Axis from Africa was one big battle, and our operations would have to be closely coordinated with those of 8th Army." Nevertheless, in February the situation changed quite suddenly. Montgomery's forces, which had accelerated their push of Rommel's forces west toward Tunisia, came to a stop. Once the British had captured Tripoli, Montgomery felt the need to pause and let his army catch its breath. He also knew that Rommel had now reached a strong defensive position. The British general was content to wait and watch for a while.

Rommel saw opportunity, however. He was less worried about Montgomery's forces behind him than Alexander's forces ahead of him. Having had some success at outwitting his opponents, he decided to try again. Thus he left a minimal defensive force facing the Eighth Army to the south and planned a surprise attack to the north. His objective was to hit the Allied lines, punch through, and capture their supply depot. Once he severed their supply lines, they would find ammunition, fuel, and food hard to come by.[13]

On February 12 Eisenhower made his first visit to his advanced command post. Truscott arranged for an escort by a mechanized cavalry platoon to provide security throughout the visit. Eisenhower was anxious to confer with Major General Fredendall, who commanded the II Corps. The following day, ever alert for Luftwaffe aircraft, Truscott, Eisenhower, and their small staff journeyed to Fredendall's headquarters. Truscott had forewarned his commander about what to expect at the corps command post, knowing that his own concept of a general's headquarters was strikingly different from what Fredendall had built. "I will never forget my first visit to General Fredendall's command post," he remembered. "Although it was sheltered by towering mountains and concealed among the trees, the corps engineers were blasting away at the mountainside to build underground shelters for the operational staff—and this was a good 60 or 70 miles from any point where there was contact with the enemy." He recalled Fredendall saying that "he would exercise control by means of communications; he did not need to be any closer to the front!" Truscott knew that maps and good communication were essential parts of any command-post operation, but he also firmly believed that "there can be no substitute in command for personal visits and reconnaissance by commanders and staff officers alike. The actual sight of soldiers, guns, ground, and sky will often erase the pessimism created by the pictures drawn in grease pencil upon maps." When Eisenhower visited II Corps headquarters, it was obvious that he was not pleased with what he saw. Fredendall was operating a command post that General Bradley would later describe as "an embarrassment to every American soldier." According to Truscott, Eisenhower uttered some "acid comments" but chose not to relieve Fredendall on the spot. In the near future, however, the two hundred combat engineers who for weeks had dug ever deeper into the side of a mountain, using skills and equipment needed elsewhere, would have a new commander.[14]

About this time, Truscott learned that Eisenhower would reassign him in the near future to command the 3rd Infantry Division, now slated to be one of the invasion units for Sicily. Truscott's tenure in North Africa was near its end. He was elated.[15]

Valentine's Day near Faïd Pass seemed like any other early morning in Tunisia. Anxious American commanders guarding the pass continually scanned the hills, but thus far they had seen little activity by German forces. Their first clue that a blitzkrieg was coming was when Luftwaffe dive bombers screamed down from the clouds. Next, like angry arrows from a renegade Cupid, racing panzers punctured Allied lines. Still green, spread too thin, and clearly outgunned, many American soldiers fled from what they saw as certain death or capture. At noon another attack came at Sidi Bou Zid. There a frontline colonel radioed his senior headquarters and reported that the American line had broken and that troops were in flight. Headquarters staff assured him that it was probably just some units changing positions. Disbelieving what he was hearing, the colonel interrupted and shouted, "I know panic when I see it!" Poorly disposed and thus incapable of mutual support, some American units folded. Reinforcements, rushed in to pursue what appeared to be departing Germans, were shocked to discover they had fallen into an ambush. Allied personnel and equipment losses were staggering.[16]

General von Arnim was the instigator of the attacks. The plan was for him and Rommel to coordinate their forces and defeat the Allies in North Africa. Arnim, however, was a more cautious and defensive-oriented commander than Rommel. Although he had clearly achieved a success against the Allies that day, he chose not to exploit it. To make matters worse, he now refused to share his panzer divisions with Rommel. With no time to take the matter to their superior, Field Marshal Kesselring, Rommel attacked on

February 19. He intended to go through Kasserine Pass on the way to Le Kef in an effort to split the Allies and disrupt their supply chain. Without von Armim's panzer divisions, however, he had to rely on his own Kampfgruppe DAK, which was a weaker armored unit consisting of Germans and Italians. The attack hit U.S. units defending the pass and substantially pushed them back. But with the assistance of British units, the Americans managed to set up blocking positions north and west, thus slowing—but not stopping—Rommel's drive. The general won Kasserine Pass but accepted that in doing so he had overextended his resources. He regretted having to abandon his drive but knew that he needed to race back south to keep Montgomery's tanks from breaking through German defenses there.[17]

The Americans' inadequacies were now obvious not only to the Germans but to the British as well. They now faced two giant tasks ahead of them. The first was to improve substantially their own performance; the second was to demonstrate to the British that they had done so. It would take some time for their allies to regain confidence in the Americans. Only Rommel seemed to have the vision to see that supplied with better training, equipment, and leadership, the Americans would prove unstoppable.[18]

To their dismay, senior Allied leaders now realized that capturing Tunisia was taking much longer than expected and was now affecting the timeline for the Sicily invasion, which had already been set. Consequently, certain units and commanders—including Truscott—were to return to Morocco to prepare for the Sicily landing. As the designated commanding general of the 3rd Infantry Division, Truscott would not witness the climactic battle in Tunisia. His former chief of staff, Colonel Carleton, would accompany him to the new division. Major Conway, however, had come to the attention of Eisenhower, who was looking for a talented American aide for General Alexander. Truscott hated to lose Conway but understood his need elsewhere. Before departing for Morocco, the general stopped at Eisenhower's headquarters in Algiers to say goodbye. Eisenhower took the occasion to ask Truscott for his opinion of Fredendall. He openly but respectfully replied that he thought the general "had lost the confidence of his subordinates." Truscott added that he believed II Corps would do poorly under his command; further, that Fredendall considered the British to be untrustworthy and thus would "never get on well" under a British commander. Truscott recommended that Eisenhower send General Patton to take command of II Corps.

The general already had that in mind, but because of the upcoming invasion of Sicily, he could not allow Patton to stay long. When it became time for Patton to leave, Omar Bradley would assume command of II Corps.[19]

By now, General Alexander had arrived and assumed overall command of Allied ground forces in North Africa, consisting of the British First Army of 120,000 men, a French corps of 50,000 troops, and Bradley's II Corps of 90,000 men. With the inclusion of Montgomery's Eighth Army, Allied forces in North Africa numbered more than 300,000 troops and possessed nearly 3,000 tanks and artillery pieces. The huge Allied net began to close like a purse seine around the large school of Axis forces on the continent. Rommel saw the seriousness of the situation and flew to Germany to plead with Hitler to allow the evacuation of German troops from North Africa. Hitler not only refused but also decided that Rommel must be ill, ordering him to go on sick leave immediately.

The Allies moved in from the north, south, and west until they had backed the retreating Germans to the Mediterranean coast. By May 12 the catch was complete. Abandoned by an angry Hitler, General von Arnim surrendered 250,000 German and Italian troops, which was even more than the numbers the Soviets had captured at Stalingrad. The Allied cost of capturing North Africa, including British, French, and American forces, was 70,000 killed, wounded, or captured. General Bradley's report card for the U.S. performance in the campaign was to the point: "In Africa we learned to crawl, to walk—then run. Had that learning process been launched in France, it would surely have . . . resulted in unthinkable disaster."[20]

Now a second invasion, the largest to date, would take place at Sicily. The 3rd Infantry Division would be one of the divisions going in. It now had two standout soldiers in its ranks. The first was Major General Truscott, its new commanding officer, who was about to shake things up. The second was a soft-spoken eighteen-year-old boy from Kingston, Texas, who looked to be even younger. His name was Audie Murphy.[21]

CHAPTER 15

INVASION PLANNING, SICILY

For Truscott, the invasion of Sicily, codenamed Operation Husky, would be like playing a game of lethal chess with the best player in the world—in this case, the Wehrmacht. Italian forces would be there, of course, but Truscott knew the Germans would make the important moves. He also knew that how the Americans had fared in Tunisia was not good enough to succeed in Italy. The general committed to better train, equip, and condition the soldiers of his new command, the 3rd Infantry Division. "I had observed modern war at Dieppe, I had experienced it in command at Port Lyautey, and I had just been closely associated with American troops in the first battles against the veteran Germans," Truscott recounted. He knew how much British commandos and American rangers were capable of doing, and he saw no reason why a standard infantry division could not do as well. "I had long felt that our standards of marching and fighting in the infantry were too low, not up to those of the Roman legions . . . nor even those of Stonewall Jackson's 'Foot Cavalry' of Civil War fame." The general would transform the members of the 3rd Infantry Division, one of the army's oldest, in his crucible so they could meet the challenges ahead. He was confident that the better he trained each soldier, the more likely it was that that man would one day make it home.[1]

After departing Tunisia, Truscott made a nostalgic return to Port Lyautey, the site of his first battle. He gazed at the immense ocean, the tricky river, and the once enemy-infested hills, reflecting on the lives lost there. He jingled a few coins and a key in his pocket; maybe they had brought him good luck, he thought. These items had been in his pocket during this first battle, and they would remain there until war's end. There was no logic to it, of course, but what was the harm? Perhaps they could help ensure that he would once again see Sarah and the children.[2]

The 3rd Infantry Division was in Morocco, awaiting its new commander. Truscott knew that it would take more than luck to get the division up to his standards. Moreover, it would not be just the enlisted men or junior officers who would need to measure up. "Throughout my service," he remembered, "I had heard 'you young officers' blamed for everything that went wrong, and combat had been no exception." As far as he was concerned, if the training or initiative of young officers was lacking, senior officers were not doing their jobs. "Either, we had not trained them properly," the former cavalryman reflected, "or we had held the reins so tight that the horse could not use his head."[3]

First off, he and Colonel Carleton met with the division-headquarters staff to talk about the problems in Tunisia caused by inadequate training, poor equipment, ineffective leadership, and insufficient will to fight. Truscott next began meeting with the other officers in the division, inculcating in them the value of using good common sense, of having an intimate knowledge of weapons and equipment, of being in the best possible physical condition, and of taking calculated risks. He warned his junior officers and NCOs that senior officers would correct honest mistakes, but they would punish failure to take responsibility. "Development of this individual and mutual confidence resulted in an *élan* and *esprit,*" he recalled years later with justified pride, "which was to distinguish the 3rd Infantry Division throughout the war."[4]

Among the rank and file, Private Audie Murphy, assigned to the 15th Infantry "Can Do" Regiment, also waited in Morocco, anxious to get on with the war and get it over. Ahead of him and his fellow soldiers were more than two years in a war zone. The division would experience 233 days in actual combat and receive thirty-one Medals of Honor, one of which was destined for Murphy.[5]

The Sicilians are island people. As with others throughout the world, no matter how large or small their island, they are convinced that the mainlanders are out to harm them one way or another. For Sicily, certainly, that has been the case throughout its sad history. Since ancient times, invaders have included Greeks, Romans, barbarians, Phoenicians, Byzantines, Arabs, Norman crusaders, and various European countries, including mainland Italians. Distant from Rome and buffered from the mainland by the Straits of Messina, the defacto rulers of Sicily were its powerful landowners and homegrown

Mafia, aided and abetted by pervasive poverty brought on, in part, by denuded forests, depleted soil, and absentee landlords.[6]

Aware of Allied success in North Africa, German panzers clanked, rumbled, and ferried from the mainland onto Sicily. They were not invited by the islanders but by Mussolini, albeit reluctantly. To Sicilians, the Fascist-Nazi partnership was now just another invasion of their island. Now it seemed imminent that the Allies would be next in line to invade, though ironically many Sicilians saw them as potential liberators. Yet, in the struggle to come, the island would take a pounding.[7]

Sicilians consider themselves Sicilians first and Italians second, but they are very much like their mainland cousins in one respect. Both define themselves not from the national level downward, but from the family level upward. Italian governments come and go, but the family, arms linked with its neighborhood and village, persists. The succession of various governments over the ages has served to invest Italian power not in the national or even local government but in its multitude of families. Had the Allies been more cognizant of this, they might have taken the risk and launched their invasion of Sicily as early as possible. That way, the dispirited Italian army would have been the primary enemy. Now it would be the Germans, who had rushed in just ahead of the Allies.[8]

Having waited too long, the Americans and British would have to go against what was probably the best army in the world—the Wehrmacht. To a significant degree, European leaders were to blame for this. After World War I, required by the Treaty of Versailles to reduce its officer corps from 30,000 to just 4,000 men, the Germans kept and cultivated only the very best and from that small nucleus secretly began to reinvent not only their army but also modern warfare. Some veteran officers of that elite force waited now in Sicily. Significantly outnumbered, the Germans would nonetheless execute one of the most effective defensive withdrawals in military history.[9]

Certain secret information intended for General Alexander was especially sensitive and thus could not be transmitted by radio or telegraph. It necessitated hand delivery, not by a large security force, which might invite attention, but by one man—a Royal Marine acting major assigned to Lord Mountbatten's Combined Operations Unit, with which Truscott had worked while in England. He never

Sicily, Italy, and German defensive lines. Map by Megan Postell.

had occasion to meet this young officer who, not coincidentally, was an expert in amphibious landings.

William Martin carried the sealed letter from Lieutenant General Sir Archibald Nye, vice chief of the Imperial General Staff, to Alexander, then in Gibraltar. The message addressed a number of routine issues and then broke some bad news. Troops previously intended for Alexander would go instead to British general Sir Henry "Jumbo" Wilson. It reaffirmed that the Germans expected Sicily to be the next invasion target but revealed that Wilson's mission would be to invade Sardinia first and thereafter simultaneously invade both Sicily (from the north) and Greece. The Balkan campaign required the use of the two army divisions previously promised to Alexander.

Unfortunately, Martin was killed en route when the airplane carrying him went down in the sea. Spanish fishermen saw something floating and discovered his body, life vest now deflated, with a leather briefcase still handcuffed to his wrist. Spanish authorities learned of the find and took custody. A medical examiner reported the presence of fluid in the body's lungs and determined the likely cause of death to be drowning. Authorities then presented the remains to the local British consul's office, though without the briefcase attached. The British, in something of a panic, demanded the return of the briefcase, which the Spanish sheepishly handed over. By then, of course, agents had secretly opened it and photographed the letter therein for the Germans. The information, deemed by Nazi agents to be authentic, quickly found its way to Hitler, who personally decided to maintain all existing German forces in Sardinia and to augment those in Greece. His message to Field Marshal Kesselring underscored that "the measures to be taken in Sardinia and the Peloponnesus have priority over any others." The job of the Allies had now become much more difficult.

Or so Hitler thought. The whole thing had been cooked up by British intelligence—the XX Committee of MI5. They used the body of a man who had died of pneumonia, in many ways similar to drowning, and planted it with the identification of a William Martin. They then deposited it by submarine in Spanish waters, where wind and tides would take it to shore. The rich imaginations of MI5 lieutenant commander Ewen Montagu and flight lieutenant Charles Cholmondeley, authors of this deception, constantly churned out other ruses, but their "Major Martin" gambit remains among the best instances of military disinformation in history. Code-named Operation Mincemeat, it has now morphed into the story of "The Man Who Never Was." Once it seemed certain that the ruse had fooled the Germans, MI5 sent a short message to Churchill, then meeting with Roosevelt and others in Washington, D.C. It read, "Mincemeat swallowed whole."[10]

On March 8, 1943, General Truscott was taking a close look at his division. "I saw much, but said little," he recalled, "and that little usually only to officers on the subject of standards. . . . I had been in command for about a week when there came an opportunity for which I was waiting." He intended to inculcate into his soldiers the notion drummed into every successful army in history—physical fitness is essential for success in combat. First however, he had to get everyone's attention, perhaps with some bit of information that would fly through the ranks as surely as a rumor that Betty Grable was coming to entertain them. This rumor, however, would foster such statements as, "Have you heard what that new hard-ass general wants us to do?"[11]

Lieutenant Colonel Ben Harrell, the division's operations and plans officer, approached the general with a routine order for his signature, the sending of one battalion to an outpost and the return of another, a distance of ten miles. Truscott read the order and saw his opportunity. He instructed Harrell to have the two battalions march at four miles an hour. The colonel cautiously reminded the general that army troops march at two and a half miles an hour. He acknowledged that and again said he wanted the troops to march at four miles an hour. The colonel, more than a little puzzled, left and returned moments later with a copy of the pertinent field manual, which clearly stated that infantry troops march at two and a half miles an hour. Quietly, though with less patience, Truscott said: "Colonel, you can throw that field manual and that order, too, in that wastebasket there. Will you issue the order or shall I detail someone else to issue it?"[12]

The march was not easy. In the battalion of about one thousand men heading to the outpost, more than one hundred fell out and straggled behind. But of the returning battalion, which had been training on sand dunes daily for two weeks, only twelve fell out. "The difference was simply a matter of physical conditioning," Truscott noted. "I was confident that an average infantry battalion could approximate ranger and commando standards for marching." The wakeup call was not just for the troops but for the officers as well. "You can't lead your men from a command post in the rear," he told his officers more than once.[13]

On May 14 Lucian shared some news with Sarah. "You will be interested to know that you are now reading the first letter I have ever written while wearing glasses." Another catch-up letter to her on May 23 mentioned Lucian III at West Point and Jamie still at home but used their nicknames. "I am so glad that Doodie will be home this summer. How long does he have at home? I'll bet Jas will be thrilled." He also mentioned the speed marching he required of his division. "The men call it the Truscott Trot." Private Murphy would get a taste of it when his regiment trotted across Sicily.[14]

Truscott did not have much time to get his troops ready before the invasion fleet sailed, so he would invest every moment possible in training and planning. Even though the 3rd Infantry Division had already made one invasion landing and had seen battle, a quarter of its veterans were reassigned when it became necessary to augment other units then fighting in Tunisia; newcomers had taken their place. Perhaps worse, Truscott observed, the men had been in the rear long enough that their discipline and enthusiasm had softened. In short, the 3rd Infantry Division was standing at ease and needed to be called to attention.[15]

The general moved his division to the Invasion Training Center at Arzew, Algeria, where Brigadier General John W. "Iron Mike" O'Daniel, who would later become Truscott's assistant division commander, ran the program. There and elsewhere, the soldiers speed-marched, ran obstacle courses, lifted logs, did calisthenics, climbed ropes, practiced street fighting, and negotiated bayonet courses. They participated in beach landings both day and night against aggressor forces. They practiced how to follow closely behind artillery barrages, sometimes within one hundred yards. Separate schools taught specialist soldiers the essentials of landing craft, transport, communications, maintenance, supply, beach organization, and waterproofing vehicles and equipment. A separate school near Pont du Cheliff taught mountain warfare, which consisted of "mountain walking and marching, tactical formations for mountain fighting, combat firing for all weapons for mountainous terrain, and day and night combat exercises."[16]

Truscott viewed planning as every bit as important as training. He established an innovative planning board and charged Lieutenant Colonel Albert Connor, division personnel, with running it. His group was fashioned somewhat after the planning syndicates he had seen at work in London. In addition to the principal representatives for the usual staff sections of personnel, intelligence, operations and training, and logistics and supply, Truscott added representatives from the navy, Rangers, airborne, artillery, armor, beach engineers, and later, a commando-trained British officer, Major Robert Henriques. Planning board members had no other duties except to meet daily in the "War Room," in actuality a fenced and guarded hospital tent. While Truscott had never heard such terms as "participative management" and "getting buy-ins from principal stakeholders," he was doing exactly that. He later said of the process, "It was effective because it insured the utmost in cooperation among all the branches and services involved and the careful and coordinated planning of an infinite number of details."[17]

There was one thing that Truscott would not consider. When Allied Forces Headquarters suggested that troops receive training in how to escape if captured, the general balked. They could train his men how *not* to be captured if they liked, but not how to escape. He had no interest in any exercise that suggested that surrendering was somehow permissible under anything but the most desperate of circumstances. He did, however, accept a silk escape map of Sicily when offered one—it would be a good neck scarf for his increasingly personalized uniform. It even had something of cavalry flair to it.[18]

Ironically, at a higher level there was too little planning in progress for the Sicily invasion. General Montgomery had been aware of this for some time and had sounded the alarm more than once. Eisenhower, Alexander (ground-force commander), Royal Navy admiral Sir Andrew Browne Cunningham, and Royal Air Force air chief marshal Sir Arthur Tedder, all separated geographically, were each too busy to pay close attention to what Task Force 141, the assigned interservice planning group, was doing. While that group was working hard, it was essentially rudderless. Montgomery was as busy as the others were, but he could see that what passed for progress was not good. Not even one high-level commander was devoting his full time to overseeing the developing plan, which proposed splitting Allied forces and underestimated enemy resistance.

At some risk to his career, Montgomery wrote a letter to General Brooke, calling the existing plan for Sicily something similar to what a dog might eat for breakfast. He also simply announced that he intended to land his Eighth Army in southeast Sicily. He sent General Alexander a similar message and later personally delivered the message to Eisenhower's chief of staff, General Smith, in of all places the men's room at Eisenhower's headquarters. In essence, Montgomery announced where he intended to land his army regardless of Task

Force 141's intentions. Alexander and Eisenhower, now presented with Montgomery's over-the-transom plan, had little choice but to start paying attention to the situation. The British general also complained about a critical element that would become a contentious issue as the invasion progressed: "The planners, and everyone else, had been concentrating on *where* to land; nobody had considered how the campaign in Italy should be *developed*."[19]

After considerable spirited debate and more than a few muttered epithets about Montgomery, the senior Allied commanders accepted his proposal. The original plan had been for Patton's U.S. Seventh Army to land in northwest Sicily and take Palermo, while Montgomery's British Eighth Army landed in southeast Sicily and took Syracuse. Both armies, Patton's moving east and Montgomery's moving north, would battle their way to Messina in northeast Sicily, situated less than a half mile across the Straits of Messina from mainland Italy.

The revised plan now called for Montgomery's army to follow essentially its original route but for Patton's army to land west of it, basically doing little more than capturing airfields and protecting the British flank. The Allies would ignore Palermo—not surprising, Patton was irate. The Americans viewed this as Alexander giving in to his general's complaints. Montgomery disagreed and saw his plan as consolidating rather than dividing Allied forces. Although unintended, the change renewed hard feelings and left Patton plotting to enlarge the American role in the campaign.[20]

Had Field Marshal Kesselring been able to eavesdrop on Operation Husky planning, he might have smiled and shaken his head. By his measure, the Allies were invading the wrong island. "The enemy would gain more from an operation against Sardinia and Corsica if the Allied objective were the speedy capture of Rome," he believed. "The possession of the islands, especially Corsica as an 'aircraft carrier,' would facilitate an offensive directed against the south of France."[21]

Like most other American commanders, Truscott was miffed at what he described as Montgomery's "bitter opposition to the original plan." He and his staff had been doing considerable planning, much of which now had to be tossed. Especially irritating, Truscott's revised assignment called for him to land his troops at beach positions where there was a dearth of intelligence, few aerial photographs, and the most detailed map his staff could lay hands on was dated 1883.[22]

Truscott needed new information about his target beaches, but senior planners ignored his almost daily requests for photographic surveillance. Finally, a senior intelligence officer in Eisenhower's headquarters made it clear that aerial photos of the area would not be taken for fear that doing so might expose Allied intentions. "Then I was desperate," Truscott recalled. "This photographic intelligence was essential to our planning." Knowing that the U.S. Army Air Forces' Eighth Bomber Command was doing some surveillance flights over Sicily, Truscott went to see its commander, Major General James H. "Jimmy" Doolittle, hoping he might have some useful photos. His command had no photos that would aid the division commander, but being a man of action, Doolittle ordered air missions to acquire some. In a few days Truscott had the photos he needed as well as an on-loan aerial-photograph interpreter to assist his planners. Thanks to General Doolittle, Truscott recalled, his planning staff had "far superior photographic intelligence for this operation than any other Sub Task Force—far better than I was ever to have again."[23]

Truscott's planning-board members considered, tested, and included many innovations for the landing. Suspecting the beach would contain rows of barbed wire and other obstacles, some of the landing craft were equipped with mortars that could fire grappling hooks to snag and pull away such obstructions before the troops departed their boats. Tanks were loaded into landing crafts in such a way that their crews could fire their powerful guns onto the beach during the approach if necessary. Chief of Staff Carleton suggested modifying two larger landing craft by attaching metal runways long enough to launch two small, lightweight observation aircraft that would later land onshore. Truscott authorized the 30th Infantry Regiment to purchase forty Arab burros or donkeys to carry ammunition and other supplies as troops moved inland. One test involved overloading the landing craft so as to transport soldiers and equipment more quickly yet still provide for their safety. Truscott, remembering the information vacuum he had suffered at Port Lyautey, added a personal requirement—the assignment of one officer from each battalion, equipped with radio and Jeep, whose sole mission was to keep division headquarters informed.

Each of the above was acceptable to the navy except one. It balked at allowing "mules" on its vessels. "You are making a cavalry stable out of my ships," an exasperated Rear Admiral Richard L. Conolly, commanding the Amphibious Force, Atlantic Fleet, told Truscott. "I will be the laughing stock of the Navy." It took some smooth talking by the former cavalryman to persuade Conolly that the beasts of burden were actually weapons of war. "Dammit, General you are right," the admiral finally acceded. "We will carry the goddam mules and anything else you want carried." Truscott was sure that no other army general ever had a navy opposite who was more capable and willing to help. His soldiers were fond of Conolly as well, apparently because he insisted that the covering ships and landing craft operate as close to shore as practical. The soldiers nicknamed him "Push 'em up Closer" Conolly.[24]

Excepting Doolittle's excellent assistance, similar cooperation was not forthcoming from the U.S. Army Air Forces. Truscott was disappointed that the air command, then still a part of the army, was much less willing to assist than the navy. Repeated requests for assistance went unanswered.[25]

During preparations for the operation, so realistic was one invasion rehearsal that some soldiers thought it was the actual event. With understandable pride, Truscott noted, "Never was any division more fit for combat and more in readiness to close with the enemy than the 3rd Infantry Division when we embarked for the invasion of Sicily." To make the situation even better, Eisenhower offered him an additional general, knowing that Truscott's command, Joss Force, totaled 50,000 soldiers, triple the strength of a standard division. He wasted no time in requesting "Iron Mike" O'Daniel.[26]

Truscott was a proud general, but he was still a concerned father. In the middle of preparing for Sicily, he received a letter from Sarah reporting that young Jamie's grades were slipping. Lucian replied on June 23, saying, "I am distressed about Jamie's marks, but I suppose there is nothing I can do about it." Apparently, there was. On June 25 he wrote directly to his son. "Mother wrote me that . . . your marks were straight B instead of straight A. That has surprised and disappointed me. You must know that doing your part in school, and at home, is your contribution to the war." Jamie must have taken his father's words to heart, for he later graduated from West Point.[27]

Truscott reviewed the overall plan for Operation Husky. To begin with, the navy had to transport everyone and everything to Sicily and in such a manner that continued the ruse that Sardinia was the real target. Then it would deposit the two armies onto the beaches. Montgomery's Eighth Army, consisting of British and Canadian troops as well as commandos, paratroopers, and glider troops, would land in southeast Sicily between Pachino and Syracuse. Patton's Seventh Army would also land in southeast Sicily but west of Montgomery's troops. Under Patton, General Bradley's II Corps, consisting of the 1st Infantry Division, the 45th Infantry Division, and two ranger battalions, would splash down near Gela and Scoglitti. Truscott's sub–task force, code-named Operation Joss Force, would report not to Bradley, but directly to Patton. Truscott's large command would handle its own maintenance and supply for at least a month. Joss Force consisted of Truscott's 3rd Infantry Division, one ranger battalion, and one combat command of the 2nd Armored Division. The night before the landing, paratroopers of the 82nd Airborne Division, a unit under Patton, would fly from North Africa and drop behind enemy lines. Remaining shipboard in floating reserve would be one armored combat command of the 2nd Armored. Standing by in North Africa for deployment, if needed, would be the 9th Infantry Division.[28]

Invasions are replete with complexities, and Sicily was no exception. It would be the largest amphibious assault force to date, using 2,600 navy ships and landing craft to carry 115,000 British troops and 66,000 American troops as well as 1,800 large guns, 600 tanks, and 14,000 other vehicles. The 1st Infantry Division would arrive by ship from North Africa, and the 45th Infantry Division would arrive combat-loaded by ship from the United States. Truscott's troops would also come from North Africa, but they would motor the ninety miles in landing craft. It would be the first test of this concept. A complication for Truscott was that the three kinds of landing craft carrying his troops traveled at different speeds.[29]

The night before he sailed for Sicily, Lucian penned a letter to Sarah. He was going into combat again, and he knew she was worried. He assured her that he would take good care of himself, but he could not resist talking about his soldiers: "These men I believe are better prepared than any in all our military history. They are fit, serious, and anxious to get the job done—and get home." He would do his best to get as many home as he possibly could.[30]

The USS *Biscayne,* serving as the general's initial headquarters, pulled its North African moorage lines on July 8 and pushed its bow through the blue Mediterranean under equally blue skies. The sea was calm, with the prospect that the passage would be as pleasant as could be expected, considering that the intent was to forcefully land on an enemy shore. All that changed about 3:00 A.M., when the ship's general alarm sounded. A hurtling Mediterranean wind was pushing aside everything in its path. In France this cold, severe, and unexpected wind is called a *mistral,* while in Italy it is a *tramontana.* Truscott knew no name for what he saw, but he did not like it. "The flat-bottomed, broadnosed landing craft were buffeted about; breaking waves drenched everyone and everything on board," he recalled. The speed of every craft—purposely overloaded—slowed, with some able to motor at only two or three knots. Admiral Conolly did some quick calculating and changed the course of the slower craft to a more direct route. The troops, described by Truscott as now being "sea sick, sea weary, and thoroughly drenched," were ready to trust their fate to a hostile beach rather than drown at sea. This tramontana had a side benefit, however. The Italian navy had advised the overall military commander of Sicily, Generale d'Armata Alfredo Guzzioni, that the high seas and bad weather precluded any Allied landing. Many soldiers of the Italian coastal-defense units, officers and enlisted men alike, thus slept while the winds howled outside.[31]

On July 10 Lieutenant Bill Phillippi, a U.S. Army Air Forces pilot, received notification that his C-47 aircrew would be dropping one stick (two dozen paratroopers) into Sicily. It would be a night drop the evening before the invasion. The mission of these 82nd "All-American" Airborne Division paratroopers was to land inland from the beach and then do everything possible to delay German and Italian reinforcements rushing to the beaches to push the Allied invaders back into the sea.

For Phillippi, his journey to Sicily had begun on December 7, 1941, when he had been a law student at the University of Wisconsin. Upon hearing the news of Pearl Harbor, he muttered to himself, "Well, there goes my deferment." He knew that if he waited for the draft, he might serve in the infantry; instead, he enlisted in the Army Air Forces air-cadet program. By February 1943, after graduating from basic and multiengine flight training, he transferred to North Carolina to help train the men of the 82nd Airborne in their new duty, which included many takeoffs but no landings. Dispatched to North Africa, Phillippi and his crew in their new C-47, a modified DC-3, flew the southern route, landing in Marrakech before traveling on to Oran. He later briefed squadron flight crews on where the airborne drops would take place and offered additional information about Sicily's history, recent events, language, and culture.

More than a half century later, when asked about his experiences in Sicily, he remarked, "The first drop went fine. The second drop didn't. We won't talk about the second time we went in."[32]

CHAPTER 16

JOSS FORCE ASSAULT

The tramontana would be a problem not only for the beach landings but also for the U.S. paratroopers, who would descend from the clouds beneath wind-pushed parachutes. General Eisenhower, now working from his new command post on Malta, knew the risk for the airborne troops, but he feared that the entire invasion might fail without their assistance. Sitting at his desk, uneasy at the thought of possible outcomes and well aware of the loss of life that might result from his decision, he made the hard call. It was merely one of many to come. With each tough decision, he matured as supreme commander, growing into the impossible job now entrusted to him. The airborne portion of Operation Husky would continue as planned. On the night of July 9, the first flight of C-47s lifted into the skies. It would mark the first time an entire American airborne division jumped into combat.

During World War I, the 82nd Division was a highly regarded infantry unit, perhaps best remembered as the division in which Medal of Honor recipient Sergeant Alvin York served. Now it was an airborne command, the only one so far, and it would make history. In Patton's Seventh Army area, 3,500 paratroopers would drop behind enemy lines near Gela, intent on seizing key ground inland from the beaches to slow the response of enemy reinforcements.

For the men doing the jumping, things turned nasty even before the first planes lifted off. Colonel James M. Gavin, the young, handsome commander of the 505th Parachute Infantry Regiment, was already seated in his assigned C-47, engines revving, when a weatherman ran up to the plane and asked to speak with him. Shouting over the noise of the two engines, the weatherman yelled, "I was told to tell you that the wind is going to be thirty-five miles an hour, west to east." Gavin had routinely canceled training jumps when the wind was over fifteen miles an hour, and now it was more than double that. There would be no cancellation of this jump, however. It would go on.[1]

In Montgomery's Eighth Army area, an airborne glider force would ride the air currents downward, hoping to find forgiving turf for landings. The men inside hoped to seize a key bridge, the Ponte Grande. Just south of the city of Catania, the Ponte Grande made an ideal chokepoint for the Germans, situated between the likely British invasion area and the probable route the Tommies would take north to Messina. Tragically, the unkind winds blew the descending gliders off course, resulting in many releasing too early from their towlines. Almost half the powerless aircraft ditched into the sea. Enemy fire downed other gliders, while some suffered serious damage when they crash-landed in rough terrain. Only a small portion of the attack force arrived at the objective. Fewer than one hundred of an original force of two thousand men gathered to seize the bridge. Even if they could take it, holding it would be an almost impossible task.[2]

The luck of the Americans was no better. Gusting winds and murderous flak resulted in otherwise tight aircraft formations expanding upward and outward. For most of the pilots, this was not only a night drop but their first combat drop as well. They intended to deliver three thousand paratroopers to four specific drop zones, but as each man left the doorway, the wind seized his destiny. The result was a dispersed landing over one thousand square miles.[3]

Gavin jumped from his C-47 into the night wind and seconds later looked up at the just-opened canopy above his head. Then he looked down at the ground, straining to see as much as possible in the dark, but even the distance to the ground was hard to judge. After a hard landing, he gathered his parachute and hoped that the ground on which he stood really was Sicily, though he was not willing to bet on it. He knew that it was quite possible the winds had blown him and his regiment somewhere over mainland Italy, perhaps even to the Balkans. It had been a difficult jump. "Some of us met heavy fighting at once, others were unopposed for some time," Gavin later recalled, "but all were shaken up by the heavy landings on trees, buildings, and rocky hillsides. I managed to get together a small group and start cross country, searching for combat team objectives."[4]

An orphan adopted by a coal-mining family, Gavin made it through the eighth grade before his adopted father ordered him to quit school and go to work. The teenager pumped gas at a local service station for a while, then at age seventeen enlisted in the army.

Within two years he won admission to the army's West Point prep school and later to West Point itself. Now he was doing what he had been taught years before as a cadet—move to the sound of the guns. The original mission of the paratroopers had been to somehow regroup in the dark and delay the arrival of German and Italian reinforcements headed for the invasion beaches. That was impossible now, but their fallback mission worked almost as effectively. They fought as small, roving bands of guerrillas, creating so many problems that German and Italian units throughout southeastern Sicily thought thousands more paratroopers had descended.[5]

On July 10 at 1:30 A.M., the *Biscayne*, one of several hundred ships in just one part of the invasion fleet, dropped anchor several thousand yards offshore. General Truscott felt about as comfortable as he could under the circumstances. Unlike Dieppe and Port Lyautey, his invasion force had had sufficient planning and training, and many of the soldiers were combat veterans. Of course, anything could happen, he reminded himself. Just then four large searchlights onshore flashed bright, their beams swept along the water's surface, did a double take, and came to rest on the gray hull of the *Biscayne*. Admiral Conolly was about to have the lights shot out when Truscott suggested that they wait a moment to see if enemy fire came. None did. Twenty minutes later, one by one, the searchlights went black. Simultaneously, two U.S. Navy cruisers and escorting destroyers many miles to the north began shelling the town of Agrigento, a diversion intended to make the enemy think the invasion would occur there.[6]

At 2:45 A.M., H-hour, landing craft motored forward, their metal ramps providing a modicum of protection to the very wet, cold, and nervous soldiers scrunched inside, each knowing he would soon have to run up a still-dark beach replete with machine-gun pillboxes, obstacles, trenches, barbed wire, and mines.[7]

The decision to forgo preinvasion shelling in hopes of making a surprise landing turned out to be a good one. Even better, the wind calmed. All along the beaches, American landing craft dropped their ramps, spilling out young soldiers, some still teenagers. Bradley's II Corps, consisting of the 1st and 45th Infantry Divisions, landed southeast of Truscott's troops. Bradley's mission was to capture airfields near Ponte Olivo, Comiso, and Biscari. The 1st Infantry Division had experience from the North Africa invasion, but the

45th Infantry "Thunderbird" Division, a National Guard unit from Oklahoma, Colorado, New Mexico, and Arizona, did not. Many of its soldiers were Apache, Cherokee, Choctaw, Sioux, and Seminole Indians whose grandfathers and great-grandfathers had likely once battled the U.S. Cavalry. The division had been combat-loaded in the United States for what would be its first bitter taste of battle. Truscott would later say that the "45th Infantry Division had made a record of which any division could be proud. This was their first campaign . . . , yet it had taken every objective and in the long drive across Sicily had kept pace with the veteran divisions."[8]

For Bradley, the invasion would be a pain in the behind—literally. Hemorrhoids caused him excruciating pain, requiring shipboard surgery. The naval doctor confined the general to the ship, which sufficiently suited Bradley. He could not remember when he had felt worse.[9]

Truscott's battle plan for his augmented command called for a landing near Licata. His ranger force and the three regimental combat teams had the responsibility of anchoring the left flank of II Corps and the rest of the Seventh Army. They, in turn, would anchor the left flank of the British Eighth Army. Truscott's force of 50,000 men would use four beaches. Red Beach and Green Beach were west of Licata; Yellow Beach and Blue Beach were east of it. His soldiers needed to capture several hills about five miles inland from the beach and town so that more troops and equipment could land safely. "The keynote of the operation was therefore speed and momentum," Truscott remembered, "and the key to speed was simplicity." He jingled the lucky coins and key in his pocket. With luck, everything would go as scheduled, and his armored combat command of tanks could land at whichever beach afforded the best opportunity to exploit success. His immediate targets were Licata's port, town, and airfield.[10]

Each of Truscott's regiments had previously trained one battalion to serve as a special team of infantry and engineers. Their job was to land first, clear the many beach obstacles, and if need be, engage enemy defenders. Other battalions could then pass through on their way to the high ground. Everyone knew the plan. At Red Beach the 7th Infantry Regiment would seize the hills and open the routes to Campobello and Palma di Montechiaro. At Green Beach the 2nd Battalion, 15th Infantry Regiment and a ranger battalion would capture Mount Sole, including its coastal battery, army fort, town, and port. At Yellow Beach the remainder of the 15th Regiment would capture the bridge over the Salso River and the hills above it, then help take the port and town. At Blue Beach the 30th Infantry Regiment would capture the hills overlooking the Salso River. Staged within some landing craft were tanks, self-propelled artillery, antiaircraft weapons, and machine guns, all loaded so they could fire directly onto the beach while still afloat. Backing all these troops when needed were the heavy guns of the navy destroyers and cruisers, along with antiaircraft weapons of varying sizes.

The landing craft began their journey to the designated beaches; Truscott could only watch and wait. By 5:00 A.M., darkness submitted to a hazy dawn that brought enough light for the general to launch his two small observation aircraft from their special seaborne ramps. For two hours the unarmed pilots flew over the beaches and beyond, reporting everything they saw, which provided Truscott with a reasonably good picture of the situation. When opportunities arose, they also directed naval gunfire. Later, they safely landed on the beach.[11]

To Truscott's delight, it took little more than sixty minutes for his rangers, ten infantry battalions, and tanks to get onshore. Within seven hours all objectives, including the town, port, and airfield, were secure. Casualties were light, about one hundred, but already more than two thousand Italian prisoners were in custody. Truscott recollected with pride, "Careful planning and preparation, rigorous and thorough training, determination and speed in execution, had paid dividends in success." Several officers and soldiers confided to the general that "fighting the battle was a damn sight easier than training for it."[12]

Now was not the time to rest, however. When your opponent staggers from a punch, you hit him again. Truscott's troops pushed forward. The next day the 15th and 7th Infantry Regiments took Campobello and Palma di Montechiaro. Both units encountered resistance from German troops for the first time. Truscott queried Patton's headquarters about his division's next objectives. Major General Geoffrey Keyes, former cavalryman and now Patton's deputy army commander, revealed that General Alexander's headquarters had no additional objectives. Apparently, General Montgomery had been right all along—no one was paying any attention to what to do once everyone was onshore.[13]

Three days later Truscott met someone who would become a lifelong friend. The meeting, however, would be under unusual circumstances. Colonel Carleton reported to the general that a war correspondent had been discovered living among the soldiers of the 7th Regiment. Truscott remembered briefing a number of correspondents on the ship, but none had come onshore, or so he thought. He sent his provost marshal to arrest the man and bring him to division headquarters. A short time later Brigadier General William W. Eagles, the deputy division commander, brought the correspondent, Michael Chinigo, to Truscott. Chinigo quickly admitted that he had not reported to division headquarters, wanting instead to ride a landing craft with infantrymen and land on the beach. He had talked himself aboard a landing craft and splashed ashore just like any soldier.

Truscott's anger was about to erupt when Eagles and Colonel Harry B. Sherman, the 7th Regiment's commander, gave the general some information that put Chinigo in another light. It seemed that enemy soldiers had fired on Sherman's troops during the landing, but the men managed to make their way a kilometer inland to a vacated railroad station. While in the station, Chinigo heard a telephone ringing. Fluent in Italian, he answered. The voice on the other end, a train agent somewhere in the interior, sought confirmation of several reports that there had been an Allied landing. In perfect Italian, the correspondent assured him that no such invasion had taken place and that things were perfectly calm. His quick thinking likely canceled at least some enemy reinforcements that might have otherwise responded. Truscott not only forgave Chinigo his trespass but several months later, based on Sherman's recommendation that Chinigo had "distinguished himself during the action on the beach," awarded him a Silver Star. Chinigo would accompany the 3rd Division while it was in Sicily. Eventually, with Truscott's help along the way, he would become the first correspondent to arrive in Palermo and Messina, and still later in Rome. "We became close friends," Truscott remembered. "His intimate knowledge of Italians and Italy was to be invaluable to me."[14]

Overall, the Allied landings had been successful. Montgomery's Eighth Army continued to encounter resistance, but it had already taken Syracuse and Augusta. Patton's Seventh Army was now fully ashore. Troopers of the 82nd Airborne Division, fighting in small, pestering groups here and there, had slowed German and Italian reinforcements. Eventually, however, the Italian Livorno Division and the Hermann Goering Panzer Division arrived on the scene. The Germans brought with them more than one hundred tanks, seventeen of which were the behemoth Tigers, requiring Patton to call for naval assistance and employ his reserves. Thundering naval guns temporarily chased the Italians and Germans back into the hills, but the enemy had no plans to leave permanently. They came back the next morning but were again repulsed. By then Patton had decided he needed to call for another drop from the 82nd Airborne.[15]

Gavin and his 505th Parachute Infantry Regiment were already on the ground, scattered about but being remarkably effective. The 504th Parachute Infantry Regiment, commanded by Colonel Reuben H. Tucker III, would make the next drop on June 11. Both Major General Matthew B. Ridgway, commanding general of the 82nd Airborne, and General Patton had taken efforts to ensure that Allied troops on the ground were aware of the inbound paratroopers and would hold their fire. Still, Patton had a bad feeling. He noted in his journal that he had gone to "the office at 2000 [8:00 P.M.] to see if we could stop the 82nd Airborne lift . . . found we could not get contact by radio. Am terribly worried." Also worried were the troops on the ground and on the ships, who had been under German air attack most of the day. The C-47s of the 52nd Troop Carrier Wing were due to come through later that night. Altogether, the 144 planes carried 2,300 paratroopers.[16]

There were nine planes in the 14th Squadron and nine planes in the companion 18th Squadron. Lieutenant Phillippi, a pilot with the 14th Squadron, later recalled how they dropped the 82nd's paratroopers:

> A normal drop is at night. You have to stay close, with no lights on except the cup lights along the top of the wings, visible only from the sides and the back. You have to stay as tight as you can. You fly at 400 to 500 feet, depending on the terrain. Your air speed is at 160 until just before the drop, and then you decrease it to 120 or 130. As you approach the drop zone, you push the light for the troopers to stand and hook up to the static line. There are twenty-four troopers in a stick. You have to cut the left engine to limit the prop blast, but still stay in formation. It's tricky. It's real tricky. You need to put the second engine to all power and maintain the line. You push the green light and they all go out. After the drop you put the power back on and the crew chief pulls in the static lines.[17]

As the green light above the jump door illuminated, the first flight of 504th paratroopers plunged into the darkness below. Everything seemed to be going as planned. Then the second flight of paratroopers arrived overhead. Below, nervous soldiers and sailors of antiaircraft units, their necks aching from continually looking up, scanned the night sky for yet another German attack. Then in the pitch black, a gunner somewhere on the ground or on a ship heard the drone of low-flying aircraft. The Germans were coming again, he must have thought. He saw the planes in the distance, assured himself that he saw German markings, and took aim. His trigger finger clinched tightly, rhythmically pumping rounds into the night air. Within seconds, hundreds of other gunners engaged their trigger fingers; the contagion had spread. The night sky became almost day-like with the glow of flares and tracer rounds. Seemingly, every ground weapon fired upward, and sailors on ships began to deliver a stream of rounds. The first wave of paratroopers was already hitting the ground. The second wave was about to experience hell in the air.[18]

Chaplain Delbert Kuehl, 82nd Airborne, wearing his parachute wings on his chest and his chaplain's insignia on his collar, was standing at the door of his C-47 talking with the first sergeant when they saw the light show below begin. Suddenly, it seemed, the Fourth of July arrived. Hundreds of lines of tracers crisscrossed in the night, some coming at their aircraft. Many other planes had already been hit, some exploding in the air and others simply plunging into the dark water below. Kuehl's plane was hit as well, killing several soldiers and the crew chief and wounding the pilot. The chaplain and the surviving paratroopers raced to bail out before the plane exploded. Colonel Tucker's C-47 was in the third wave and managed to drop its stick, including Tucker, and fly back to base. Its crew later counted more than a thousand bullet and flak holes in the plane's thin skin. The crew of Kuehl's C-47 counted more than five hundred holes.[19]

Some pilots turned on their exterior lights, hoping the ground troops could identify the wing markings of the C-47s, but the shooting continued. What had been a convoy formation quickly disintegrated as pilots attempted every conceivable maneuver to escape the kill zone. Of 144 planes on the mission, 8 aircraft at the back of the column managed to break off early and return to North Africa. Twenty-three others were shot down, and 37, though substantially damaged, limped home. Some C-47s had managed to drop their stick, but others had not. In all, sixty pilots and crewmembers and eighty-one paratroopers perished. More than 150 aircrewmen and paratroopers were wounded or missing.[20]

When the sky seemed to explode, Lieutenant Phillippi's paratrooper stick was already out the door and descending into who knew what below. The pilot pushed and pulled the big C-47 until he could aim its nose away from the firestorm. One engine was severely damaged. Phillippi knew each crewmember depended on him to get them out of the maelstrom. "We could see that all hell had broken loose, but we didn't know why," he remembered many years later. "We could see flares and tracers—all kinds of stuff. Orders were always to go ahead with your mission no matter what. Germans had bombed them an hour before. You can't get information to all the troops." The damaged engine of his C-47 refused to cooperate, and no amount of cursing or praying was going to make it do so. Phillippi had no choice but to set his plane down in the Mediterranean—not something he had been able to practice in flight school. "The C-47 is a good plane to land in the water," he discovered. "The engines go down into the water and the tail goes up, but the wings support the plane, and the rear door is about six to 10 feet above the water." Phillippi and his crew scrambled up to the elevated tail, jettisoned bulky parachutes, inflated life vests, and jumped into their inflated life raft. It was all over in a matter of minutes. Slowly but inexorably, the black waters swallowed the C-47 whole. Then it got quiet. They waited in first-quarter moonlight, able to make out land on the horizon and to hear distant rafts somewhere out there filled with other aircrews who were in the same fix they were. Phillippi saw by his watch that it was about 2:00 in the morning. It would be a long time until dawn. German or Italian aircraft or boats could arrive at any moment. Would they be captured, shot, or blown out of the water? They wished it were darker. Dawn finally broke, and at about 10:00 A.M. Phillippi could just barely see in the distance what appeared to be a small torpedo boat speeding toward them, bouncing along the water's surface. If it was a German E-boat, they were probably finished. Fortunately, it turned out to be a British PT boat sent to rescue the downed aircrews. If the twenty-five-year-old pilot had ever had a happier day, he could not recall it.[21]

Despite the airborne catastrophe, the Americans still held the beachheads. At Patton's position, tanks and artillery sometimes had had to fire point blank at the enemy. Any soldier on the beach, regardless of his usual assignment, often found himself fighting as an infantryman. Navy guns continued to hurl huge rounds beyond the beach, forcing the Germans and Italians to withdraw into the surrounding hills. Still, they could see that the GIs had no intention of evacuating the beach. German lieutenant general Fridolin von Senger und Etterlin, binoculars to his eyes, looked through the smoldering ruins of what had once been a panzer division. Beyond the wreckage of fifty-five tanks, he could see hundreds of Allied ships offshore, ready to deposit even more reinforcements and equipment. He proposed to Field Marshal Kesselring that the time had come to move to the next phase of their defensive strategy for Sicily. Kesselring agreed and set in motion a plan that would make the Allied advance as slow and painful as possible.[22]

Truscott waited impatiently for his next objective, which he assumed would be the capture of Agrigento to the north. There was a problem, however. While General Alexander had some ideas for follow-on missions, nothing yet was clearly defined. As General Bradley recalled, "Astonishing as it seems in retrospect, there was no master plan for the conquest of Sicily." Alexander's strategy never ventured beyond getting the British and American troops ashore, taking the high ground, and capturing the airports. With a lack of confidence in the Americans, and with Montgomery's situation still developing, Alexander seemed content to wait and see what transpired.[23]

The situation was potentially implosive in that two aggressive commanders, Montgomery and Patton, would fill any vacuum in strategy. Montgomery was in the stronger position because Alexander knew him well, whereas Patton was still something of a mystery. Additionally, Eisenhower had harshly censured Patton for the 82nd's tragedy, holding him personally responsible for having not ensured notification to all ground forces. Patton still suspected that he might be relieved of his command, thus he was gun-shy about questioning Alexander's lack of direction. The only thing apparently settled was that the American role would continue to be limited to protecting the flank of the British advance.[24]

Montgomery now found himself stalled on the Catania Plain, situated between Mount Etna and the Mediterranean Sea, where the Germans parried each British thrust to the north. The general concluded that his next move should be to send part of his forces around the back of Etna. He apparently did not clear this with Alexander first, nor did he bother to notify Patton, but simply set his plan in motion. Bradley was outraged at this and amazed that Patton readily acquiesced to it.[25]

On July 14 Patton visited Truscott's headquarters for the first time to talk about next steps for the operation. Truscott knew that "Palermo drew General Patton like a lode star," being Sicily's biggest port and city. The two generals agreed that the possession of Porto Empedocle, the seaport near Agrigento, would be necessary for any effort to take Palermo. Then Patton shook his head, reminding his subordinate that they were under orders not to attack Agrigento for fear that their troops might get bogged down and thus be out of position to support Montgomery. Truscott, no doubt reflecting back to his instructor days at the Command and General Staff School, made a proposal. "I suggested," he later wrote, "that the high command would probably have no objection to my making a reconnaissance in force toward Agrigento on my own responsibility." A reconnaissance is taking a close look at something to get information, but one done "in force" is more of a limited attack to help clarify an unknown situation. Patton, eyebrows raised, concurred that such a thing might be appropriate. As the general departed, Truscott fired up his Joss Force machine. The "in force" part of the probe would involve the 7th Infantry Regiment, a ranger battalion, and seven battalions of field artillery totaling 148 big guns. When this force later approached Agrigento, a motorized enemy column appeared in the distance. "It was an artilleryman's dream!" Truscott remembered. The result was the destruction of more than fifty vehicles and one hundred enemy soldiers. Shortly thereafter, small white flags appeared in the hills near the town, and more than four hundred Italian soldiers emerged and surrendered. Eventually, the tally for this reconnaissance in force included more than one hundred enemy tanks and other vehicles, fifty pieces of artillery, and six thousand prisoners.[26]

Patton knew that Montgomery was not having much success, for neither his forces on the Catania Plain nor those working their way around Mount Etna were making significant progress. No doubt encouraged by Truscott's success, and perhaps now feeling that Eisenhower had no plans to relieve him after all, Patton went unannounced to Alexander's headquarters on July 17. Surprised to see the American, Alexander rather quickly acceded to his proposal to initiate a drive north to Palermo on the north coast, the objective being to split Axis forces in Sicily. Since Agrigento and its port were now secure, the plan made sense. Patton, not surprisingly, declined to mention to Alexander that following this, he intended to arrive in Messina before Montgomery.[27]

CHAPTER 17

THE BLOODY PURSUIT THROUGH SICILY

On July 18 Truscott learned that Joss Force would disband and that he and his 3rd Infantry Division and various other units would become part of a provisional corps under Patton. Technically, they would be under General Bradley, but in actuality, Deputy Army Commander Keyes would oversee them. The major general, an intellectual, had studied at the French War College between the wars and had later taught French at West Point. The basic plan, as related by Keyes, was for the 3rd Division to move northwest and then curve back northeast to attack Palermo. While Truscott and his troops headed for Palermo, the 82nd Airborne Division, two ranger battalions, and a regiment of the recently arrived 9th Infantry Division would trek northwest and take Marsala and Trapani. The 2nd Armored Division would wait until called and then drive to wherever it was most needed. Patton envisioned Palermo as America's first armored victory.[1]

While Patton was confident that he could take Palermo and still do his job of protecting Montgomery's flank, the military necessity of taking that city and northwestern Sicily was questionable. Bradley was especially critical, concluding that the effort was "taking the main weight of the 7th Army off in the wrong direction in what was essentially a public relations gesture." Nonetheless, he knew that Patton, the old warhorse, "had the bit in his teeth; there was no stopping him now." The essence of Bradley's complaint was that now his own II Corps, consisting of the 1st and 45th Infantry Divisions, had to handle the assignment previously intended of the entire Seventh Army. Yet even he later admitted that the drive to Palermo boosted spirits for soldiers and Americans alike.[2]

Field Marshal Kesselring would have agreed with Bradley. He saw no need for the Allies to take Palermo, later commenting that the lackluster performance of his Italian partners had led him to

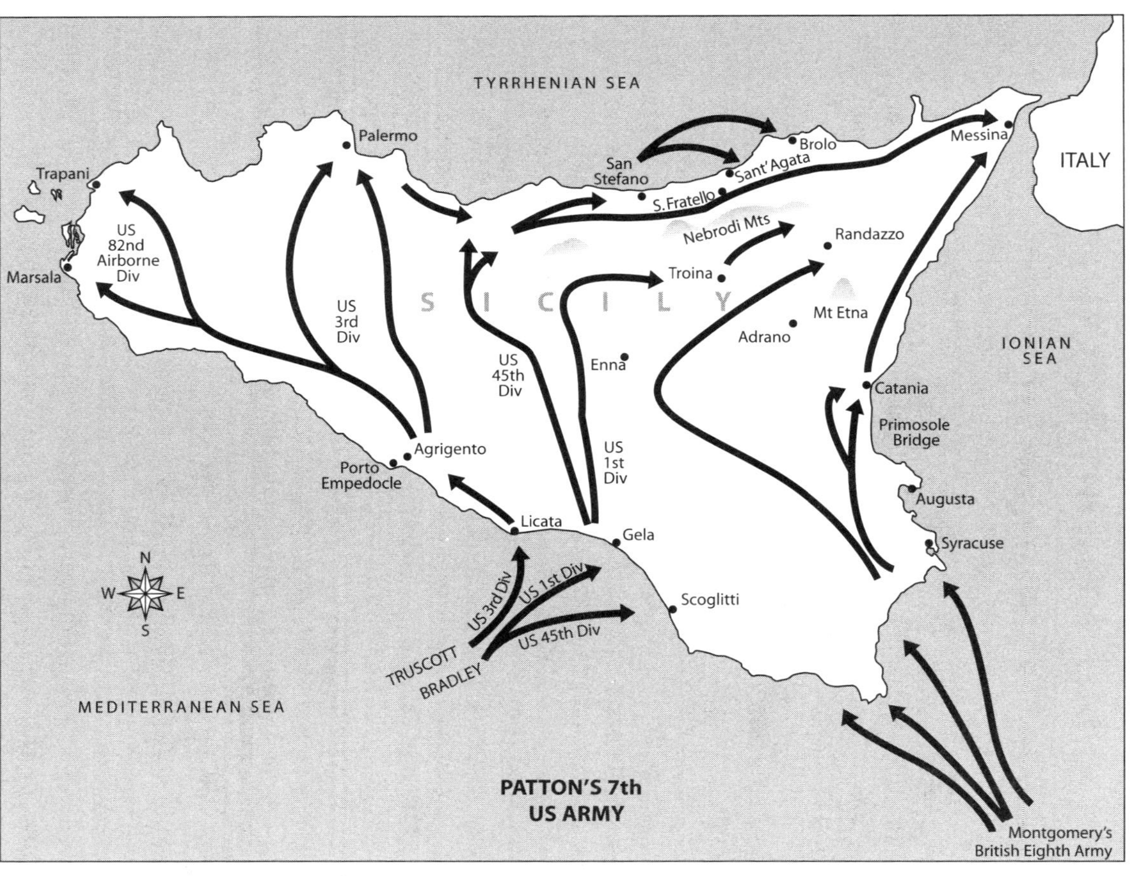

The Allied invasion of and follow-up campaign in Sicily. Map by Megan Postell.

conclude that "the west of Sicily had no further tactical value and had to be abandoned." For Patton, however, taking Palermo not only meant a victory that would please all Americans but also one that would likely result in some personal headlines for him. No doubt he was particularly pleased at the thought of the British eyebrows it would raise.[3]

While debating the military need for this operation might have made for enlivened cocktail discussion at the Command and General Staff School, on the ground in Sicily, Truscott had a tough mission ahead. He intended to take Palermo and not pause until he had done so. He was pleased that he had trained his division for just such a mission. Whatever enemy forces existed in western Sicily would likely be waiting along the one hundred miles of twisting roads between Agrigento and Palermo. The route itself was a challenge. Recalling this years later, Truscott said, "Our three tortuous roads northward had steep grades, numerous hairpin turns, and many bridges which would be rendered more difficult by enemy demolitions and delaying actions." Forty of these miles snaked through jagged mountains several thousand feet high, and the next forty led through open plateau country. Thereafter, the troops would negotiate more jagged mountains surrounding Palermo. Truscott's plan was one of speed and mobility; the sooner his troops got to the city, the less time the enemy had to demolish and delay. On July 18 he met with his regimental commanders, broke open a bottle of Scotch so they could toast the American combat soldier, and gave them five days to get to Palermo. Private Audie Murphy later recalled: "The march toward Palermo became virtually a foot race. We had to average from twenty-five to thirty miles a day over rugged terrain. Dust lay over the highways like a smoke screen; not a cloud appeared in the sky. Often we could not stop even to eat. We gulped our rations as we walked." It was a tall order: three regiments, five days, one hundred miles. It was the Truscott Trot in action—but even Truscott would be surprised when his soldiers accomplished the feat in three days.[4]

The 15th Infantry Regiment would use the eastern road while the 30th Infantry Regiment would take the center road. The rangers would use the western road, maintaining communications with the 82nd Airborne, which would use a coastal road farther west. The 7th Infantry Regiment would remain in ready reserve. The units all left the starting gate at 5:00 A.M. on July 19. By the evening of July 20, soldiers had captured San Stefano di Quisquina along with 1,000 prisoners and many vehicles and weapons. Their pace never slackened. Truscott later described what he saw. "In blistering heat and stifling dust, these soldiers plowed their way forward like waves beating on an ocean beach and at a rate which Roman legions never excelled." The general queried his chaplain and surgeon, wanting to know how many of his soldiers had fallen out. "None" was the answer. Truscott moved his command post from Prizzi to Corleone just to keep up. Before he knew it, he was peering through his binoculars at Palermo, where Italian soldiers had seen the approaching vanguard and were more than ready to surrender. At a cost of 272 American casualties, several thousand Italian soldiers were killed or wounded and 53,000 surrendered.[5]

Patton had made it clear that he wanted no formal surrender until he arrived, although Truscott did manage to get permission to allow some of his soldiers to enter the city to prevent the destruction of its port facilities. The next morning he wanted to see Truscott. No doubt having heard rumors of the speed-marching being done by the soldiers, Patton greeted him by saying, "Well, the Truscott Trot sure got us here in a damn hurry." That night Lucian wrote to Sarah: "I do not believe that the equal of these men has ever existed in our Army—though I will admit that I may be somewhat prejudiced!"[6]

The news was both good and bad. The good news was that Truscott and his soldiers would get a break. The general, in fact, had already selected for his headquarters a castle near the sea, more or less lent to the Americans by an Italian princess. The bad news was that Patton was now more than anxious to get to Messina in hopes of beating Montgomery there. "This is a horse race, in which the prestige of the U.S. Army is at stake," he wrote to Major General Troy H. Middleton, commander of the 45th Infantry Division, who would endeavor to lead the drive. "We must take Messina before the British." Noting his commander's obsession with getting to Messina, Truscott brashly pointed out that if Patton *really* wanted to get there, he should send the 3rd Infantry Division. Patton agreed. The 45th Division, which had acquitted itself well in its first series of battles, got a well-earned rest, and the 3rd was on the move again.[7]

It would be a much slower pace than anyone anticipated. The 98 miles to Palermo had taken just three days instead of the anticipated five. The 105 miles from San Stefano di Camastra (where the 45th Division had ended its push) to Messina would take seventeen.

General Bernard L. Montgomery, commander, British Eighth Army, shakes hands with Lieutenant General George S. Patton, Jr., commander, U.S. Seventh Army, upon Montgomery's departure from Palermo Airport, July 1943. Courtesy of the U.S. Army and the National Archives.

These would be days of penetrating sunshine, unforgiving temperatures, and a fine dust that coated everything—especially one's throat—during which death could happen at any moment from any direction while going up against terrain perfect for defense and terrible for offense. Even water was scarce, having to be carried in cans on the backs of mules. Perhaps more important, the enemy would no longer be reluctant Italians but intransigent Germans. Modern movie legend aside, the only army-level commander regarding Messina as a race was Patton; Montgomery was simply trying to win a much tougher battle than he had expected. He, in fact, agreed that it would be best for the Seventh Army to take the city. A disbelieving Patton simply concluded that Montgomery had something up his sleeve. Nonetheless, the American commander had managed to infect both Truscott and Bradley with race fever. Montgomery had little time for such thoughts, concerned only that *someone* needed to capture Messina.[8]

Truscott had two routes to Messina available, and he would need both. The primary route was a modern highway meandering along the narrow northern coast. At best the coastal plain here was a few hundred yards wide, affording little room to maneuver around German forces and no parallel roads for use by artillery, reinforcements, or supply vehicles. The Wehrmacht, of course, had no interest in sharing it. Its soldiers demolished any bridge they had already used and thoroughly mined the approach. In addition, the immediate area was preregistered by artillery and machine-gun fire, allowing them to zero in and take out anything on the highway that moved toward the bridge site. Truscott's division specialists in construction and demolition, the 10th Engineer Battalion, would need to work practically nonstop to reconstruct these destroyed bridges. He knew that the longer it took his engineers to rebuild, the more time the Germans had to set up their next defensive position.

Truscott's secondary route was a single-track, treacherous, often cliffside trail through the Nebrodi Mountains, about 5,000 feet high. The track paralleled the Tyrrhenian Sea about a dozen miles or so inland. This route was replete with sheer cliffs and steep gorges and was barely negotiable by mules, sometimes only by men on foot. "The weather was hot," Truscott recalled. "Each day dawned clear and bright, and the blazing sun was merciless. There was no wind but an occasional *sirocco* which seared like an oven blast." Every step kicked up a fine, peppery dust that seeped into engines and irritated eyes and throats.[9]

Fortunately, the former horse cavalryman recalled the class taken many years earlier at Camp Jones, Arizona, on how to pack a mule train. Early on in Sicily, he had instructed his troops to confiscate every horse and mule they came upon and add them to a growing herd. The roundup totaled more than four hundred mules and one hundred horses. The general formed a provisional pack train and a provisional mounted troop, appointing as its commander another former cavalryman, Major Robert W. Crandall, with whom he had served in the 5th Cavalry at Fort Bliss. "In ordinary times," Truscott said, "the distance to Messina would be a few hours' drive of great scenic beauty." That would not be the case now. It was slow, painful, and deadly, and it would have been even more so without the mounted troop. Not long before this, Major General Kenyon A. Joyce, Truscott's former commander from the cavalry days, had paid him a visit. Truscott greeted the general with a salute and a twinkle in his eye, announcing that he had six hundred mounted soldiers in his infantry unit.[10]

The going was impossibly tough. The Americans attacked defensive positions, the Germans fell back, and then Truscott's troops attacked the next set of defensive positions. The Germans blew up bridges and cliffside trails at the last moment, then simply drove away. The Americans would have to rebuild the bridge or trail to pursue. When the mules could not find footing to carry their packs and sometimes fell to their deaths, soldiers had to shoulder the loads.[11]

On August 3 General Keyes alerted Truscott that Patton had made available some navy landing craft to move one reinforced battalion by water around the Germans. It seemed like a good idea—an end-run around the defenders to attack their flank or rear. Truscott concurred as long as he would have command authority over the seaborne battalion. It was critical that it move in concert with the division so that it did not become isolated. Once assured that he would have due authority, the general gave the assignment to Lieutenant Colonel Lyle Bernard's 2nd Battalion, 30th Infantry Regiment. Aside from troops, the lift included tanks, artillery, and engineers, all landing at Sant'Agata de Militello. The remainder of the 30th Infantry and its mule train dodged artillery and picked its way through minefields, encountering significant resistance at San Stefano di Cemastra and nearby Caronia. The 15th Infantry Regiment pushed forward as well and on August 3 met the Germans along the Furiano River near the 2,200-foot-high Mount San Fratello. The defenders were embedded on the mountainside and in the small town of San Fratello. Mines protecting the approach route were supported by artillery, machine guns, mortars, and rifles that rained fire down on the soldiers. From observation positions high in the hills, the Germans watched and countered every move the Americans made.

"The enemy is entrenched and determined," Private Murphy later wrote. The Americans responded by using round after round of smoke until very little was visible to the Germans. The 10th Engineers then rushed in and began building a road that permitted the artillery units to emplace their guns. Some help came too from air support. Colonel Bernard's seaborne battalion arrived and provided additional assistance. It took four days for the three regiments to drive out the Germans. "It had been the toughest fight we had had so far," Truscott remembered. The booty was several enemy artillery batteries and more than 1,600 prisoners as well as many tanks destroyed. Murphy recalled, "I acquired a healthy respect for the Germans as fighters."[12]

Truscott had no doubt that the terrain around Mount Fratello was tough, but its steepness took on new meaning when he encountered Major Crandall coming up a trail. Amid the battle for San Fratello, the general had been at an observation post overlooking some gorges and hoped to meet with General Eagles and Colonel Arthur H. Rogers, who were about a mile down the mountain. Knowing that Crandall and a mule train had just come up a cliffside path from their position, Truscott asked him how long it would take to hike down to Eagle's command post. "Well, sir, I made it in a little over an hour," Crandall replied. When Truscott mentioned that he would go down to see Eagles and Rogers, the major cautioned him, saying, "Well, General, it has taken me just three and a half hours to come back from there hanging onto the tail of a mule." The general changed his mind.[13]

The 15th Infantry next moved overland toward Naso, where it hoped to eventually connect with Bernard's battalion, which would make yet another end-run by landing craft and beach at Brolo. A complication was that difficult terrain had delayed the regiment, which disrupted timely emplacement of the artillery needed to support the operation. Truscott postponed the landing by one day, informing General Keyes of this. Keyes cautioned him that Patton had already assigned a number of war correspondents to accompany the landing craft, and he would probably want the landing to go on. They checked with General Bradley, Truscott's immediate commander, who authorized the one-day delay. Keyes called Patton to advise him of the situation but met immediate rebuke. The army commander ordered the landing to go on. Truscott next took the telephone and tried to explain as well, but Patton would hear none of it and slammed down the receiver. An irritated Truscott complied with the order and told Bernard to load the landing craft.

Within the hour, Patton arrived and stormed through division headquarters like a tank through a stone wall, yelling at everyone who happened to be in his way. Truscott recalled him as "screamingly angry." Upon seeing Truscott, he bellowed, "Goddammit Lucian, what's the matter with you? Are you afraid to fight?" Bristling at the comment, he shot back: "General, you know that's ridiculous and insulting. You have ordered the operation and it is now loading." Patton returned fire: "General Truscott, if your conscience will not let you conduct this operation, I will relieve you and put someone in command who will." Truscott held his ground. "If you don't think I can carry out orders, you can give the Division to anyone you please. But I will tell you one thing, you will not find anyone who can carry out orders which they do not approve as well as I can." Patton cooled, put his arm around the general's shoulder, and said: "Dammit Lucian, I know that. Come on, let's have a drink—of your liquor." Patton's recollection of the conversation differed substantially. He recalled that Truscott had said: "This is a war of defile, and there is a bottleneck delaying me in getting my guns up to support the infantry. They—the infantry—will be too far west to help the landing." The general remembered himself replying: "Remember Frederick the Great: L'audace, toujours l'audace! [Boldness, always boldness!] I know you will win and if there is a bottleneck, you should be there and not here." In his diary Patton admitted being perhaps a little obstinate about the matter.[14]

Bradley was not present during the exchange, but his recollection of the affair was more to the point. "Patton arrogantly overruled me. . . . For the sake of a favorable headline, Patton was placing the lives of many men in jeopardy." Ironically, it was Bradley who had first suggested the "leapfrog" end-run, an untested concept at the time, as a way to beat Montgomery to Messina, although he stressed the need for tight control. An aide to Truscott made an August 10 journal entry that walked a fine line: "Gen Patton arrived at 2100 and personally endorsed the orders to go ahead with previous plan." Considering the relative ranks of the generals, it seems likely that the person who felt most put upon—Truscott—recollected the conversation more accurately.[15]

On August 11 the end-run landing proceeded. Bernard's battalion of about 650 soldiers went ashore at Brolo, situated not far behind the German lines running from the beach at Cape Orlando to Naso. The Americans moved toward Mount Cipollo and the high ground overlooking the only escape route for the defenders. Every command in the 3rd Division, including the rangers, would assist the battalion, but the nearest unit was at least ten miles away, with rugged mountains in between. Unfortunately, the Germans detected Bernard's force early on. What Truscott had wanted to avoid —a trapped seaborne battalion—now came to pass.

A fierce battle ensued. Anticipating that Bernard would be too busy to keep him informed, Truscott had sent along a staff officer, Captain Walter K. Millar, whose sole job was to inform division headquarters on a regular basis. Millar's formerly routine messages quickly took on an urgent tone when the Germans discovered the battalion. "Enemy counterattack massing east Brolo 1,000 yards. Request air mission on that position. . . . Urgent. Also navy." For some reason, Bernard could not contact naval support offshore. Three of Truscott's senior staff members ordered naval and air assistance. The messages from Millar kept arriving, though: "Request all possible artillery support on Brolo . . . motor vehicles and M-6 tanks. . . . Must have everything. . . . Must have [navy] now. Air not here. Situation critical. . . . Enemy counterattacking. Do something. . . . How about other dogfaces. Can Toms reach cape? . . . ammo very short." Truscott ordered his 155-mm Long Tom artillery to fire. Elements of the 7th, 15th, and 30th Infantry Regiments and a ranger battalion were already on the way, but the going was slow. Another message arrived from Millar: "Must have navy and air on 702504 or we are lost." A final transmission came across: "Give navy priority and let them—." Then Millar's radio went silent. By then, the USS *Philadelphia* began acting on Truscott's fire mission, its crews delivering the needed fire support. According to *Time* correspondent Jack Belden, who had accompanied Bernard's battalion, the soldiers began to cheer, with one shouting: "The goddam navy. The good old navy. Jesus, there ain't nothing like navy guns." By that time, though, the battalion had suffered 167 casualties. Truscott later reflected that these efforts had "rescued the battalion, but the enemy escaped." He later greeted Bernard by saying, "Thank God, Bernard, for I am certainly glad to see you." The colonel replied, "General, you just don't know how glad I am to see you."[16]

The 3rd Division pushed on. Beyond Cape Calava, the Germans had blown away a road that had hung precipitously to the steep mountainside, leaving a sheer cliff with a hundred foot drop to the sea below. Truscott's 15th Regiment and the rangers were already beyond the cape, having carefully stepped single file along a tiny ledge, but now they were forward and without artillery or tank support. "Days would have been required to blast another road from the cliff, and building one passable for motors over the mountains would have required many weeks," Truscott remembered. His engineers went to work on another plan. War correspondent Ernie Pyle was there and watched the complicated process of building an emergency bridge. It started with holes blown at the lower slope to accept installation of two vertical timbers, then small ledges were jackhammered out at the crater's ends. Then engineers bolted in more timbers, then sunk steel hooks into the rock to support cables, with more timbers bolted together to span the crater. Pyle wrote, "Huge uprights were slid down the bank, caught by a group of men clinging to the steep slope below . . . , and worked into the blasted holes." They added more timbers before "a half-naked soldier, doing practically a wire-walking act, edged out over the timber and with an air-driven bit bored a long hole down through two timbers." Next came more bracing and more sledgehammers driving huge spikes. Finally, the men strung cables across the gap and winched them tight. Twenty more bare-chested soldiers in the blazing Sicilian sun began working with spliced timbers, wooden spans, big stringers, and heavy flooring. Other soldiers used stones to build up the approach to the bridge so vehicles would be able to drive onto it. Infantry vehicles lined up ready to cross, with reconnaissance platoons and machine gunners given lead positions.[17]

Truscott had arrived the day before and had stressed the importance of getting the bridge built by noon the next day. The next morning an impatient general sat on a log and talked with the officers directing the project. He watched the combat engineers—his favorite soldiers next to the infantry—do what looked to be impossible. First Sergeant Adilard Levesque had promised him that the bridge would be ready on time. Indeed it was, with a few minutes to spare. Truscott and his driver, Sergeant Louis Barna, drove to the lead, where the virgin bridge spanned the hundred-foot drop to the sea below. The engineer officers intended to use another Jeep to test it before sending anyone across. The test vehicle, much to the dismay of and over the protests of the engineers, turned out to be that of Truscott and Barna. Pyle later wrote, "when it was ready, the general just got in and went. . . . It showed that the Old Man had complete faith in his engineers. I heard soldiers speak of it appreciatively for an hour." The correspondent recalled that the bridge was rickety and bent, squeaking as vehicles drove over it. Engineers monitored the timbers below, gauging their sag, and temporarily shut it down after the vanguard had passed to strengthen it so that trucks and even a huge bulldozer could cross. The engineers had worked on the bridge for thirty-six hours without sleep. Pyle's Scripps-Howard wire copy of September 6, 1943, said about these men: "They had built . . . the kind of bridge that wins wars. . . . The general was mighty pleased."[18]

Later Truscott learned that Patton had ordered a third seaborne landing, this time of a regiment of the 45th Infantry Division. He advised General Keyes that 3rd Division troops were already beyond the point intended for the landing. Keyes said he understood but that "General Patton was not averse to profiting from such a spectacular operation." Visualizing the potential for friendly fire casualties, Truscott just shook his head and arranged for two senior officers of the division to meet the 45th Division's battalion as it beached, not unlike Hawaiian greeters welcoming tourists.[19]

Elsewhere in Sicily, Montgomery continued to push up the eastern coastline while Bradley's II Corps and other elements of the British Eighth Army battled around behind Mount Etna toward Messina. The time had come for the Germans to initiate their phased evacuation. There was no embarrassment in their departure. Sixty thousand soldiers, with little help from their air force or navy, had held off more than 465,000 Allied troops.[20]

On August 16 Truscott's troops entered Messina. The next day the general awaited Patton's arrival, as directed by General Keyes. Patton arrived with his usual retinue of motorcycles, scout cars, and correspondents and bellowed: "What in the hell are you all standing around for?" He later accepted the surrender of the city. Truscott and his key staff drove back to Palermo and lunched at their headquarters. It had taken two and a half bloody, miserable weeks to get to Messina. "We had returned in just three hours," he reflected. After lunch they continued on to Trapani, where the 3rd Division would rest and refit. Another general would later say of the operation, "What Truscott did in Sicily was to turn his infantry into cavalry."[21]

On August 25 Lucian wrote to Sarah, letting her know that he was fine. He mentioned, "Georgie sent a barrel of cognac today—on the barrel is the division insignia about a foot square . . . and a banner, 'First in Messina.'" Eisenhower was also pleased with Truscott. On July 23, when Truscott was in the midst of battle, the supreme commander had concurred with Patton regarding Truscott's officer-efficiency report, adding, "I know of no major general who has more efficiently performed as a Division Commander." Patton had rated Truscott 5th out of 153 generals.[22]

The Allies had learned much in Sicily. Their mistakes were visible—no single headquarters for command and control, inadequate leadership at the highest levels, use of ineffective tactics, and too little air and naval assistance. The latter was painfully obvious as German and Italian troops and their equipment evacuated across the Straits of Messina. The price paid in casualties included more than 5,500 killed, 14,000 wounded, and 2,900 missing. Mainland Italy awaited arrival of Allied forces, though without Mussolini in power—King Victor Emmanuel III had removed him from office. The Italian government would continue to profess partnership with the Nazis while secretly working on a surrender offer to the Allies.[23]

Perhaps those most victimized were the Sicilians, whose villages were damaged or destroyed by both sides. Civilian fatalities ranged in age from infants to the elderly. Private Alberto Testaecca, an Italian artillery soldier, recalled his own fate along with those of the Sicilians he encountered. He remembered that the residents were destitute and hungry and had hoped to get food from the army. The soldiers were just as hungry and went to the villages looking for food. All left empty-handed. Omar Bradley, aware of pervasive poverty in the villages and the desire of most Sicilian soldiers to quit the war, had earlier come up with his own solution. In violation of President Roosevelt's order of unconditional surrender, Bradley simply paroled any Sicilian soldier who surrendered: "I declared a local 'amnesty' policy: any Sicilian in the Italian Army who wanted to defect was free to go home." The result was that more than 33,000 Sicilian soldiers, who needed no U.S. troops to guard them, quit fighting to return to their families to help avert starvation. Patton said of the Sicilians, "they are a very cheerful people and seemingly contented with their filth, and it would be a mistake in my opinion to try to raise them to our standards, which they would neither appreciate nor enjoy." Audie Murphy's recollection probably echoed that of most Sicilians: "The Sicilian campaign has taken the vinegar out of my spirit. I have seen war as it actually is, and I do not like it."[24]

While the Allies were moving slowly across Sicily, the Germans were implementing a four-phase evacuation operation that would remove most of their soldiers and equipment from the island to mainland Italy. Kesselring's commanders removed 55,000 soldiers, 10,000 transport vehicles, fifty tanks, and 160 big guns—usually in broad daylight. The Italians, in their own evacuation, removed 70,000 troops. An Allied air and naval campaign could have trapped these forces on the island, but the effort exerted was only minimal, perhaps viewing their airplanes and ships as too valuable to risk losing. But Eisenhower did not order the U.S. Army Air Forces or the U.S. Navy to impose a more vigorous blockade either. Instead, the evacuated Germans would be waiting on mainland Italy to take another crack at American and British forces. The killing would continue.[25]

For the Allies, the trip up Italy's beautiful spine would not be pretty, and it would ignore Napoleon's sage advice that Italy is a boot and should be entered from the top.

CHAPTER 18

SALERNO AND THE ROAD TO ANZIO

In August 1943 Allied leaders met in Quebec for the Quadrant Conference. The British still wanted to put off the cross-channel invasion until the Soviets had whittled down the German army, and the Americans still wanted to avoid a potential stalemate on mainland Italy. Only two agreements were worthy of a handshake. The first was that the cross-channel invasion, now called Operation Overlord, would occur in the spring of 1944, with a concurrent invasion of southern France. The second was that Italy would take a backseat to Overlord. The Americans saw the Italian campaign as doing little more than tying down German divisions, though at the significant cost of tying down Allied divisions as well. The British—especially Churchill—wanted to take Rome and the rest of Italy. Allied commanders, who by now should have known better, were seduced by the line that the Italian army's surrender would force the Germans to evacuate north of Rome, possibly farther. General Truscott, who had witnessed the great loss of American soldiers required to push the Germans back even a little in Africa and now in Sicily, knew better.[1]

The boot of Italy runs north to south for 750 miles and east to west for 85–120 miles. The Apennine Mountains run almost its full length, with peaks as high as 6,000 feet. Jutting off east and west from the spinal ridgeline are thousands of peaks, mountains, hills, ridges, ravines, rivers, and streams. Any travel north or south along the Apennines requires much climbing, descending, and river crossing. Roads are few and straight roads nonexistent. The summer weather swelters and the winters are windy, rainy, muddy, snowy, and bone-penetratingly cold. The two coastal plains are narrow, about 25 miles wide on the Tyrrhenian (western) side and about 10 miles wide on the Adriatic side. For a defensive commander, Italy is a dream; for an offensive commander, a nightmare. For the Allies in the winter of 1943–44, all roads did *not* lead to Rome. Indeed, from Naples only two main roads did, and Kesselring held both with a tight fist. Highway 7, the Appian Way, ambled up and down the Mediterranean side of western Italy, squeezing in between the mountains and the sea. Highway 6, the Via Casilina, climbed, descended, and snaked inland through the hostile western side of the Apennines, about 35 miles from the sea.[2]

The job of the Germans was to ensure that the Allies remained in the south, well away from Rome. In doing this, the crown jewel of their defenses was in the area of the town and monastery of Cassino, high in the mountains. If the Allies could break through there, the Liri Valley provided an eighty-mile open sprint to Rome. The Germans were determined not to let that happen. Getting to and through Cassino would become the greatest challenge of the Mediterranean war.[3]

The Allied plan for the conquest of Italy was simply enough: start at the bottom and push north. On September 3, following the capture of Sicily, Montgomery's Eighth Army landed on the boot toe of mainland Italy near Reggio, more than three hundred miles south of Naples. The Germans did not challenge the landing, and for five days Montgomery advanced north about a hundred miles before stiffening resistance stalled him. On September 9 another British landing went ashore at the boot heel of Italy at Taranto. With German attention focused on these two landings, Lieutenant General Mark Clark landed his Fifth Army, consisting of two British divisions and one American division, at Salerno, about fifty miles south of Naples. This was the main attack, intended to spur the anticipated German retreat. Once that happened, Clark's forces would link up with Montgomery's forces, and together they would pursue the retreating enemy north. Clark had liked the plan from the start; Montgomery went along with it, but to him it seemed unnecessarily complex. If the Salerno landing went well, Montgomery argued, there was no reason to continue fighting the Germans in the south. Why not evacuate all Allied forces from the south, he asked, and send them to augment the Salerno landing? He suspected that those Germans still south of that position could be left to decay, or at least would have to expend considerable effort to fight their way north. He later reflected in his memoirs, "This was not done."[4]

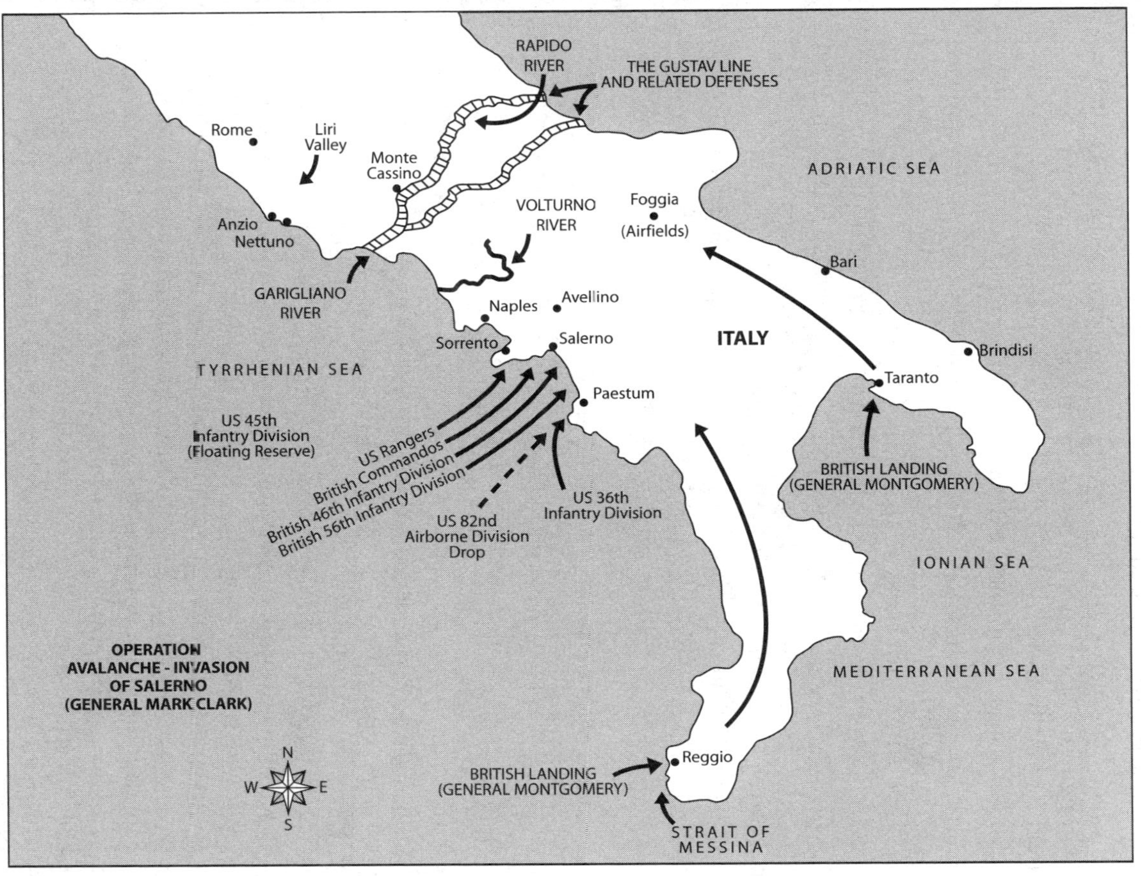

The Allied invasions of southern Italy, including Operation Avalanche at Salerno. Map by Megan Postell.

An understanding of General Clark and how he invaded Salerno is instructive in understanding the next campaign, Anzio, which would occasion the fall of Major General John P. Lucas and the continued rise of Major General Truscott.

Clark had formed the Fifth Army in the spring of 1943. He had not fought in North Africa or Sicily and thus had received little direct benefit from what the Allies had learned there. At age forty-eight, tall, slender, and possessing a determined, hawkish face, Clark was hard to miss. His height, overseas cap, green neck scarf, tanker jacket with Fifth Army patch, and trousers bloused into paratrooper jump boots made him easy to recognize.[5]

Eisenhower considered Clark, a friend, to be his best planner of amphibious operations, based on his considerable experience. Others likely concluded that the commanders who had just fought in North Africa and Sicily—Montgomery, Patton, Bradley, and Truscott—were just as able and now much more experienced. Clark, however, was hungry to lead an invasion and pestered Eisenhower for a combat command. He knew that his fellow generals had each made a fine combat showing and now found himself in the shadows and in need of some limelight; taking Naples and Rome would give him just that. Eisenhower finally acceded to Clark's entreaties for an invasion command.[6]

Clark was one of the best staff officers in the U.S. Army, although shy on senior line command and combat experience. During World War I, as a twenty-two-year-old acting battalion commander, he suffered a wound during his second day in combat. When he returned to full duty, it was as a staff officer in a supply section. It was his misfortune that his staff work was so good that he found himself in demand for such assignments between the wars. Such experience often resulted in promotions but did little to prepare for leading troops in battle. Those staff officers now working under General Clark in Italy—his combat planners—had already developed a reputation of formulating operations by studying maps and photographs. Critics suspected that they gave too little eyes-on study to the actual terrain and too little thought to how the Germans would react. For Clark, provided with seductive Ultra intelligence that the Germans seemed bent on withdrawing north, there seemed to be little necessity to scrutinize southern Italy's many natural barriers, predictably bad weather, and limited space for armor and artillery maneuver.[7]

The general selected Salerno, less than fifty miles south of Naples, as his invasion site. It was not his first choice, but it would have to do. He needed the port facilities of Naples for any advance north, and Salerno was still within range of Allied air cover, though just barely. Clark was not particularly worried, however, concluding that there would be little opposition. Others, notably Truscott, thought otherwise. Truscott and his troops had remained in Sicily for rest and refitting, but the general stayed tuned in to the developing situation on mainland Italy. He knew the Germans would give a good fight.[8]

The Salerno invasion force consisted of 70,000 troops. Clark's plan called for the British X Corps, consisting of rangers, commandos, and the 46th and 56th British Infantry Divisions, to land west of the Sele River and capture the high ground, the town of Salerno, a nearby airport, and a key rail junction. The American VI Corps, initially consisting solely of the 36th Infantry "Arrowhead" Division with tank support, would land its troops east of the Sele River at Paestum, to seize the main roads and protect the right flank. Two regimental combat teams of the U.S. 45th Infantry Division, in floating reserve, would go in the next day when landing craft became available. The 36th Division, also known as the "Texas" Division, was commanded by Major General Fred L. Walker. Since it had yet to see combat, the unit was something of an unknown in terms of performance. Clark, however, realized that the other American divisions were either resting from recent fighting or in reserve for Operation Overlord. He also knew that in a crisis he could call on paratroopers of the 82nd Airborne Division.

His assault plan had serious flaws. In hopes of achieving surprise, Clark ordered no preinvasion bombardment of the VI Corps beaches. Vice Admiral Hewitt, in disbelief, argued that surprise was impossible and that any military officer who could read a map and use dividers could predict that the Gulf of Salerno was as far north as Allied air cover would allow. Clark saw it differently. Another flaw in his plan, aside from the dangerously wide beachhead, was the Sele River, which flowed from the surrounding mountains down to the gulf. The river would pose a natural obstacle between the British divisions and the American division until crossed. To be on the safe side, Clark ran his concerns by General Patton, designated as backup commander should anything happen to Clark. Patton immediately pointed out the problem of the river, which had steep banks and little bridging. With it and a seven-mile gap between the British and the Americans, neither side could support the other. Nevertheless, Clark still thought the situation manageable. Later confiding to his diary, Patton jotted that he "told him that just as sure as God lives, the Germans will attack down that river."[9]

Field Marshal Kesselring, continuing in his role as chief nemesis of the Allies in Italy, had predicted about where landings would occur and had only to wait and shift troops to the specific location just prior to the invasion. His 16th Panzer Division, 17,000 strong with about one hundred tanks and sufficient artillery, was in position not far away. He had also just recently commandeered from the Italian army elevated coastal batteries whose emplaced guns looked directly down on the Gulf of Salerno. German 88-mm cannons would do the serious work at the beaches, assisted by tanks, antitank guns, antiaircraft guns, mortars, machine guns, mines, and rockets. Available for fast response were reinforcements from other Axis units in Naples and Rome as well as the Luftwaffe. Kesselring believed that any beach landing would be a fatal operation for the invaders.[10]

On September 5, just days before the launch of the Salerno invasion, code-named Operation Avalanche, Clark called General Truscott and other senior commanders to a meeting aboard the USS *Ancon* in Algiers Harbor. The general informed them that he expected little resistance. He alerted Truscott that in the future his 3rd Infantry Division might land somewhere to the north, perhaps as far as Rome. Truscott was skeptical. Even had he been privy to Ultra reports, which he was not, he would have urged caution, having just witnessed the skill with which the Germans had gradually loosened their grip on Sicily. "I had already had enough experience with the Boche," he recalled, "to believe the landing at Salerno would bring a violent reaction of some sort even though the landing itself might be unopposed." He returned to Sicily in anticipation that sooner or later he and his troops would be summoned. Truscott knew his soldiers were "fit and ready," but he worried that due to losses on Sicily, his command was down by at least 2,000 officers and men.[11]

Three days later, as the invasion fleet churned its way north toward the Gulf of Salerno, Kesselring already knew they were coming. German planes had sent out an alert as soon as the ships had left harbor. The field marshal would need only to hold the Allies at Salerno for a while, for he was building a supreme defensive system to the north. When finished, it would belt Italy from the Tyrrhenian Sea to the Adriatic Sea. For the Allies, getting through it would be a herculean challenge.

Situated north of Naples in steep mountains, the Gustav Line afforded an excellent defense to the entrance of the Liri Valley, the path to Rome. Eighty miles south of the Eternal City, it spanned the narrowest part of Italy. The terrain was already an impressive natural defensive position, but Kesselring's augmentations would entail an ambitious effort of obstacles and weapons. When the Allies eventually passed through Salerno, which the field marshal knew would happen, they would encounter an elaborate series of successive defensive lines and positions. Planted in front of the Gustav Line were 75,000 landmines backed by interlocked machine-gun fire from armor-plated pillboxes. Command-post operations and artillery operated from cave-like recesses. Mortars launched from behind protective ledges. Some of the tanks, lacking mobility in the mountainous terrain, were buried up to their turrets so they could still fire but would be difficult to detect and destroy. Even before the Allies actually reached the main position, they would have to negotiate their way through other obstacles: the Volturno River defenses, the Barbara Line, the Garigliano River, the Mignano Gap, and the Rapido River. It would be a marathon journey.[12]

On September 9 at morning twilight, German lookouts in the mountains were able to discern the darkened fleet of hundreds of ships that had come to rest about twelve miles offshore in the Gulf of Salerno. Supported by naval fire, U.S. rangers and British commandos beached at 3:10 A.M., followed by the main force at 3:30 A.M. Gun emplacements in the hills directly above the landing site began to fire; German commanders had already summoned reinforcements. With engines whining and tracks clanking, mechanized forces carved grooves in roads and fields as they straightened the curves on the way to the area.

Even before Allied soldiers touched dry land, a torrent of deadly metal descended from the sky. Opposition on the British beaches was significant but manageable. That was not the case for the soldiers of the 36th Infantry Division, who were in their first combat. Flares burst in the air, removing what little darkness had existed to conceal the first waves of soldiers; later waves motored forward in clear view on a cloudless day. Racing up the beach, many soldiers suddenly threw themselves to the ground, seeing and hearing a tracer-lit storm of whooshing, cracking, buzzing, and zinging indiscriminate metal above them. Thunderous sounds and exploding earth surrounded them, leaving deep holes in the beach and body parts scattered about. The ground quivered, shook, and rocked in ways that terrified every fiber in one's body. Soldiers developed tunnel vision, seeing only what was directly ahead of them, their peripheral vision useless. The first loud detonations had shut down their ears, causing ringing so loud that everything became a dense fog. Officers yelled for the men to move forward. Sergeants barked orders to go, go, go! Those who were lucky missed the mines, negotiated the barbed wire, and found a sand dune or a bit of scrub or some other heaven-sent piece of cover.

With pounding hearts, the survivors realized they had somehow made it across the beach; a peek back toward the water revealed the dead and bruised bodies of comrades who had not. Sucking in air to pay off huge oxygen debts, the soldiers hugged whatever piece of protection they had found. German machine-gun crews scanned for any movement in their interlocked sector and squeezed their triggers, pumping out a constant stream of tracer rounds that showed them exactly where their rounds were going. Snipers scoped their targets, took a breath, let half out, and often watched an enemy fall. Fire from prowling Mark IV tanks, 88-mm artillery batteries, mortars, and machine guns pummeled the Americans. The Luftwaffe also joined in the action. Allied commanders on the beach yelled over the din for more fire support. Allied planes zipped in, unleashing their fire into the defenders. Navy gunboats and destroyers moved in close and fired low. The Germans moved back a little and regrouped. By day's end, Allied troops had achieved their initial objectives. For the moment, they were safe.[13]

The next day, September 10, with landing craft once again available, Clark landed the two floating-reserve regiments, sending them to protect the Sele River gap. At this point he had no other reserves to commit. Two days later Kesselring, at the controls of a twin-engine Ju-88 airplane, landed just inland from the beach. He inspected the front and discussed the situation with his subordinates. Thus far, they had not discovered the separation between the Allied forces, though they would soon enough. Clark continued to work the beach as he had done since coming ashore, shuffling resources and imploring his troops to hang tough. He muttered to an aide that the situation was still bad and he did not know what to do. The general finally realized that if the Germans came down the Sele gap, they might split the 45th Division from the 36th Division, turning the flanks of each. A crisis was at hand. Clark considered ordering an airborne drop. He was well aware of the significant problems with wind and friendly fire that had occurred over Sicily. Even so, he was now contemplating dropping paratroopers on a slender strip of beach just behind his front. They might land exactly where he wanted them, as he hoped, or they might drop in the water or well behind the enemy lines. Nonetheless, he feared that German counterattacks could push his troops back into the sea if he did not do something. He considered a second measure, even more drastic: withdrawing the Americans and then relanding them on the British beaches.[14]

His first step was to order Major General Ridgway to drop two regiments of his 82nd Airborne Division along the beach that very night. The mission fell to Colonel Tucker's 504th Parachute Infantry, the same regiment mangled by friendly fire over Sicily. With less than twelve hours, preparation consisted of quick notes scribbled by dim light. Briefings cut to the chase, with variations of: "We've got no choice; our guys are dying on the beach. We're jumping in." A gasoline-fueled fire in the form of a giant T marked the Texas Division drop zone. On September 13 the incredibly risky nighttime jump took place. It required timing, communication, coordination, skill, and luck. Somehow, it worked. A second drop the following night, this time of Colonel Gavin's 505th Parachute Infantry Regiment, succeeded as well. Troops on the ground cheered as paratroopers floated to the ground. Later, glider troops, additional infantrymen, and an armored force arrived by ship. In less than two days, 3,400 paratroopers and other soldiers were on the beach, bolstering the 36th and 45th Divisions along the Sele River. Clark's luck was holding. A third paratrooper drop, this time behind enemy lines at a key crossroads, failed miserably. This wave of paratroopers dispersed over one hundred square miles. During the following two weeks, more than 500 of them managed to work their way to friendly territory; the others were killed, captured, or missing.[15]

While the airborne drop was brewing, Clark ordered preliminary planning for the possibility of a withdrawal. He contemplated reloading the 36th Division into landing crafts and off-loading it to the more quiet British beaches, or perhaps bringing the British troops to this beach. None of his British or American commanders supported the idea. Admiral Hewitt was shocked. He knew it was one thing to beach a loaded landing craft and then back away an empty one—doing the opposite was much more difficult. Major General Troy H. Middleton, commanding general of the 45th Infantry Division, seemed to sum up the collective feelings of the other commanders. He told Clark that the 45th was not leaving—just leave them some supplies and ammunition. Generals Alexander and Eisenhower, when informed of this possibility, opposed it. The best result of Clark's proposed withdrawal was that it removed any reluctance by more-senior Allied officers to commit additional naval and air support.[16]

The general had looked around for other assistance. The evening of September 13, Truscott received the urgent call he had anticipated. Patton informed him that the Salerno beachhead needed help and that the 3rd Infantry Division should prepare to land there at once. While Truscott and his staff went to Italy to meet with Clark, the 3rd Division readied for embarkation. Still short of men, the division called on the 1st and 9th Infantry Divisions to transfer in replacements.

Viewing the distant beachhead from a full-throttled British PT boat, its bow slamming up and down on the black water, Truscott had no doubt that he was looking at Salerno, the "ring of fire that flamed and glowed and sparkled in the distance." Booming cannons onshore, streaking rockets, and illuminating flares overhead seemed uncomfortably close as the small boat weaved its way through the fleet to the flagship *Biscayne.* Truscott and Carleton spent the night onboard, getting an initial briefing on the situation before bedding down. They went ashore in the morning and located Major General Alfred M. Gruenther, Clark's chief of staff, who was directing operations at the beach command post while Clark was away. Gruenther told them that the invasion had met immediate resistance by the 16th Panzer Division, now reinforced by other units. Earlier, the Germans had driven a wedge between the invading forces and had overrun two battalions of the 36th Division. The following day Truscott sought out Major General Ernest J. Dawley, commanding VI Corps, and Major General Walker of the 36th Division. As they briefed him, it was clear that neither was pleased with the situation, which they blamed on "disorganization of Command."[17]

By September 17, after more than a week of fighting, the GIs and Tommies secured the Salerno beachhead. The following day Truscott began landing his three regimental combat teams. No longer needed at Salerno, they moved inland. Kesselring, having consolidated his troops from southern Italy and Salerno, now gave the order to withdraw to the mountains, instructing his troops to demolish bridges and lay landmines as they backed away. Clark focused on finding a route to Naples.[18]

The Allied butcher bill for Salerno was high: more than 2,000 soldiers and sailors killed, 7,000 wounded, and 4,000 missing, with 3,000 of the missing presumed captured. Also feeling captive in a more metaphorical sense were General Marshall and his chiefs of staff. Ultra intelligence intercepts had enticed them into thinking that the Germans would withdraw in the face of another invasion. Now disengaging from Italy and moving the war to France, Marshall's preference, had become a lot tougher. The Americans would pay a surcharge for problems with the invasion. The quality of American fighting on Sicily, orchestrated by Patton, Bradley, Truscott, and others, had erased much of the British contempt left over from North Africa. Now U.S. leadership was once again suspect, British officers likely concluding that their performance in Sicily was a fluke. Clark knew he had just avoided disaster at Salerno and now grew more cautious. Nonetheless, he believed that his leadership had saved the day. Others thought that his inexperience had necessitated that the day be saved.[19]

The VI Corps now had a new boss, John P. Lucas, an old cavalry friend of Truscott's. The major general had taken over for General Dawley, who had crossed swords with Clark at Salerno. Lucas had graduated from West Point in 1911, served in the cavalry and artillery, and was almost killed when Pancho Villa raided Columbus, New Mexico. He cheated death a second time during World War I when he recovered from a serious head wound. Between the wars he came to the attention of Marshall, Eisenhower, and Patton, all of whom thought highly of him. By the time he took over VI Corps, however, he was fifty-four. What hair he still had was turning white to match his mustache, and a double chin had made an appearance. His penchant for Ben Franklin glasses and a corncob pipe gave him the look of a professor, perhaps a farmer. Clark would have preferred someone younger and bolder—like himself. At best it would be an uneasy partnership; at worst, an unworkable one.[20]

With the Germans demonstrating yet another skilled withdrawal, moving Allied troops from Salerno to Naples proved an effort.

The British 46th and 7th Armored Divisions pushed through the Sorrento Peninsula, passed by the ruins of Pompeii, and approached Naples from the south. The British 56th Division bypassed Naples and went straight to the Volturno River. Truscott's 3rd Division and the 45th Division, both now under Lucas, worked their way through the mountains toward Naples.

On October 1, three weeks after landing, the Fifth Army marched into Naples. It was a shell of a city. Before evacuating, the Germans had gone on a ransacking mission, destroying, disabling, or booby-trapping anything that might be of use to the Allies. The populace hid in buildings, uncertain when it might be safe to emerge. That same day Montgomery took Foggia and its needed airfields. The Allies now had a major seaport for supplies and a number of airports for air support. Eisenhower expected to reach Rome in a month or two. Little did the Allies suspect that the toughest fight was still ahead. Hitler, persuaded by arguments proffered by Kesselring, had changed his mind. His original plan had been to delay the Allies in the north of Italy, hence, the misleading Ultra messages. Instead, the Germans would delay them in the south. Hitler believed he had the right commander in place to do just that.[21]

CHAPTER 19

CASSINO

NO LIGHT AT THE END OF THE TUNNEL

On October 3, 1943, Montgomery launched an end-run amphibious invasion at Termoli, on the Adriatic side of the boot of Italy north of the spur. He succeeded in landing behind German lines but then bogged down because of adverse weather. The winter months darkened the sky and agitated the previously peaceful rivers into rolling, roaring torrents. Soldiering was now not only dangerous but also cold, wet, muddy, miserable work, all in the most appalling of landscapes: mountains, cliffs, and poor roads with no shortage of hairpin turns. Until recently, bridges had spanned many of the rivers, streams, and ravines. Now the British found only raging waters or yawning holes, courtesy of Kesselring's demolition specialists.[1]

As for Truscott and the Americans, their next obstacle was the Volturno River defenses, thirty-five miles north of Naples and fifty miles south of Rome. Although the river valley made for an excellent, though only temporary, defensive position, Kesselring knew it would have to hold until mid-October, when the impressive Gustav Line fortifications to the north were completed. When that happened, he would withdraw his troops there.

The officers and soldiers of the 3rd Infantry Division were by now old hands at advancing against withdrawing Germans. The Italian terrain was as unforgiving as that of Sicily. As he had done there, Truscott reverted to cavalry mode, setting up horse-mounted infantry for scouting and mule teams for packing ammunition and supplies. Even at that, he recalled, "we were to find many places that pack mules could not climb where supplies had to be carried on the backs of men."[2]

He had honed his battle tactics in Sicily, where the narrow plain and dense mountains provided little room for envelopment. Here as there, one of his regiments pushed the Germans along the route until a destroyed road or bridge, coupled with fire from ambush, halted the American advance. Then, as one of his battalions maintained contact with the enemy, the other two battalions attempted flanking movements. Truscott's division artillery moved as close as practical, then forward observers called in rounds on German positions until the defenders fell back to another line. As quickly as possible, his engineers rushed in to clear the road or mend the bridge. Then the process began again. A relatively small number of soldiers could defend a position near a destroyed bridge over a deep ravine for some time. In contrast, Truscott might need to employ his entire regiment to push the enemy back, during which his units often suffered more than a few casualties.[3]

Lucas's VI Corps, part of Clark's Fifth Army, now included the 3rd Infantry Division, the 34th Infantry Division, and the 45th Infantry Division. Each unit continually engaged the Germans while clearing various villages along the approach to the Volturno. Following a struggle, Truscott's 3rd Division dislodged the defenders from the town of Acerno but found five bridges beyond it demolished. By then, however, a British invention was in the hands of the combat engineers. Called a "Bailey bridge," it consisted of sections of steel bridging pinned together and pushed across a divide up to 240 feet wide. For two months Truscott's 10th Engineers assembled and emplaced Bailey bridges; they also, when necessary, cleared roads, carved trails, bulldozed runways for observation aircraft, rendered minefields safe, and sometimes fought as infantry. "There was no weapon more valuable than the engineer bulldozer," Truscott remembered, and "no soldiers more effective than the engineers who moved us forward."[4]

In early October the Fifth Army mission was to cross the raging Volturno. Any river crossing in enemy territory is a challenge, but Clark, Lucas, and Truscott agreed that the troops could likely cross the Volturno without significant delay. About this time, however, the defenders received the assistance of a good friend—rain. It was not just a shower, but a cold, constant, sleeting rain, night and day, day after day. Kesselring had anxiously awaited the start of the wet season as a kidnapper awaited the arrival of an accomplice. He had refined his tactics as well. Having observed that Truscott and other Allied commanders used purchased or commandeered mules to transport supplies, the Germans now killed all mules and potential transport animals they came across. They also downed large trees into a basket-weave pattern, which choked roads and required days to clear, especially when the whole mess was mined and booby-trapped. In many villages the withdrawing soldiers demolished the fronts of stone buildings so that the stones tumbled onto and blocked the narrow streets, often several feet deep. Truscott's engineers did not have the time or maneuver room to clear the immense piles; instead, they smashed paths over the tops of the rubble for vehicles to drive on.[5]

Clark intended that his British X Corps and the VI Corps cross the Volturno during the night and early morning hours of October 12–13. Truscott and his soldiers well knew the difficulty of river crossings, but the rain-swollen Volturno looked formidable. It was as much as three hundred feet across and six feet deep, with steep, ten-foot banks, and flowed with alarming ferocity. Enough troops and support weapons had to reach the other side to hold off the Germans temporarily while the main force of soldiers, already cold, wet, and miserable and increasingly affected by a wide range of physical ailments, had to tackle the torrents as quickly as possible. A few soldiers had the unenviable duty of stripping down and wading or swimming to the other side to gather intelligence or to attach safety ropes for the others to use. At the designated moment and location, almost certainly under enemy fire, the remaining soldiers had to cross using rafts or assault boats or by wading or swimming; a few lucky ones might have a footbridge to use. Getting vehicles and heavy weapons across was even more difficult.[6]

In preparation for the crossing, Truscott's troops were ensconced in the dark trees along a seven-mile stretch of the river. He briefed his regimental commanders, going over their instructions a final time. "Our plan was simple," he recalled, "as all good tactical plans must be. Our aim was to clear enemy fire from the river line to permit bridge building so that the entire division could cross over in the shortest period of time." In concert with a British attempt to cross the river farther away, the 30th Infantry Regiment would feint a crossing at the point where the Germans most likely expected one. A short time later, with enemy attention focused elsewhere, the 7th and 15th Infantry Regiments would cross and seize the nearest high ground. Division artillery would initiate the plan by bombarding potential crossing points for an hour. Then shortly before the GIs emerged from their dark hideouts, soldiers of the 84th Chemical Battalion would shroud the area with a heavy smokescreen.

"Every officer and man knew the part he was to play," Truscott remembered. "All preparations had been completed with great secrecy." Soldiers had already staged in the woods everything they would need to ferry, ford, or bridge the river. At the same time that the infantry crossed, engineers would race forward to construct three bridges: a small one for Jeeps and light vehicles, a larger one for bigger trucks and artillery, and an even larger span for tanks, heavy artillery, and bulldozers.[7]

The division's feint attack began at midnight. At 1:00 A.M. the artillery sent forth its shower of exploding metal into all likely German positions. On Truscott's order an hour later, with heavy smoke saturating the area, the main crossing began. The Germans might not be able to see much, but that did not stop them from unleashing their preregistered fire.[8]

British soldiers of the 56th Division, crossing at Capua, failed in their attempt, retreating to the relative safety of the deep woods. The Americans had better success, and by 5:30 A.M. most of the 3rd Division and part of the neighboring 34th Division were over. Reinforcements and supporting fire were now essential. If trapped on the other side, the soldiers faced death or capture.[9]

Bad news arrived. Of crisis proportion was that German fire was preventing unarmored bulldozers from breaking down steep riverbanks so that tanks and tank destroyers, desperately needed on the other side, could cross a shallow part of the Volturno. Truscott knew the outcome if his armor could not get across—the infantry already across would be lost in a few hours. He first ordered his artillery to concentrate its fire on likely threats, then he gathered an engineer platoon. The general made very clear to his wet and shivering engineers what they needed to do, his raspy voice straining to be heard over the sounds of gunfire and the roaring river: "You've only got picks and shovels, men, only your hands, but right now they're better than guns. For God's sake, let's get the job done. We've got a whole regiment of men over there. They'll get wiped out unless you get tanks across." Truscott later praised the effort of these engineers as "immediate and inspiring." This was not a heavy-equipment operation, however. It was men, armed with basic tools, who double-timed to the river and began the backbreaking work of swinging picks and stabbing shovels to bust down the steep banks. When the earth finally surrendered, the engineers stepped aside and the armored vehicles rolled forth.[10]

A short time later Truscott came upon some of his tank crews huddled in nearby woods, waiting while engineers assembled a pontoon bridge over the muddy Volturno. Jumping from his Jeep, the general pounded on the sides of the tanks. "Goddammit, get up ahead and fire at some targets of opportunity. Fire at anything shooting our men, but goddammit, do some good for yourselves." The tanks emerged almost instantly and fired over the heads of the engineers into enemy positions beyond. With each round fired from their steel tubes, the immense sound deafened the ears of the engineers, but there would be no pause until the bridge was ready for use. Truscott felt elated, though only for a moment, for he had more problems to tackle. His officers occasionally felt the sting of his tongue: "What do you mean, it can't be done? Have you tried it? Go out and do it."[11]

Truscott moved on to check the progress of his other bridges. The Jeep bridge was almost finished, but work had stopped on one of the larger ones. German artillery fire had damaged it, destroyed some vehicles, and wounded a number of engineers. The general huddled another group of engineers and calmly but firmly explained that the bridge had to be built, even under fire. He watched with pride and admiration as the men went back to work without as much as a grumble. They finished the span by that afternoon. Soon the last bridge was also completed. When the smoke finally lifted, the 3rd Division had conquered the Volturno River in sufficient strength that they were across to stay. By October 19 the rest of the Allies were north of the Volturno too. For Truscott, the crossing had come with a steep price: 314 officers and men killed or wounded.[12]

The Volturno River might be at their backs, but more rivers and mountains were ahead. Progress was slow and the work never ending. The rain proved incessant as the mud became deeper and more difficult. General Lucas wrote in his diary: "Rain, rain, rain. . . . [T]he roads are so deep in mud that moving troops and supplies forward is a terrific job. Enemy resistance is not nearly as great as that of Mother Nature, who certainly seems to be fighting on the side of the German."[13]

Truscott's men began to suffer from jaundice, various fevers, and respiratory illnesses. Noncombat losses began to exceed battle casualties. Many, including Audie Murphy, had contracted malaria in Sicily and now suffered renewed symptoms. Because no one had thought the campaign would last into winter, the soldiers fought not in winter clothing, but in the same uniforms they had worn

Major General Lucian K. Truscott, Jr. (*left*), commander, 3rd Infantry Division, and British general Sir Harold Alexander (*right*), commander, Fifteenth Army Group, near forward-observation posts in the vicinity of Caserta, Italy, November 1943. Courtesy of the U.S. Army and the National Archives.

when they had been rushed ashore a month earlier. The cold was the kind that went into and through the bones. The Great Depression years of hunger, followed by army physical training and subsequent combat, had removed any body fat from the young soldiers. Without it, they had little natural insulation and thus little defense against the cold.

The winter of 1943–44 came decades before the availability of wick-away long underwear, fleece of varying weights, quilted vests and jackets of down and fiberfill, and waterproof parka shells. By today's standards, the army's hats, gloves, socks, and boots were pathetic. Blankets were too few and, invariably, got wet and never quite dried out. The army had supplies of long underwear, overcoats, and more blankets, just not on mainland Italy. Vast quantities of such items remained on the docks in Sicily, where lack of shipping—the bane of the Mediterranean theater—kept them there. Nor did the soldiers have sleeping rolls or shelter halves with which to make tents. Some items, such as rubber overshoes to keep boots dry, could not be found anywhere in the Mediterranean.[14]

Trench foot, the nemesis of infantry soldiers from World War I through Vietnam, appeared on the scene. Immersion foot, the medical name for the condition, results when feet are confined in wet shoes or boots. Left untreated, it can require amputation of the infected foot. Prevention sounded simple enough: keep your feet dry and change your socks often. Of course, a soldier had to get his boots and socks dry first. As for extra socks, they seemed as unlikely to appear as hot food. From time to time visitors showed up at the division's command post, including Clark and Eisenhower. Truscott was especially pleased to see Eisenhower, who could now see for himself the deplorable conditions under which the soldiers lived and fought. He never doubted that "one personal inspection is worth a thousand reports." The general noticed, however, that his visitors never stayed very long.[15]

Truscott's other complaint was the continued lack of air support. He and Colonel Carleton recalled the fine air support the navy had provided at Port Lyautey. Now Army Air Forces commanders dismissed Truscott's request to have some of its officers assigned on the ground with his units. He later reflected with some bitterness, "Air Force officers were extremely reluctant to establish this ground control, and would never permit a ground officer to direct any aircraft to a target."[16]

The next obstacle for Truscott's troops was the Mignano Gap, which Generals Alexander and Clark saw as the next gate to Rome. The Allies had thought that having crossed the Volturno, progress would be faster. What they failed to see was that Kesselring had merely withdrawn his troops to the next natural barrier, now augmented with fortifications. Worse, they had not yet even made it to the Gustav Line. What little momentum the British and Americans had was about to halt. "This last operation," Truscott remembered, "which began on October 31, was to be a heartbreak for me." The Mignano Gap, a narrow valley several miles across and seven to ten miles deep, is bounded by mountains on both sides, each from nearly 1,000 to 3,000 feet high and quite steep. Mounts Cesima, Difensa, Maggiore, Camino, Rotondo, and Lungo were all ideal for defense.[17]

On November 2 Truscott met with Lucas and Clark to discuss his plan for attacking the Mignano Gap, which they approved. The 3rd Division's regiments moved forward over extremely difficult terrain. Truscott later wrote, "Conditions on the mountain tops were appalling." Nonetheless, his soldiers had to take the gap, which meant conquering each mountain that served as a base of German fire. Truscott had no doubt that his troops could do it, but he knew it would not be quick or easy. Private Murphy agreed: "The terrain over which we advance is a nightmare for offensive troops. The narrow trails, frequently on the edge of sheer cliffs and deep gorges, are so treacherous that pack mules often lose their footing and tumble to their death. Sometimes the mules cannot make it at all. Supplies have to be dragged up the slope by men inching their way on all fours."[18]

On the evening of November 5, General Lucas, sounding somewhat stressed, called Truscott and instructed him to transport the 30th Infantry Regiment through the lines of the 45th Division that very night so they could attack Mount Lungo early the next morning. Truscott was incredulous. The mountain was twenty miles away through terrible terrain, and his troops would have to attack without reconnaissance or sufficient artillery support. He balked, whereupon Lucas shot back: "Yes, Lucian. I know it, but I can't help it. This is the Army Commander's order." He then asked to speak directly with General Clark, but Lucas replied: "No, Lucian. Dammit, you know the position I'm in with him. That would only make it worse, and put me in a helluva hole. You have just got to do it."[19]

There was nothing left for Truscott to say. Early the next morning, as directed, he launched his attack. By November 8, after three days of bitter, deadly fighting, the 3rd Division managed to achieve a foothold on top of Mount Lungo. German counterattacks came and were beaten off, but the division was spent; it simply could not advance. From the top of the mountain, Truscott's troops could see Monte Cassino, which would be an even tougher nut to crack. Ten days later Clark pulled the general and his soldiers out; he also withdrew the 34th and 45th Divisions as well as the British divisions. "Every other Division in the line both British and American was in a condition comparable to that of my Division," Truscott remembered. On November 15 General Alexander ordered a halt. Murphy later wrote, "Crawling with filth and sodden with weariness, we are pulled out of the lines in mid-November." Truscott reflected, "So ended our fifty-nine days of Mountains and Mud."[20]

It would be up to the 36th Infantry Division to cross the next obstacle, the Rapido River, which was part of the Gustav Line. Soldiers of the division would come to know the Rapido as "Bloody River."[21]

Truscott used the time away from the front to beg for more mule units and supplies. On November 24 he wrote to Eisenhower: "My pack train, pack battery, and mounted troop have been worth their weight in gold. You may recall I organized these in Sicily and started them in this campaign before their organization was complete and before they were trained. . . . [E]very division in this theater has need for a similar organization." On December 1 he wrote another letter to the general's chief of staff, Bedell Smith, stressing the need for mules: "They have been worth their weight in gold. . . . They are certainly needed." Two weeks later a response gavc Truscott the bad news. Smith said he understood that the provisional pack trains were essential, but the War Department was determinedly against any new units. Truscott could see that the focus was now on Operation Overlord. Inexorably, the Italian campaign was drifting into a sideshow.[22]

The push up the Ionian Peninsula thus far had been an immense struggle but had resulted in the capture of the port of Naples and the airfields of Foggia. Italy had surrendered, and most of its reluctant army had melted back into a thousand villages. With the southern half of the country now held in a tight Allied grip following a tough and miserable fight, the immediate capture of Rome seemed less important, at least to some people. General Marshall and his chiefs of staff saw better ways of getting to Germany than going through an Italian meat grinder all the way up to the Alps. Stalin's thinking was much the same. Having won at Stalingrad, he now advocated for the cross-channel invasion and perhaps a Mediterranean invasion of France as well, even if that meant the forces in Italy having to go on the defensive. Prime Minister Churchill, however, had no interest whatsoever in holding tight in southern Italy and switching focus to southern France. For him, Rome's capture had become symbolic. He saw it as the first wooden stake in the heart of the Axis. He seemed to miss what Marshall, Stalin, and others saw: that after a significant sacrifice in Allied blood, Rome's capture would mostly mean more Italian mouths to feed.[23]

Marshall and Stalin were committed to Operation Overlord, whereas Churchill was not. He hoped to delay it. Nonetheless, one important detail needed to be decided, and that was who would command Overlord. With Roosevelt unwilling to give up Marshall, the two Western leaders agreed that Eisenhower should become supreme commander. As a result, the Allies now needed to shuffle some top generals around. Those who would lead Overlord, Eisenhower, Bradley, and Montgomery, shuttled to England. Patton would join them later but first needed to serve penance for having slapped two soldiers in Sicily whom he regarded, with scant evidence, as cowards. The resulting media flap had enraged Eisenhower, but he felt he could not get by without Patton. British field marshal "Jumbo" Wilson, six feet, seven inches tall and with noticeably large ears, replaced Eisenhower as commander in the Mediterranean. Wilson had been running the show in the Middle East, and now he would command the Mediterranean as well. Generals Alexander and Clark would remain in the region. Thus, it appeared that any drive to Rome would be with Wilson at the wheel, Alexander riding shotgun, and Clark taking a back seat.[24]

In late 1943, when Eisenhower lay awake at night, it was because he worried about France, not Italy. He expected little to happen in southern Europe until spring. Bad weather, too few landing craft, determined German resistance, and a stalled Allied offensive combined to shift his thoughts northward. Alexander and Clark, however, had no interest in quitting the Mediterranean. Having overseen the Dunkirk evacuation, Alexander preferred tackling northern Italy to evacuating northern France a second time. Clark considered the capture of Rome as the way to ensure his place in history. The problem for them was that high-level discussions in Cairo and Teheran had now subordinated everything—everything—to Operation Overlord. An unintended result of this was that the British became the controlling partner in the Mediterranean effort. These commanders, prodded by Churchill, still hoped that success in northern Italy, followed by a Balkan invasion through the Ljubljana Gap in the Alps, would obviate the need for a cross-channel invasion.[25]

Now, if anything were going to happen in Italy, there would need to be something of a catalyst. The previous November Eisenhower had sought permission from the Combined Chiefs of Staff to retain in Italy sixty-eight landing craft that were scheduled to return to England. He sought to retain them there to support the possibility of an end-run seaborne invasion. The chiefs reluctantly agreed to his request, though only if certain conditions were met. *If* the Allies could reach Cassino, *if* they could break through, and *if* they could push on the twenty-five miles to Frosinone, then Eisenhower could launch the end-run amphibious invasion. Hoping that these conditions were achievable, he authorized Alexander to undertake planning for such an operation. Alexander determined that any end-run would work best at Anzio, a small Italian resort town on the Mediterranean. It was beyond Cassino but still thirty-five miles south of Rome. The general hoped that this would destabilize and isolate Kesselring's forces on the Gustav Line and perhaps threaten Rome itself. He authorized Clark to begin preliminary planning for an amphibious assault on Anzio. Clark understood that an essential component of this operation was that the Allies had to crack the Gustav Line first. Once that happened, and *only* if it happened, forces near Cassino could push north to Frosinone and link up with the Anzio invasion force, which by then should have pushed in from the beachhead. Once conjoined, they would roll on as one to Rome.[26]

Planning for Anzio proceeded long enough for Clark to realize that its concept was simply unworkable. At this point his troops were completely exhausted; they could not even reach the Cassino defenses, much less breach them. He shook his head and on December 19 folded the plan: invading Anzio with too little time for planning, too few troops, and not enough equipment and supplies would invite failure. When he put the plan on the shelf, he should have stamped it "Do not resuscitate." It was there less than a week before Churchill pulled it out and administered CPR.[27]

With "Jumbo" Wilson now taking Eisenhower's position, Marshall thought it appropriate for Commanding General Brooke, the most senior British military officer, to assume executive oversight of the Mediterranean. He likely assumed that Brooke had the same relationship with Churchill that he himself had with Roosevelt; that is, the president provided direction but Marshall and his generals ran the war. But unlike Roosevelt, Churchill stayed very involved in his generals' business. A December 19 meeting in Tunis between the prime minister and Brooke established that the general would concentrate on the many problems in England while Churchill would take care of the Mediterranean and oversee the commanders there.[28]

One of Brooke's self-appointed duties had been to serve as a brake on some of the more outrageous ideas fired up by the prime minister. Now, with the general focused at home, Churchill went full throttle. On December 22, 1943, he sent a telegram to the Imperial General Staff lambasting the lack of action in the Mediterranean as nothing less than a scandal. Perhaps for Churchill, who had had a starring role in the British disaster at Gallipoli during World War I, there had come a chance for redemption.[29]

On December 24 the prime minister met with his most senior British commanders. His agenda was not whether to invade Anzio, but when. Eisenhower and Bedell Smith sat in on a follow-up meeting on Christmas Day, but since they would not be involved, they participated little in the discussion. Churchill persuaded the others that the capture of Anzio was essential to the capture of Rome. Through his superior intellect, legendary eloquence, and a willingness to be a deceitful bully when it suited him, he seized control of the Mediterranean theater. He sent a message to Roosevelt asking to retain the needed landing craft and, assuming the president would agree, signaled the green light for the operation. If Churchill felt a little uneasy, it was because he had just recently agreed with Roosevelt and Stalin that absolutely nothing could interfere with the cross-channel invasion. With the British leader determined to have Rome, Alexander ordered Clark to reignite Anzio planning. The American general was more than willing to do so, but he could not ignore that the situation had not changed in the least from when he had shut down invasion planning just days before. Without more resources, the assault would fail. Perhaps—yet another conditional word—with a few more resources, it might not. Churchill finessed the holding of even more landing craft and acquired a parachute regiment for the region.[30]

On January 8, 1944, in Marrakech, Morocco, Churchill chaired another meeting. British generals Wilson and Alexander attended as did U.S. lieutenant general Jacob Devers, General Smith, and other senior British and American officers. The prime minister saw no need to invite General Clark, who he knew supported the invasion.

Incredibly, he also chose not invite General Lucas, who would lead the Anzio assault force. Lucas later said that he never learned why he had not been invited, though in all likelihood Churchill viewed him as a naysayer. Instead, he invited two of Lucas's colonels, an operations officer and a logistics officer. Clark, concerned about the general's absence, carefully instructed the two colonels on what to say. Each made a strong argument for, among other things, the need for additional amphibious training for recently arrived replacement soldiers and for a few extra days to conduct a critically important rehearsal. Churchill dismissed their concerns with a wave of the hand, saying that they had already trained the troops. When they countered that the U.S. 3rd Infantry Division had absorbed many replacements since its last action, he rejoined that one experienced officer or NCO per platoon was sufficient. The colonels exchanged glances of helpless frustration.

Churchill knew that Eisenhower's intelligence chief, British brigadier Kenneth W. D. Strong, would be critical of the invasion. The brigadier would likely contend that the entire operation hinged on a breakthrough at Cassino, which was anything but certain. Only after Churchill had made quite clear to those in attendance that he and Alexander fully supported the invasion did he allow Strong to speak, suggesting to the others that the latter would be negative in his view. Indeed, Strong argued against the landing, though not as effectively as Churchill had argued for it. With the plan more or less approved, the prime minister cabled Roosevelt on January 8, reporting, presumably with a straight face, that the two conferences had resulted in full discussions involving all responsible officers from both countries and all branches and that the group fully supported the proposed action. According to him, the group also believed that available resources were sufficient. How could the president possibly say no?[31]

Clark's planners were quickly back at work. Hundreds of details had yet to be decided. A rehearsal resulted in considerable disappointment for Lucas and Truscott, but Clark's response to their request for a second practice run was that there was simply no time. "You have just got to do it," he told Truscott. Lucas found himself as little more than a spectator in the planning efforts. Truscott recalled that "any further delay would be flatly refused."[32]

The consensus of Churchill and Alexander seemed to be that faced with the landing of *two* Allied divisions, the Germans would give way rather quickly. Yet these were the same opponents who had held off more than seven times their number in Sicily, had almost kicked the Allies back into the water at Salerno, and now had them stopped cold at Cassino. Clark's own intelligence officer reminded him that the Germans could probably muster 14,000 troops to immediately resist the landing, 22,000 by D-day plus two, 31,000 by D-day plus three, and more than 60,000 in a little over two weeks.[33]

The amphibious assault at Anzio, code-named Operation Shingle, was given a launch date of January 22. Somehow, its three major commanders, Alexander, Clark, and Lucas, had vastly different views of the objectives. Alexander saw it as the first step in capturing the Alban Hills just south of Rome. Doing so would lead to cutting the two highways that supplied Kesselring's Cassino defense, the collapse of which would allow for the capture of Rome itself. The key, he knew, was to take the Alban Hills.

General Clark, still sporting a black eye from Salerno, had a more modest appetite. He would have liked General Lucas to do all that Alexander hoped for, but he knew that Anzio's shoestring allowances made that impossible; he would be happy with just a secured beachhead. The last thing Clark wanted was another potential seaborne evacuation. In fact, he intentionally softened his written orders to Lucas, changing language from "advance *and* secure Colli Laziali" (the Alban Hills) to "advance *on* Colli Laziali." Clark underscored this when he later said to the general, "You can forget this Goddamned Rome business." His take-home lesson from Salerno had been that the best way to hold a hostile beach is to land and immediately go on the defensive.

General Lucas, now infected with a dose of his commander's pessimism, felt a measure of relief nonetheless. He knew his invasion force was too small to advance to Rome or even the Alban Hills. Now, however, his mission was clear: his job was to take the beach and hold it, moving forward only when the situation permitted. Lucas concluded that his superiors did not really want him to capture the Alban Hills and beyond, for had that been the objective, they would have given him an army instead of a beefed-up corps. Official naval historian Samuel Morison later concluded: "That was the fundamental weakness of Operation Shingle. Either it was a job for a full Army, or it was no job at all; to attempt it with only two divisions was to send a boy on a man's errand."[34]

On January 20, two days before the scheduled landings, Clark launched a major attack south of Cassino, part of which was sending the U.S. 36th Infantry Division across the icy Rapido River. It was a night operation designed to work in conjunction with the Anzio assault, but its plan had serious flaws. The result was that too few troops with too little cover and artillery support went up against overwhelming German firepower across a minefield. The first attempt was a deadly failure. The next day Clark ordered a second attempt, this time in daylight. Before long the freezing river took on a noticeable red tinge. These failed attacks resulted in 143 killed, 663 wounded, and 875 missing, of which more than 500 were in German custody. The 36th would not forgive Clark for the Bloody Rapido.[35]

At this point, one thing should have been clear. There would be no linking up between the Allied forces at Cassino and those at Anzio anytime soon. This, of course, had been an essential component of the invasion plan. With the link up still not possible, why land at Anzio at all? Historians Dominick Graham and Shelford Bidwell suggest that with all the fuss over holding landing craft and assigning additional troops, any cancellation of the Anzio invasion would have cost Alexander and Clark their jobs. That was likely the case for Alexander. Churchill wanted Rome, and he would have found another commander willing to accept the risks. Clark might have survived, however. Marshall, Eisenhower, and the Combined Chiefs of Staff were focused on the invasion of France. Maintaining a good defensive line north of Naples, the Rapido River, for instance, might have been acceptable to them. Considering the number of Allied deaths likely to result from a continued crawl up the spine of Italy, the possibility of cancelling the Anzio operation deserved more discussion than it got. In practical terms, the assault force was mounted and ready to launch, and nothing under heaven would stop it now.[36]

By December 28, 1943, the Anzio plan identified the two assault divisions. These would be Truscott's 3rd Infantry Division and the British 1st Division. Five battalions of rangers and commandos and four battalions of paratroopers would assist. A few days after the initial assaults, one regiment of the 45th Infantry Division and part of the 1st Armored Division would land. Even at that, Truscott was certain that the invasion force could not achieve the results that Alexander and Clark desired. "No one below Army level," he later wrote, "believed that the landing of two divisions at Anzio would cause a German withdrawal on the Southern [Cassino] front, or that there was more than a remote chance that the remainder of the 5th Army would be able to cross the Rapido River and fight its way up the Liri and Sacco valleys to join us within a month." Truscott must have shaken his head in disbelief. He knew that Alexander had been in Sicily and that Clark had been at Salerno. By now they should have known better. Thus began a four-month operation that would resemble the closest thing to the Great War's trench warfare occurring during World War II. Slightly more than 36,000 troops would get the Allies on the Anzio beachhead. It would take more than 150,000—more than four times as many—to get them off. As incredible as it sounds in retrospect, Clark's initial plan had been for just *one* division—the 3rd Infantry—to land, and with only enough supplies for seven days. Upon hearing this, Truscott had reminded the general that in Sicily his troops had averaged only two miles per day. Then he stated his position as clearly as possible: "We are perfectly willing to undertake the [Anzio] operation if we are ordered to do so and we will maintain ourselves to the last round of ammunition. But if we do undertake it, you are going to destroy the best damned division in the United States Army for there will be no survivors."[37]

CHAPTER 20

ANZIO, A HALFWAY MEASURE

On January 22, 1944, at 1:50 A.M., in unruffled waters near the sibling Mediterranean towns of Anzio and Nettuno, two naval rocket craft launched a brief but intense barrage along the beaches. By then, Allied landing craft had already motored away from their mother ships on what would become a surprisingly warm winter day. Almost unbelievably, the invasion at Anzio came as a surprise. Enemy opposition was light and ended with the surrender of more than two hundred German soldiers, members of two tired and bruised battalions of a panzer grenadier division recently sent to rest from harsh duty at Cassino. The Abwehr, Hitler's military intelligence agency, had misled Kesselring. Its director, Reichsmarine Admiral Wilhelm F. Canaris, had assured the field marshal that there was no reason to suspect that the Allies would invade in the near future. Despite this bad information, within three hours of the amphibious assault, Kesselring had a full report, affirming that an invasion force had landed, not just a raiding party. He thought it at least possible that the Allies would strike for the Alban Hills, and thus he initiated his prearranged response plan. By 8:30 A.M. German reinforcements were on their way from Rome, northern Italy, France, Germany, and the Balkans. As the Allies had hoped, a few even came from Cassino.[1]

Situated about thirty miles south of Rome, Anzio and Nettuno had been beachfront resort towns since Roman imperial days. Anzio also boasted a small port. In the 1930s Benito Mussolini had drained much of the nearby Pontine Marshes to create farmland. He had posed for a 1936 commemorative photograph astride a Fiat tractor, wearing a determined look as though he were about to personally scrape out the boundaries for Aprilia, a model farming settlement. Aprilia and several communities like it would increase Italy's food supply by creating three thousand new farms. He also reforested nearby areas. Soon crops grew where marshland had existed before.[2]

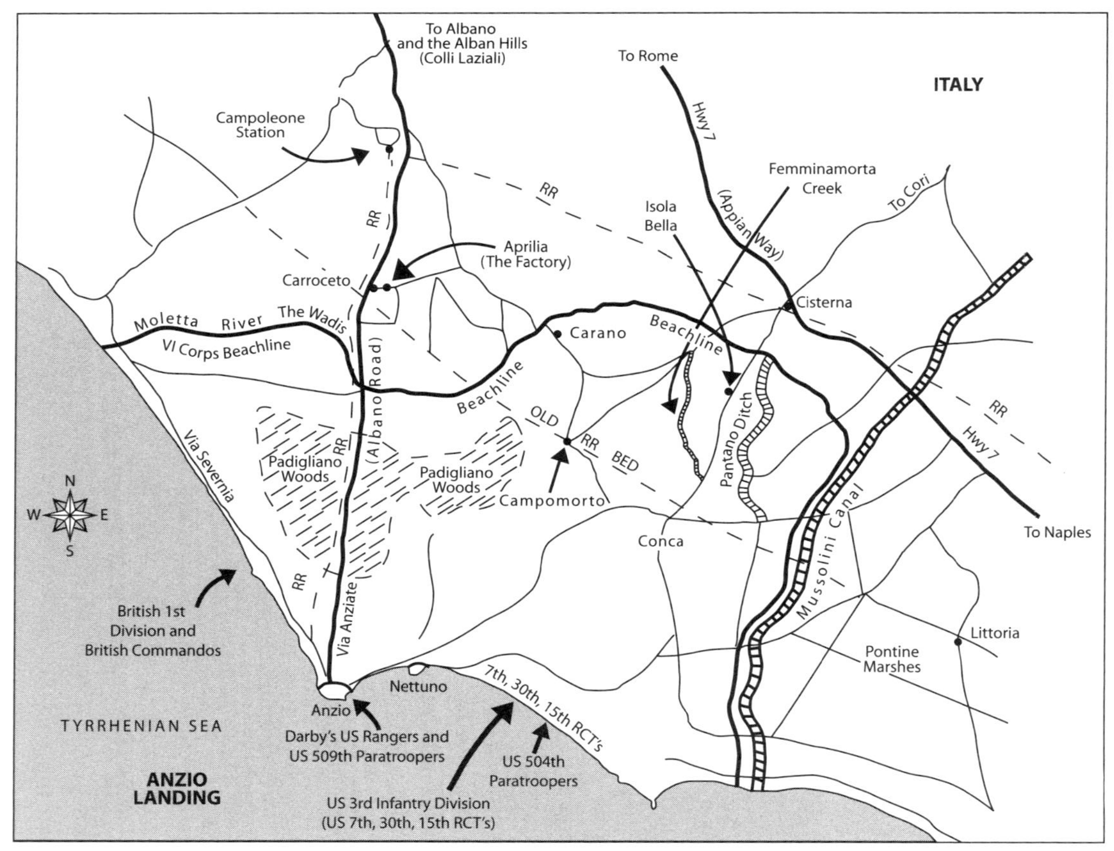

The Allied landing at Anzio, Italy. Map by Megan Postell.

The year that British and American troops waded ashore, the Via Anziate ran from Anzio to Albano, a village situated at the foot of the Alban Hills and just eighteen miles southeast of Rome. On the way north from Anzio, the road passed near Carroceto, which had a train station, and Aprilia. Allied soldiers would call Aprilia "the Factory" because of its very visible bell tower, which resembled (to them) an industrial smokestack. Beyond Aprilia, the road passed through Campoleone, an important road-and-rail junction, and farther still it intersected with Highway 7 (the Appian Way), the main coastal route from Naples to Rome. Northeast of Anzio, lesser roads intersected to form a network running to Cisterna. Highway 6, farther inland, also ran from Naples to Rome. It paralleled Highway 7 through interior hills and valleys. From Naples, that road passed through Cassino, the Liri Valley, Frosinone, and Valmontone, before reaching Rome. In the months ahead, each of these towns would witness the deadly contest between the Allies and the Germans.[3]

The landscape just north of Anzio was mostly flat and open except for a small area called the Padiglione Woods, which had been Mussolini's reforestation project. To the northwest beyond the Moletta River, the land became deep-gully country. East of Anzio, on the other side of various canals, lay the remnants of the Pontine Marshes. Other natural and artificial features in the vicinity included about a dozen small villages as well as various farm roads, railway tracks, and a disused railway bed. The canals and ditches were products of Mussolini's drainage program, with the largest canal named in his honor. Although the area had become arable, its water table remained high, a mere two feet beneath the surface. For soldiers whose lives depended on digging deep foxholes and required firm roads and fields capable of supporting heavy armored vehicles, this was not good news. More than a half dozen small villages existed not far from Anzio and Nettuno. Most of the local population had evacuated, leaving numerous two-story farmhouses and other buildings vacant. These *poderi,* as the Italians called them, consisted of walls of stone covered with plaster. In the flat, open, and coverless land coveted by lethal foes, these amazingly well-built structures offered considerable safety to those inside and substantial risk to those who had to attack them. Second only to the prize of Rome were the Alban Hills, about three thousand feet high, which rose between Highways 6 and 7. The elevated terrain was ideal for observation and indirect-fire weapons.[4]

Having landed, the 36,000 members of Lucas's invasion force, with 3,200 vehicles, wasted no time in setting up defenses and making the port of Anzio, seized with minimal effort, operational. Over the next few months, this Allied force would grow to 150,000 men. The expression "there's never enough time to do it right, but always enough time to do it over," had a corollary at Anzio. There were not enough Allied troops available to actually seize and hold the Alban Hills, but enough would become available once it appeared that another Dunkirk or Salerno was at hand.[5]

Darby's 1st, 3rd, and 4th Ranger Battalions and the attached 509th Parachute Infantry Battalion captured the small towns of Anzio and Nettuno, respectively. Truscott's 3rd Infantry Division went ashore southeast of Nettuno. Most of Major General W. R. C. Penney's British 1st Division, with two commandos (battalions) attached, beached to the northwest of Anzio. As soon as turnaround shipping allowed—about three days—one regiment of the 45th Infantry Division would land, if needed, followed by a portion of the 1st Armored Division.[6]

Lucas's troops had taken a sixteen-mile stretch of beach and had pushed inland several miles to their intended corps beachhead line. Emanating in a semicircle from the sea, his left flank was the Moletta River, his right flank was the Mussolini Canal and the nearly impenetrable Pontine Marshes, and his back was to the Tyrrhenian Sea. The Allied front—at least for the moment—appeared to be free of German troops. It was tempting to push farther inland, the general knew, but if he tried for the Alban Hills, he would likely be unable to hold the port at Anzio. Lucas could do one or the other, he reasoned, but not both, so he concentrated on getting the harbor working, installing an antiaircraft system, and scraping out an airfield. The lesson from Salerno seemed to be that holding the port was the more important objective. The GIs and Tommies wasted no time in preparing their defenses and now awaited the inevitable counterattack. Alexander and Clark visited the beachhead that first day. Alexander was pleased and concurred with Lucas's decision not to go for the Alban Hills. Clark was pleased as well and warned his subordinate: "Don't stick your neck out, Johnny. I did at Salerno and got into trouble."[7]

Kesselring had done his homework. His defensive strategy was to have small observation units stationed at likely invasion sites, with larger mobile units staffed, equipped, and on alert to roll within eight to twelve hours. "The first hours of 22 January 1944 . . . were full of anxiety," he recalled, but the field marshal relaxed somewhat as he observed the "hesitant advance of those troops which had landed." It did not take him long to read Lucas's mind. "Yet as I traversed the front I had the confident feeling that the Allies had missed a uniquely favorable chance of capturing Rome and of opening the door on the Garigliano [Cassino] front. I was certain that time was our ally." He could see that Lucas intended to secure the beachhead before moving forward. Kesselring seemed pleased by something else too. As he would later conclude: "The landing force was initially weak, only a division or so of infantry, and without armor. It was a half-way measure as an offensive that was . . . [the Allies'] basic error." German reinforcements arrived in plenty of time. Had Lucas commanded a sufficiently large landing force, the remaining war in Italy might have taken a different course. Of course, as Truscott later admitted, "what we did not know and failed to appreciate was the technique which the German command had developed for rapid concentration against, and the sealing off of, any such landing."[8]

By 10:00 A.M. on invasion day, Truscott had inspected his lines and found everything in order, so he returned to his command post for a late breakfast. Over the years he had grown to appreciate good food and, when time allowed, even played chef. Since that was not possible now, he relied on one or more soldiers to operate the mess service for his command staff. This practice had begun at Port Lyautey, where Truscott had drafted a young Chinese American soldier, Phue P. Lee, to be his personal cook. His mistake back then was inviting General Patton to dine with him. When Patton left, he took Lee with him. When Truscott later took command of the 3rd Division, he drafted another Chinese American soldier—a Private Taw S. Hong—as part of a complement of four soldiers to operate his mess; Hong had the additional duty as serving as Truscott's personal orderly. For the general's first Anzio breakfast, the private arranged for bacon, eggs, and toast—where the three dozen fresh eggs came from was a mystery Truscott chose not to investigate. He and Colonel Carleton ate their first breakfast while standing next to the general's Jeep, using its hood as their table. During this meal, General Clark and a few of his staff arrived, followed by General Lucas and his chief of staff. None could resist the smell of bacon, eggs, and toast and inveigled an invitation from Truscott. A couple hours later, as Truscott

Corporal Allen Frederick (*left*) and Private First Class George Mezich (*right*), B Battery, 39th Field Artillery Battalion, 3rd Infantry Division, share C-rations with an Italian boy named Adrione near Anzio, January 1944. Courtesy of the U.S. Army and the National Archives.

prepared to leave, he overheard Hong in conversation with Sergeant Barna, the general's driver, saying, "Goddam, Sergeant, General's fresh eggs all gone to hell." The soldiers soon found themselves feeding not only the division's staff but also many visitors, who quickly dubbed Truscott's mess service the "Canton Restaurant."[9]

During an air raid on January 24, a shell exploded near Truscott's foot, sending shrapnel through his heavy wool jodhpurs and tall leather boot into his left leg. "Had it not been for the cavalry breeches and boots which I always wore during battle," he recalled, "the wound would have been far more serious than it was, which was bad enough by the time the surgeon had finished cutting out the fragments and had encased my leg in an adhesive cast." Along with the coins and key in his pocket, breeches and boots became the general's lucky battle attire, soon combined with a leather bomber jacket. The leg wound was a concern, of course, but perhaps more serious was a case of laryngitis. Truscott could issue his firm commands only in a whisper, but what worried him was that it seemed to hang on much longer than it should have.[10]

General Lucas focused on acquiring reinforcements, food, ammunition, equipment, and supplies. These, and a solid defense line, were his priorities. He would not strike for the Alban Hills until he had enough troops to give the thrust a good chance of success. Truscott later wrote, "I suppose that some arm chair strategists will always labor under the delusion that there was a 'fleeting opportunity' at Anzio during which some Napoleonic figure would have charged over the Colli Laziali [Alban Hills], played havoc with the German lines of communication, and galloped on into Rome." Truscott knew the time was not right to go that far. General Penney, the other division commander at Anzio, agreed, saying that one day in Rome would have led to eighteen months in a prisoner-of-war camp. Major General Harmon, who would arrive in a few days with his 1st Armored Division, concurred. In Naples he had originally proposed pushing for Rome but afterward said: "I am glad now I was overruled. . . . The Allies would have had Rome for twenty-four hours. After that the Germans would have had us." British general Gerald Templer would later join in this opinion, saying that Lucas could have taken Rome, but within two weeks every British soldier would be dead, wounded, or captured. Finally, even Kesselring later conceded, "It would have been the Anglo-American doom to over-extend themselves." Taking Rome might have been possible; holding it was not.[11]

While unaware of how many troops the Germans had marshaled, Truscott was certain that many had arrived. Within two days his front of twenty miles and Penney's front of seven miles were in contact with German armored units. Truscott recalled, "Any reckless drive to seize the Colli Laziali with means then available in the beachhead could only have ended in disaster and might well have resulted in [the] destruction of the entire force."[12]

Not tackling the Alban Hills was one thing, not trying for Campoleone and Cisterna was another. Each town had key road junctions not yet adequately defended that Allied soldiers easily could seize and block. Now that some reinforcements had arrived, one regiment of the 45th Infantry Division and the 504th Parachute Infantry Regiment (detached from the 82nd Airborne Division), it might be possible. Truscott met with Lucas on January 26 and proposed using the entire 3rd Division to attack Cisterna, later followed by using the British 1st Division and part of the 45th Division to attack Campoleone. Lucas liked the idea but wanted to delay a day. That was all he needed—one more day—to get part of the 1st Armored onshore before moving forward.[13]

Clark, who on January 22 had urged Lucas not to stick his neck out, managed to change his mind the next day. Instead of just one regimental combat team of the 45th Division going in, he authorized the remaining two regiments, the entire 1st Armored, and a regiment of the highly regarded 1st Special Service Force, a Canadian and American commando regiment under Brigadier General Robert T. Frederick. Soon, Lucas would have more than four divisions on the beach. Clark had dismissed caution and wanted his subordinate to do the same, encouraging him to take some chances and send his troops forward. Lucas was close but not quite ready. He also had to consider the larger picture. By now he was well aware that the Rapido River crossing had failed miserably, which could only mean that Clark would make no progress on the Cassino front anytime soon. Thus, Lucas could not help but believe that he should wait at least for the 1st Armored to get on shore before launching an attack. He jotted in his diary, "This is the most important thing I have ever tried to do and I will not be stampeded."[14]

General Alexander had previously complimented the landing, declaring it "a splendid piece of work." Now, disappointed with Lucas's hesitation, the British general told Clark that the corps commander needed a push. Clark agreed to do so but resented Alexander's interference, even though he knew that much of the pressure was coming via Churchill's distant view from 10 Downing Street. Lucas, in fact, was very close to launching his attack, but he needed to line up a few more things. Previously, based on faulty intelligence, he had overestimated the size of the German forces facing him. That would not be the case now, for Kesselring had rolled in more than 70,000 troops to oppose the Allies' 40,000.[15]

By January 30, a little more than a week after landing, Lucas was ready to move forward. He would time his breakout to coincide with an attempt by Clark to puncture the Gustav Line at Cassino. He had been ready to launch the attack the day before but had assented to a day's delay to allow Penney's 1st Division and Harmon's recently landed 1st Armored Division to complete last-minute preparations. During those twenty-four hours, the 26th Panzer Grenadier

Division arrived unnoticed to assist the Hermann Goering Division. "As it turned out," Truscott lamented, "this delay was most unfortunate for us."[16]

The plan was to have a naval, air, and artillery bombardment precede the ground assault. Then, the 1st Division would make the primary attack on the left flank and take Campoleone. The 1st Armored would follow with a left hook, pass through Penney's division, go on to Albano, and then seize the Alban Hills. Truscott's 3rd Division, Darby's rangers, and the 504th paratroopers would make a secondary attack on the right flank and take Cisterna, then continue on to cut Highway 7 at Velletri. Possibly, these forces could also press on and cut Highway 6 at Valmontone. The 45th Division, corps engineers, and other units would protect the flanks. It was an ambitious plan.[17]

Penney's 1st Division pushed forward for three days until a curtain of bullets and shellfire cut down the British and blew them apart. Harmon's tanks tried to assist but learned a lesson the hard way. The copy of the plan provided to Harmon when he came ashore relied on maps and aerial photographs, not on detailed scouting of the actual ground. Thus, what appeared to be small marks suggesting trenches on the map were actually gullies up to fifty feet deep. When his tanks tried to skirt these, they bogged down in mud. An armored wrecker sent to pull out four tanks became stuck itself and needed more tanks to aid it. These too then required help from still more tanks, which in turn required assistance from even more tanks. Harmon confessed, "Because I was stubborn, I lost twenty-four tanks . . . to succor four." The following day the general went forward to the British position to see if he could do anything to help them. Upon arriving and climbing out of his tank, he could not believe the scene. "There were dead bodies everywhere. I had never seen so many dead men in one place. They lay so close together that I had to step with care." Upon seeing Harmon, a muddy corporal of the 2nd Sherwood Foresters Brigade stepped forward and said that while his unit had gone in with 116 men, there were now only 16 left. The British attack on Campoleone was a tragic failure.[18]

Truscott's secondary effort, which had spearheaded the whole attack, had done worse. To the best of his knowledge, at the time of his intended attack, only the Hermann Goering Division opposed the 3rd Infantry Division. The general's previous reconnaissance suggested that the Germans were along a wide front, situated at

Major General Ernest N. "Ernie" Harmon, commander, 1st Armored Division, April 1946. Courtesy of the U.S. Army and the National Archives.

a number of strongpoints with mobile units in between. He and Colonel Darby prepared a plan that would send two ranger battalions on a night infiltration mission between the strongpoints and into the town of Cisterna. Once behind German lines, the Americans would create as much havoc as possible. An hour after the two battalions departed, Truscott's 15th Infantry Regiment and a third ranger battalion would follow, becoming the primary force that would break through the enemy lines and support the first two battalions. At the same time, the 504th Parachute would make a diversionary attack on the right near the Mussolini Canal, and Truscott's 7th Infantry

Regiment would attack on the left along the Feminamorta Canal and attempt to cut Highway 7 northwest of Cisterna. Artillery, tanks, and tank destroyers would assist.[19]

One member of the 15th Regiment slated for the assault was Audie Murphy. He had missed the landing because a temperature of 105 degrees had necessitated malaria treatment at a hospital. Now he had rejoined his unit at Anzio and was surprised to learn that the army had promoted him to staff sergeant in charge of a platoon. He was nineteen years old but still looked sixteen. Murphy described his feelings of going into yet another battle. "The weather is sunny; and though it is January, beads of sweat roll off our skin. Fear is moving up with us. It always does . . . , fear is right there beside you. . . . I am well acquainted with fear. It strikes first in the stomach, coming like the disemboweling hand that is thrust into the carcass of a chicken. I feel now as though icy fingers have reached inside my mid-parts and twisted the intestines into knots."[20]

On January 30 at 1:00 A.M., in complete darkness the two infiltrating ranger battalions crept north single file through the German lines along the Pantano Ditch. The dry gully was part of the Mussolini Canal system and ran southeast of the village of Isola Bella. It was deep enough that the rangers evaded detection as they passed enemy sentries in the darkness. Truscott's intelligence officers had suspected only the usual German activity in the area, but they had not noticed that the 26th Panzer Grenadier Division had just arrived to join the Goering Division.[21]

Colonel Darby set up his command post in a farmhouse along the road, hoping to maintain contact with all three of his battalions. As the two infiltrating ranger battalions reached the end of the Pantano Ditch and emerged less than a half mile from Cisterna, they found themselves amid enemy paratroopers. A sudden hailstorm of German firepower slammed into them. In the early morning hours, two German divisions, about to launch their own attack, had detected the rangers and began pouring everything they had into them. Flares and tracer rounds lit the night as rifles, machine guns, tanks, mortars, direct artillery, rocket launchers, and self-propelled antiaircraft guns opened up. The rangers scrambled about, using bazookas and sticky bombs to stop some of the tanks. By the afternoon, their rifle ammunition ran out. German paratroopers shot some of the Americans at close range and took many others captive.[22]

Ranger Carl Lehmann recalled firing his M-1 rifle so fast and for so long that the wood stock began to smoke. Ranger Frank Mattivi remembered the desperation of being surrounded by Germans and being very low on ammunition. All of the officers in his company were now dead, with only about thirty men still alive, and Mattivi realized that he was the highest ranking among them. Ranger captain Chuck Shunstrom recalled seeing the Germans marching eighty captured Americans in four columns toward his position, shouting that they would shoot the captives if Shunstrom and his men did not surrender. Eventually, the Germans captured Lehmann, Mattivi, Shunstrom, and many other rangers. The captain later escaped from a prison camp and eventually received a Silver Star for his actions in battle.[23]

Truscott and Darby were powerless. A sergeant major, whom the colonel had known since training days in Northern Ireland, reached him by radio, saying that he hoped they would meet again someday. It was clear that the man was saying goodbye. Darby shouted back, pleading, telling him to not let the rangers surrender, to hang on to his radio no matter what, that troops were coming through, that the men could stay together or evade individually, that the sergeant major could do what he thought was best. He added that he wished he were there with them, and he meant it. Finally, when there was nothing left to say, Darby offered a final "God bless you."

The two infiltrating battalions had left Anzio with 767 men; 6 came back. This was a casualty rate of 99 percent. Between 250 and 300 rangers were killed and more than 450 captured. The Germans later paraded the captives through the streets of Rome. The remaining battalion, at a different location, had encountered its own resistance and lost half its men. The 1st Ranger Battalion, the original unit created by Truscott and Darby in Northern Ireland, ceased to exist, as did the 3rd Ranger Battalion. It was a heartbreak for Truscott; it was the loss of a family for Darby. He had fought with those men in North Africa, Sicily, and Salerno. Now they were gone. Today in the small town of Isola Bella, a street is named Via dei Rangers.[24]

CHAPTER 21

TAKING CHARGE

Kesselring, of course, knew that Campoleone and Cisterna were obvious objectives. He would need all his resources to resist an attack—and already had slipped in another division surreptitiously—but he knew that if he were patient, the Allies would come to him. When they finally arrived, Kesselring was ready. And with Clark's push at Cassino having failed, Anzio, intended as the answer to Cassino, now became its own question.

For Clark, the ranger catastrophe meant more bad press. He had plenty of that following the Rapido River crossing, and now he anticipated more media criticism. He met with Lucas and Truscott. Clark accused the latter of misusing the rangers and threatened an investigation to fix responsibility. Truscott was not only surprised but also angry: "I reminded him that I had been responsible for organizing the original ranger battalion and that Colonel Darby and I perhaps understood their capabilities better than other American officers." He added that there was no need for an investigation as the responsibility was his entirely. Lucas disagreed, saying responsibility for the mission was his, jotting in his diary later, "I told Clark the fault was mine as I had seen the plan of attack and had OK'd it." Clark apparently dropped the issue. Perhaps much of the responsibility rested with Allied intelligence, which had predicted that fewer Germans would be available to resist the attack.[1]

Matters had not gone well for the 3rd Infantry Division, either. Each of its regiments, the 7th, 15th, and 30th, had battled for two days with little progress. Since landing, Truscott had sustained more than 3,000 casualties and had lost a third of his tanks and tank destroyers. The overall British picture was not much better, holding Campoleone but with a weak grip. What the Allies did not know was that the Germans had suffered as well.[2]

On January 31 Clark noted in his diary that he was disappointed with the lack of aggressiveness by VI Corps, meaning General Lucas, of course. Lucas had already picked up the signals, and by the next day he suspected that neither Alexander nor Clark was happy about the overall situation. He noted in his diary: "My head will probably fall in the basket but I have done my best. . . . I was sent on a desperate mission, one where the odds were greatly against success, and I went without saying anything because I was given an order and my opinion was not asked." Coincidently, during this time, Alexander called Clark and told him that the Germans were massing for a major counterattack, a conclusion likely based on Ultra intercepts. The American commander immediately told Lucas to put his corps on the defensive. Indeed, two weeks after the Allied landing, Kesselring was ready to launch his own counteroffensive, doing so on February 4 in hopes of driving the Allies back into the sea. The Germans snatched Campoleone from the British and pushed them back to Aprilia, where the Tommies stemmed the advance but nothing more.[3]

Informed by Lucas about the upcoming attack, Truscott bolstered his front. "We made extensive use of mines, wires, and obstacles as is usual." Over the initial objections of his crews, he placed his tanks and tank destroyers near the front lines to be immediately ready to support the infantry. Before long, the tank officers supported the concept. The general coordinated his seven battalions of artillery so that at any moment, when called upon by a forward observer, artillery officer, or infantry commander, every gun in the division could deliver rounds simultaneously to any location. Potential targets were preregistered, and any disruption of communications called for repeated fire until communications resumed.[4]

The VI Corps anxiously waited. On the eastern flank, the 1st Special Service Force held six miles along the Mussolini Canal. Sharing the center area, Truscott's 3rd Division, with attached paratroopers, held ten miles, and the 45th Division held another five. Sharing the western flank, the British 56th Division (having relieved the 1st Division) held three miles along the Via Anziate—its southern portion—and the U.S. 36th Engineer Regiment defended three miles along the Moletta River. The battered British 1st Division, along with Harmon's 1st Armored Division, moved to reserve in the rear. Backing these units were four hundred artillery pieces, three hundred tanks, three hundred tank destroyers and antitank guns, and four hundred machine guns.[5]

Operation Fischfang, the anticipated German counterattack, began on February 16 with six to eight divisions. Aided by bad weather, the Germans cleverly concealed their initial point of attack. Truscott suspected it would come down the Via Anziate, but his troops had to be ready nonetheless. Several enemy thrusts did come at his 3rd Division, but the heaviest assaults drove at the 45th Division's sector near Carroceto and Aprilia. For three days the Germans pushed down the Via Anziate. Like sharks invading a school of fish, their objective was to split VI Corps and then attack its flanks; their goal was nothing less than pushing the Allies back into the sea. Fortunately, Allied artillery proved superior to that of the Germans and assisted the British and American infantry in staving off the attacks.[6]

After midnight on February 17, Colonel Carleton brought bad news to Truscott. "Boss, I hate to do this, but you would give me hell if I held this until morning." The general rubbed his eyes and read the message. In a copy of an order from Clark to Lucas, Truscott was instructed to hand off his 3rd Division and take over as deputy commander of VI Corps. Truscott saw the action for what it was: a lack of confidence in Lucas by Alexander and Clark.[7]

Truscott and Lucas had been friends for many years, and their working relationship had always been good. "Nevertheless," Truscott acknowledged, "our methods of command were different. I was not blind to the fact that General Lucas lacked some of the qualities of positive leadership that engender confidence, and that he leaned heavily upon his staff and trusted subordinates in difficult decisions." Still, the general regretted leaving his divisional command of almost a year to fill what was essentially a staff job. However, "There was a job to be done, and I was a soldier. I could only carry out the order loyally." His own deputy commander, Brigadier General O'Daniel, would take over the 3rd Division. Truscott thought highly of him, later describing him as a "rugged, gruff-voiced Irishman, who thoroughly enjoyed fighting, and had no equal in bulldog tenacity or as a fighting infantry division commander. He well merited the sobriquet 'Iron Mike' by which the Division knew him." O'Daniel had come by his nickname during World War I, when as a young lieutenant he continued to fight for twelve hours after a bullet had slammed into his cheek, leaving a deep scar for life.[8]

When Truscott reported to VI Corps headquarters, Lucas and his staff were visibly concerned about the recent penetrating attacks down the Via Anziate against the British 56th and U.S. 45th Divisions,

Major General John W. "Iron Mike" O'Daniel, December 1950. Courtesy of the U.S. Army and the National Archives.

which showed a serious potential for the Allies to lose the beach. Lucas had recalled the British 1st Division and the 1st Armored from corps reserve and sent them forward to bolster the line. Truscott recalled: "There was a feeling of desperation, of hopelessness. . . . My optimistic assurance that nothing ever looked as bad on the ground as it did on a map at Headquarters did little to dispel the pall-like gloom." Still, he had to admit, "the situation was far graver than we had realized in the 3rd Infantry Division."[9]

Truscott needed to see for himself what the other parts of the front looked like. Going forward, he found General Harmon and Major General Eagles, commander of the 45th Division. Neither seemed overly alarmed, although it was clear that the six German divisions had pushed a serious salient into the corps beachhead line four miles wide and four miles deep. By that evening Truscott concluded that it was time for an Allied counterattack. He suggested to Lucas that all corps reserves and a recently arrived British brigade be included in the action. Clark arrived about this time and concurred with his proposal, as did Harmon and General Templer. Lucas, still hesitant, also agreed.[10]

Now Truscott wanted to find out just how the Germans had managed to achieve their salient. His investigation concluded that too little use of artillery by the 45th Division was the primary reason. It had resulted after communications broke down following casualties among those officers who normally called for fire support. Truscott arranged to meet with Brigadier General Carl A. Baehr, corps artillery officer and newly arrived at the beachhead, and with his former artillery commander with the 3rd Division, Major Walter T. "Dutch" Kerwin. At the meeting Truscott said to Kerwin, "Major, do you know what I mean when I say that I want all of the artillery fires of the Corps organized and coordinated just as they are on the front of the 3rd Division?" When Kerwin said he did, Truscott turned to Baehr. "General, your sole duty tonight is to accompany this young officer. If anyone questions his authority or any order that he may issue, you are to say, 'That is the Corps Commander's order.' Do you understand?" Baehr said he did, and to his amazement, he would see it all happen in one night. The following morning he reported to Truscott, saying, "I wanted to tell you that I have had the best lesson in artillery that I have had in thirty-five years' service in the artillery." Cavalryman Truscott suspected that it was not what the Artillery School taught, but it seemed to work well in this situation. Another former cavalryman agreed. Harmon later wrote: "The American artilleryman wrote a page in history at Anzio. His aim was deadly." On February 19 at 6:30 A.M., four hundred artillery and naval guns and more than two hundred U.S. Army Air Forces bombers supported the Allied advance as proposed by Truscott. The attack gained only a little territory, but it was enough to break the enemy offensive. Three days after its beginning, Operation Fischfang fizzled. The Germans had sustained more than 5,300 casualties; the Allies lost 3,500 men. The Germans attributed more than three-quarters of their casualties to artillery. Indeed, VI Corps had fired more than fifteen to twenty shells for each one the Germans fired.[11]

On February 22, in conversation with Truscott, Clark said he was relieving Lucas of command. Truscott protested, saying that relieving him would anger American officers, who would suspect that British criticism was the root of the replacement. He added that he and Lucas had a good working relationship, which could continue as such. Clark replied that the decision was final. Afterward Truscott went to give his regrets to his friend. "While Lucas was deeply hurt," he remembered, "he had no ill feeling toward me, and our friendship was unbroken up to the time of his death. But he was bitter toward General Clark and blamed his relief upon British influence. It was one of my saddest experiences of the war."[12]

Criticism of Lucas has lingered, citing his failure to attack the Alban Hills in particular, even though the evidence is more than sufficient that senior commanders had rushed the undersized invasion force ashore. The general became the designated scapegoat for Anzio, with some historians giving Churchill, Alexander, and Clark a pass. A promotion for Lucas disguised his relief, and he returned to the United States to begin a new assignment. He noted in his diary: "Alexander said I was defeated and Devers said I was tired. . . . And I thought I was winning something of a victory." To Lucas's credit was the accomplishment of keeping the port of Anzio working throughout bombing, shelling, and miserable weather and to bringing ashore 4,000 tons of supplies daily. Had he not done so, the eventual breakout, still months away, would not have been possible. General Marshall offered Lucas's services to Lieutenant General Lesley McNair, now commanding general of army ground forces, stating that he wanted to save Lucas's pride and reputation and yet still allow him make a meaningful contribution. McNair agreed completely.[13]

With the departure of General Lucas, the only reason Eisenhower did not send Patton to Anzio was that Truscott was already there; Truscott was also Clark's preferred choice. The general was not only very familiar with the situation, but Clark also likely viewed him as more manageable than the intractable Patton. Eisenhower had hoped to bring Truscott to England to lead a corps during the cross-channel invasion, but that would not be possible now. Had he known of Eisenhower's intentions, Truscott would have been disappointed to miss working for him again. Nonetheless, he fully understood the need for him to remain in Italy. His short assignment as deputy corps commander had already given him a much bigger picture of the Anzio operation than he had seen.[14]

The beachhead remained in serious trouble. Truscott knew he needed to make some substantial changes to renew confidence in the officers and men. He began by sitting down with Colonel Carleton and comparing notes. One thing on their list was reducing the anxiety among the corps headquarters staff regarding the incoming commanding general. Truscott later reflected: "Commanders are rather like old garments; the well-worn ones are usually the more comfortable. Commanders differ in personality and methods of command and few staff welcome the disruption of accustomed and established procedures." For this problem, the general brought with him several of his key staff from the 3rd Division. Their presence would aid the transition, letting the corps staff know informally what the new commander liked and disliked. Of course, the staff members needed to accept that a new general brought with him new rules. For one thing, corps headquarters general and special-staff sections would need to stay continuously up to date on all aspects of the beachhead. "I explained to them," Truscott recalled, "gently but *firmly* that I would expect full and accurate reports at eight o'clock the following morning and every day thereafter." From then on, the section chiefs and various commanders met each morning to present their reports, which kept not only Truscott informed but everyone else as well.[15]

It was also important that the British feel more welcomed at headquarters. Truscott's experience with Mountbatten's staff helped a great deal with this. In light of the American belief that British officers were behind Lucas's relief, Alexander sent Major General Vivian Eveleigh to help reduce tensions. Truscott could not have been more pleased. "It was General Eveleigh," he reflected, "who was primarily responsible for removing all previous causes of friction," adding that Eveleigh's "knowledge, boundless energy, and rare personal charm . . . were of inestimable value in establishing command relationships which were thenceforth to be a model for every Allied command."[16]

A symbolic effort inspired confidence among the troops. Previously, corps headquarters had operated from old wine-cellar caves in Nettuno. Since all division headquarters, the beach hospital, and other operations were above ground, it made sense that corps headquarters should be there as well. While not requiring all staff operations to do the same, Truscott, Carleton, and their immediate staff moved their own headquarters to an aboveground location, where they also maintained their sleeping quarters. It was less safe but demonstrated to the troops the general's willingness to share the danger they faced daily. Truscott later professed: "We learned to sleep through the nightly cannonading. But there were some narrow escapes."[17]

The next task was to improve antiaircraft defenses. Truscott gave this assignment to Major General Aaron H. Bradshaw. With the commander's assistance, Bradshaw was able to obtain just-developed, jam-resistant radar. Thereafter, he organized, directed, and controlled the sixty-four rapid-fire 90-mm antiaircraft guns and hundreds of smaller guns onshore and offshore. For those enemy aircraft that came in under the radar beam, Truscott suggested a "standing barrage." Bradshaw concurred, identified five firing sectors, and used a central gun-operations room employing radio and telephones to direct all fire. With all the guns in any one corps sector firing upward at the same time, any low-flying German plane would have to pass through a lot of lead, even if not well aimed. Within a month the beachhead defenders had shot down or damaged up to four hundred enemy aircraft. Faced with the now-organized defenses and the standing barrage, the Germans essentially gave up air strikes and relied instead on artillery.[18]

Although the Germans at Anzio used the monster Krupp Works 210-mm and 280-mm railway guns, dubbed by GIs as "Anzio Annie" and "Anzio Express," the Germans relied primarily on the plentiful and lethal 170-mm guns. Emplaced on surrounding hills, these guns had an accurate range of seventeen miles. The biggest VI Corps artillery weapon was the 155-mm Long Tom, which had a range of less than fifteen miles.[19]

General Baehr and his staff established the VI Corps Fire Direction Center to handle counterbattery operations. The Fire Center identified and mapped possible enemy artillery positions by aerial reconnaissance and photographs, sound and flash ranging, and observation. When one enemy gun began to fire from somewhere, every corps gun in range immediately fired on a preidentified target. This method expended a lot of ammunition, but the German tactic of advancing their guns from cover, firing up to thirty rounds in ten minutes, and then returning them to cover was defeated. Additionally, in an effort to confuse distant enemy guns that were out of range of Allied artillery, two army chemical-warfare companies handled another part of Truscott's antiartillery plan. Each day

A soldier of the 179th Chemical Smoke Company operates a smoke generator to conceal Fifth Army operations from German observation, Anzio beachhead, March 1944. Courtesy of the U.S Army and the National Archives.

these specialists pumped out a giant smokescreen that shrouded the beachhead during daylight hours.

A final effort brought some conflict with General Clark. All the various Fifth Army gasoline and ammunition dumps were dangerously concentrated without any concealment attempted. Truscott ordered army staff (Clark's command) to correct the problem. The immediate result was a message from Clark instructing him to stop telling army-headquarters personnel what to do. Truscott's protests that Clark had previously confirmed that the corps commander was in charge of all beach operations did not dissuade him. Truscott then suggested putting the units under VI Corps or perhaps assigning him as deputy army commander, but Clark declined both. Finally, the general sent Colonel L. K. Ladue to Anzio as senior Fifth Army representative. Truscott was pleased that Ladue made himself part of the team, effectively resolving the problem.[20]

With these matters attended to, Truscott set about reconfiguring his defenses. In particular, the British forces had suffered a severe mauling. Because they had been battling for years before the Americans had joined the war, the British army had depleted its pool of service-age men. Thus, as a consequence, the 56th Division was operating at about a quarter of its normal strength. Between February 24 and February 28, Truscott sent Clark messages detailing the desperate need for reinforcements. Exacerbating the problem was new information that the Germans were preparing yet another major attack. Clark eventually arranged for the British 5th Division to relieve the 56th Division and promised to send the U.S. 34th Infantry "Red Bull" Division in the near future.[21]

By February 28 Truscott was certain that the German attack was coming. He believed they would feint a push down the Via Anziate, but this time their strongest effort would come against the 3rd Division's front southwest of Cisterna. Truscott and artillery chief Baehr mapped every location where the enemy would likely assemble troops, tanks, and artillery; station reserves; position supply dumps; and establish command posts. He later remembered, "I now decided we should surprise the enemy before the assault began." On February 29 at 4:30 A.M., an hour before German artillery was expected and before any infantry emerged, every VI Corps gun began an hour-long barrage on the designated targets. Nonetheless, the Germans launched Operation Seitensprung. Truscott had previously called Clark to arrange all-out air support, and that evening he went forward to witness the result. "Our arrival on the 3rd Division front was timed beautifully with an Allied air mission over Cisterna as 100 or more medium bombers soared over the town and released bombs which fell fair and square on the target."[22]

Five VI Corps divisions now faced nine understrength enemy divisions, of which five were poised in front of the 3rd Division. A German feint came at the British sector to the west, but the American front between Carano and Isola Bella received the biggest punch—right where Truscott had expected it. The best success of Operation Seitensprung came against the 509th Parachute Infantry

Battalion attached to the 3rd Division. There, specially trained German pioneer (engineer) units used Bangalore torpedoes and wire cutters to eliminate the barbed wire, after which troops, shouting and even singing, poured through. Allied artillery and other guns responded. German estimates were that 66,000 shells—double that expended during Operation Fischfang—fell on them, causing nine hundred casualties. A second attack the next day also failed.[23]

Kesselring was not happy with the situation and fired off an angry and critical missive to his subordinate at Anzio, Colonel General Eberhard von Mackensen. The latter was in no mood for criticism and fired back a retort that his new replacement troops were young and undertrained. He suggested that a large breakout from the beachhead was inevitable, and that in order to be ready for it, the Germans would need more troops, additional supplies, and better tactics. Kesselring relented. He replied that since the weather would soon turn rainy anyway, German units should halt all operations except minor attacks intended to keep the Allies at a distance.

Realizing the Germans were in need of rest, Truscott planned a limited-objective attack, code-named Operation Panther, but canceled it when air support became unavailable. The general, well aware that his own men were also in need of rest, followed Kesselring's lead. A stalemate followed.[24]

Amid this, Truscott's throat condition worsened. On March 5 Carleton teletyped General Gruenther, Clark's chief of staff, requesting that a "laryngologist with equipment for complete laryngoscopic examination be sent to the beachhead for approximately one day's stay at 56 Evac hospital in order to do a complete examination of General Truscott's throat." An early dose of carbolic acid followed by decades of smoking, a steady supply of alcohol, the beachhead smokescreen, and unrelenting stress did not help his condition.[25]

Things were still not in hand at Cassino. The Benedictine monastery there, founded in A.D. 529 and now inaccurately thought to be a German artillery-observation point, had been bombed without mercy in mid-February. Even so, the Allied offensive there remained stagnant. Alexander reorganized his forces, telling his commanders to expect to launch an attack in early spring. Clark went to Anzio on March 19 to ensure that Truscott would be ready to initiate his breakout operation in conjunction with the Cassino push. Truscott said he would be ready and used the intervening weeks to reorganize, conduct further training, and rest his troops. He expected the 34th Infantry Division, the remainder of the 1st Armored Division, and possibly another division to arrive at Anzio in the near future. When that occurred, the 504th and 509th paratroopers and what remained of Darby's rangers would rotate out. Truscott anticipated that his breakout plan would employ the 3rd Infantry Division—in which he had the most confidence—as its spearhead. He withdrew the division, along with the 1st Armored, to the rear for special training. The remaining units would hold the front. The Germans rested and prepared their units as well. Neither side expected a big attack, but small attacks, supported by bombing and artillery, ensured that neither side got too comfortable.[26]

On March 22 a German artillery barrage of sixty 88-mm rounds fired from many miles away struck the Anzio hospital. The complex was not small, consisting of several hundred tents, each marked with a large Red Cross symbol, and collectively containing 2,500 hospital beds. The shelling killed five patients and a nurse and wounded about twenty patients, nurses, and doctors. When Truscott and his staff visited the compound, an irritated chief nurse marched up to the general and showed him a large shell fragment. She demanded to know what he was going to do about the situation. Truscott agreed to do more. Later during the tour, several injured soldiers took the occasion to ask if they could return to the front—where they thought it was actually safer. The general ordered his engineers to lower the hospital tents two feet into the ground, the maximum allowed by the high water table, and to sandbag the excavated earth around the sides of the tents to a height of four feet. For surgery rooms, his men were to cover the tops with timber and sandbags. It was an improvement and about all they could do.[27]

Over the months, the medical staff had somehow grown accustomed to working in the dangerous environment. Lieutenant LaVerne "Tex" Farquhar of the 33rd Field Hospital Group, when interviewed by a Red Cross correspondent, commented that the air and artillery attacks had become routine. What she found exhilarating now was helping save the lives of soldiers so severely injured to be near death. Not long after her interview, a German artillery barrage of the hospital area on February 10 killed Tex Farquhar. Three other Anzio nurses who remained at their operating-room stations during the bombardment later received Silver Stars for gallantry—the first World War II nurses to be so honored.[28]

In response to an artillery barrage that struck the 56th Evacuation Hospital, army combat engineers lower the medical tents into the ground and mound excavated earth around them, Anzio beachhead, April 1944. Courtesy of the U.S. Army and the National Archives.

Nurse June Wandrey received a "Dear Jane" letter from her army-officer boyfriend—safe and comfortable back in America—demanding that she come home or else. In a letter to her family, she complained that she could not just go to General Clark and demand a stateside assignment. Instead, she continued to live in a muddy tent, ducked when artillery shells exploded nearby, and went prone when German planes strafed the compound. When she finally made it home, her dress uniform displayed the battle stars she had earned from service in North Africa, Sicily, Naples, Anzio, Rome, southern France, and Germany.[29]

"No one who served at Anzio," Truscott later wrote, "will ever forget the gallantry of the medical personnel there, particularly the Army nurses. . . . At Anzio, there were no safe regions; every part was within range of German guns." These attacks killed doctors and nurses as easily as infantrymen. The hospital area, dubbed "Hell's Half Acre," treated over 26,000 battle casualties, 4,000 accidental injuries, and 18,000 cases of disease or illness, especially trench foot. One of the nurses who served at Anzio occasionally dined at the general's mess. She was 1st Lieutenant Mary Walker Randolph, Truscott's sister-in-law.[30]

Another witness to the miserable conditions at Anzio was war correspondent Ernie Pyle. "On the beachhead," he wrote, "every inch of our territory was under German artillery fire. There was no rear area that was immune, as in most battle zones." Those who did not have a stone building—and most did not—relied on digging to survive. Pyle remembered, "Italy was the first time our entire ground force had had to burrow beneath the surface. . . . [T]here must have been tens of thousands of dugouts, housing from two to half a dozen men each."[31]

Usually the front was flat and open, requiring soldiers to remain in shallow holes from daylight to dark; lifting one's head invited a sniper shot or machine-gun fire. Anyone slightly wounded might have to treat himself and then wait for dark to move to the rear. When they could, medics dashed forward to provide treatment. Of course, getting out of one's hole even at night could be risky. Sleep seldom came. After a week, the soldiers might rotate back. It was a subterranean existence reminiscent of World War I.[32]

Audie Murphy recalled his own foxholes in the rain and mud. "We slant the bottoms of our foxholes. Water drains to the lower ends; and we dip it out with our helmets. But when the storms really strike, we give up. For hours we crouch in ankle-deep water." Since the water table was high, not every location was suitable for digging. Shallow holes at the front usually had water at the bottom. When on occasion dry socks arrived at the front lines, soldiers had to change quickly lest their feet swell too large to get their boots back on. Murphy later wrote: "In the constant cold and wetness, feet turn blue, and flesh rots. I send the worst cases to the rear for treatment. The men are given cans of foot powder and promptly returned to the lines, still shivering and hobbling." Suffering for several days from a malarial attack, frustrated, and irate, Murphy called back to speak with one of the doctors, a captain, to tell him that soldiers came back to the front with minimal treatment. The doctor hesitated but said that he was aware of that. Surprised and livid, Murphy shouted: "You do! Well, goddammit don't shove them back up here with a couple of aspirins and a pack of foot powder." The captain shouted back, "Who do you think you're talking to, sergeant?"[33]

War correspondent Ernie Pyle visits soldiers of the 191st Tank Battalion attached to the 45th Infantry Division, Anzio beachhead, circa April 1944. Courtesy of the U.S. Army and the National Archives.

When taken off the line after a week or more, soldiers moved back to holes that were more elaborate. Because the soil was sandy, digging was not difficult. Men might cover the tops of the holes with logs or boards or occasionally a wood door from a bombed-out building. They scrounged material to keep the sides of their holes from caving in. Some shelters, if carefully selected, might stay dry. If not, the soldiers covered the bottoms with wood, straw, or whatever suitable material was available. Once candles became plentiful, they provided light and surprising warmth, though not quite as much warmth as the infrequent arrival of a bottle of cognac. Ernie Pyle recalled spending three nights in various holes and not waking up even though bombing or shelling was going on in the area. "That's what the combination of warmth, insulation against sound, and a sense of underground security can do for a man."[34]

Soldier-cartoonist Bill Mauldin with the 45th Infantry Division tried to give the folks back home just the slightest inkling of what it was like to be an infantryman at Anzio:

> Dig a hole in your back yard while it is raining. Sit in the hole until the water climbs up around your ankles. Pour cold mud down your shirt collar. Sit there for forty-eight hours, and, so there is no danger of your dozing off, imagine that a guy is sneaking around waiting for a chance to club you on the head or set your house on fire.
>
> Get out of the hole, fill a suitcase full of rocks, pick it up, put a shotgun in your other hand, and walk on the muddiest road you can find. Fall flat on your face every few minutes as you imagine big meteors streaking down to sock you.
>
> After ten or twelve miles (remember you are still carrying the shotgun and suitcase) start sneaking through the wet brush. Imagine that somebody has booby-trapped your route with rattlesnakes which will bite you if you step on them. Give some friend a rifle and have him blast in your direction once in a while.
>
> Snoop around until you find a bull. Try to figure out a way to sneak around him without letting him see you. When he does see you, run like hell all the way back to your hole in the back yard, drop the suitcase and shotgun, and get in.
>
> If you repeat this performance every three days for several months you may begin to understand why an infantryman sometimes gets out of breath. But you still won't understand how he feels when things get tough.[35]

CHAPTER 22

THE WAIT

Truscott waited for word from Clark on the expected push at Cassino. Whenever the attack order came, the troops at Anzio would not have much time and thus needed to maintain constant readiness. The heart of the breakout plan rested with Generals O'Daniel and Harmon, whose divisions would lead the assault. The two generals had the additional task of developing methods for getting through minefields, pillboxes, and the other death-inviting obstacles ahead. Tank drivers practiced lowering treadway bridges over antitank ditches and pushing Bailey bridges across divides. Creative soldiers designed various contraptions to either be pushed ahead over minefields or fired forward by mortar and dragged back, detonating mines before tanks or troops encountered them. Instructors provided special training in commando tactics, reconnaissance, and sniper response. Everything was ready by April, but no call to attack came.[1]

The Germans also waited. They had finished placing more landmines and stringing additional barbed wire. Near Cisterna, commanders positioned frontline platoons every three hundred yards, with up to eight machine guns interlocked and aimed low, mere inches above the ground. Reserve units waited to the rear in ditches and dugouts. Behind them were the big-gun emplacements.[2]

During the stalemate, despite daily shelling and occasional ground and air attacks, the days at Anzio calmed just slightly. "Life was tense as it always is when men live close to death," Truscott later reflected, "but we learned how to survive." Fresh meat and fish mysteriously appeared. Bill Mauldin recalled, "One rifleman at Anzio insisted that a cow had attacked him and that he fired in self-defense." He further noted, "It's astounding how many soldiers before cleaning their rifles squeezed off a couple rounds to loosen the dirt in the barrels and a cow just happened to be standing there." Truscott recalled that some of his soldiers dug up German landmines, exploded them in the sea, and collected the floating fish.

Comic signs appeared, bearing such wit as, "Beach Head Hotel, Special Rates to New Arrivals." Spring flowers decorated anything worth decorating, and the beachhead denizens played baseball and volleyball and enjoyed swimming in the blue Mediterranean, even when artillery rounds landed within five hundred yards of them. Truscott ordered flowers cut and delivered to the hospital area, where an occasional musical instrument, radio, or singing performance raised spirits. On occasion, a Scottish regiment played its bagpipes, the members sometimes wearing kilts. Axis Sally, ably assisted by her accomplice George, played music for the troops and spilled forth with laughable propaganda. Anzio was a deadly place to live, but even there, some relaxation was possible. "Without this," Truscott remembered, "I do not see how men could have survived the terrific nervous tensions under which they lived at Anzio."[3]

By mid-March General Alexander had completed reorganization of his forces at Cassino. The British V Corps, detached from the Eighth Army, would now handle the Adriatic side of the advance. Other Eighth Army troops, including Polish and New Zealander soldiers, would take a turn at the Cassino sector, emplacing on the line running from the Apennines to the Liri River. The main body of Clark's Fifth Army, consisting of the II Corps and the French Expeditionary Corps, would assume the fifteen-mile Garigliano sector from the Liri River to the Tyrrhenian Sea. It would be up to the Eighth Army to make the primary drive through the Liri and Sacco valleys, while Clark's forces, excepting Truscott's VI Corps, drove north along the western seacoast. At some point the Cassino forces and Anzio forces would meet up, so Clark hoped, on the road to Rome.[4]

The innovative plan was not a product of Alexander or of Clark but of Lieutenant General Sir A. F. "John" Harding. Unlike most senior British officers, Harding came from a middle-class family and a World War I commission in the Territorial Army. General Montgomery had noticed that Alexander needed a strong chief of staff and suggested to General Brooke that Harding might be the most capable candidate. By this time Alexander was ready to try anything that might pierce Kesselring's Gustav Line. Once on board, Harding quickly studied the situation and the Allied troop dispositions, reorganized them, and planned an elaborate ruse to make the Germans think another amphibious assault was coming. He next developed the tactics for the plan, code-named Operation Diadem, that would break through the Gustav Line. Clark, of course, saw

Major General Lucian K. Truscott, Jr., commander, VI Corps, and Lieutenant General Ira C. Eaker, commander, Mediterranean Allied Air Forces, inspect wine-cask-and-sandbag revetments used to protect the airport at the Anzio beachhead, April 1944. Courtesy of the U.S. Army and the National Archives.

Diadem as yet another British plot to steal from him the glory of Rome's liberation.[5]

The II Corps now had a new unit, the 85th Infantry "Custer" Division. It consisted primarily but not exclusively of draftees who were the products of accelerated combat training. Soldier Bill Hanrahan was typical of these young men. In 1942 he had enrolled in his college's

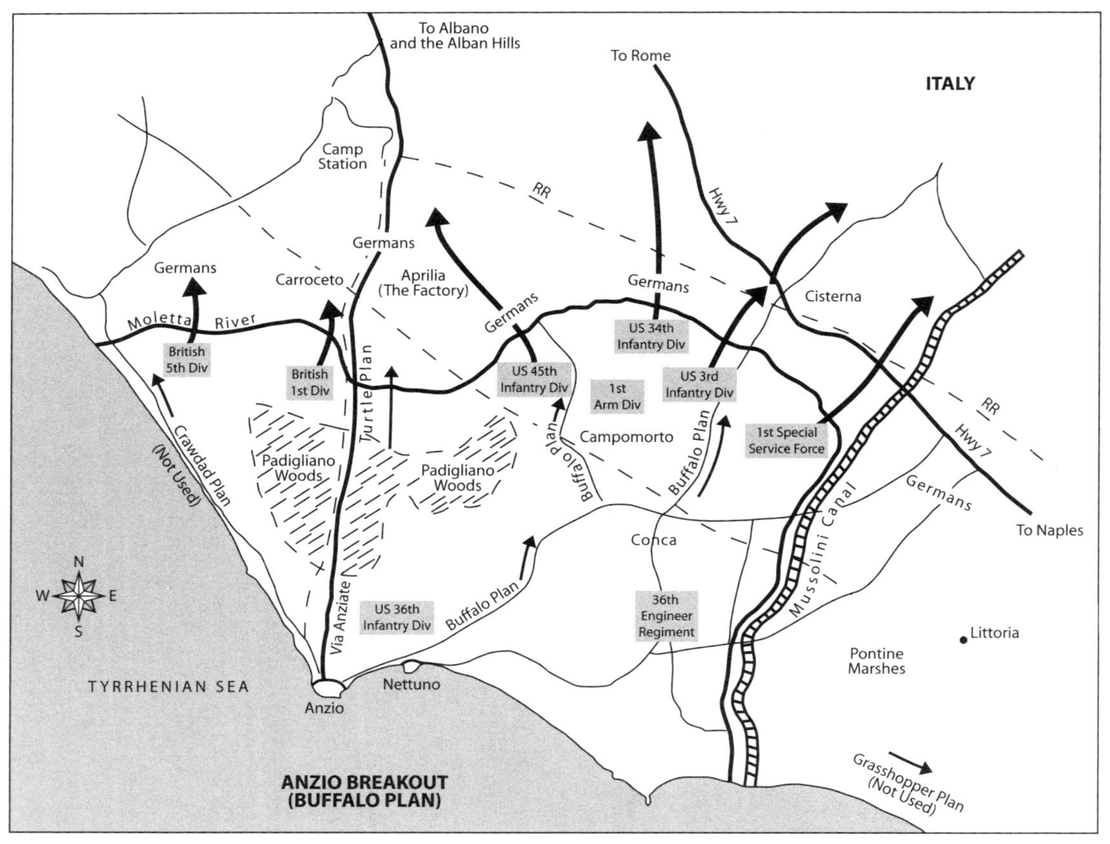

Buffalo Plan and the Allied breakout from the Anzio beachhead. Map by Megan Postell.

Reserve Officer Training Corps and enlisted in the reserves as well. Activated in February 1943, he attended basic and artillery training at Fort Bragg, North Carolina. He next found himself in North Africa, assigned to the 85th Infantry Division. Following mountain and amphibious training, he and his fellow soldiers expected to invade Yugoslavia but instead disembarked at Naples. Two days later his division arrived at a narrow coastal plain along the Tyrrhenian Sea near the mouth of the Garigliano River. There they assumed positions previously dug by British troops but then did more digging of their own. The vast majority of these soldiers had little interest in becoming senior NCOs or officers or in receiving battle decorations. Many would do so, of course, but most simply accepted that they had to fight and win the war before they could return home. As Hanrahan recalled: "The Germans shelled us occasionally, both day and night. In the Italian campaign, almost all the action was in the mountains. It was like starting at the Columbia River in Oregon and fighting your way along the Cascade Mountains to the Canadian border. . . . It was the kind of terrain where small, skilled enemy units could hold off ten times their number of attackers." After a while, Hanrahan and his fellow artillerymen even began to recognize some of the German units.[6]

Operation Diadem continued to call for troops from Anzio to break out and join with the Cassino forces once the latter punched through that position. Timing the Anzio breakout would be important, but any such plan would need to have built-in flexibility. In discussion with Clark, Truscott and his planners developed four breakout scenarios, each with its own code name. Turtle and Buffalo would be the primary plans, with Crawdad and Grasshopper as the backups. Turtle would be a fast grab for Rome, taking the Via Anziate through Aprilia and Campoleone to Albano on Highway 7, then following that road northwest to Rome. Truscott's troops were not keen on this plan because it was, essentially, what they had been trying to do without success for months. They had the casualty lists to prove it.

Buffalo would drive northeast to Cisterna, cross Highway 7, and then continue north to Highway 6 but remain east of the Alban Hills. The advantage here was that most of the German units would be positioned to defend against the objectives of Turtle. Buffalo also led to Rome, though indirectly via Highway 6, the inland road from Cassino to Rome. An additional advantage was that Highway 6 was the German communications and supply route as well as the likely line of retreat from Cassino. An added enticement was that it might result in the entrapment of an entire German army.

The other two plans were just-in-case scenarios. Crawdad would take the coastal route to Rome. It was the shortest distance, but its surrounding marshland precluded tank support. Grasshopper would be an attack in the opposite direction from Rome should it become necessary to join with Allied forces somewhere south of Anzio. Planners thoroughly fleshed out each option, which necessitated working twenty-four hours a day during the last two weeks of March. This extra effort was wasted, however, when the main attack at Cassino was delayed until April, then to May.[7]

On March 29, after Clark departed from a visit to Anzio, more than forty German bombers dropped their loads on the Allied positions. Truscott later noted why it was memorable for him. "This date . . . happened to be my twenty-fifth wedding anniversary. Just after I saw the General off in his plane that afternoon, the Germans provided the noisiest serenade in my twenty-five years of wedded life. . . . It was quite a show."[8]

In early April Alexander convened his generals and laid out the final plan. On May 10 part of the British Eighth Army would attack through Cassino and on into the Liri Valley. The U.S. Fifth Army (less the VI Corps at Anzio) would attack through mountainous terrain west of the Garigliano River and hit the flank of the German army, which the general hoped would be focused on stopping the Eighth Army's advance. Within twenty-four hours of receiving the order to break out, Truscott would push the VI Corps through Cisterna to Valmontone on Highway 6, cutting off the German retreat and capturing or killing as many of them as possible. Whatever remnant of the enemy evaded the trap would endure a high-risk flight to Rome. Truscott had no doubt that Rome was an objective, but he was certain that defeating the enemy was the goal."[9]

O'Daniel's 3rd Infantry Division, Harmon's 1st Armored Division, and one regiment of the newly arrived 34th Infantry Division would lead the attack. Other divisions would support the wedge that O'Daniel and Harmon hoped to hammer through the German defenses. There was much to do: orders prepared, continual reconnaissance conducted, hundreds of gun emplacements dug, thousands of rounds of ammunition delivered to concealed positions, telephone lines laid, and assembly areas and routes identified.

The limited road network at Anzio, including one that engineers had named "Truscott Boulevard," had to be used to full capacity without congestion, necessitating the strictest discipline on who could drive and when, all enforced by officers and military police. Everything, of course, had to be done quietly and invisibly so as not to arouse German suspicion.[10]

When he could, Lucian wrote letters to a worried Sarah. On April 7 he scribbled: "I'm damnably healthy except for my voice. Apparently I've got some kind of infection developing. . . . I thought of you and 25 years ago on our anniversary—I only wish that I could have sent you something, but there's no selection at the moment in Anzio Beachhead shops." Another letter on April 13 said: "I am afraid that the doctors will finally succeed in making me stop smoking. I stopped for ten days and . . . can notice myself that it affects my voice. I'm going to lay off another ten days and see what happens then." On April 16 he penned: "Do you realize that I have been gone now for two years? . . . I do get dreadfully homesick for you at times but fortunately for me I have work that has required complete concentration—and with the result that I have lack of time." His letter of April 19 was dreamier. "I can close my eyes and imagine Virginia countryside now . . . , the blue mountains and green trees."[11]

On May 5 General Alexander visited Anzio. Unlike Clark, who always appeared with a small force of correspondents and photographers, Alexander arrived with only one aide. After Truscott explained with some pride the four breakout scenarios possible, he recalled, "General Alexander . . . let me know very quietly and firmly that there was only one direction in which the attack should or would be launched, and that was from Cisterna to cut Highway 6 in the vicinity of Valmontone in the rear of the German main forces [at Cassino]. He had, he said, reserved to himself the decision as to when he proposed to initiate it." Only later did it occur to him why Alexander had come to tell him personally that Cisterna to Valmontone (Buffalo) was the *only* route to be taken. Truscott's routine report to Clark summarized this conversation and reported the general's stated desire for Buffalo. A furious Clark arrived at Anzio the next day, declaring that he was "irked at General Alexander's 'interference.'" Clark acknowledged the clear benefits of Buffalo but ordered Truscott to keep all four scenarios up to date. He reminded his subordinate that Rome was the important objective and the British wanted to get there first.[12]

General Sir Harold Alexander, commander in chief of Allied armies, awards the Honorary Companion of the Most Honorable Order of the Bath to Major General Lucian K. Truscott, Jr., San Marco, Italy, April 1944. Courtesy of the U.S. Army and the National Archives.

Alexander's main drive from Cassino began on May 11. Bill Hanrahan recalled that things had been static at his position near the Garigliano River, but at 11:00 P.M. that day things changed drastically. The engineers had built a bridge over the river on which artillery trucks pulling the big guns and ammunition now rumbled. On occasion, the vehicles came to villages where the engineers had leveled demolished building fronts into a roadbed, sometimes seven feet high. Everyone knew the job was to get to Rome. Hanrahan's 329th Field Artillery Battalion had three batteries, each of which had four (and later six) 105-mm howitzers. His job was that of fire-control coordinator for one of the batteries. "The Germans fell back but in a very skilled and orderly way," he recalled. The Germans were certainly not fond of Allied air and tank attacks, but most of all they had come to dread the volume and accuracy of American artillery fire.[13]

On May 17, three months after the bombing of the monastery and after a week of bitter fighting, Polish, French, British, Canadian, and American troops broke through the Cassino line and began the drive north through the Liri Valley. Keeping in mind the possibility of having to respond to yet another amphibious assault near Rome, Kesselring had no choice but to pull one of his best divisions from Anzio and send it south in hopes of blunting the Allied attack.[14]

Clark gave the order to launch Buffalo on May 23 at 6:30 A.M. Truscott's artillery had been routinely firing barrages every morning for weeks. The Germans had become used to the shelling and regarded it as a routine annoyance. The shelling on May 23 was seemingly no different. Truscott recalled there had been "no sight or sound to indicate that more than 150,000 men were tensely alert and waiting." The general looked at his watch and jingled the lucky coins and key in his pocket. "For better or worse," he knew, "the die was cast as the minute hands of watches moved slowly toward the zero hour." Truscott studied the sky just before dawn. The night rain had stopped and the still-faint sunrise promised a clear day. At precisely 5:45 A.M., more than 1,000 VI Corps big guns let loose. Tanks, tank destroyers, mortars, and cannons shot forth. Next, hundreds of machine guns began firing. After forty minutes, Army Air Forces fighters and bombers arrived and for five minutes pummeled the Germans below. Then the artillery resumed. The time for the infantry to leave their foxholes now arrived. Each soldier hoped it would be the last time he left his particular hole and that by the end of the day he would still be around to climb into another one elsewhere, hopefully farther ahead. The Germans waited in ditches, behind barriers, and within fortified stone buildings. The land over which the Allied infantrymen slogged would lead to graves for many.[15]

Truscott's plan was to send forth his troops in four major and two minor attacks. The 1st Armored and part of the 34th Division would attack between Cisterna and Velletri, aiming to cut Highway 7. The

3rd Division would attack Cisterna and encircle it. The 1st Special Service Force would attack northeast along the Mussolini Canal toward Highway 7, staying southeast of Cisterna and protecting the right flank of the breakout. The 45th Infantry Division would expand the breakout to the west toward Carano. The remainder of the 34th Division would hold the frontline as needed, then move to corps reserve. The just-arrived 36th Infantry Division would stand by to pass through the 3rd Division when ordered to do so. Per Alexander's instructions, Truscott would not use the British divisions, now at 60 percent of their normal strength, as part of the breakout. Instead, they and the 36th Engineer Regiment would make limited attacks along their fronts to hold the Germans in place. Thus, the breakout assault would consist exclusively of U.S. troops.[16]

Staff Sergeant Audie Murphy readied his platoon. "Under the spinning shells we turn from the holes in which we have cowered for nearly four months and march toward the enemy. Directly overhead our 50-caliber machine guns lay a cover of bullets that crack in their passing like millions of bullwhips. . . . The first major task of my company is to cut the railroad running south of Cisterna." The initial attack would be over canals and ditches, up hills, and down ravines. Beyond these, the land would open up, allowing tanks to come up and operate. Then the troops would encounter more ravines, woods, streams, and vineyards. German resistance was intense, but by day's end most VI Corps units had achieved their objectives. Fighting continued the next day, with U.S. fighter-bombers arriving to help beat off enemy counterattacks. German defenses began to collapse, though not everywhere. Overall, Truscott was satisfied, yet his troops still had much to do. "It was clear we were through the main German defenses," he recalled. Now the tantalizing possibility of capturing an entire German army lay before them.[17]

That afternoon Clark arrived at Truscott's command post and asked him if he were considering any shift in his attack toward the northwest and Rome. Truscott said it was still at least a possibility, but only if the Germans reinforced in strength around Valmontone. Clark ordered continual updates and left.[18]

By May 25 the 3rd Division had taken Cisterna. It had required three brutal days of fighting, during which soldiers of the division carried the heaviest load. For four of these men, one of whom had just arrived and was in his second day in combat, the battle resulted in Medals of Honor. Coincidently, on that same day, two

Colonel William O. Darby, original commander of the U.S. Army Rangers, shown here as commander of the 179th Infantry Regiment, 45th Infantry Division, San Marco, Italy, April 1944. Courtesy of the U.S. Army and the National Archives.

U.S. engineering units encountered each other: the 36th Engineer Regiment of the VI Corps and the 48th Engineer Regiment, along with the 91st Reconnaissance Regiment, of General Keyes's II Corps. With this link up of two parts of the Fifth Army, the struggle at Anzio had ended and the battle for Rome was on. Clark raced from his command post to be at the meeting of these two units. It took him three hours to arrive, necessitating a restaging of the event for the general and the more than two dozen correspondents and photographers who traveled with him.[19]

U.S. soldiers near damaged railroad station at Cisterna, Italy, northeast of the Anzio beachhead, following the breakout of May 1944. Courtesy of the U.S Army and the National Archives.

When a cheerful Truscott returned to his command post late in the afternoon, he found Brigadier General Donald W. Brann, Clark's chief of operations, waiting. "The Boss," Brann began, referring to Clark, "wants you to leave the 3rd Infantry Division and the Special Force to block Highway 6 and mount that assault you discussed with him to the northwest as soon as you can." Truscott could hardly believe what he was hearing. "I was dumbfounded," he remembered. The enemy was in strength where Clark wanted him to go. The only sane thing to do, Truscott protested, was to get his forces to the Valmontone Gap to be in position to destroy the retreating German army, the same force that had escaped from Sicily and Salerno and had held the Allies at bay at Cassino and Anzio. Allowing them another chance to escape would mean fighting them all the way to the Alps, with many Allied deaths guaranteed. Truscott refused to comply with the order until he could talk personally with Clark. Brann said the general was away from the beachhead and unreachable—even by radio. He repeated that Clark wanted it done: "There's no point in arguing. It's an order." "Such was the order," Truscott later wrote, "that turned the main effort of the beachhead forces from the Valmontone Gap and prevented the destruction of the German X Army." In essence, Clark was ordering Truscott to take part of his units from Buffalo and use it to conduct Turtle, all contrary to Alexander's explicit instructions to Truscott.[20]

Even though Clark was supposedly traveling from Anzio to the southern front and out of radio contact, Brann radioed him at 4:00 P.M.—only a short time after the meeting with Truscott—to say that Truscott was in complete agreement. Clark's diary indicates that he was meeting with his chief of staff at his main command post that afternoon. Historians Graham and Bidwell assert that the army commander had gone to what became the restaging of the link up of the 36th and 48th Engineer Regiments.[21]

The bulk of Truscott's troops were to turn northwest toward Rome; a smaller force was to continue on to Valmontone. Thus, Clark could tell Alexander with a somewhat straight face that he was still pushing in the direction that Alexander had ordered. Yet what had been a flow of troops toward Valmontone now became a dribble. By splitting Truscott's forces, Clark sent too few troops to the northwest, where the strongest force of Germans remained, and too few troops to Valmontone, where the Germans from Cassino were in retreat. Perhaps he had forgotten his West Point reading of Carl von Clausewitz's classic book, *On War,* which asserts, "The destruction of the enemy's military force is the leading principle of War, and for the whole chapter of positive action the direct way to the object."[22]

Truscott met with his division commanders and presented Clark's redirection, mustering as much enthusiasm for it as he could. His aide, Captain James M. Wilson, was present and recalled a "fairly stormy session, and both Iron Mike and Ernie Harmon, who were not known for their reticence, protested loudly, as did the others, but to no avail." Several divisions and miscellaneous units, all charging forward, had to be stopped, pivoted, and redirected by sidestepping and crisscrossing on limited and congested roads. Truscott recalled, "A more complicated plan would be difficult to conceive."

Only a good staff coupled with trained and disciplined troops allowed it to work.[23]

Having sent Brann to break the news to Truscott, Clark now broke it to Alexander, though twenty-four hours later. The news came not in person but through routine report distribution via his chief of staff, General Gruenther. It did not address either violating the spirit of Alexander's orders or splitting of Truscott's forces. When informed of the change of plans, a perplexed Alexander proceeded directly to Clark's command post. There, he found only Gruenther present to explain literally the turn of events. Clark, by absenting himself from any discussion with an incredulous Truscott and by presenting Alexander with a fait accompli, succeeded in his desires. The British general said to Gruenther that he assumed that Clark would continue his push to Valmontone. Gruenther replied that his boss had in mind the undertaking of a vigorous action. It was not quite the direct "yes" that Alexander preferred.[24]

Along the route to Rome designated by Clark, German units waited in strength and exactly where Truscott thought they would be. The 3rd Panzer Grenadier Division, the 65th Division, and part of the 4th Parachute Division blocked the Turtle route. While the 3rd Division and 1st Special Service Force pushed on to Valmontone, the 1st Armored Division; the 34th, 36th, and 45th Infantry Divisions; and associated units attacked northwest for two days, suffering heavy losses while making little progress. Then on May 30 Truscott got some good news. Major General Walker of the 36th Division reported that his scouts had discovered a gap in the German lines that might allow units to reach the tops of the Alban Hills near Velletri on Highway 7. He thought that with engineers doing some fast work, even tanks could climb their way through. Truscott gave permission to proceed. A turning point was at hand. The task was not easy, however; the engineers had to turn a path for wagons and pedestrians into a tank road. Correspondent Eric Sevareid watched them do it: "Scrambling around the tanks, we found the ubiquitous bulldozer, simply carving the trail into a road, roaring and rearing its ponderous way at a forty-degree angle upward. This was all madly impossible and yet it was being done."[25]

Near Valmontone, Hanrahan and his comrades in the 85th Infantry Division, II Corps made contact with the 3rd Division. By June 3, units were approaching Lake Albano, and reports were coming in that the Germans were retreating. A small gap in the enemy line, a fortuitous discovery, had pulled Clark's bacon from the fire once again. Perhaps ironic, the same division that he had sent across the Rapido River had made the discovery.[26]

On June 3 Truscott's friend, correspondent Mike Chinigo, met with him in the evening. He had heard at an Anzio press conference that General Clark and II Corps would enter Rome the next morning; Chinigo intended to go along with them. Truscott suggested that if he wanted to get to Rome before the other correspondents, he should stay with VI Corps. Chinigo knew the general well enough by now to take the advice.

The next day units of the 36th and 85th Divisions and the 1st Armored converged on the outskirts of Rome. There was some disagreement between General Walker and Lieutenant Colonel Louis V. Hightower of the 1st Armored as to who should proceed first into the ancient capital. Truscott arrived and reminded Walker that he was out of position, then spoke to Colonel Hightower and asked if he knew his orders. Hightower replied that he was to capture the bridges over the Tiber River. "Well, Colonel," Truscott asked, "what are you waiting for?" The general then turned to Chinigo and said, "Well, Mike, if you want to be the first correspondent in Rome, you had better follow that leading tank." Chinigo did—and was.[27]

The following morning Clark ordered Truscott to meet him in the city. Truscott had never before been to Rome, nor had his aide, Captain Jack E. Bartash, who fortunately spoke Italian. The next day, with an Italian boy voluntarily perched on the Jeep hood pointing out turns, Truscott and Bartash navigated the urban roads to Capitoline Hill, where Mussolini had so often harangued the crowd. Along the way, large crowds offered flowers, wine, bread, fruit, and hugs. Clark was supposed to be there but was nowhere in sight. With the young Italian hood ornament still in place, Truscott and Bartash drove around until they encountered the general's unmistakable entourage of scores of staff officers and hundreds of correspondents and photographers. Before he knew it, an uncomfortable Truscott found himself standing with Clark and others on a building balcony from which the army commander was giving a speech. Truscott listened but heard little. Let Clark posture, he likely thought, I need to get back to the war.[28]

Correspondent Sevareid was in Rome that day and heard Clark say, "This is a great day for the 5th Army." Given no recognition by the general were the British, French, and other Allies who had fought just as hard as the Americans. Sevareid later wrote: "That was the immortal remark of Rome's modern-day conqueror. It was not, apparently, a great day for the world, for the Allies, for all the suffering people who had desperately looked toward the time of peace. It was a great day for the 5th Army."[29]

Truscott went back to work, taking his corps eighty-five miles north of Rome. Along the way they captured two of the despised Anzio Annie/Anzio Express railway guns, each sixty-five feet long and capable of firing 700-pound, 280-mm projectiles. Truscott then paused to prepare for his next assignment. A few days after Rome's liberation, Clark had informed him that he would next land his VI Corps on the southern coast of France while Clark and the rest of the Fifth Army continued northward in Italy. Truscott's journey to France would be a temporary one, for the war in Italy would call him back. A terrible winter waited.[30]

More than a few military leaders, historians, and biographers have commented on Clark's actions in his desire to be first in Rome. Truscott later wrote: "There has never been any doubt in my mind that had General Clark held loyally to General Alexander's instructions, had he not changed the direction of my attack to the northwest on May 26, the strategic objective of Anzio would have been accomplished in full. To be first in Rome was poor compensation for this lost opportunity." General Harmon recalled: "The First Armored could—and should—have rolled onto Highway 6 and been in Rome in an hour and a half. . . . Unfortunately, on May 26 General Clark changed the battle plan." General Alexander said, "I had always assured General Clark in conversation that Rome would be entered by his army; and I can only assume that the immediate lure of Rome for its publicity value persuaded him to switch the direction of the advance."[31]

Senior German commanders were also critical. Kesselring later said that turning the French Expeditionary Corps and VI Corps would have encircled the German Tenth Army. German general Heinrich von Vietinghoff said that continuing the attack toward Valmontone would have resulted in the capture of Rome and most of the German units as well as the isolation of two German armies.[32]

Perhaps most ironic was the conclusion of Winston Churchill, who had rekindled the Anzio invasion in the first place and had sought Rome perhaps even more than had Clark. In a cable to Alexander, he stressed that cutting the German line of retreat was more important than capturing the city. A second cable a few hours later stressed that the capture of German divisions was the measure of the battle, not the capture of the Italian capital.[33]

Ironically, Clark outsmarted himself. Had he continued his full force to Valmontone, he almost certainly would have reached Rome earlier. Indeed, he could have captured a German army *and* been first in Rome.

As historian Martin Blumenson notes, Anzio had been a rush job: too few had invaded too quickly. Eventually, additional forces became available from the United States, the Middle East, and North Africa. Had the Allies postponed the operation until a larger force was available, taking the Alban Hills might have been possible immediately after landing. Alternatively, had those additional troops been assigned at Cassino, Anzio might have been unnecessary. Also, had Roosevelt supported Marshall instead of Churchill, the Allies would have held a line south of Cassino and launched the invasion into southern France closer in time to the Normandy invasion, as was originally intended.[34]

Clark's moment of glory was brief. The day after he liberated Rome, the Allies invaded Normandy. For him, the day was less happy than he had anticipated, seeing that the headlines featured Normandy rather than Italy. Rome's capture had become yesterday's news almost literally. Perhaps not sure who all he wanted to include in his epithet, he simply muttered, "The sons-of-bitches."[35]

Truscott was not Clark's favorite general. While General Lucas had consistently rated Truscott as number one on his officer-efficiency report, Clark rated him 7 out of 20, and 20 out of 250. That would change in the future, when Truscott once again served under Clark. By May 24, 1945, he would write of Truscott: "He has a thorough knowledge and quick grasp of military problems, particularly in combat, and makes sound and rapid decisions . . . , abundantly demonstrated strong physical and emotional stamina over long and very trying periods . . . , a quiet but forceful personality, coupled with obvious personal courage and determination, which inspires confidence and loyalty in all personnel associated with him." He rated Truscott as 1 out of 71 generals.[36]

On May 30, 1945, Truscott returned to Anzio to speak at a Memorial Day ceremony held at the as yet undedicated Sicily-Rome American

Cemetery and Memorial at Anzio-Nettuno. Bill Mauldin was there and heard the general speak. "When Truscott spoke, he turned away from the visitors and addressed himself to the corpses he had commanded here. . . . It came from a hard-boiled old man who was incapable of planned dramatics. The general's remarks were brief and extemporaneous. He apologized to the dead men for their presence here. He said everybody tells leaders it is not their fault that men get killed in war, but that every leader knows in his heart this is not altogether true. . . . Truscott said he would not speak about the glorious dead because he didn't see much glory in getting killed in your late teens or early twenties." The seventy-seven-acre Sicily-Rome American Cemetery and Memorial at Nettuno continues to honor the remains of 7,861 Americans.[37]

CHAPTER 23

SOUTHERN FRANCE, THE PERFECT INVASION

The 1944 Allied campaign in southern France might have been the perfect invasion except for two complications. The first involved a French commander who endeavored to run the show himself, regardless of General Truscott's wishes. The second involved one of Truscott's division commanders managing to irritate the general once too often. Eisenhower's original intent had been to invade both Normandy and southern France concurrently in June 1944. The concept was simple. While Hitler held one hand against the front door in the west and the other hand against the back door in the east, another Allied force would climb up from the basement stairs.[1]

By April 1944, however, Eisenhower had had to cancel the southern France operation. There were too few landing craft to carry and support two distant invasion forces at the same time. Now, a month after the Normandy landings, an invasion of southern France seemed to be a possibility after all. Forces in northwestern France had bogged down among the hedgerows of the *bocage,* while the Italian campaign was crawling on its hands and knees north of Rome. Eisenhower needed a catalyst to rattle the Germans, and an attack somewhere on the French Riviera might do it. By late June the second invasion was back on, with a target landing date of August 15. Not surprising, it would have to be another rushed amphibious assault. Previously code-named Operation Anvil, it became known as Operation Dragoon once the previous name appeared to be compromised. "As an old cavalryman," Truscott seemed to smile later, "I took this change of name to be of good omen."[2]

The plan called for the VI Corps and a reinvented French army of seven divisions to kick open Europe's basement door and seize the needed ports of Marseilles and Toulon. Thereafter, the Allies would roll north through the Rhône River valley, liberate Lyon and Dijon, and lock arms with the Normandy force, which by then should have debouched from the hedgerows. The coup de grâce would be to shove the Germans eastward into the monster jaws of the Soviet army, which by then would have broken through Germany's back door.[3]

All the lessons Truscott had learned from the invasions of North Africa, Sicily, Salerno, and Anzio would benefit the campaign in southern France. It was too late for him to be the invasion designer, but his experience would be invaluable in detecting problems and correcting them. Bill Mauldin remembered this operation as "the best invasion I ever attended." Sergeant Murphy was equally impressed, saying, "France had been calculated and prepared to the smallest detail; and it moved with the smooth precision of a machine."[4]

If Mauldin and Murphy saw it that way from ground level, why would anyone at the top have tried so hard to obviate the invasion? The answer was that the person at the top in question was Winston Churchill. Previously the biggest proponent for the Anzio landings, he was now the biggest opponent of invading southern France. He maintained that the Allies should finish Italy first and then move into the Balkans, not southern France. His frequent references to the soft underbelly of Germany took on a crusade-like urgency. Churchill peppered Eisenhower with every argument he could muster, but the general refused to budge. He had not succumbed to the prime minister's argument to forgo Operation Overlord, and he was not about to do so for Operation Dragoon. Not having much luck selling his Balkan strategy, Churchill rephrased his argument and advocated that Eisenhower should seize the ports in Brittany instead of the French Riviera. One of Eisenhower's aides, U.S. Navy captain Harry C. Butcher, recalled that during the marathon meeting, "Ike said no, continued saying no all afternoon, and ended saying no in every form of the English language at his command."[5]

Eisenhower's recollection of the difference of opinion was that it "brought up one of the longest-sustained arguments that I had with Prime Minister Churchill throughout the period of the war." He considered Churchill's argument to be political, not military. If the prime minister's concerns were political, Eisenhower rejoined, he should take them up with President Roosevelt. "But I did insist," he wrote, "that as long as he argued the matter on military grounds alone I could not concede validity to his arguments." The general argued for Operation Dragoon because he needed the major ports of Marseilles and Toulon to bring more troops, equipment, and supplies into France. Eisenhower acknowledged that the Port of Antwerp was desirable but reminded Churchill that the Allies had not yet captured it and that when they did, they would likely find it heavily damaged. He saw Dragoon as being more attractive because it would protect the right flank of the primary Allied invasion force as it rolled east through France and into Germany. He also argued that French troops, equipped at considerable American expense, could quickly depart Italy and North Africa and participate in operations; further, that once on French soil, they would fight hard for home and country. Finally, Eisenhower reminded Churchill that Roosevelt and the Combined Chiefs of Staff supported Dragoon. Churchill had little choice but to accept that he would not win this one; he later quipped that he had been "dragooned" into going along with it. Since he could not stop the invasion, he decided to attend what promised to be quite a show.[6]

The overall commanding general of the operation would be Lieutenant General Alexander M. "Sandy" Patch, who had recently commanded U.S. Army troops on Guadalcanal. With Patton's transfer to the Third Army, Patch assumed command of the Seventh Army. The general who would be in charge on the beach, however, would be Lucian Truscott, who probably knew more about leading amphibious landings than anyone else in Europe, maybe the world. Because his experience was vast, planners would need to listen to him, and he had more than a few things to tell them. Despite Churchill's resistance, ongoing planning for the landings never ceased. Even so, formal approval arrived just days before Dragoon's launch date.[7]

The VI Corps would continue to include the 3rd and 45th Infantry Divisions, both highly experienced. Truscott had also selected for his command the 36th Infantry Division. The latter's "hard luck" reputation from Salerno and the Rapido River, he suspected, had more to do with Mark Clark than with its soldiers, whose road from rookie to veteran had been fast and bumpy. He also knew firsthand that their performance during the Anzio breakout had been first rate.

Major General O'Daniel still commanded the 3rd Division, and Brigadier General Eagles still led the 45th Division, both of whom had been with Truscott at Anzio. Major General Dahlquist, who had taken General Walker's place, now commanded the 36th Division. Dahlquist's command experience was limited, and this would be his first command of troops in combat. He had served in the occupation army following World War I and, during the years between the wars, had worked mostly as a logistics, staff, or training officer. Back when Truscott had first arrived in England, Dahlquist had been one of the two generals in Northern Ireland who had professed wariness at American officers—including Truscott and his staff—working as part of British planning units. Now he was working for Truscott, and he soon would find himself on the wrong side of the general's temper.[8]

Prior to leaving Italy to plan another invasion, Truscott had accepted an invitation to visit the Vatican. In a June 15 letter to Sarah, he mentioned casually, "Yesterday I had an audience with the Pope." It was not a bad rise for a poor boy from frontier Oklahoma.[9]

Perhaps unnoticed by many was that the American officers and soldiers of the invasion force were far more experienced than most of those who had just landed at Normandy. Of some concern to Truscott was that the French forces, which would follow his VI Corps ashore, had less experience than his own soldiers. Compounding this was that many of these divisions consisted primarily of colonial soldiers from other countries under French dominion. Many of them could not speak French—which their officers spoke—or English. Even more problematic was that the commander of the French force, General Jean de Lattre de Tassigny, was adamant that he would serve under the U.S. Seventh Army only until Dragoon forces made contact with Patton's forces in the north. The odds of some sort of clash between Truscott and de Lattre were high.[10]

Upon arrival in Algiers, the general and his key staff met with planners already working on Operation Dragoon. It would be the first meeting between Truscott and General Patch. The two would not see eye to eye on everything but would get along well enough. "I came to regard him highly as a man of outstanding integrity," Truscott recalled, "a courageous and competent leader, and an unselfish comrade-in-arms." He was pleased to learn that General Marshall happened to be in Algiers at the time. In a subsequent visit between the two, Marshall made a point of telling Truscott that Eisenhower had earlier requested him for the Normandy invasion, which would have meant an army-level command. Of course, Truscott was up to his neck in Anzio at the time, Marshall lamented, and he had had to tell Ike that the general would remain in Italy. "I was deeply touched," Truscott recalled years later, "for there was no call upon General Marshall to tell me this. It was one of those generous and thoughtful things that always distinguished him in his dealings with his subordinates."[11]

Patch informed Truscott that the preliminary targets of Operation Dragoon would be Toulon and Marseilles. For political reasons, the capture of these two cities would be reserved for the French troops. The VI Corps would land first, seize the beachhead and inland areas, and maintain the front until the French came ashore the following day. From there Truscott's troops would protect the right flank of the French army as it moved west to capture the two port cities. None of this caused concern for Truscott, but he took occasion to stress the importance of a few things having to do with the initial landings. The first item was the need for the invasion-planning headquarters to relocate to Naples as quickly as possible and for the army, navy, and air forces planners to assemble there straightaway. He also emphasized the need for comprehensive training and, perhaps most important, a clear understanding of "undivided command responsibility during the initial phase." Patch and Truscott were in complete agreement.[12]

Originally, the French had wanted command of the entire invasion force, but senior officials disabused them of that notion early on. One U.S. general remarked to Truscott that if the French were in charge, they would be "insufferable." General de Gaulle, in fact, had sought overall command for the sake of French "honor." Since the French would eventually command seven of the ten divisions, and de Gaulle was on the ascendancy, Eisenhower and Patch had little choice but to permit accommodation where they could. After several iterations the general invasion plan was ready. The VI Corps would land on the Côte d'Azur, which Truscott later fondly recalled as "rather wildly beautiful," though the site was not selected for its beauty; direct assaults on Toulon and Marseilles were inadvisable. The good news was that military intelligence, maps, aerial photographs, and partisan assistance were all excellent. Fortunately, the thoroughly trounced German navy and Luftwaffe would not be a big factor during the operation.[13]

Beyond the famous Riviera rose the formidable two-thousand-foot Maures and Esterel Hills. Truscott was thankful that exits from the beaches were good and that a substantial interior road network allowed for movement west toward Toulon and Marseilles—even eastward to Cannes and Nice, if necessary. If airborne forces could seize the two hill masses, their possession would enhance protection of the seaborne landings.[14]

The invasion plan was comprehensive. For the month preceding the D-day of Operation Dragoon, Allied bombers would pound every potential target on the southern coast so as not to tip off where a landing might come. Then, some days before D-day, Marseilles would be bombed intensely to suggest that the invasion would go ashore there. The night before the main assaults, 1st Special Service Force commandos and French commandos would sneak ashore at two small islands and a mainland location to neutralize enemy coastal batteries. At the same time, French naval-demolition crews would block routes coming from the east to prevent any unwanted access to the invasion area. On August 15, invasion D-day, at 4:00 A.M., American and British airborne troopers from a provisional task force would drop down onto the rugged hills near Le Muy and attack enemy positions from the rear. In an effort to confuse the Germans, the Allies anticipated using some psychological warfare too. Small human-like dummies, clad in paratrooper uniforms, would drop by parachute. Later, Allied naval patrol boats would speed about offshore, presenting the appearance of conducting critical missions but assigned there simply to confuse the defenders. One of the patrol-boat captains would be cinema star Lieutenant Commander Douglas E. Fairbanks, Jr.

Just before 8:00 A.M., air and naval bombardment would soften up the targeted beaches for the invading divisions, which would land abreast along thirty miles of shoreline. On the left, near Saint-Tropez, the 3rd Infantry Division would land; in the center, in the area of Sainte-Maxime, the 45th Infantry Division would go ashore; and on the right, close to Saint-Raphaël and Frejus, the 36th Infantry Division would hit the beach. Once the beachhead was under control, a French armored brigade would land farther to the left of the VI Corps; the rest of the French forces would arrive on D-day plus three. The entire invasion force then would move toward Toulon and Marseilles. Following capture of those two ports, the VI Corps and the French force would turn north and drive through the Rhône Valley, eventually linking up with Patton's Third Army. The photo-perfect route, adorned with tree-covered slopes and accessorized with small towns and villages studded with steepled churches and overlooked by the famous Mont Ventoux, would not be too beautiful to suffer war.[15]

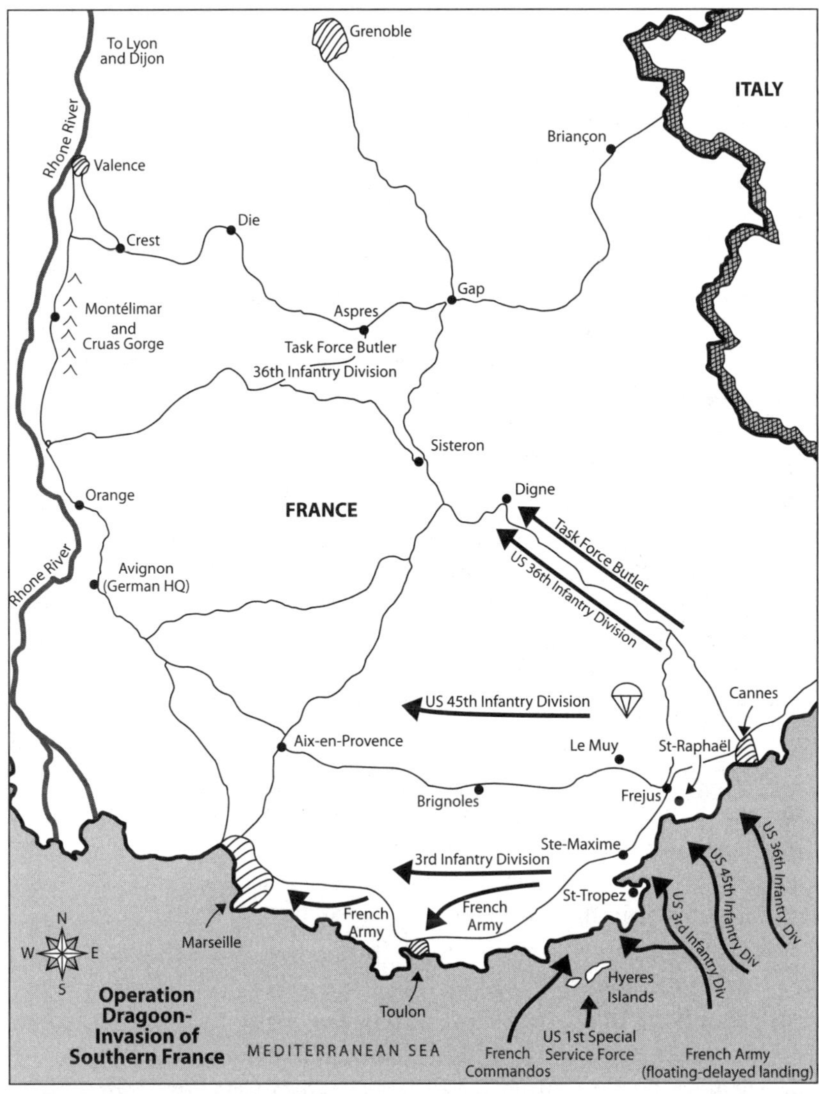

The Allied invasion of and early follow-up campaign in southern France. Map by Megan Postell.

Waiting onshore for an anticipated Allied invasion was the Nineteenth Army, headquartered in Avignon and commanded by General Friedrich Wiese. This force consisted of eleven divisions, including two panzer divisions, and miscellaneous units of artillery, tanks, and coastal guns. Wiese had little doubt that a Riviera invasion was coming, but exactly when and where was a guess. Thus, he and his superior, General Johannes Blaskowitz, commanding Army Group G and charged with protecting all of southern France, had to determine how best to defend Toulon, Marseilles, and the southern beaches. Wiese and Blaskowitz had other problems as well. They had already sent some of their units north to prevent the Normandy breakout, and other units were already dedicated to preventing another seaborne invasion along the French Atlantic Coast. German air and naval support was essentially unavailable, and French Resistance fighters had become emboldened by Allied progress. The Resistance, in fact, had blossomed into quite a force. German soldiers at risk of capture much preferred that such happen by the Americans rather than these French fighters. As Bill Mauldin later noted: "The Germans know how much the people hate them. When they surrender, most Germans say, 'we are regular Army—not SS.' Maybe they feel a little less guilty."[16]

"Frejus was a critical area," Truscott remembered. "Our best route inland followed the Argens River valley northwest from Frejus." His forces needed to take the whole valley, but first they needed to capture the German airfield at that town. Doing so would allow for closer Allied air support, ensure a safer beach and harbor for the initial landing and resupply, and protect the primary route inland. The job of taking the airport fell to thirty-seven-year-old Major General Robert T. Frederick, a 1928 West Point graduate who had created and until recently led the airborne- and commando-trained 1st Special Service Force. Even before Anzio, the regimental-size unit had received praise for its aggressive night- and mountain-combat ability. While fighting there under Truscott, it had earned the sobriquet of "Black Devils of Anzio," with Frederick himself dubbed the "Head Devil." Bumped up a star from brigadier, he now commanded 10,000 men of the 1st Airborne Task Force. He had turned down command of the 36th Infantry Division to stay with an airborne unit. His concept of being a leader was to be out in front, which he usually was. By war's end Frederick would hold two Distinguished Service Crosses, two Distinguished Service Medals, and not one or two but eight Purple Hearts. His newly assigned task force included various units of American and British paratroopers, his own 1st Special Service Force of Americans and Canadians, a Japanese American antitank company, and recently assigned glider troops, whose only training had been a quick-study program given them near Rome by the general himself. As this amalgam of units had never before fought together, its mission success was a gamble, though one Frederick was comfortable taking.[17]

While the 36th and 45th Divisions trained at the Invasion Training Center, the 3rd Division, by now the pros of amphibious landings, conducted its own training. Truscott insisted on a full-dress rehearsal for all three divisions, of course, and afterward remarked, "Few divisions have ever been better prepared for the task which lay ahead." The armor for the VI Corps would come from the French. Brigadier General Aime M. Sudre, commander of an armored brigade of the French 1st Armored Division, who would work under Truscott, came to see him on July 5 to clarify the French mission. Truscott said that the French armored force would land on the beach near Frejus and then most probably strike west to assist in taking Toulon and Marseilles. Enthusiastic about his new assignment, Sudre departed but first extended to Truscott an invitation from his superior, General Jean Touzet du Vigier, commanding general of the 1st Armored Division, to inspect French troops, then at Oran. Truscott agreed to do so, and on Bastille Day, July 14, received a formal invitation signed by General du Vigier. On July 18 Truscott and several of his staff flew to Oran for the review. "Brigade looks very good indeed. Men alert, and new equipment," Truscott's aide jotted down in the corps journal afterward.[18]

On July 20 de Lattre, whose French forces would follow the Americans onshore, returned to Naples and sent an officer to invite Truscott to lunch that very day. The general made time in his schedule so that he and French-speaking Lieutenant Colonel Conway, who had rejoined Truscott's staff, could present themselves for lunch at de Lattre's plush villa. The lunch also included Sudre and du Vigier as well as twenty or so of de Lattre's staff and his division commanders. Truscott's first impression of de Lattre was that he was very fit and displayed a strong military bearing. The disconcerting thing about him was the cold stare he gave the American; also, every French officer present appeared as nervous as a child just scolded by a raging parent.

Following lunch, de Lattre and Truscott, with Conway interpreting, retired to a side room along with the French officers. As the door closed behind them, Truscott was startled when de Lattre "launched into a tirade." An impatient Truscott could hardly wait for Conway's recitation of de Lattre's vehement comments. "As translated by Conway," he learned, "I found I had violated the normal niceties of military and diplomatic protocol by inspecting one of his units without his permission and without his presence." When Truscott heard something about "a slight to him and to the honor of France," he stopped the tirade right there. Thereafter, Conway worked overtime, letting de Lattre know that Truscott thought it entirely proper to inspect French soldiers who would be under his command; furthermore, the inspection had been arranged by formal invitation. "If that was all that he had to discuss," the American general fumed, "we were wasting our time." De Lattre, somewhat collected, invited Truscott to discuss other issues more privately, with Conway and de Lattre's chief of staff the only other officers in the room. The others officers remained in the outer room, appearing stunned by their boss's scathing ambush. In a few moments of translated French, Truscott realized that what de Lattre was really upset about was that *his* French armored brigade would serve under Truscott's command. The French general remonstrated that de Gaulle himself had promised the armored unit to him whenever he wanted it, most certainly by D-day plus three. De Lattre now demanded to know what the American intended to do with the brigade. In a reasoned voice Truscott said he would be happy to keep de Lattre informed of all plans but clarified that "any idea he should review and approve or disapprove them was of course entirely unacceptable." The Americans then excused themselves.[19]

Truscott reported this episode to General Patch. The latter, obviously irritated at de Lattre, assured him that the French general commanded three colonial divisions and the remainder of an armored division but not the French armored brigade assigned to Truscott. Furthermore, whenever Truscott released the brigade, it would move to Seventh Army reserve, not to de Lattre's command. By the time Truscott returned to his headquarters, apologies were already in from Generals Sudre and du Vigier. Sudre, in particular, stressed to Conway that he looked forward to serving under the American's command and would do so until released.[20]

Nevertheless, Truscott had a bad feeling about the continued availability of the armored force. It was like sticking a weakened cotter pin back into an unexploded grenade: it was safe for the moment, but enough pressure could easily release it. Truscott needed a fallback plan. He attempted without success to get an American armored brigade assigned to his corps, nor could General

Patch assure him with certainty as to how long he would be able to keep the French unit. Truscott elected to assume that once ashore, de Lattre, perhaps assisted by General de Gaulle, would manage to pull the release pin on the French armored brigade. Since having some kind of an armored force was essential for any drive north, he decided to piece together his own armored force from the American units at hand. He had become used to matching wits against German commanders, placing himself in the other's position and then rethinking his own. Now it appeared that he might have to do the same with his French Allies.

Truscott elected to appoint his assistant corps commander, Brigadier General Fred B. Butler, to lead "Task Force Butler," a provisional armored force. Truscott's headquarters would supply its staff and communications, and the 36th Division would provide cavalry and reconnaissance squadrons, armored field artillery, motorized infantry, various general-service troops, and engineer, tank, and tank-destroyer battalions. The task force would not assemble immediately but would be preassigned and on alert to converge immediately when called upon. The limitation of such an ad hoc unit was that it would never be as strong as a regular armored brigade would be, nor would its troops and commanders have the opportunity to train together. Nonetheless, at least Truscott would have something of an armored force when he needed one. He discussed with Butler three likely armored missions and told him to begin preliminary planning.[21]

CHAPTER 24

ATTEMPTING A CANNAE

The invasion machine fired up. Various parts of what would become a combined fleet set a course for the rendezvous site. Ironically, the soldiers who would splash ashore had no idea where they would land. Everyone knew an invasion was at hand, but most thought it would be somewhere in northern Italy. The VI Corps shipped out from Naples and various small ports from Salerno to Pozzuoli; the French II Corps departed from Taranto and Brindisi at the heel of Italy's boot; Sudre's French armored brigade sailed from Oran; and other ships eased away from docks at Palermo and in Sardinia and Corsica. On August 12 Truscott and Patch stood together on the deck of their command ship, USS *Catoctin,* where Patch emphasized that Truscott would run his own battle. It was just what the general wanted to hear. The total fleet consisted of 885 ships and landing vessels, 1,400 landing craft, 150,000 soldiers and sailors, and more than 20,000 armored and transport vehicles. Truscott's portion included 450 ships carrying 95,000 soldiers and more than 11,000 vehicles. They all gathered near Corsica and then in the late evening pointed bows toward southern France. Battleships, cruisers, and destroyers prepared to provide fire support on request. It would take only a matter of hours to deposit the soldiers and their vehicles on the beaches. More than once having been critical of the U.S. Navy, Truscott was more than pleased this time. "Our admiration for the professional ability of our Naval comrades was boundless, and our respect for their achievement in this complicated operation was profound." Finally, he had an invasion that pleased him. "Few operations of such magnitude have been planned more cooperatively or mounted more efficiently than [Operation] Anvil [Dragoon]," he recalled.[1]

The night before the main landing, in pitch dark 2,300 soldiers of the 1st Special Service Force, with blackened faces, used small rafts to approach two small islands housing coastal artillery that threatened the landing. Several times a German searchlight swept over the force, requiring the soldiers to stop paddling and get low in their rafts. Herbert Morris remembered paddling up to the side of a cliff about fifty feet high. A small ledge below the waterline allowed the soldiers an assist in ascending the cliff with ropes. Once on top they discovered that the artillery they had intended to destroy were actually dummy guns—with a little creative disguise, drainpipes had passed for artillery. The German soldiers had withdrawn to nearby forts protected by thick walls. It would take three days of fighting before they surrendered.[2]

Next in were the airborne and glider contingents. More than 500 C-47 troop planes carried sticks of paratroopers or towed more than 450 troop-loaded Horsa and Waco gliders. As the green light came on to indicate arrival over the drop zone, one of the first paratroopers out the door was Lieutenant Colonel William P. Yarborough. He later remembered that he jumped into darkness so complete that he could see nothing; in fact, his landing was something of a surprise. He remembered that the only thing he could hear was his own heart, which was beating quite loudly.[3]

The Germans had prepared a special welcome for the fragile gliders: antiglider poles with impact-sensitive explosives attached, which protruded from the ground like deadly spines on a humongous cactus petal. The pilots touched down without brakes at ninety miles per hour, doing their best to miss not only the deadly poles but also the many rocks and trees. Even worse would be running into another glider, which was very possible as each pilot descended while hyperfocused on finding his own patch of forgiving turf on which to land. Passenger Bill Leas recalled that his glider's pilot was just about to set down when another aircraft came from the left and landed just in front of them. Leas's pilot pulled hard on the stick and gained just enough elevation to clear a group of trees. It then sliced the surface of soft, recently plowed dirt, resulting in the glider nearly doing a nose stand, stopping just short of vertical before falling back to the earth on its belly. Leas wasted no time in getting out of the plane, the first soldier on his side to do so.[4]

At first light on a hazy morning, U.S. Army Air Forces planes and navy ships greeted the Germans. The bombers pummeled the beaches and interior locations. They had hardly finished when the battleships, cruisers, and destroyers released their own steel-encased destruction. The soldiers who would land soon cheered at the sight of flashes and rising smoke onshore, hoping the show would go on much longer than it did. Watching from the railing of a British destroyer in the morning daylight, Prime Minister Churchill stood mesmerized. He had not been able to witness the bombs dropping and the ships firing, nor had he seen the panorama of parachute canopies popping open as airborne troops descended or gliders detaching from their mother ships in search of a soft place to land. He had not even been able to see the first waves of landing craft motoring forward to drop their troops on some of the most beautiful beaches in the world—even if now the most dangerous. But he was able to see many soldiers in the later waves going ashore. Soldiers filling a few craft nearby saw and instantly recognized the British leader, complete with trademark cigar; he beamed as they cheered. At noon one hundred bombers and the navy ships gave a repeat performance. Truscott wondered if anyone could survive such a bombardment.[5]

Sergeant Murphy's view of the French Riviera as he motored forward was narrower: "We do not see the gigantic pattern of the offensive as we peer over the edge of the landing boats that are nearing the coast of France. We study the minute detail of the front that lies immediately before us." For him and his squad, the white sandy beaches at the edge of the spectacular turquoise-and-blue water would not be as inviting as usual.[6]

Standing at the railing of the *Catoctin,* Truscott watched as the landing craft of his 3rd, 36th, and 45th Infantry Divisions approached their assigned beaches. Finally, he thought, everything is proceeding as planned. Then for no reason he could fathom, the boats carrying one regiment of the 36th Division, now a few thousand yards off the beach, turned and headed back out to sea. The general's disbelief turned to anger. In a few moments the *Catoctin* received a message that underwater obstacles at the intended beach had resulted in a navy decision to land the troops at an alternate location. Truscott was aware that the navy had already undertaken a significant effort to clear the obstructions, using radio-controlled drones, various explosives, and underwater-demolition teams. Exasperated and with Colonel Carleton and Captain Wilson in tow, he lost no time in finding a landing craft to take them to confer with the 36th Division's commanding general, John Dahlquist. It was fortunate for Dahlquist that it had not been his decision that resulted in the turnaround and that he had ensured that the errant regiment got ashore elsewhere as quickly as possible. It might have ended there had Truscott not learned that Dahlquist had sent a congratulatory note to the admiral who had made the decision. "I made known to Dahlquist," Truscott steamed, "my complete displeasure with this procedure. It was in fact almost the only flaw in an otherwise perfect landing." The turnaround caused a delay in clearing the original beach, which required a change in the landing of the French armored brigade. It further affected bringing ashore ground elements of the Army Air Forces as well as the capture of the airfields near Frejus and in the Argens valley, which in turn resulted in delayed air support for the drive north. A still-irritated Truscott reminded the division commander that it was a "grave error which merited reprimand at least, and most certainly no congratulations." Strike one for General Dahlquist.[7]

Upon landing, Truscott made his way to his beach command post at Sainte-Maxime, accompanied by his French liaison officer, Colonel Jean Petit. It was ironic history that both Truscott and Petit had been at Port Lyautey in North Africa, where Petit's soldiers had opposed the American landing, though they were allies now. By late afternoon Truscott had a good picture of the status of his various VI Corps units. The 3rd and 45th Divisions had already achieved their objectives for the day, and the 36th Division would likely achieve its objectives before morning. At a cost of 183 VI Corps casualties, 2,000 Germans were captive and an unknown but substantial number were dead or wounded. "It was, I thought, a fitting celebration of the twenty-seventh anniversary of my original commission as an officer in the United States Army." Truscott recalled with satisfaction that "speed and power, thorough planning, training, and preparation, had paid off." First, though, he took a moment to gaze at the beauty of the place he had just invaded. Perhaps someday in the future, he likely hoped, he could bring Sarah here to see the low mountains, rolling hills, broad fields, and the villages, with their winding, cobbled streets and ancient churches. They could do it someday, but not anytime soon.[8]

Perhaps reflecting on General Lucas's caution at Anzio and criticism that followed, Truscott weighed his options. His own calculations suggested that a fast punch inland was very possible and would keep the Germans reeling. Poring over his maps, he studied the situation from every prospective. The critical elements were coming into place. He reminded himself of something he had learned early in his career, something General Clark had chosen to ignore during the breakout from Anzio. "In an offensive battle," Truscott knew, "the object is to destroy the enemy." In Sicily the highly mobile Germans had avoided being trapped by the Allies and also had done remarkably well in staving off disaster after Salerno, Cassino, and Anzio. Now Truscott saw that it might be possible to do something every commander dreams of achieving—trapping an enemy army in such a way that it cannot escape, a checkmate move in the lethal game of war. General Patch had no objection to the plan, but Truscott knew that making it happen would be a challenge. The concept was simple. If his invasion force landed with focused intensity, the Germans would have to rush in troops from the surrounding area to resist it. While they were so occupied, Truscott could send an armored force north to set a trap. Then as he forced the Germans to retreat, which he knew he could do, an ambush would greet them.[9]

About 150 miles to the north, the French Alps on the east approach the wide, deep, and fast Rhône River on the west. The path between the mountains and the river is narrow. The countryside enchants with its beige stone farmhouses, poppy fields, and, even during war, vineyards. Truscott, of course, surveyed the scene not with the eyes of a tourist, but with those of a warrior. If the Army Air Forces could take out all the bridges over the Rhône, he reasoned, retreating Germans on either side of the river would find it nearly impossible to support those on the other. Those on the east side, Truscott's bailiwick, could move north only through a narrow and likely suicidal route. His trap would best be set just north of Montélimar, where the route north squeezes through the narrow Cruas Gorge. Studying his map from south to north, the general could see that with the river on the west and a commanding ridge on the east, the highway and railroad competed for what little space remained in the gap. All he needed to do was to push the Germans north and then, from elevated positions above Montélimar, attack their flank. Of course, if the Germans got there first, they could mount an excellent defense that might allow most of their forces to slip away. The way to prevent that, Truscott reasoned, was for an Allied armored unit to identify the best route through the mountains, then race northwest from the invasion beaches, through the town of Sisteron, and emplace above Montélimar. The Seventh Army planners had not considered this possibility, he noted, but he had already seen the possibility while still in Naples. What was frustratingly uncertain was whether he would continue to keep Sudre's French armored brigade under his control or if de Lattre would succeed in siphoning it off. Truscott calculated that the latter was the more likely scenario. He thus gave the order to activate Task Force Butler.[10]

So far, the situation was even better than expected. Truscott had his three divisions ashore and moving inland, and his airborne task force had had a serendipitous landing that practically surrounded a German corps headquarters, allowing for the capture of several hundred soldiers. The German corps commander and his staff had evaded the paratroopers, but two days later the troops of Task Force Butler netted them. Robert Frederick had had less than a month to assemble and train his airborne task force, but the general had still produced amazing results. Truscott regarded their landing as one of the "remarkable exploits of the war. It was one of the most successful airborne drops." In addition, the 45th Division had captured a communications center, leaving the German command in the dark at a most critical time of the battle. This was all good news for Truscott. The bad news came when Patch alerted him that the 11th Panzer Division was now rolling hard and fast to halt the Allied advance at Brignoles, north of Toulon. Even so, Truscott knew his troops were in position.

With Task Force Butler crouched in the starting blocks at Le Muy, Truscott and Butler checked and rechecked their plan. Deputy corps commander since Anzio, Butler knew the general's predilections, and Truscott regarded him as "one of the most fearless men I ever met." Butler would depart Le Muy with his mélange of armored vehicles and roll northwest to the Durance River, then on toward Montélimar. How far his task force could get was a guess, but Truscott knew that if anyone could do it, Butler could.[11]

Something new to Truscott was the assistance provided to his troops by the Maquis, key resistance fighters within the French Forces of the Interior, which American troops were already calling the "Mackeys." Early on, the Maquis had worked with nearly 800 British MI (Military Intelligence) and American OSS (Office of Strategic Services) officers who had parachuted behind enemy lines to bring guns, provide coordination, and help destroy bridges and other infrastructure of use to the Germans. De Gaulle, operating from London, had sent another 850 of his own agents. The Maquis had become so effective that German soldiers moved cautiously, fearing ambush at any time, any place.[12]

By D-day plus four, enemy reinforcements arrived at Brignoles and engaged the 3rd Division, though with little success. Iron Mike

O'Daniel had things under control. General Sudre was also making progress, having taken Le Val and cut the coastal road to Toulon, where he would join with other French forces. When Truscott stopped by Sudre's temporary headquarters at Cabasse, there was something of a celebration going on. The mayor, the local Resistance leader, and numerous townspeople, abundantly supplied with Côtes de Provence wine, food, and flowers, were making speeches and offering toasts. For the Provençal people, blessed with the perfect mixture of French reserve and Mediterranean exuberance, life was finally about to resume.[13]

The German high command in Avignon could read the writing on the wall even if Hitler turned a blind eye. Allied troops in Normandy had now broken out at Saint-Lô and were rolling east, and Truscott and the French would soon be pushing up from the south. On August 16 Berlin relinquished and gave its commanders the order to withdraw from France. Not included in the general pullback, however, were those units assigned to defend Toulon, Marseilles, and some of the Atlantic port cities—Hitler's order to them was to defend to the end.[14]

Messages from Patch to Truscott indicated that General de Lattre had not yet managed to get his full complement of troops ashore, and he was refusing to move forward until everyone was collected. Knowing Patch was frustrated at the delay, Truscott offered to have the 3rd Division take Toulon, which he thought they could do in less than two days. While Patch would have liked to give him the nod, each knew that the politics of the situation necessitated that the French make the capture. Truscott concurred but suggested that he have the division cut incoming roads, effectively isolating Toulon and Marseilles from German reinforcements. His only request, to which Patch agreed, was that de Lattre relieve the 3rd Division from its blocking position at the earliest opportunity so that it could join the drive to Montélimar. The Germans might be restricted from moving west by the river and from moving east by the ridge, but Truscott still needed the 3rd Division to help push them north to ensure that none filtered back south.[15]

Not long after their conversation, Patch advised him that Sudre's armored brigade would need to return to the French II Corps. Truscott had anticipated as much and already had Task Force Butler assembled and waiting. From here forward, the Allied campaign divided along three routes. The French would head west to assault and capture Toulon and Marseilles. Truscott's main force would protect the French right flank until capture of these ports. Thereafter, the Americans would take the primary route north to Montélimar, pushing the enemy ahead of them. Task Force Butler would take the shorter but more mountainous route to that town, endeavoring to arrive well ahead of the retreating Germans. For Patch, things were happening almost too fast. While approving of and pleased with Truscott's progress, he could already see that logistics, a Seventh Army responsibility, was about to become an intense headache.[16]

By the time Truscott returned to his command post, which had moved to Vidauban, one of Butler's lieutenants was standing by with an important message. The general could hardly believe his ears: "Butler was at Sisteron!" Now almost halfway to Montélimar, Butler had had to overcome some resistance, but he had already taken 1,000 German prisoners and was now coordinating with the Maquis. Truscott immediately alerted General Dahlquist to have his 36th Division prepare to follow Butler's route. One regimental combat team was to start the next day, with the other two thereafter. Truscott told Butler to hold at Sisteron until the 36th Division arrived but to go ahead and scout to determine how best to seize the high ground north of Montélimar. The situation was pregnant and near delivery. The 45th Division was waiting at the Durance River for the order to move forward. The 3rd Division was holding in Aix-en-Provence, having isolated Toulon and Marseilles for the French. The U.S. Army Air Forces reported that Germans were streaming north along the west bank of the Rhône and that all bridges previously leading to Lyon had been destroyed. How many Germans the French could kill or capture inside Toulon and Marseilles was hard to say, but it was likely that many others, perhaps three full divisions, five partial divisions, and miscellaneous other enemy units, were still south of Montélimar and rapidly evacuating toward Truscott's trap.[17]

The general knew it was time to strike; any delay meant the escape of more Germans. The night of August 20, he scribbled an emergency message to Butler: "You will move at first light 21 August with all possible speed to Montélimar. Block enemy routes of withdrawal of the Rhône valley in that vicinity. 36th Division follows you." Trapping a huge number of Germans was possible, but any slipup would allow many to escape. The emergency message was hand-carried by Colonel Conway and his Jeep driver, climbing, descending, and bumping over one hundred miles of rough, tortuous mountain roads in the black night.[18]

Truscott was attempting to do something of historic significance. He later wrote that his plan was "to set the stage for a classic—a 'Cannae'—in which we would encircle the enemy against an impassable barrier or obstacle and destroy him." (The tactic is so named because Hannibal had used it to defeat the Romans in 216 B.C. near the village of Cannae in southern Italy.) First, Truscott had to ensure that he had enough troops pushing the Germans north to keep them from evading south. Good news arrived when the French reported that they were ready to take over the area north of Marseille. That evening, August 21, Will Lang, a correspondent with *Life* magazine, joined Truscott for dinner. Would the general care to answer a few questions? Of course, he replied. Little did Truscott suspect that a *Life* cover story about him would appear in the not-too-distant future.[19]

Then, at the worst possible time, secret information arrived that the 11th Panzer Division had arrived below the Durance River, a lesser waterway running from the Alps west to the Rhône, north of Aix-en-Provence and well south of Montélimar. A heavy counterattack against either the 3rd or the 45th Divisions, while unlikely, could be a problem as Truscott's backup command, the 36th Division, was already on its way to Sisteron. As much as he hated to do so, Truscott had to tap the brakes on the 3rd and 45th Divisions and one regiment of the 36th Division. As it turned out, the threat was not significant, but Truscott had lost valuable time.[20]

He and aide Captain James Wilson flew by Cub airplane on August 24 to Aspres, nearly halfway between Sisteron and Montélimar, to meet with Dahlquist for final details. When they arrived, Truscott learned that the division commander was not there. Dahlquist's chief of staff, sent to Aspres to meet the general, said that the 141st Regiment and the corps artillery battalion, which were supposed to be nearing Montélimar by now, had not been sent forward because Dahlquist was concerned by reports that Germans were moving south from Grenoble and Gap. Truscott's mood turned sour. "I was angry," he later wrote. He immediately sent one regiment from the 45th Division to counter any threat at Grenoble, while the bulk of the 36th Division focused on getting to Montélimar as quickly as possible. On August 22 Truscott blasted off a note to Dahlquist, its contents leaving no doubt that he was unhappy:

"Apparently, I failed to make your mission clear to you. The primary mission of the 36th Infantry Division is to block the Rhône Valley in the gap immediately north of Montélimar." For Truscott, blocking the Rhône Valley meant taking control of every route, especially to the east, which the Germans could use to evade the trap. "Keep in mind," he underscored, "that your primary mission is to block the Rhône Valley."[21]

Truscott's irritation was visible, his graveled voice sharp. Admittedly, this was Dahlquist's first combat command, but he had not carried out an order specifically given to him, nor had he immediately alerted Truscott about the developing situation. The corps commander made clear that he did not want it to happen again. Strike two for Dahlquist. Elsewhere, Truscott learned that one of his attack orders had not yet begun. Now downright angry, he warned: "Don't you understand? This is the opportunity of a lifetime. We can trap the entire German corps and the 11th German Panzer Division with a few men and guns. Now get goin'!" Truscott had lost the capture of one German army on the breakout from Anzio and did not want to let another opportunity slip away.[22]

The next day Truscott received a note from Butler saying that his task force had gained more high ground north of Montélimar. Even so, the following day the U.S. Army Air Forces reported that Germans were still fleeing north on *both* sides of the Rhône. Truscott concluded that whatever Dahlquist and Butler were doing was not enough. It turned out that Butler had not taken a high ridge between La Coucourde and Montélimar, which the Germans had seized and were now using to resist his forces. To perplex the situation, Dahlquist had arrived in the area and disbanded Task Force Butler, returning its various units to their former regiments. Truscott immediately countermanded this order and reassembled the special command. He pointed out their mistakes but did not dwell on them. The general reminded both Butler and Dahlquist, "The essential task was to occupy the long ridge overlooking Highway 7 north of Montélimar."[23]

For General de Lattre, there had been good news. The Maquis reported that the Germans in Toulon had prepared to resist an invasion from the sea but not an attack from the land. De Lattre attacked Toulon on August 21, with much street fighting resulting. By August 28 the Germans had surrendered. Marseilles fell the same day, squeezed between the attacking French army and the Maquis fighters erupting within. In all, the French netted 27,000 Germans. Both sets of port facilities sustained some serious damage, though; getting them up and running would take some time and effort but would still happen weeks earlier than expected.[24]

The next day Germans were still withdrawing north of Montélimar along the Rhône. "I was most unhappy about the situation at Montélimar," Truscott fumed. In what must have been something of a Pattonesque moment, the general stormed into Dahlquist's command post. "John, I have come here with the full intention of relieving you from your command. . . . You have just five minutes in which to convince me that you are not at fault." Dahlquist talked fast, explaining that his subordinates had misinformed him as to where some of his units were located but that he had now corrected the situation. He pointed out that he had four battalions of artillery aimed at the road, which he thought would stop enemy movement. His conclusion, which he proffered to his commander, was that except for the initial mistake, he had done all that he could. "I did not fully concur," Truscott recalled, "but I decided against relieving him." It was not quite strike three for Dahlquist, but a swing and a tick. One positive note was that the 11th Panzer Division was itself now attempting to evade north with the other German units.[25]

Released from blocking for the French, the 3rd Division pursued the Germans north from August 25 through August 27, finally pausing about five miles south of Montélimar. To the north of that town, Task Force Butler and the 36th Division's artillery and tanks were continually blasting the road from above, as did American fighter-bombers from time to time. Truscott flew over the area in his observation plane, studying the gorge below where his artillery and the warplanes had raked the road repeatedly. Stalled bumper to bumper, with no organization or control apparent, the long lines of German troops and vehicles suffered near-total destruction. Two battalions of the 3rd Division captured 350 enemy vehicles and large guns as the retreating convoy reached the blockage. Even though most of two German divisions had transited what would become the blood-soaked stricture, the scene of death and destruction was difficult for even Truscott to witness. Hundreds of bodies, dead horses, burning hulks of vehicles of every kind, wrecked railway cars, and damaged artillery, including seven of the "Anzio Annie" type, littered the road and adjacent tracks, making travel impossible. Truscott's engineers came forward with bulldozers to clear the road so U.S. troops could continue the pursuit. The corps's ground weapons had done most of the damage. "I know of no place where more damage was inflicted upon troops in the field," Truscott confessed. "And the sight and smell of this section is an experience I have no wish to repeat." Captain Wilson labeled it "carnage compounded."[26]

One of the soldiers who passed through the hideous scene was Audie Murphy, who remembered: "In their haste to escape, the doomed vehicles had been moving two and three abreast. Our artillery zeroed them in. The destruction surpasses belief. As far as we can see, the road is cluttered with shattered, twisted cars, trucks and wagons. Many are still burning. Often the bodies of men lie in the flames; and the smell of singed hair and burnt flesh is strong and horrible."[27]

Truscott's plan resulted in the destruction of 4,000 vehicles and the capture of 5,000 prisoners at Montélimar alone. Since landing, the VI Corps had advanced one hundred miles and taken 23,000 prisoners, essentially destroying two German divisions. "Even if Montélimar had not been a perfect battle, we could still view the record with some degree of satisfaction," Truscott recounted. The cost to the Americans during the two weeks since the invasion had been 1,300 killed or wounded.[28]

Truscott's divisions continued north. Taking a moment to catch his breath, and with feelings of homesickness running strong, Lucian wrote a letter to Sarah on August 29. "This is an anniversary too—just twenty seven years ago this morning I rode the Drummen's Special [train] into Douglas and actually entered upon my duties as an officer. And it was not too long after that we met! Do you remember?"[29]

In early September the VI Corps pushed northeast while the French moved northwest. For political reasons, the French army and the Maquis were to take Lyon, but scouting by officers of the 36th Division had determined the city to be free of Germans. The French would continue north to join with Patton's forces, while the VI Corps headed for the Belfort Gap in yet another effort to trap German forces.[30]

Having anticipated a major battle at the original invasion beaches, Seventh Army planners had supplied Operation Dragoon with more artillery and ammunition than transport vehicles and fuel. Now with the French and Truscott's VI Corps battling well to the north, Patch's supply line snaked several hundred miles from beaches to mountains and beyond. Trucks packed with food, gasoline, and ammunition rolled twenty-four hours a day. The most critical item was gasoline, the lack of which threatened to cease all Allied movement. Truscott needed fuel and had no time to deal with requisitions through channels. On August 22 he took aside Colonel Edward J. O'Neill, his G-4 (logistics) officer, and told him to solve the problem. O'Neill returned to the invasion beaches and located a beach master with a sympathetic ear who agreed to unload an oil tanker if one could be located. The colonel borrowed a landing craft and motored throughout the many ships at anchor, asking if anyone had gasoline. One ship did, and its captain was willing to move to shore for unloading, though only if Admiral Hewitt consented. O'Neill took his case to the admiral, who once again came through for Truscott. "Had O'Neill attempted to solve this problem through Army G-4," Truscott knew, "delay in unloading would have had serious implications on the battle at Montélimar and elsewhere."[31]

While O'Neill's actions demonstrated the make-it-happen attitude that Truscott expected of his officers, the overall supply situation remained critical. Commandeering a railroad line helped, but when the French army began demanding gasoline, the problem intensified. O'Neill winced when his commander agreed to give the French 10,000 gallons. Truscott's gift did not keep everyone happy, however. When General Marshall later visited American and French troops, General de Lattre seized the moment to rage against Truscott, accusing him of stealing gasoline intended for French troops. Marshall, as Truscott later learned, did not take kindly to de Lattre's complaints. "General Marshall set him right back on his haunches," Truscott later said.[32]

By now the Germans could see Patch's long supply line as easily as he could. Using the Doubs River as their defensive line, the Germans cobbled together every available unit so they could make a stand near Besançon. If they could hold the town until late September, other German units farther west could slip out through the Belfort Gap. That was not going to happen if Truscott could help it. The general repositioned his forces for the showdown. The VI Corps, with its three divisions abreast, moved northeast along the French-Swiss border, intending to take Besançon and then move on to Belfort. Capturing Besançon might be quite difficult, however. Bordered on three sides by the Doubs River, it was crowned with a centuries-old fortress—La Citadelle—that held commanding views of the countryside. Its high walls of gray stone had protected the city through the ages, resisting attack after attack, most of which had come from the east. Its elevation and fortifications, within a deep loop of the river, would be tough to crack. On September 6 Truscott told General O'Daniel to have his 3rd Division study the situation and then either attack the city or hold the surrounding heights until Truscott could deliver reinforcements. The German force within was hunkered down, intending to make the best of the city's defensive attributes. The fighting was difficult, but Iron Mike's division took Besançon within two days, netting seven hundred prisoners.[33]

On September 12 Truscott briefed General Patch on the VI Corps plan to attack Belfort. The three divisions would wheel to the right and approach the city abreast from the west, with each division keeping one regiment in reserve. The army commander approved the plan and underscored its importance by noting, "The Belfort Gap is the Gateway to Germany." Situated between the Vosges and Jura Mountains and the Rhine and Rhône Rivers, Belfort had figured in many of Europe's wars. Once again, it would suffer the clash of armies.[34]

On September 15 the Seventh Army and the French army were both placed under command of the newly formed U.S. Sixth Army Group, commanded by General Jacob Devers. At first, this reorganization seemed merely to involve an additional layer of oversight. Closer study, however, suggested that a major new strategy was brewing, one that would conflict with what Patch and Truscott had in mind. A new plan, promulgated from Devers's army-group headquarters, arrived at Patch's headquarters, which immediately sent a copy to Truscott. In the VI Corps journal, Captain Wilson noted Truscott's reaction to the news: "General [Truscott] both surprised and disappointed, plan being entirely contrary to his conversation with General Patch on 12th. Plan sacrifices valuable time in Belfort attack, relegates [7th] Army to minor role with possibility of complete bogging down in Vosges [Mountains] during the winter. [Commanding General] spends morning stewing over it." His troops had already fought battles in the mountains during the winter months, and no one wanted to do it again.[35]

On September 15 Truscott sent a thoughtful but apparently unappreciated letter to General Patch. In it he assured Patch that

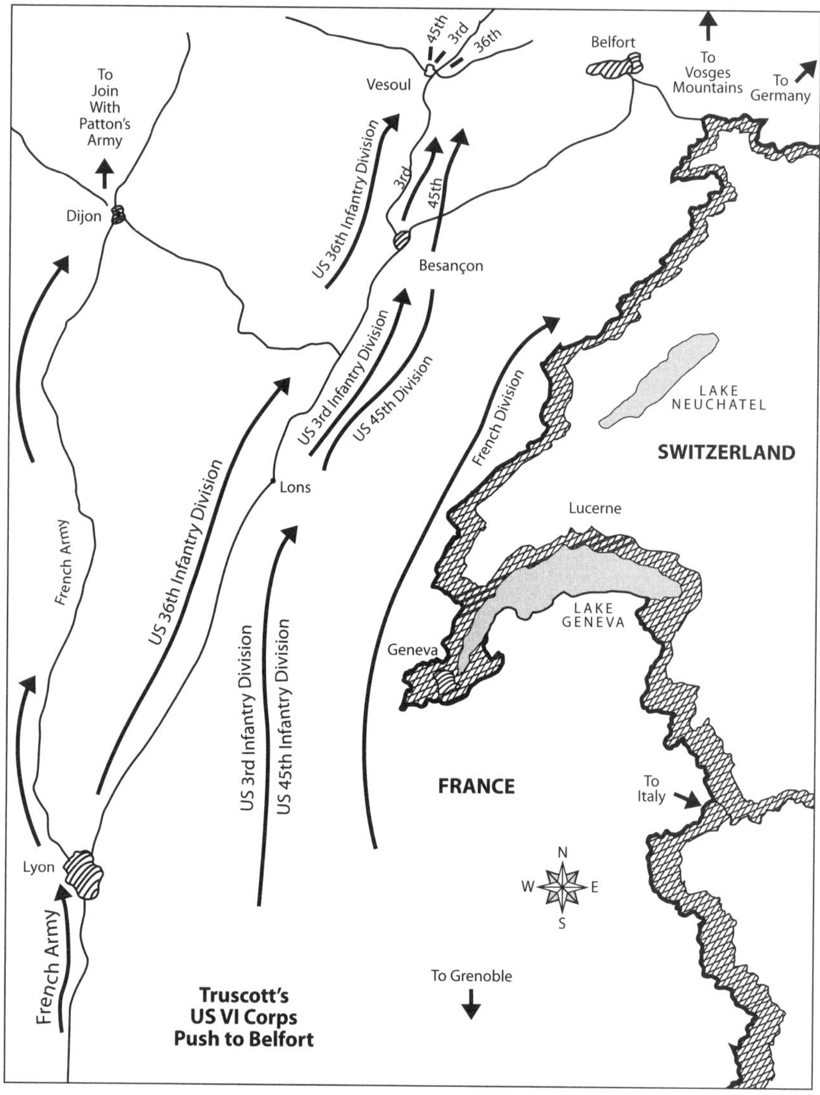

Later follow-up of the campaign in southern France. Map by Megan Postell.

VI Corps was already complying with the new order but pointed out that any delay in attacking the Belfort Gap would merely allow the Germans more time to set up and enhance their defenses in the Vosges Mountains. He added that winter in the Vosges brought considerable rain and snow, making the country ideal for the defender and simply terrible for the attacker. Taking the Belfort Gap immediately would avoid a protracted winter campaign. Truscott's proposal, of course, was an alternative that was counter to Devers's plan. Putting it forth was a risky move. While Field Marshal Montgomery might get away with such a thing in the British army, where subordinate-commander negotiation was acceptable, Truscott knew he had only a slim chance of finding success with this in the U.S. Army. Nonetheless, he proposed using several French divisions, soon to arrive, to attack the gap immediately. Concurrently, the VI Corps would move east through Nice and Genoa and attack the Germans in northern Italy. Such an effort, Truscott proposed, would bring about a quicker demise to the Germans than would keeping VI Corps in the Vosges, and it might even break the stalemate in Italy. Inherent in this proposal was the suggestion either to use VI Corps now to attack the Belfort Gap before it became fortified or to let the French handle it while VI Corps pursued a flanking invasion of northern Italy. It was innovative thinking by Truscott, who was a master of detail but who also kept his eye on the big picture.

Patch was not impressed. He responded the next evening, not by message but by telephone. "I don't think that letter of yours was advisable." The army commander then pointed out that the letter suggested that the corps commander had no confidence in his superiors. Truscott assured Patch that preparations were ongoing in compliance with the Seventh Army order and that the proposal was simply something to consider.[36]

His exasperation softened when good news arrive for both him and Carleton. Truscott had been awarded a third star, making him a lieutenant general, and Colonel Carleton had received his first, making him a brigadier general. Putting frustrations aside for the moment, the two generals, along with seven or eight staff members, clinked glasses of champagne that evening.[37]

On September 23 Patch again met with Truscott, this time providing some startling news. He had just come from a meeting with Eisenhower in Versailles, and it now seemed that the British would lead the main Allied attack through northern Europe, with that flank allotted most of the available supplies, including gasoline. Patton's Third Army and Patch's Seventh Army would get little fuel or other materials. To Patch and Truscott, this was a major and disappointing change in strategy. In fact, the change was the result of Eisenhower's acceptance of Montgomery's argument that going across northern Europe would mean a quicker dash to Berlin.

Codenamed Operation Market Garden, the effort would include the largest airborne operation ever, quickly followed by an armored assault. A livid Omar Bradley had tried to persuade Eisenhower not to approve the scheme, but without success. Even so, Bradley did say of Montgomery's idea: "The Market-Garden plan was a dazzler, one of the most daring and imaginative of the war . . . dangerously foolhardy—the wrong plan at the wrong time and the wrong place." Indeed, the operation failed. A senior British commander had predicted as much when he cautioned Montgomery at the beginning of the endeavor, suggesting that it might be "a bridge too far."[38]

Truscott already knew that Italy had become a sideshow, and now it looked as if southern France might follow. For his troops, it would mean another winter in the mountains. Unfortunately, General Devers had something of an offense in mind. He told Patch to keep VI Corps moving through the Vosges under the assumption that the Germans in position there were but a shallow force of little depth. Truscott complied, knowing much better than Devers the reality of what awaited his men. The attack began on October 15 with the intention of capturing the castled hill town of Bruyères. The 45th Infantry Division would come from the west while the 36th Infantry Division moved up from the south. When a breakthrough occurred, the 3rd Infantry Division would exploit it, pushing toward Saint-Dié. Throughout this effort, the rain and cold assaulted the Americans, who by now were tired, understrength, and short of supplies. The troops trudged through the thick forests that covered the steep hillsides, the veterans telling the replacements what was coming and the replacements not liking what they were hearing. "It is the prelude to another long, grim winter," Sergeant Murphy lamented. "My regiment is on the verge of some of the hardest fighting of the entire war."[39]

The 36th Division now received an additional regiment, which until recently had been securing the French-Italian border. The 442nd Regimental Combat Team was unlike any other regiment created during the war. The family members of many soldiers and junior officers looked out through barbed-wire enclosures in a number of forced resettlement camps in the United States. Perhaps without saying as much, these men were on a mission to show their fellow Americans that the members of the 442nd were not "Japanese Americans" but "just Americans." Along the way they would become one the most decorated regiments of World War II.

Truscott would see more of them later, but for now the army had something else in mind for him.[40]

The 3rd Division joined with the 442nd Regimental Combat Team and other VI Corps units in the attack. Murphy, who had already received numerous medals for bravery by now, recalled combat in the Vosges: "At night the fog closes in. Under its cover, the Germans infiltrate our lines; and hand-to-hand fighting becomes commonplace. I whet my bayonet until it is razor sharp and keep it always handy." Ever the effacing hero and reluctant leader, Murphy was surprised to learn that he and two fellow soldiers would receive battlefield commissions. He recalled the comments of Colonel Hallett Edson as he pinned gold bars on their collars: "'You are now *gentlemen* by act of Congress,' he says, smiling at our muddy uniforms and bearded faces. 'Shave, take a bath, and get the hell back into the lines!'"[41]

On October 17 Truscott, wearing the three shining stars of a lieutenant general on an otherwise weathered uniform, was called to Epinal, France, to meet with Generals Patch and Eisenhower. While Eisenhower's greeting was friendly, his comments sounded disconcerting. "Lucian," he began, "I am going to relieve you from VI Corps. You are an embarrassment to me now that you have been made a lieutenant general." He now had Truscott's focused attention. "All of my Corps commanders now want to be made lieutenant generals. I am going to assign you to organize the 15th Army." Eisenhower smiled. It was an army-level command—a promotion. To his disappointment, Truscott's parade came with a little rain; his new assignment would be a training and administrative command under General Bradley. Truscott, never one to sit in an office when he could stand at the front, asked to remain a major general and stay with VI Corps. Eisenhower smiled and declined his request. On October 21 Lucian sent a quick letter to Sarah: "I suppose Mary, Doodie, and Jamie got a thrill in seeing Daddy make *Life* cover. I'll bet Doodie is glad that he's not a [West Point] plebe for he would probably have to memorize the whole thing." Truscott had made the cover of the October 2, 1944, issue in an article written by Will Lang. His photograph was impressive: Donning a steel helmet, leather jacket, silk scarf around his neck, cavalry britches, and cavalry boots, he rested one foot on a rock as he gazed off in the distance.[42]

By October 24, with Bruyères captured, Truscott and his staff said their goodbyes to the three divisions of VI Corps. The general proceeded to Supreme Headquarters Allied Expeditionary Force to begin organizing the new Fifteenth Army. He had some available time for a break, however. In early November Truscott and some of his staff returned to the United States for a visit—their first in more than two years. As the plane headed out over the Atlantic, the tension from Truscott's mind and body must have hissed as it escaped. He could not recall when he had last been so relaxed.[43]

Sarah, of course, could hardly contain her excitement.

CHAPTER 25

Return to Italy

The days and nights at home with Sarah and young Jamie were as short and sweet as those at Anzio had been long and bitter. Lucian squeezed in a visit with older son Doodie, then pushing his way through an accelerated program at West Point. Second lieutenants, expected to lead the way, oftentimes did not last long in combat, and the army always needed more. Near the end of his furlough, Lucian and Sarah visited Washington, D.C., no doubt reflecting on their Great Depression days there, both good and bad.

While in the city he called on General Marshall, who took the opportunity to invite him to sit in on the usual morning briefing. "It was intensely interesting," Truscott observed, "covering briefly, concisely, and in detail the military deployment of our forces in all parts of the world." An item on the agenda concerned the recent death of Sir John Dill, Churchill's senior representative in Washington, in that it would result in Sir Henry Maitland "Jumbo" Wilson, Allied supreme commander in chief in the Mediterranean, taking Dill's place in Washington. This would put General Alexander into Wilson's position, which in turn would lead to General Clark assuming Alexander's position. With Clark's old job open, Marshall's staff speculated, Clark would probably recommend his subordinate, Geoffrey Keyes, to assume command of Fifth Army. The question being presented was, did General Marshall concur?[1]

Marshall looked at Truscott and asked him how he would feel about going back to Italy. Truscott, almost on cue, said he would go wherever the army chief of staff needed him. Marshall, disinclined to repeat himself, replied: "I know that. . . . That is not what I asked you." Truscott, accepting this invitation for candor, answered that he would prefer to return to France, where he hoped to serve under General Eisenhower. He added, somewhat awkwardly, that he was junior to both of the Fifth Army corps commanders, Generals Keyes and Willis D. Crittenberger. Marshall ignored the latter comment and closed the topic with instruction to his staff to consult Eisenhower on the matter.[2]

Lucian and Sarah hugged goodbye, holding their embrace. Neither wanted to lose the warmth of the other, and neither wanted to say what each was thinking: that he could still die over there. His plane lifted off from Washington for New York's La Guardia Field and from there on to France. After landing in Paris Truscott hustled to Versailles, where Eisenhower maintained his headquarters. He hoped to speak with Eisenhower's chief of staff, Bedell Smith, before his boss had the opportunity to answer Marshall regarding Truscott's return to Italy. He was too late. Churchill, consulted as well, was pleased at the prospect of Truscott's return to the Mediterranean. The prime minister knew that the general got on well with the British and that he was intimately familiar with Italy. Indeed, Churchill likely recalled that Truscott had gotten the Anzio forces off the beach, the young divisional commander whom everyone praised. Eisenhower probably had second thoughts about not having Truscott on his team but was likely relieved to be able to agree with the British leader for a change. He told Marshall that Truscott was "the logical choice" to command the Fifth Army in Italy.[3]

To Truscott's disappointment, his life had taken another course correction. On December 5, before leaving Orly Air Field in Paris for Caserta, Italy, and with Eisenhower's permission, Truscott reassembled his former VI Corps headquarters staff. Most had already reported to the newly created Fifteenth Army, the command Eisenhower had previously intended for the general; now he redirected them to Italy. Truscott looked forward to again joining his "war family": Carleton, Conway, Harrell, O'Neill, Bartash, Wilson, Barna, Hong, and the others. Missing from the roundup would be General O'Daniel and the soldiers of the 3rd Infantry Division as well as those of the 36th and 45th Infantry Divisions. The 3rd Division, of course, had been Truscott's pride. He would miss all his units, but especially the "Rock of the Marne" Division, which would go on to earn the distinction of receiving forty Medals of Honor—more than any other infantry division. Over the course of several amphibious invasions and the resulting campaigns, it would also sustain the highest battle casualties of any U.S. infantry division—almost 5,000 killed and 27,000 wounded.[4]

Nor would there be paratroopers or rangers under Truscott's command this time. The war in Italy had become the forgotten front, where a medley of Allied forces continued the fight. Truscott's new command, the Fifth Army, had a number of divisions, but only five were American. He was very familiar with two of them, the 1st Armored Division and the 34th Infantry Division. They had supplied the first volunteers for the original ranger battalion and had served under him in Italy. Truscott knew less about his other American divisions, the 85th, 88th, and 91st. One thing he did know was that by now they were all very experienced at fighting the Germans in Italy. The other army in Italy was the British Eighth Army, under Lieutenant General Sir Oliver Leese. Its three corps contained sixteen divisions made up of British, Canadian, and Polish troops.[5]

Three new units had either recently arrived in the Fifth Army, or would do so in the near future. Each was unlike any other unit in the command. One thing they had in common was that, for varying reasons, Marshall's theater commanders had reservations about accepting them. They were the 442nd Regimental Combat Team, the 10th Mountain Division, and the 92nd Infantry Division.

The 442nd "Go for Broke" Regimental Combat Team consisted of Japanese American enlisted soldiers and junior officers who were commanded by Caucasian senior officers. Their combat record thus far was impressive. Notwithstanding that, much of the American population continued to mistrust Japanese Americans. Of concern to Allied theater commanders was the question of how their Caucasian soldiers might regard these Japanese American soldiers, especially if one had a brother or friend killed in the Pacific. The second unit was the 92nd Infantry "Buffalo" Division, consisting primarily of African Americans. Their combat record thus far was questionable. In addition, theater commanders might have worried that some of their Caucasian soldiers would not be tolerant of serving with these men in combat situations. The third unit was the 10th Mountain "Mountaineers" Division. It had an unusual mixture of world-class skiers, well-known mountain climbers, Ivy League students, and muleskinners. The concern of theater commanders regarding this unit differed from the other two, suspecting that the division might be too specialized and too lightly armed and likely wondering if its soldiers were too elitist or otherwise difficult to manage.

The 442nd Regimental Combat Team was born of West Coast alarm following the Pearl Harbor attack. Lieutenant General John L. DeWitt, commanding general of the U.S. Army's Western Defense

Command and the Fourth Army, had implemented President Roosevelt's Executive Order 9066, which resulted in the forcible relocation of 110,000 Japanese Americans. Of those men, women, and children eventually relocated, 94,000 had resided in California and 15,000 in Washington State. In February 1942 they arrived at ten relocation camps in which they would remain until near the end of the war. DeWitt justified his roundups by noting the difficulty of telling the "sheep from the goats." Ironically, in Hawaii, where 150,000 Japanese Americans lived and constituted 37 percent of the population, and where the initial Japanese attack had occurred, there had been no roundup nor any successful pressure to do so.[6]

In 1942, faced with ramping up a small army into a huge one, the U.S. government began looking under previously unturned stones for additional servicemen. It did not take long to notice that a number of young men in Hawaii and within the mainland relocation camps were interested in serving their country. In Hawaii the army had already segregated 1,500 Japanese American soldiers who had served in the Hawaii National Guard into the Hawaii Provisional Infantry Battalion, later redesignated the 100th Battalion. When its soldiers assembled for an aloha ceremony, family and friends gathered to wish them well. Under wind-flapped U.S. flags, they exchanged hugs and wiped away tears. It was, at the same time, a sad, patriotic, and festive affair. But the story was different in the relocation camps. There army recruits hung their heads as they departed amid disapproving looks from fellow camp residents. Each relocation recruit asked himself the same question: was it honorable to fight for an army that locked up his family?[7]

One thing was the same for the Hawaiians and the mainlanders, however. Bringing shame to the family was simply unacceptable. One recruit, Daniel Inouye, would later recall his father's earlier admonition. By that time, the young soldier lay seriously wounded, wondering if he would live or die. His father had said about the United States: "It has been good to us . . . it is you who must try to return the goodness of this country. . . . Do not bring dishonor on our name."[8]

Differences between the Hawaiian and mainland recruits emerged in April 1943, when the two groups comingled at Camp Shelby, Mississippi. Those from Hawaii already had some military experience and were generally darker, more informal, and more easygoing than the mainlanders. They also spoke a form of pidgin developed from six languages. It was not long before they felt looked down upon by the West Coast recruits, who regarded the Hawaiians as country boys. Before long, the mainlanders began calling them "Buddhaheads." The Hawaiians returned the favor and called the city boys "*Kotonks,*" the definition of which is uncertain. Although having faced more-intense discrimination, the mainlanders were more reserved, lighter in complexion, more competitive, and spoke both better English and Japanese than the Hawaiians. Early on, the soldiers, who on average were five feet, six inches tall and weighed less than 130 pounds, sometimes settled their disagreements with fists. But as the result of someone's suggestion, the friction between the two groups evaporated. Some of the Hawaii soldiers—those deemed informal leaders—were invited to visit a nearby relocation camp at Rohwer, Arkansas. For them, the camp came as a shock. The sight of fences, armed guards, poorly constructed buildings, and a stoic but obviously unhappy population was sobering. Each Hawaiian soldier wondered if he might have enlisted were he or his family held in such a place. Thereafter, the Buddhaheads and Kotonks became brothers. The nicknames remained, but only in good-natured jest.[9]

In September 1943 the 100th Battalion shipped off to the Mediterranean theater of operations, where it became a "separate" battalion within the 34th Infantry Division. The newcomers fought in the immediate aftermath of Salerno and then at Cassino and Anzio. The fighting ability of the unit was hard *not* to notice. The battalion quickly developed a reputation as a superb force. On July 27, 1944, General Clark awarded the battalion a Distinguished Unit Citation for its earlier fighting at Belvedere, Italy, north of Rome. The unit had also earned the dubious nickname of "Purple Heart Battalion." The 2nd and 3rd Battalions of what the army now called the 442nd Regimental Combat Team arrived in the Mediterranean in June 1944. In August the 100th Battalion officially joined them and became part of the 442nd. Under normal circumstances it would have been designated the 1st Battalion, but because of its distinguished record, it was allowed to remain the 100th Battalion. Clark, to his credit, had been an early opponent of Japanese American relocation as well as one of the original supporters of the 100th Battalion and, subsequently, the combined 442nd.[10]

When the 442nd joined Truscott's VI Corps in the Vosges Mountains in France, Operation Dragoon was well underway. The unit became an additional regiment within the 36th Division. In October the 442nd took part in the battle to liberate Bruyères, a key communications and transportation area for the Germans. Its soldiers had more than exceeded expectations. Truscott, also a strong supporter of the 442nd, had departed for Italy on October 25 and thus was not present to witness one of the unit's finest moments. That came when General Dahlquist, commanding the 36th Division, ordered the 442nd to rescue one battalion of the 141st "Alamo" Regiment. Although history has come to know this battalion as "the lost battalion," it was not actually lost but had become cut off from its regiment. It took four days of bloody fighting by the men of the 442nd to reach and rescue the surviving soldiers from the regiment. In the process the unit suffered forty-two killed and many more wounded. Second Lieutenant Martin J. "Marty" Higgins of the Alamo Regiment minced no words about the sacrifice of the 442nd, asserting that the rescue of him and his men could not possibly justify the loss of so many fellow soldiers; he maintained that he and the others should have been bypassed. The soldiers of the 442nd came to believe that Dahlquist had been responsible for their considerable casualties. As historian Robert Asahina notes, "To this day, the men of the 442nd blame Dahlquist for giving them this dangerous assignment, as if it had been a personal rather than a tactical decision." The general, nearly relieved of his command by Truscott, would go on to become a four-star (full) general, despite having once been formally reprimanded by Eisenhower for shaking hands and lunching with Hermann Goering following the latter's capture.[11]

On a foggy, dismal November 12, with snow on the ground, the 442nd assembled near Bruyères for review by Dahlquist. Backed by a wintry landscape, the youthful soldiers stood at attention but looked somewhat relieved to have finally received wool overcoats, neck scarfs, gloves, and rubberized shoepacs to keep out some of the mountain cold. The general was surprised at the small number of men present. He asked Lieutenant Colonel Virgil R. Miller where the others were. "That's all that's left," came the reply. The 442nd had been in combat in the Vosges for less than a month, and yet it earned five Presidential Unit Citations for its actions. It was destined return to Italy once again to serve under Truscott.[12]

The 10th Mountain Division was as unusual as the 442nd Regimental Combat Team. Its creation was the idea of Charles Minot "Minnie" Dole, the first director of the National Ski Patrol. In February 1940, well before the Pearl Harbor attack, Dole and a few friends, all prominent American skiers, had discussed news reports of how the miniscule Finnish army had somehow held off the giant Soviet army in the deep snows of winter that year. They reached the conclusion that the U.S. Army could use a "mountain" unit as well. Dole saw to it that a report by an onsite military observer in Finland found its way to Army Chief of Staff Marshall, coupled with Dole's recommendation that the general create a similar unit. Marshall replied with a polite thank-you letter. Dole persisted, however, and managed an in-person meeting with Marshall. The proposal eventually filtered down to Mark Clark, then a lieutenant colonel, as well as to General McNair, who commanded all U.S. Army ground forces. Clark liked the idea, but McNair did not. Mountain divisions used mules, said McNair. The Germans were highly mechanized, he argued, and that was what the U.S. Army needed to become. He saw little use in creating a mountain division.[13]

On October 8, 1941, Dole presented something of a manifesto to Marshall, with copies to Secretary of War Henry Stimson and President Roosevelt. He reminded them that winter snow fell every year in much of North America and that the best mountain infantrymen in the world were now in the Wehrmacht. His suggestion was that German mountain soldiers might someday arrive in Canada or the northern United States. Marshall and Stimson relented in late October, and by November—three weeks before Pearl Harbor—the army formed a battalion of what would eventually become the 87th Mountain Infantry Regiment. It began preliminary training on Mount Rainier near Fort Lewis, Washington. Truscott had been at Fort Lewis at the time and probably heard about the new unit, but he left that month to take command of the 5th Cavalry Regiment at Fort Bliss, Texas.[14]

The army next did something it had never done before. It asked Dole and the National Ski Patrol—a civilian organization—to recruit soldiers for the new unit. Dole issued a National Ski Patrol notice alerting its readers that the army needed "packers, prospectors, trappers, Forest Service men, timber cruisers, guides, and men who have mountaineering as an avocation *whether or not they can ski.*" Over the next two years, an avalanche of candidates—7,000 men—flowed in, including some of the best and most well-known skiers in the United States and Europe as well as many Ivy League students. The prospective soldiers were generally older, brighter, and more accomplished than most army recruits; indeed, two-thirds of them qualified for Officer Candidate School. Some observers suggested that the mountain recruits probably had the highest collective IQ of any U.S. Army division. Bil "One L" Dunaway, future ski racer, ski-magazine editor, *Aspen Times* owner, and media and real-estate notable, later remembered, "I joined the 10th Mountain Division because I wanted to be around some of the best skiers and climbers in the world." When asked many years later if he had seen much action during World War II, he nodded and changed the subject.[15]

The army moved mountain training from Fort Lewis, Washington, to Camp Hale, Colorado, elevation 9,224 feet, with training areas up to 13,000 feet. An early discussion surfaced about whether the snow soldiers needed downhill or cross-country ski training more. A visiting Norwegian army officer reported that German mountain troops trained on cross-country skis 99 percent of the time, which settled the argument. By July 1943 the original regiment had morphed into three regiments of the 10th Light Division (Pack, Alpine) and included 13,000 men. Eventually, 500 of the division's soldiers would be foreigners, many from Norway and elsewhere in Europe. Perhaps surprising, the 10th Light Division still had no combat mission. Theater commanders declined Marshall's offer of the troops, explaining that the unit was too small, too lightly armed, too specialized, and had too few vehicles and too many mules. They would prefer instead a standard infantry division.[16]

Dole met with Marshall again to urge a mission for the men. To make the division more attractive to potential commanders, the army increased its size and provided it with heavier weapons. By November it reconstituted the division as the 10th *Mountain* Division. Its shoulder patch, a powder keg with crossed bayonets mimicking the Roman numeral ten, now included a "Mountain" tab to be worn above the patch, putting the division on par with other elite units, such as airborne and rangers. Even more important, the 10th Mountain "Mountaineers" Division now had a new commanding general—all on Thanksgiving Day, 1944.[17]

Major General George P. Hays had received the Medal of Honor while serving as a first lieutenant with the 3rd Infantry Division in World War I. He fought as a horse-mounted liaison officer and artillery observer at the Second Battle of the Marne, during which he suffered a serious wound and had seven horses shot out from under him. By the end of that war, he had also received the Legion of Honor, the

French Croix de Guerre, two Silver Stars, and a Purple Heart. Before taking over the 10th Mountain Division, he had fought at Cassino and later landed at Omaha Beach. By January 1945 the 14,000-strong 10th Mountain was on its way to Italy.[18]

In mid-January it disembarked at Naples and boarded transport bound for the Apennine Mountains. After three years of training, it was about to be bloodied. The army had not used the division at Cassino, where there had existed a dire need for it. About that time Marshall had responded to a complaining Dole by reminding him that the army had only one mountain division. If he positioned it at one point and then needed it worse at another, Marshall wrote, in the mountains of Italy, he would not be able to move the division quickly enough. Later, the general regretted that decision, having become well aware that a unit trained for winter duty at elevation might have completely altered the Italian campaign.[19]

The saga of the 92nd Infantry Division would not be as illustrious as that of either the 442nd Regimental Combat Team or the 10th Mountain Division. While 1.2 million African Americans served during World War II, the military assigned them primarily as general-service troops, working in noncombat units as stevedores, laborers, road builders, and truck drivers. But the U.S. Army did eventually field two infantry divisions consisting primarily of African Americans. The 93rd Infantry "Blue Helmet" Division served in the Pacific, but commanders subdivided it into smaller units while it was still in San Francisco. Portions of the 93rd engaged in combat in the Pacific, but primarily in small patrol actions. Commanders never reassembled the division, and it never fought as such. The 92nd Infantry "Buffalo" Division, then identified as a "Colored" or "Negro" division, was formed in May 1943 at Fort Huachuca, Arizona, a former post of the 10th Cavalry Regiment of Buffalo Soldiers. Many of the African Americans recruited or drafted during World War II had come from geographical regions that had consciously denied them educational and employment opportunities. The result was that the illiteracy rate of the 92nd Division was about 60 percent. Wade McCree, a soldier assigned to the division, had attended Harvard Law School and was given the additional assignment of teaching reading and writing to illiterate recruits. He found it sad that a government that had not had the will to educate such men showed no hesitation in drafting them.[20]

President Roosevelt appointed William Hastie, a federal judge and dean of the Howard University School of Law, as advisor for Negro affairs for Secretary of War Stimson. Judge Hastie raised a few eyebrows when he argued that the best thing to do for African American soldiers was to integrate them fully into the military. Upon learning of this recommendation, General Marshall balked. He wrote to the judge saying that Hastie's proposed solution suggested charging the army with resolving a complex social problem as old as the country. Marshall added that the military could not accomplish such a mission and that it was unfair to expect it to do so. Further aggravating the situation, the new commanding general of the 92nd Division, Major General Edward M. "Ned" Almond, had little regard for African Americans. As late as 1959 he seriously questioned the advisability of trusting "Negroes" in important combat units.[21]

Almond continued to allow segregation at Fort Huachuca, which resulted in various separate facilities, including living quarters, mess halls, and clubs for both enlisted men and officers. One African American officer, 2nd Lieutenant Vernon J. Baker, who would later receive the Medal of Honor, recalled that African American officers who came to Almond's headquarters could enter only through the rear entrance. Another officer who served in the 92nd Division, Hondon Hargrove, recalled that by the time the division was ready to leave for the war, "there was—in constant ferment—an intangible, elusive undercurrent of resentment, bitterness, even despair and hopelessness among black officers and enlisted men in the division." Part of this was Almond's continuation of a policy that specified there would be "no black officers commanding companies, battalions or regiments and no black staff officers at battalion level or above."[22]

Because of complaints emanating from Fort Huachuca, the Office of the Inspector General sent Brigadier General Benjamin O. Davis and Truman Gibson, a civilian aide to the secretary of war, to investigate the situation. Their report, issued in July 1943 and declassified in 1978, was the result of interviewing more than eight hundred officers and thousands of soldiers. Its major conclusion was "that the morale of the 92nd Infantry Division is unsatisfactory, and that there is a feeling of resentment against the white officers as a group by many colored officers and enlisted men."[23]

Nonetheless, the army needed troops to fight the war. Consequently, it consolidated what it deemed to be the best officers and soldiers of the division's three regiments into one regiment, the 370th, and sent it to Italy; the other two regiments would follow later. The men of the 370th Regiment arrived in Naples in July 1944 and temporarily became part of the 1st Armored Division in a somewhat integrated status. A month later the men found themselves on the Arno River near Pisa, facing the Gothic Line. It was Kesselring's final defense system, which stretched across northern Italy from the Ligurian Sea to the Adriatic Sea. None of the men of the 370th had been in combat before, and their inexperience soon showed. Even so, their regimental commander, Colonel Raymond G. Sherman, 1st Armored Division, and a friend of General Almond, seemed satisfied. Just as important, the morale of the regiment was developing. Then Almond arrived with the other two regiments of the 92nd Division, and the 370th returned to that command. During his twenty-four years as an army officer, Almond had commanded troops for only three.[24]

In early October the general established his division headquarters on the Ligurian coast at Viareggio. What had previously been questionable morale among the 92nd Division's soldiers deteriorated into mutual distrust between them and their white officers. A day after Almond's arrival, the division attacked Mount Cauala, south of Massa, a major objective. For two days the soldiers attacked, but each time the enemy managed to push them back. On the third day the division reached the summit but could not hold it in the face of fierce resistance. Six days after the operation had begun, the Germans still occupied the mountain, but the 92nd Division had suffered four hundred casualties. On a number of occasions, soldiers had retreated without orders, some refusing to stay even when ordered to do so. Four months later a second major operation conducted in the Serchio Valley and around the Cinquale Canal had similar results. A third attack, code-named Operation Fourth Term, concluded much the same as the first two. Almond was certain that the problem was with the African American soldiers, NCOs, and junior officers and not with his senior commanders or himself. In February General Marshall arrived to investigate the situation.[25]

CHAPTER 26

THE FINAL PUSH

After Truscott had departed Italy for the invasion of southern France, Allied forces there had continued their advance north of Rome, though at a slower pace. Following General Wilson's departure for Washington, General Alexander became supreme Allied commander in the Mediterranean and General Clark assumed command of the Fifteenth Army Group. Clark quickly grew frustrated at the lack of progress in Italy, which resulted primarily from reduced troop numbers. Aside from the Allied divisions withdrawn earlier for the Normandy invasion, both Truscott and French general Alphonse Pierre Juin had taken their respective corps with them to southern France. Due to attrition, British battalions under Clark now had only three rather than four companies. To add to his problems, the Germans had voluntarily evacuated Greece in the fall of 1944, obligating the Allies to send three divisions there to discourage any return. Replacement troops arrived in Italy, though not enough to suit Clark, and they came from a variety of countries: England, the United States, Poland, Brazil, South Africa, New Zealand, India, liberated Italy, partisan Italy, and Palestine. The Allied force continued to be as it had been for some time—very multinational, with concomitant problems of language, customs, and equipment.[1]

While Operation Dragoon had unfolded, the U.S. Fifth Army and the British Eighth Army had advanced north until reaching the Gothic Line, Germany's final defensive network constructed to stall the Allies south of Bologna. While not as formidable as the Gustav Line, it was still an impressive series of concrete fortifications, obstacles, and tank traps set within a harsh, mountainous landscape. One temporary hole in the line opened on August 30, when the Canadian I Corps punched through. The Canadians might have been able to flank the Germans, but Eighth Army commander Oliver Leese had failed to bring forward his armor. Without tanks on hand, the Canadians could not exploit their success, and the Germans quickly patched the breach. Another crack occurred near the two ridges of Monticelli and Mount Altuzzo when regiments of the U.S. 85th Infantry "Custer" Division and the 91st Infantry "Pine Tree" Division fought small battles worthy of study by West Point cadets. As a result of the fighting, Il Giogo Pass fell, followed by Futa Pass. The Americans pressed forward, giving General Clark his first tantalizing view of the Po Valley but nothing more. The rains came, the soldiers lost what little momentum they had, and the Allied push skidded to a stop.[2]

Bill Hanrahan and other soldiers of the 85th Division had been part of the Fifth Army for some time. In May 1944, after crossing the Garigliano River, they had pushed the Germans hard, watching them retreat but noting how they fell back in a controlled and disciplined way. The division had reached Rome on June 4, the soldiers seeing for the first time in person the Roman Coliseum they had seen only in pictures; but there was no time for sightseeing. Hanrahan's artillery unit had moved on to Civitavecchia, then later to Florence to take up combat positions behind the infantry. There they saw the famous Ponte Vecchio, the only bridge left standing over the Arno River. It was fortunate that relatively little damage had occurred to Rome and Florence, resulting from Kesselring's resolve to spare these great cities. Apparently, he had felt differently about Naples, where his soldiers did their best to render the city and port useless to the Allies. The field marshal had continued to do everything he could to frustrate his pursuers until his own forces could re-form along the Gothic Line. By mid-September the 85th Division was back in combat against Kesselring's troops. The fighting was difficult, with Hanrahan's artillery unit staying tight behind the infantry regiment it supported. As always, the terrain heavily favored defensive efforts. Hanrahan recalled watching one infantry regiment go up a mountain six times and come back down six times; on the seventh try they made it to the top to stay. The campaign continued until late October, when the weather turned and offensive activity quickly slackened. The men were now physically and mentally exhausted. A final battle of the year took place at Mount Grandi by soldiers of the 85th and 88th Divisions, leaving them bloodied but still short of their objective. As the fighting lessened, the cold intensified.[3]

The Italian winter of 1944–45, when not snowing or freezing, delivered a cold, punishing, and unrelenting rain. Truscott would later recall the "bitter weather, in rugged mountains sheathed in snow and ice." Finally, U.S. troops received some cold-weather clothing. Rubberized shoepacs proved even better than the waterproof jackboots the German soldiers wore. Huge overcoats were available, but these turned out to be clumsy and remained warm only if dry; once wet, they became long, olive drab sponges. Eventually, combat jackets and pants arrived. When coupled with GI raincoats, they made a big difference. Hanrahan was thankful to be in the artillery. During the drive up Italy's spine, his unit had often found some kind of stone house to sleep in at night, which usually provided a light or two to assist the always-on-call fire-control operation. Replacements sprinkled into the division during this time. "They were mostly very young fellows, eighteen or so," Hanrahan remembered, "and they felt they were under pressure to fit in." Eventually, they did, with some assistance from Hanrahan and the other veterans, who were feeling pretty seasoned by then. The artilleryman recalled seeing only one general throughout his time in Italy, when General Clark came to address the troops. "He was what I would call a political general," Hanrahan reflected.[4]

Alexander had previously used an alternating one-two punch against the Gothic Line, with the British jabbing and then the Americans. He hoped at some point to force a breakthrough at an underattended point on the defenses. Unfortunately, the various obstacles, coupled with German tenacity and bad weather, kept the Allies just nine miles short of the Po Valley. Clark continued Alexander's alternating-jab tactic, but he had to accept that Italy would not fall by the end of the year, meaning that his troops would have to suffer through yet another cold and wet winter. Clark pushed his men hard, but he pushed himself hard as well. If the soldiers of the 85th and the other divisions had to spend the winter in the mountains, so would he. His own headquarters staff, which had looked forward to a not-too-unpleasant winter in Florence, groaned when they received word that they would be wintering in the mountains like everyone else in the army. Of course, cold weather for a general is never as cold as it is for a private: the general always has ways to warm up; the private can only shiver and swear.[5]

While Clark's troops likely appreciated his gesture, many must have wondered if warm weather in spring would bring another major offensive, and if so, what was the point. They likely pondered what was the sense in launching a deadly offensive as the snow melted when other Allied forces to the north were swinging hard from the west and punching deep from the east. It appeared that the Germans were on the ropes. The Allies in the Mediterranean had been in the fight long enough; why not stay out of arm's reach until the final bell sounded? Historians Graham and Bidwell later questioned the need for a big offensive as well, noting that the Combined Chiefs of Staff had no strategic gains in mind for Italy and that the real cost of a spring offensive would be paid with the deaths and injuries of soldiers and civilians. Of course, Clark was not happy either, though for a different reason. He was irritated that his friend Eisenhower had robbed him of Truscott's VI Corps and Juin's French Expeditionary Corps. Had the general not taken those units, he grumbled, the Allies might have finished Italy in 1944. Instead of spending another winter in the Apennines, they might have broken through Brenner Pass to Austria and Hungary and on to Germany. In December Truscott rejoined Clark in Traversa, Italy, at Futa Pass, elevation 2,700 feet, later recalling, "Here, in ice, snow, mud, and fog we spent the winter."[6]

In mid-December, when Truscott assumed command of the Fifth Army, it was in the process of resting, regrouping, and resupplying. Allied communication and supply lines stretched from north of Pisa on the Ligurian Sea to south of Ravenna on the Adriatic Sea. American-led units tended the Mediterranean side and the Apennines, while British-led units tended the Adriatic side. Before Truscott departed for France, the Fifth Army had more than 250,000 soldiers; now it numbered 150,000 men. Italy was still mountain fighting, but the only trained mountain troops in Italy had been those of General Juin, and he had taken them to France. Maybe, Truscott hoped, the new 10th Mountain Division might help. Kesselring was still Truscott's opponent, though now in name only. On October 23 Kesselring's staff car had collided with a German truck towing an artillery weapon along a darkened road outside Bologna, severely injuring the field marshal. Colonel General Heinrich von Vietinghoff now found himself directing the German defenses. Kesselring would return to Italy before February 1945, but the next month Hitler would order him to Berlin, impossibly hoping that he could somehow stop the collapse of the Third Reich. In Italy the Germans still controlled thirty-three divisions, six of which were Fascist Italian. They faced twenty-seven Allied divisions, but these were nearly equal to them in troop strength. What virtually guaranteed German defeat, however, was the complete lack of airpower, which must have grated Kesselring, a former Luftwaffe officer.[7]

Truscott's two corps commanders, Geoffrey Keyes and Willis Crittenberger, were former cavalry officers who had always been senior to him. In fact, Keyes had been one of his instructors at Officer Training Camp and had later served as Patton's deputy corps commander in Sicily, where he exercised oversight over Truscott. Likewise, Crittenberger had been one of Truscott's instructors at the Cavalry School. Fortunately, if either general resented the reversal of roles, he made no mention of it, nor was Truscott ever less than pleased with their support.[8]

The formal change-of-command ceremony occurred on December 16, 1944, with Clark handing off his cherished Fifth Army to Truscott and assuming command of the Fifteenth Army Group. He would once again supervise Truscott, who now considered himself among the "forewarned is forearmed" crowd. Coincidentally, the following day a parade of U.S. members of Congress arrived, hoping to see for themselves the progress in Italy. Clark, Truscott, and various other senior officers greeted the delegation of the House Military Affairs Committee. After introductions, followed by coffee and doughnuts, the visitors and their hosts climbed into thirty Jeeps and splashed and squished through rain and mud to visit locations of interest. Truscott spent most of his time with the acting committee chair, Representative John Martin Costello of California. Of course, he was also most impressed with the eye-catching Connecticut representative Clare Boothe Luce, famous as a writer, editor, playwright, and journalist even before her election to Congress. That afternoon Truscott gave his goodbyes to the group, then invited Bill Mauldin to ride with him back to "the hut," Truscott's name for his command post, where he and the soldier-correspondent joined the general's staff for cocktails and dinner.[9]

Another journalist covering the Military Affairs Committee reported on the congressional visit for Americans stateside. Anne O'Hare McCormick of the *New York Times* wrote an article that registered the surprise of the delegation:

> Rome: December 22—Members of the House Military Affairs Committee who concluded their tour of European battlefields with a visit to the Italian front expressed shocked surprise at the rigors of the campaign in Italy. Nothing they had seen in France, they said, could compare with the terrible terrain of the Apennines, and

Members of the House Military Affairs Committee—Representatives John M. Costello (*left*), Charles H. Easton (*center-right*), and Clare Boothe Luce (*right*)—tour the Fifth Army with Lieutenant General Mark Clark, commander, Fifteenth Army Group near Monghidoro, Italy, December 1944. Courtesy of the U.S. Army and the National Archives.

> nothing they had read at home prepared them for the inhuman conditions in which men of the 5th Army have to fight. The burden of complaint was that they didn't know the Italian battlefield was one of the toughest in the world. They had no idea of the tremendous natural obstacles the GI's have to contend with in addition to the stubbornness of the enemy stand on the best defensive positions he holds in Europe. . . . Stories have been written and have been printed. They have even been overwritten and printed so many times that readers don't see the mud or blood anymore. They don't hear the scream of shells or the thunder of fallen rockets. They don't realize what happens when towns are blasted from the earth and human beings are either buried under the debris or scattered like ants when somebody steps on an anthill. The boys they know sleep in wet holes, stand in water until their feet freeze, charge up slopes raked with machine guns, but words describing these things are not sensational enough to produce an answering sensation.[10]

On that same day, Clark summoned Truscott to Florence. Without mentioning Ultra as his source, the group commander told him that a significant German troop buildup was occurring in the Serchio Valley, about twenty miles north of Lucca. Clark suspected a strong German counterattack, not unlike that which had recently resulted in the still-raging Battle of the Bulge in Belgium, Luxembourg, and France. Although the Serchio Valley had been relatively quiet, less than two regiments of the 92nd Division defended the area. Truscott had known that a German division and an Italian division likely occupied the area, but this new information indicated that a German mountain division, an SS panzer division, and perhaps two other German divisions might attack. Any armored flanking attack against the inexperienced 92nd Division would threaten the critical Allied supply port at Livorno, about forty-five miles to the south. Truscott ordered two brigades of the 8th Indian Division, two regimental combat teams of the U.S. 85th Infantry Division, and various tank and artillery units into the general vicinity, with the 1st Armored Division holding in reserve at Lucca. These reinforcements were on the move but were not yet in place when the enemy struck.

In fact, the Germans *were* planning a counteroffensive at the behest of Mussolini, who prayed that it would be the Italian equal of the Bulge. On December 26 two Italian divisions and a German division struck the 92nd Division's positions, hoping to slice through and race on to Livorno. As Truscott later recalled, five or six battalions of Germans attacked two U.S. battalions. It was a shattering experience for the American troops, and more than a few of them "melted away." General Crittenberger rushed in the Indian brigades and called for air support. Through these efforts, Crittenberger was able to regain lost territory and secure Livorno. Officers and military police of the 92nd Division rounded up the "stragglers" and returned them to their units.[11]

Clark, still hoping to ignite some kind of offensive during the winter months, was irritated that the Serchio Valley situation had now caused a delay. Worse, he discovered that in November and December the Germans had managed to remove two of their divisions from Italy to reinforce in France, which was exactly what the Italian campaign was supposed to prevent. To complicate matters, flooding on the Adriatic side of the line had stopped the Eighth Army, and heavy snow and icy conditions were immobilizing the Fifth

Army. The turn in the weather, coupled with an already inadequate supply of ammunition, prompted Truscott to recommend postponing any offensive until the following month, when more ammunition would arrive. Clark was not pleased but had to agree. He went a step further and called off any major offensive until spring. He, however, did permit two limited-objective offensives, intended to hold the enemy to that front.[12]

Neither the Allies nor the Germans remained inactive during the winter. Artillery barrages ensured that everyone slept fitfully, if at all, and patrols from each side probed the other each night to discourage any surprises and to capture prisoners who might provide information. When not focused on incoming rounds or infiltrating Germans, the Allied troops did their best to stay warm but never quite succeeded. For some it was their first Apennine winter. Any complaint made by a replacement within earshot of a veteran was sure to invite a comment such as, "This is nothing, kid. It gets worse." Jaundice and various respiratory problems quickened the pace of the already overworked medical teams; even so, careful attention reduced the incidence of trench foot by two-thirds. Mail call and chow time were the highlights of the day, with every commander knowing well that troops would accept a lot of hardship as long as their mail found them. It was a soldier's only touch—literally—with his former life. The supply line trailed all the way back to the United States, with everything coming first to Naples or Livorno by ship; then to Florence, Pistoia, Lucca, or Pisa by truck; and then up deadly mountain roads by truck or Jeep. Anywhere beyond that meant hauling supplies on the backs of four thousand mules organized into fifteen pack trains or on the backs of the soldiers themselves.

Winter snows and rains brought mudslides, which meant that just keeping the roads and trails open became a continuous effort. Army engineers and Italian laborers put in countless hours keeping the roads drivable and the supply chain in motion. "No troops in the Army performed more valiant work than the engineers," Truscott remembered. Because Italy was the forgotten front, sometimes supplies and equipment were simply unavailable, no matter how much a commanding general pleaded. Consequently, nothing was discarded if it could be repaired, and some items critical to operations had to be manufactured from scratch in ad-hoc factories to the south. On the positive side, these activities employed thousands of starving Italians.[13]

Morale was always a concern for Truscott. "It is not hard to maintain morale when troops are advancing and winning victories," he recalled. "Then it is always high; and spirits soar in spite of the worst privations, physical exercise, and dangers." Soldiers who were cold and miserable resented news reports, even letters from home, that suggested that the real fighting was taking place in the north and questioned why the soldiers were still in Italy. "Prolonged absence brought personal problems—usually family distress, business or financial troubles, or affairs of the heart," Truscott later wrote. It was an unpleasant, even if not tremendously dangerous, time, and everyone from the newest private to the general himself suffered its effects. One thing that helped was the Fifth Army's rest-center program. When Truscott had commanded the 3rd Infantry Division, he had established a rest center in Naples. Now he opened other rest centers in Florence, Rome, Capri, and Sorrento. The army could furlough only a small percentage of the soldiers, but everyone knew there was at least a chance. It was a diversion for men who saw their future as an unending and deadly mountain road. In December Truscott received a letter from General Marshall, who realized that Christmas would find Truscott once again battling in Italy. Marshall added that he knew Truscott would have preferred to be fighting in the western front but reaffirmed that his vast experience had made him the exceptional choice to command the Fifth Army. He assured the general that the army had full confidence in him. Once again, Truscott was pleased with and reassured by Marshall's kindness, especially since two more months of winter conditions followed.[14]

General Keyes submitted a proposal to Truscott suggesting that the army should send the senior men from one particular division home. The 34th Division had been the first to arrive in Europe, and its soldiers had seen a lot of combat. Many of its original veterans resented that they were still in the war. The command had high rates of soldiers absent without leave (AWOL) and other offenses. According to Keyes, many of the older men felt they had done their job over the last three years and deserved rotation stateside. He finished his letter by saying, "The attitude of the men would seem to stem, not from 'combat' weariness, but from general 'war' weariness." Truscott was sympathetic but not persuaded. He countered that the morale of the 1st, 3rd, and 9th Divisions was good and that they had been in Europe almost as long. "I cannot but feel that their difficulty is entirely one of discipline and command responsibility," the army commander replied. "If there are officers in the 34th Division who have lost their usefulness and their efficiency and feel that they have done their part in the war, I think General Bolte should take corrective measures." Truscott did agree, however, that two and a half or three years at the front was long enough and suggested that such longtime veterans could rotate to the rear as other troops were sent forward. He nonetheless forwarded Keyes's letter to General Joseph McNarney, deputy chief of staff for Marshall. McNarney, while also sympathetic, pointed out the logistical impossibility of Keyes's proposal, which would, he reminded, have to apply to many divisions in Europe and the Pacific. He closed by saying that Keyes's letter suggested "definite indications of command failure particularly in the lower echelons."[15]

Truscott had a somewhat different view. "Command failures do not stem from the lower ranks, although they may exist there. Usually they originate among the higher echelons and are merely reflected downward." He did not think there was anything wrong with the soldiers, declaring, "If the Division was made to feel that only the best was expected of it, as with other divisions, it would not fail us in the test." Truscott seemed certain that it was the failure of high command, coupled with low expectations for troops, that set the stage for a division's personnel problems. In the near future he would have an opportunity to test his theory on the 92nd Division.[16]

During the winter of 1944, the 10th Mountain Division, having been declined by other theater commanders, became part of the Fifth Army. Truscott, no doubt smiling, later recalled, "it was one of the best combat divisions I knew during the war." He was equally pleased with its commander, Major General George P. Hays, whom he considered "one of the ablest battle leaders I ever knew" and who "fitted the Division like a well-worn and well-loved glove."[17]

With no major offensive permitted until spring, Truscott worked on setting up the two limited attacks permitted over the winter. The 92nd Division would conduct one of them, which Clark and Truscott saw as a way "to test further the battle worthiness of the colored troops." The 10th Mountain Division would conduct the other limited attack. These newcomers had been on defense along the high and rugged thirty-mile front between the Serchio Valley and Mount Belvedere. Now the division would attempt to capture Belvedere. The forbidding terrain around the mountain provided last-ditch accommodations for the many German units that controlled access to Highway 64, one of two major approaches to Bologna. Truscott's hope was that Hays's climbers could bag Belvedere and thus improve the army's launch position for the spring offensive. The previous November and December, Clark had attempted three times to take Mount Belvedere but without success. Its 3,900-foot peak remained clutched in the tight fist of the Germans, who knew that if the Allies knocked them off its summit, they essentially knocked them out of the war.[18]

General Hays studied the surrounding area. Because of its rugged features, he concluded that the Axis did not expect an attack to come through there during the winter. Nonetheless, the fresh eyes of Hays saw something that Clark, Truscott, and other senior commanders must have missed. The problem was not just Mount Belvedere, but also the Serrasicca-Campiano Ridge to the west, which the army had dubbed Riva Ridge. Hays suspected that German artillery observation posts positioned on the four-mile-long ridge, 3,200–4,800 feet high, surveilled the approach for any Allies and provided precise coordinates for artillery barrages delivered from protected positions on Belvedere. The key, Hays thought, would be taking out the artillery observers.[19]

Since the back of Riva Ridge was almost a walk-up, German troops abundantly protected that approach, but the front side had such a steep face that they placed few guards there. Hays, having elite mountain troops at his command, chuckled. Air reconnaissance and several ground patrols confirmed that relatively few Germans monitored that face. The 10th Mountain soldiers subsequently identified five routes, two of which allowed for previously positioned olive drab nylon climbing ropes, piton anchors (driven in by cloth-wrapped hammers), and snap rings (carabiners), all of which would serve to guide climbers in the dark. Hays prepared his plan. First, he would take Riva Ridge by surprise as quickly and quietly as possible. Then, he would take Mount Belvedere, which would not have supporting observation from the ridge. Since German mountain troops protected both heights, it would be a test of opposing mountain men.[20]

On February 16—two days before the attack—Hays met with his officers and men to discuss his plan, using a natural amphitheater for the briefing. Including such a large number of troops in a briefing was an exceedingly rare thing for a commanding general. But

Hays recognized that the soldiers were the expert climbers, not he or his officers. They seemed to collectively concur that both Riva Ridge and Mount Belvedere would be difficult but doable missions. Then Hays dropped the other boot: they would make the ascent in the dark, without air or artillery support, and with their weapons unloaded. He repeated this last point to assure their disbelieving ears, for it was the critical element for complete surprise. He allowed bayonets and grenades, but no weapons firing. In his diary mountaineer-soldier Dan Kinnerly jotted down Hays's bullet points on just how they were going to achieve this mission: They were to always move forward; they were never to go back; if they were ordered to go back, they must regard it as a false order; they were to shoot, stab, and brain the Germans; they could take trophies—anything—to one day show their grandchildren; they were to go up the mountains and do what had to be done. The general assured them that he was absolutely confident that they would do damn well. When he gave his soldiers a final "Good luck," they were ready to follow him anywhere.[21]

For weeks bright Allied lights had shone at night on Riva Ridge and Mount Belvedere. These were necessary not only to blind the Germans but also to provide the equivalent of partial moonlight for preparatory activities below. On February 18 at 7:30 P.M., the night climb up Riva Ridge began. The 1st Battalion, 86th Mountain Regiment, with some of the best climbers in the division, imitated the stealth of an Apache approaching an enemy's camp to steal horses. One thing very welcomed was the propitious arrival of a dense and quieting fog. Frequently looking up, feeling for the prepositioned ropes, stepping as silently as they possibly could, the soldiers worked their way up the face. By the time the Germans realized that the Americans had scaled the 3,876-foot face of the ridge, it was too late. The mountaineers had summited. With one exception, the Germans had understandably but foolishly vacated their observation posts for the night. Now the mission of the 86th Mountain was to defend the dark, freezing ridge from Germans who would desperately want it back. Soldiers and pack animals lugged a pack howitzer and four .50-caliber machine guns up to assist. The anticipated counterattack began about 10:00 A.M. and lasted all day and into the night. When it was over, the soldiers of the 86th Mountain were still in charge. Now they could direct their own artillery fire onto Mount Belvedere. Five teams of one thousand soldiers of the 86th Mountain Regiment had climbed the ridge. None died during the climb, but twenty-one fell during the counterattacks, with another fifty-two wounded and six captured or missing.

Late the following night, 12,000 soldiers from the three mountain regiments assaulted Mount Belvedere. As with the attack up Riva Ridge, surprise was critical. In the dark the soldiers relied on knives, bayonets, and grenades, not rifles. Again, there would be no air cover or artillery support until daybreak. The soldiers slipped by enemy units whenever possible, their sole objective being to capture and hold the summit. After brutal fighting, Mount Belvedere came under Allied control. The 10th Mountain Division suffered more than nine hundred casualties in the operation. Truscott ordered strong air and artillery support and assistance from nearby Brazilian troops. It was just as General Hays had promised: his soldiers had done damned well. Truscott was also proud, noting that in their first battle in Italy, the mountaineers had "performed like veterans." The fighting from Riva Ridge through Mount Belvedere had lasted six days instead of the anticipated two weeks. This time the Germans would not be able to retake ground, leaving the Fifth Army in good position for its spring offensive.[22]

The limited attack of the 10th Mountain Division proved much better than the 92nd Division's limited strike, which began on February 8. That unit's efforts continued to fall short. In the three-day attack in the Serchio Valley and Cinquale Canal area south of Massa, about two hundred "stragglers" had "melted away" during the night and now needed to be rounded up. The Germans had killed or wounded more than five hundred Americans. In his report to Clark, Truscott attributed the situation to infantry units lacking in reliability. While the situation was clearly much more complicated than that, he was more interested in results than causes. Of note was that the Italian naval seaport at La Spezia to the north had pounded the area of the division's assaults with fire from six 155-mm guns and four 128-mm fixed coastal guns.[23]

Truscott was no stranger to disorderly retirements under fire. He had seen one for himself at Port Lyautey, when his own officers had had to search for and round up more than two hundred "stragglers" of his 9th Infantry Division. He was also aware that similar flights had occurred at Faïd Pass in Africa. There a U.S. colonel in the field had shouted over a field telephone to doubtful officers at a higher headquarters that troops were fleeing, adding for emphasis, "I know panic when I see it!" More recently, during the Battle of the Bulge, significant numbers of recently arrived and inexperienced soldiers, many eighteen-year-old high-school graduates of the class of 1944, fled from the onslaught of a major German counteroffensive. As the green troops dropped their rifles and fled, some encountered incoming paratroopers of the 101st Airborne Division, who were moving forward to a place called Bastogne. One airborne officer recalled feeling ashamed of the mumbling and obviously panicked soldiers.[24]

Not long before, Truscott had inspected the 92nd Infantry Division and awarded nearly forty Bronze Stars and Combat Infantry Badges. He recalled a remark by General Devers, who "was convinced colored troops had not yet had a fair chance." Truscott was in a quandary. He held many positive memories of working with the 9th and 10th Cavalry Regiments over the years, but he knew the spring offensive had to succeed. He later wrote, "Our colored soldiers were the product of heredity, environment, education, economic and social ills beyond their control—and beyond the sphere of military leaders." The general also knew of the significant contribution performed by many African American general-service troops who had unloaded cargo at Anzio while under continual German artillery and air bombardments. What he may not have known was that some of the U.S. Army Air Forces fighter pilots flying missions over Anzio were African Americans who later gained fame as the Tuskegee Airmen. Truscott ordered a comprehensive investigation into the conduct of African American soldiers in 92nd Division noninfantry units. He reported to General Clark his conclusion: "The Division had been satisfactory in every respect except the one element which justified its existence—the combat infantry."[25]

Truscott was a man of his times, and in his era racism tended to be blatant and pervasive. The most obvious difference between the 92nd and his other divisions, he surmised, was the race of its soldiers. At the same time, while the general had had no difficulty holding the senior officers of the 34th Division responsible for the recent poor conduct of its soldiers, he seemed less inclined to do so when it came to the 92nd Division. Additionally, having come very close to relieving Major General Dahlquist for perceived command failure in southern France, Truscott seemed reluctant to consider relieving Major General Almond, though one factor may have been Almond's close relationship with General Marshall, whom Truscott admired and respected. Both Almond and Marshall were graduates of the Virginia Military Institute and went back a long way together

Lieutenant General Lucian K. Truscott, Jr., commander, Fifth Army, inspects soldiers of the 92nd Infantry Division near Viareggio, Italy, December 1944. Courtesy of the U.S. Army and the National Archives.

in the army. The responsibility for the conduct of these soldiers did not end with Almond and Truscott, however. Clark, Eisenhower, and Marshall were complicit as well. As a group, these five generals held low expectations for the 92nd Division. Many of its soldiers, distrustful of their white commanders, delivered what the generals expected of them. Historian Daniel Gibran makes an interesting observation.

While the percentage of illiterate white soldiers in the army was less than the percentage of illiterate black soldiers, as a whole, there were more illiterate white soldiers. With this in mind, Gibran wondered how any other division would have performed in combat had the army assigned to it illiterate white soldiers equal to the proportions of illiterate troops (around 60 percent) in the 92nd Division.[26]

In his postwar writings, Truscott advocated integration of African Americans into all units of the army, which was then in progress but still meeting pockets of resistance. Nevertheless, it is very doubtful that he supported such in 1944, never recommending it or trying it himself even on a limited basis. Yet this was the same general who occasionally barked to some of his junior officers: "What do you mean, it can't be done? Have you tried it? Go out and do it." In fairness, he may have concluded that it would be highly improbable for the soldiers then assigned to the 92nd Division to overcome a history of slavery, vivid memories of lynchings, denial of education, limitations on employment, distrust of white officers, and very low expectations from army leadership. Even considering all this, it is still fair to consider how the division might have performed had its commander been the caliber of George Hays, Bill Darby, Jim Gavin, Robert Frederick, Ernie Harmon, or John O'Daniel. More to the point, when Truscott commanded a division, he had elevated a standard infantry division close to commando and ranger quality. Now as an army's commanding general, however, he had eight to ten divisions under him and only limited time to devote to each. Still, had he been the commanding general of the 92nd Infantry Division at some point, there is little doubt that the performance of its infantry would have been heads and shoulders above what it was under Almond.[27]

While in Europe to meet with Eisenhower, General Marshall took the occasion to investigate personally the situation of the 92nd Division in Italy. There was little doubt that the unit had not performed well, but Marshall wanted to know why. In the meantime, he ordered the division reorganized. The army once again consolidated the best troops of the three regiments into a single one, the 370th; the other two regiments then assumed engineer general-service duties. The 92nd Division would now consist of the mostly African American 370th Regiment, the white 473rd Regiment (retrained as infantry from now-unneeded antiaircraft duties), and the highly praised Japanese American 442nd Regimental Combat

Team, brought back from France by Marshall for this purpose. Additionally, within the division, African Americans staffed two of the four tank battalions as well as various artillery units. In later combat the division as a whole did well, but the 370th Regiment's performance was, in Truscott's opinion, "disappointing."[28]

Truman Gibson, civilian aide to the secretary of war, arrived in Italy at Marshall's request to look once again into the conduct of the 92nd Division. He had previously assisted Brigadier General Davis with the 1943 review of the unit, then at Fort Huachuca, Arizona. Gibson found that not much had changed since that first review. His second confidential report on the division, declassified in 1978, revealed several areas of concern. For instance, both white and black officers of the 92nd Division interviewed expressed concerns about the 2,600 replacements that had recently come into the command. These African American soldiers had previously served in general-service units, doing such duties as ship unloading, and had subsequently volunteered for duty with the 92nd Division. Somehow, it seems, they had received little if any infantry training. Their officers were stunned when first told that many of the soldiers did not know how to load or fire their M-1 rifles. General Almond "denied emphatically" that such was the case, but Gibson's investigation noted, "The fact remains that no other single observation was repeated in more instances than this one." The army's General Comprehensive Test, he further noted, had relegated over 90 percent of these replacements to Classes IV and V, the two lowest levels. There was little doubt that their country had denied most of these soldiers even basic education. Gibson's conclusion was that "for the most part they were sent directly into combat teams for training. Very few had the benefit of the Infantry Basic Training Courses. No similar situation has ever existed in any white units." His other findings were that both white and black officers complained about the promotion system within the division; that white officers reported that "any type of close association with Negro officers is discouraged in the division"; that two black officers escorted to an officer's club by a white officer were asked to leave, the white officer being officially reprimanded for having "an improper social attitude"; and that black officers complained that the reconstituted 370th Regiment now had no African American company commanders. Gibson, when interviewed fifty years later by historian Daniel Gibran, concluded that the division had been designed to fail.[29]

Until his death in 1975, Almond opposed integration in the armed services and never repudiated his earlier statements. He might have been surprised to hear of the World War II experience of the 78th Infantry "Lightning" Division in northwestern Europe. There, following the Battle of the Bulge, a call for replacements had resulted in many African American soldiers volunteering. Within the semi-integrated 78th Division, these soldiers served in segregated platoons within companies of white soldiers. Major General Edwin Pearson Parker, Jr., said of his African American platoons: "Morale: Excellent. Manner of performance: Superior. Men are very eager to close with the enemy and to destroy him. . . . When given a mission they accept it with enthusiasm, and even when losses to their platoon were inflicted the colored boys pressed on." One of Parker's battalion commanders added, "White men and colored men are welded together with a deep friendship born of combat and matured by a realization that such an association is not the impossibility that many of us have been led to believe."[30]

After the war the opposing German commander, Brigadier General Fretter Pico, issued an indirect critique of Almond's battle tactics. In speaking of the Allied defenses in Almond's area, he asserted that "the weaknesses of your deployment in the Serchio Valley in December 1944 [was] that your troops were deployed on a front which was too long for the number of troops available, and your reserves were too far in the rear areas which prevented their being deployed immediately."[31]

Military-service integration, ordered by President Truman in 1946, did not take effect throughout the army until 1954. Since that time, African American service members have fought in Vietnam, Grenada, Panama, the Persian Gulf, Somalia, Bosnia, Kosovo, Iraq, and Afghanistan. They now constitute more than 22 percent of the U.S. Army.[32]

CHAPTER 27

Last Battle

For General Clark, February 1945 brought more bad news from the Combined Chiefs of Staff. Five Eighth Army divisions, including the Canadian corps, would depart the Mediterranean to join Field Marshal Montgomery's forces in northern Europe. Many U.S. Army Air Forces fighter-bombers would leave as well. The remaining Mediterranean units would go on the defensive, at least temporarily, attacking only if it appeared that the Germans were withdrawing. Clark now anticipated launching no offensive until April, at which time Truscott's Fifth Army would make the primary thrust west of Highway 65, not west of Highway 64 as Truscott advocated. Of course, the general had been down a similar road before and took the precaution of developing a secondary plan. "I had not forgotten the change of direction in the breakout from Anzio," he later wrote.[1]

As the toes and fingers of the army's soldiers began to thaw, and the men continued to worry about what the spring offensive might bring, a visitor arrived at a portion of the front held by the 10th Mountain Division. Connecticut representative Clare Boothe Luce had returned to see more of the Fifth Army, which she did. Riding in a Jeep and attired in an Eisenhower-style jacket, she surprised forty soldiers of the 10th Mountain as they waited in line to use a large portable shower. The division's local newspaper, *The Blizzard,* suggested that she could easily have been mistaken for a USO star rather than a member of Congress.[2]

By the end of March, the Allies in Italy knew that the enemy had no intention of withdrawing as twenty-four German divisions and five Fascist Italian divisions remained in place. Seventeen of these units were at the front, with the rest in reserve or elsewhere in northern Italy. The British Eighth Army retained eleven divisions and a collection of brigades and Allied Italian units. Truscott's Fifth Army had nine divisions, of which seven were American, one South African, and one Brazilian, as well as an Allied Italian group and miscellaneous units. While Allied and Axis troops were comparable in number, the former had much better air support, armor, resources, and morale than their deteriorating opponents.[3]

Clark's revised plan for the spring offensive differed from Alexander's previous intentions. In three phases his two armies would debouch from the mountains into the Po Valley, capture Bologna, and then spread throughout northern Italy. Four days before the main Allied attack, however, the 92nd Infantry Division, now including the Japanese American 442nd Regimental Combat Team, would attack north along the Ligurian Sea to capture Massa and the Italian naval base at La Spezia. Clark and Truscott hoped this diversionary strike would confuse the Germans enough that they would move forces in that direction, or at least hold those already there in place. Most important was that the enemy not reposition forces to the east, which could blunt the main attack.

According to the plan, on April 5 the 92nd Division would launch its diversion. On April 9, on the east, the Eighth Army would lead out with its portion of the main attack. On April 12, on the west, Fifth Army would follow. Generally, the Eighth Army would fan out north and northeast, while the Fifth Army would fan out north and northwest. Both commands would have full air support. Truscott's IV Corps, aside from the 92nd Division, consisted of the 1st Armored, 10th Mountain, and 1st Brazilian Divisions; his II Corps consisted of the 34th, 85th, 88th, and 91st Infantry Divisions; the 6th South African Division; and an Italian group. He would hold the 85th Division in reserve until he was ready to employ it. The II Corps would take or isolate Bologna and link up with the Eighth Army while the IV Corps protected the left flank. Much to Truscott's liking, Clark's revised plan now called for the Fifth Army to use Highway 64 instead of Highway 65. It also stressed speed, boldness, and the exploitation of successes—just what Truscott did best.[4]

The U.S. Army Air Forces, and in particular the XXII Tactical Air Command, struck the first blow of the offensive. Its commander, Brigadier General Thomas R. Darcy, provided excellent ground support, using forward air-control officers in small aircraft and Jeeps. General Darcy worked hand in hand with Truscott, even moving his own headquarters to Futa Pass, near the army's headquarters. Truscott was confident that Darcy would provide excellent close air support throughout the offensive.[5]

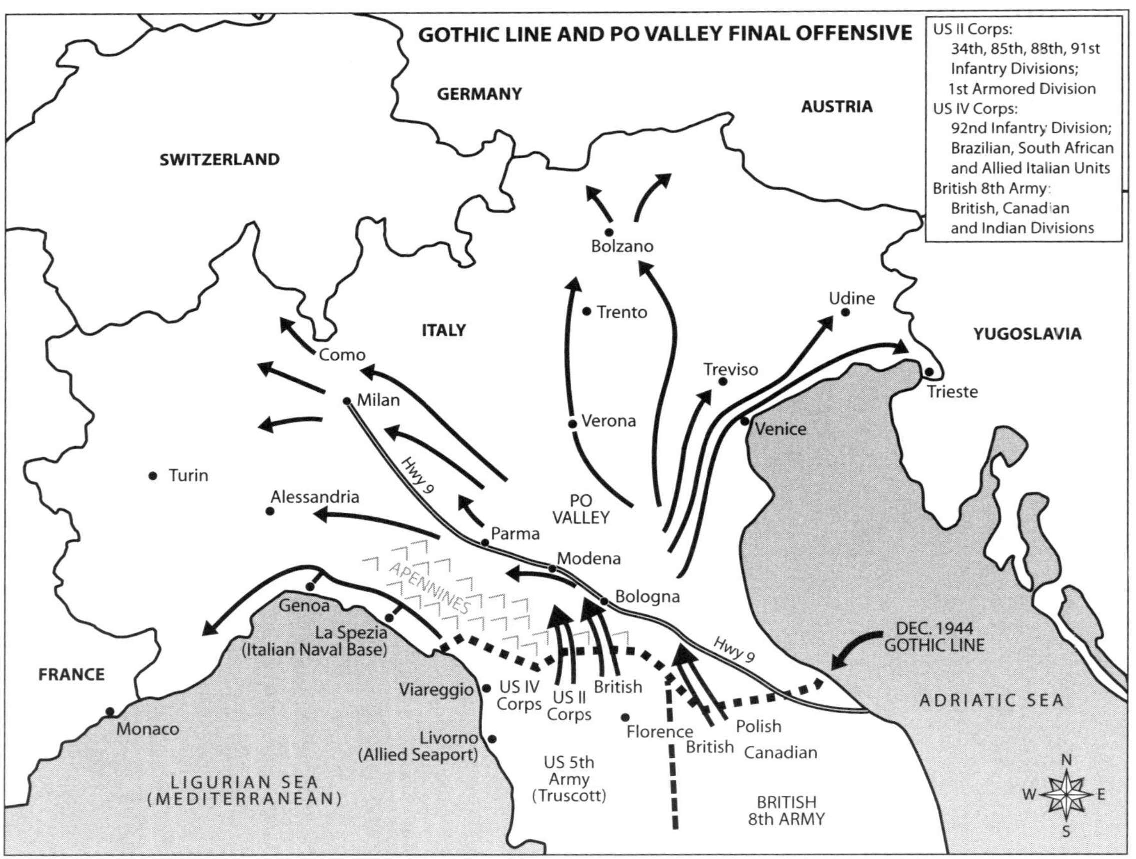

The Gothic Line and the Po Valley final offensive in Italy. Map by Megan Postell.

Lieutenant General Mark Clark, commander, Fifteenth Army Group, and Major General George P. Hays (*wearing helmet*), commander, 10th Mountain Division, at a forward-observation post, Po Valley, April 1945. Roy O. Bingham Western History Collection, Denver Public Library, Denver, Colorado.

On April 5, as planned, the 92nd Division attacked, taking Massa by April 7 and Carrara by the eleventh. The Germans took the bait and held units in the west to counter this advance. The division, despite steep mountains, bad weather, and tough resistance, went on to capture La Spezia and Genoa. Truscott later praised the unit's good work: "As a diversionary measure it was wholly successful."

Farther to the east, the Eighth Army moved out on April 9 as scheduled. To Truscott's disappointment, however, the rest of the Fifth Army would not roll forward on April 12 as planned. Bad weather kept the warplanes grounded, and he declined to launch his army's attacks without air support. April 13 brought more bad weather and the disquieting news that President Roosevelt had died.[6]

Truscott, immobilized in Traversa, cursed as he looked out from a mess tent. A thick and heavy fog spoiled the early morning hours of April 14. Generals Darcy and Carleton, along with now-Major Wilson, muttered epithets at the nasty weather that kept visibility at zero. All of Darcy's planes remained grounded. From 5:00 A.M. on, Sergeant Hong likely never let a coffee cup get empty. Darcy, sometimes with a telephone in each hand, received only bad news from each of his fighter bases. Pilots stayed close to their planes, ready to sprint to cockpits the moment their commander gave them the go. Finally, about 8:00 A.M., the fighter base at Grossetto called: "Can see end of runway. They're taking off." Other bases soon checked in with similar reports. Truscott called General Crittenberger and told him to advance at 9:00 A.M. Two days later than its commander would have preferred, the Fifth Army's attack was rolling forth.[7]

Elsewhere in Europe, the noose tightened around the German neck. The Soviet army was passing through Vienna and heading toward Berlin. American and British forces had crossed the Rhine River and were moving into Germany. Now in Italy, Allies were rushing forward as well. Truscott and Wilson flew by Cub to an observation post sited on Mount Castellana. From that vantage point, they watched the 10th Mountain Division, against heavy opposition, summit Mount Rocco Roffino. The general signaled the 1st Armored Division to fire up its tanks and rumble forward. He later wrote, "The 10th Mountain Division would carry the brunt of the attack to the Po Valley—and beyond." Ironically, by this time perhaps half of the soldiers in the 10th Mountain were replacements who had not gone through mountain training in Colorado; in addition, the unit as a whole had much less combat experience than any of Truscott's other American divisions.[8]

Within the Fifth Army, a twenty-one-year-old, ninety-day-wonder second lieutenant, fresh from Officer Candidate School, arrived as a replacement officer in the 10th Mountain. A boy from Kansas, he shook his head and wondered how he had ended up in the 85th Mountain Regiment. At the onset of the spring offensive, he found himself southwest of Bologna near Castel d'Aiano and the now-captured Mount Belvedere. On April 14, while moving forward near Mount Della Spe, his company was stopped when Germans on Hill 913 sent forth artillery, mortar, and machine-gun fire. One machine gun, secreted in a farm building ahead, delivered a constant stream of rounds. The company commander sent for the shavetail lieutenant and his platoon sergeant and said, "Take the platoon around the left flank and stop that machine gun fire." Butterflies ricocheted off the walls of the lieutenant's stomach. Personally leading a squad of soldiers, he crawled forward toward the enemy position, not daring to stand up where gunfire and explosions were sending small bits and large chunks of metal through the air. When he was fifty or sixty feet from the building, the young officer pulled the pin from a grenade, scrambled up the rocky grade, and hurled it at the machine-gun crew. He cursed as it exploded short of its target. Suddenly, a shell exploded very close by. His radioman, separated in the confusion, appeared wounded. The lieutenant crawled on hands and knees to his injured man, grabbing and dragging the young soldier toward nearby shell hole. "Too late," he remembered, "I felt a sting, as something hot, something terribly powerful crashed into my upper back behind my right shoulder. . . . Then the horror hit me—*I can't feel anything below my neck!*" Sergeant Aulis Olavi "Ollie" Manninen, a future Olympics marathon runner, arrived and dragged the lieutenant behind a wall. Then Manninen and the company continued forward as previously ordered. The seriously wounded officer remained on the ground for six hours until medic teams could make their way to him. Another less seriously wounded soldier stayed with him. The lieutenant felt no pain from his ripped shoulder, shattered bones, blood loss, and damaged spinal cord. Arriving at an evacuation hospital three hours later, he knew one thing for sure: "I was paralyzed from the neck down." He would struggle for more than three years in hospitals, working to recover the use of his body and undergoing multiple surgeries and intensive therapy. Afterward he managed with great physical difficulty to attend college and law school, then went into politics. Bob Dole, who would become a U.S. senator, would never regain full use of his right arm.[9]

While recovering in an army hospital early on, Dole became friends with another young lieutenant, then a member of the 442nd. Only a week after Dole sustained his injury, that officer had lost an arm in a battle that happened on April 21 at Colle Musatello, near

San Terenzo, five miles south of La Spezia and not far from Hill 913. Just twenty years old, the lieutenant led his platoon through rifle and machine-gun fire, seeking to capture German defenses on a ridge. At forty yards away, they were too close to call for artillery fire. As he rose up to throw a grenade, something hard slugged him in the side. "Then I counted off three seconds," he later recalled, "as I ran toward that angry splutter of flame at the mouth of the nearest machine gun." His grenade found its mark. As the German gun crew staggered out, he blasted them with his Thompson submachine gun. Wanting to avoid getting his platoon pinned down, he led the men forward while moving toward a second machine-gun nest. Knowing that he had a stomach wound, the lieutenant nevertheless lobbed two more grenades at another bunker. Then his legs gave out and he fell to his knees. Somewhere in the background someone shouted, "Come on, you guys, go for broke," the motto of the 442nd. The lieutenant forced himself forward, pulled the pin from his final grenade, and lifted his arm to throw it at a third machine gun. At that instant a German soldier fired a rifle grenade from ten yards away, its impact shredding the young officer's right arm. Using his left hand to grab the now-armed grenade from the clench of his useless right hand, he hurled it forward and watched it explode in the face of the German soldier, who was frantically reloading. He continued forward, using his left arm to fire his Thompson, his "useless right arm slapping red and wet against [his] side." The young lieutenant from the 442nd, Daniel Inouye, also became a U.S. senator. Although he and Dole would be members of different political parties, they would always share a bond.[10]

Another officer had better luck than Dole or Inouye. First Lieutenant Paul M. Bennett had joined the 86th Mountain Regiment from his home in Texas. He later recalled: "We traveled by mules. There was one per platoon and we took turns holding on to his tail to sleepwalk." On April 21 his platoon was advancing through mountainous terrain southwest of Bologna near the tiny crossroads of Sulmonte. He had just captured four German soldiers, which he handed off to some of his own soldiers. He then knelt down on the ground and used the soft dirt as an ad-hoc map to direct the next movements of his men. Just then a mortar round landed in front of him, killing two soldiers beside him and seriously wounding the lieutenant. A large piece of shrapnel had slammed into his outer thigh, passing through his cargo pants' pocket and into his leather wallet. Bennett later discovered that his wallet—and a thick wad of Italian lire from a recent payday—had stopped most of the hot metal. The jagged shell fragment had burned a hole in the wallet and almost torn it in half, but it had kept the fragment from doing far greater damage to his femoral artery than it might have. His soldiers conscripted the four captured Germans to carry Lieutenant Bennett back to an emergency medical station. Tragically, the same day that Bennett's mother received word of his serious wound, she learned that another son, Percy Bennett, had been killed while fighting in the Philippines just three days earlier. The lieutenant survived not only his wound but the war as well and returned home to raise a family. The shell fragment remains held in that wallet today. It was just as General Hays had mentioned—a souvenir to take home for his grandchildren. Bennett's daughter would one day marry the son of Lieutenant Bill Phillippi, the C-47 pilot shot down after dropping his stick of 82nd Airborne paratroopers over Sicily.[11]

For the first time in his life, Truscott watched Army Air Forces bombers deliver their payload not from below, but from 20,000 feet in the air while sitting in the back seat of General Darcy's modified P-51 Mustang fighter. Truscott had been bombed many times, and he had seen many planes overhead releasing their loads, but this was different. "It was the first bombardment I had ever watched from above. It was a breathtaking sight and an unforgettable experience." Darcy descended and circled so tightly that the Mustang's wings were vertical to the ground, allowing Truscott to see that every bridge over the Po River was gone. It was beneficial to the army commander to watch the action from 10,000 feet or so, but he later confessed, "I was careful never to let the fact be known among the higher echelons, for I had some doubt that these activities would be viewed with favor." On April 15 and 16 the Fifth Army continued to move forward, taking mountain peak after mountain peak and town after town. Because the 1st Armored Division had little infantry and was needed elsewhere, Truscott brought up the 85th Infantry Division to replace it and to stay abreast and to the right of the 10th Mountain Division. Later, viewing the action from a small observation aircraft, Truscott could see that his divisions were all out of the mountains and into the Po Valley, with the 10th Mountain and 1st Armored already in pursuit of their next objectives. He sent other units east to cut off the retreat routes of the Germans.[12]

General McNarney, deputy chief of staff to General Marshall, visited the front for a few days. During this time, he flew with Truscott by Cub to visit Crittenberger's IV Corps. Before McNarney departed for Caserta, he asked Truscott when he thought the Fifth Army would reach Highway 9, the main northwest-to-southeast route that crossed the Po Valley from Milan to the Adriatic Sea. Truscott estimated by 1:00 P.M. on April 20. McNarney bet a quart of scotch that it would not happen by then. Truscott took the wager but lost the bet by an hour and soon after forwarded a bottle of scotch. McNarney returned it with a note asking that it go to the first soldier who had crossed Highway 9. Private 1st Class B. L. Lessmeister of Montrose, Missouri, a lead scout with the 86th Mountain Regiment, had done just that at about 2:00 P.M. on April 20. Thereafter, at least for a while, he became very popular within his squad.[13]

On April 21, from separate directions but at about the same time, Truscott's 34th Division and the Polish Corps of the Eighth Army entered Bologna. With the Germans now on the run, Truscott ordered no letup of the pursuit. Both of his corps were to cross the Panaro River, move on to the Po River, seize crossing sites, and cut off those enemy units that had not made it that far north.

By the twenty-third, Lucian had a few moments to share his thoughts in a letter to Sarah. "The death of President Roosevelt at this particular time is one of the great tragedies of history. I think it is on a par with Lincoln's loss after the Civil War. I cannot help but fear for the future." Later came more bad news for Sarah. Lucian's April 24 letter said, "You are going to be sadly disappointed, if you received my last letter, to hear that I shall not be able to see Doodie graduate." Perhaps what worried her more, as well as Lucian, was that the army would do its best to rush the new West Point–educated second lieutenant to war, perhaps in the Pacific.[14]

Antifascist Italian partisans, previously organized, trained, and equipped by the Allies, now rose up within Bologna and helped root out German soldiers. Others were doing the same in other villages and towns. "Bologna was the first place where they distinguished themselves during the campaign," Truscott recalled, "but their assistance thereafter was widespread. In fact, Partisans took over some of the cities before our arrival, on the heels of the departing Germans."[15]

Clark notified Truscott that he, General Keyes, and General Crittenberger were to come to Bologna for a "triumphal entry." Truscott had no interest in attending a media event but followed orders. There, Clark's Jeep caravan, led by military police with screaming sirens, entered the city in yet another triumph. "What we were supposed to accomplish, I do not know," recalled a disgusted Truscott. Apparently, the Bolognese agreed, for only a few of them watched the parade pass. Truscott later wrote, "It was a far cry from the tumultuous reception in Rome the previous year."[16]

By April 23 General Hays and his 10th Mountain Division were preparing to cross the Po, and others units of the II and IV Corps were nearing the river. Thousands of Germans were surrendering, but thousands more were still in flight, sometimes moving in opposite directions. Truscott and General Darcy, once again in the modified P-51, were in the air viewing the spectacle. Suddenly, the Mustang dove steeply. Truscott, who knew Clark, Eisenhower, and Marshall would be livid if they knew of his airborne antics, was relieved when he saw that the object of the rapid descent was to strafe a German column. After several more strafing runs, which left vehicles burning and soldiers scrambling, Darcy moved on to find other targets, with Truscott thoroughly enjoying this midlife hot-rodding.[17]

In something of a sleight of hand, the 10th Mountain Division gained possession of riverine assault boats intended for use by the 85th Division. Two 10th Mountain engineer officers from the 85th Mountain Regiment managed to convince those bringing up the five trucks carrying fifty plywood assault boats to follow them. Thus, General Hays established the initial bridgehead when two of his regiments, under heavy fire, paddled across the Po near San Benedetto. Truscott was delighted with their success and ordered his engineers to install bridges across the river so that other units could cross and continue the pursuit.[18]

Colonel Darby now reappeared at the front, coming to see his old friend General Hays. Now assigned to the War Department in Washington, D.C., Darby was in Europe accompanying General "Hap" Arnold and other dignitaries on an inspection tour. By coincidence, Hays's assistant division commander had sustained a serious wound earlier in the day, and the general asked Truscott if it would be possible for Darby to take over his duties for the 10th Mountain Division. Truscott was delighted to approve and to see his old friend again, recalling both the early days of ranger training in Northern Ireland and the dark days of tragedy at Anzio. Clark and McNarney, queried about Darby's transfer, supported it too. Darby himself was more than pleased to leave a desk job and be back in command at the front. He was perhaps the only soldier in World War II to have been both a ranger and a mountaineer.[19]

By April 26 three engineer-constructed bridges, along with a ferry, carried troops, vehicles, and equipment over the Po River. Troops from both the Eighth and the Fifth Armies poured into the valley, capturing Verona, Padua, Vicenza, and Treviso and sealing off German retreat routes into the Alps. During this hectic time, the 10th Mountain gained information regarding Mussolini's hideout and raced across Lake Garda by watercraft to capture him. They just missed nabbing the former dictator. Italian partisans had detected him in the back of a German truck, bundled up in a greatcoat and hoping to pass as a common soldier. Partisans arrested Mussolini and his mistress, Claretta Petacci, and others with them. They immediately shot them with machine pistols and took the bodies to Loreto Plaza in Milan. There the partisans strung up Mussolini and Petacci feet first near an Esso service station where the previous year Axis authorities had executed Italian partisans.[20]

In the last few days of the war, Truscott came close to death once again. He was riding in a small, unarmed, single-engine observation plane with wing overhead and an abundance of cockpit glass all around, when he and his pilot entered a barrage of German flak. Truscott later remembered, "[the pilot] twisted and turned his way earthward through a hail of lead to tree-top level, and we made our escape with no more damage than a few holes through wings and fuselage of the L-5."[21]

On April 30 General Clark contacted Truscott and informed him that the Germans would surrender at noon on May 2. The Fifth Army had already taken more than 80,000 enemy soldiers into custody. The morning of the second arrived clear, but afternoon rainstorms turned violent. Truscott remained at his command post and handled routine matters, pleased when his correspondent friend Mike Chinigo dropped in from Rome to offer congratulations. At 5:30 P.M. word came that the Germans had surrendered. Carleton, Darcy, and a dozen staff members later gathered at the command post, situated in an olive grove not far from Verona. Major Wilson recorded the scene in the Fifth Army log: "Few magnums of champagne are cracked open to celebrate the victory. News is broadcast to troops in the area and there is a great deal of noise, fireworks, and so on from all Army and civil personnel in the Verona area. . . . Very late dinner and bed."[22]

The Germans actually surrendered on May 3. Kesselring's successor, German general Heinrich von Vietinghoff, dispatched Lieutenant General Johann Schlemmer and others to meet with General Clark, stopping first at Fifth Army's command post. Truscott had no interest in meeting with them and sent them on to army-group headquarters. Clark's staged photo session took place the next day, May 4, with German representative General Fredolin von Senger und Utterlin, a former Rhodes scholar and Cassino defender, formally saluting the American general. British Lieutenant General Richard L. McCreery, Eighth Army, and Lieutenant General Truscott stood in the background, the latter appearing unimpressed. Still wearing his well-worn cavalry britches and leather jacket, Truscott saw no more reason to "dress" for the German surrender than he had done for the French surrender at Port Lyautey. "The meeting struck me as pointless," Truscott recalled, "for the only purpose was a photographic record in Hollywood tradition."[23]

The marathon bloodletting up the Ionian Peninsula had lasted over twenty months and had inched along for more than 1,100 miles. Between 400,000 and 500,000 Allied soldiers had fought in Italy at one time or another. Of the 312,000 Allied casualties, 189,000 were from the Fifth Army. Almost 20,000 American soldiers died as did 6,600 British Commonwealth soldiers and more than 5,000 French soldiers. More than 48,000 German soldiers died. Officials could only estimate the number of Italian civilians killed, which was dwarfed by the number who were homeless.[24]

Correspondent Eric Sevareid reflected on the war in Italy: "[S]ome day people will want to know whether the returns balance the enormous investment of Allied lives, ships, transport, and planes. They will ask if we could not have achieved almost as much by stopping in southern Italy at the Volturno line, securing our ports and our bases and using the bulk of our forces in more fruitful encounters elsewhere. . . . Did not the Italian ground fighting really become a war of attrition and nothing more?"[25]

Kesselring's chief of staff, General Siegfried Westphal, proffered his opinion of the Allied tactical conduct of the war in Italy: "If, in September 1943, the Allies had landed not at Salerno but near Rome—and in January 1944 not at Anzio but near Leghorn—it would have cost them fewer casualties. This cautiousness caused them to miss other opportunities. But, in the end, the Allied victory came from a frontal attack, after the troops had gnawed their way from the toe of Italy's boot and up the leg."[26]

On April 30, a few days before the end of the war in Italy, Colonel Darby, who personified everything the U.S. Army could ask for in a leader, died when two 88-mm shells exploded near the small town of Torbole, near Lake Garda. He died not from an artillery barrage that lasted for twenty minutes or more but from one of two rounds delivered by a nearly defeated German army with little ammunition left. One piece of shrapnel punctured his chest and killed him instantly. Truscott noted with sadness, "Darby was one of the outstanding leaders whom I knew during the war." The army promoted the legendary ranger posthumously to brigadier general.[27]

Bill Hanrahan was thankful to be alive. During the spring offensive, the 85th Division had moved forward east of Bologna and into Verona. The retreating Germans were falling back, using trucks and horse-drawn equipment to flee, and the pursuing Allies caught many in the open. The smart ones surrendered; the others suffered their final fate. When word of the German surrender reached them, Hanrahan's unit was on its way to Innsbruck, Austria, anticipating having to plow through four feet of snow at Brenner Pass. It was only then that he felt sure that he would make it home. There was the possibility of going to the Pacific, but that turned out not to be the case for him. The army transferred him to the 34th Division when it finally sent home the senior veterans of that long-serving unit. Some partisan activity required Hanrahan and his fellow soldiers to deploy to Trieste for a short time. Once the hostilities had ended, he managed to visit Venice, and still later he won a raffle that allowed for a week's leave in Switzerland; he even worked in a visit to Milan. While seated in a railway car on his way back to camp, he heard something about an extraordinary bomb having exploded in Japan.[28]

CHAPTER 28

The End of a War and Other Affairs

When Clare Boothe Luce glided into a salon where a group had gathered, conversation ceased and eyes followed her. Moreover, she knew how to work a room. If she did not already know whom she would greet first, she scanned those assembled and settled on someone, usually a man, likely wealthy or powerful—or both. An acquaintance said of Luce, "She was no vamp, but all she had to do was just smile at a man and the guy would fall down dead." At evening's end, when the women surrendered the room and the men pulled out cigars and opened the brandy, she remained—if so inclined. She was the wife of Henry Luce, founder of *Time* magazine.[1]

Clare Boothe was born in 1903. Her formal education was unimpressive, but she gained considerable knowledge from books and by harvesting the experience of men who came into her life. Her first husband proved to be an abusive alcoholic but gave her a child, Ann Clare Brokaw, born in 1924. Divorce followed at Clare's request, resulting in a comfortable settlement from her wealthy ex-husband.[2]

She invaded New York society heavily armed with beauty, brains, and a determination to get whatever she sought. At one of the many posh parties she attended, Clare met Condé Nast, owner of *Vogue* and *Vanity Fair* magazines. Later invited to some of Nast's parties, she met other famous and powerful people. Without Nast's help or knowledge, she landed a job at *Vogue* writing photograph captions, but quickly moved on to *Vanity Fair.* Donald Freeman, managing editor at *Vanity Fair,* fell hard for her and did whatever he could to polish her already considerable luster. When he died in an accident (that some speculated was actually suicide), she inherited his job.[3]

Clare later met and fell in love with Bernard Baruch, who was sixty-one. She was less than half his age, but he was a man of considerable substance, a requirement for her. What was not required of him or any other man was that he be single; in fact, she could manage married men more easily, especially those who worked a great deal. Her ability to attract men was a gift, but using it to advantage was a skill taught to her by her mother. Somehow each man in Clare's life thought he was special and did not notice until later that he had given much but received little. Others, who would have liked to be in her life but could not make the cut, consoled themselves with witty slams, such as: "I didn't sleep with her. Not everyone can say that." She especially liked literary men, including Eugene O'Neill, Somerset Maugham, Ernest Hemingway, Irwin Shaw, Sinclair Lewis, and Walter Lippmann, and became friends with other famous men, such as George Gershwin and Buckminster Fuller. Baruch introduced her to Winston Churchill, who matched her up with his son, Randolph. They hit it off, but he was a drinker. She moved on.[4]

Helen (Brown) Lawrenson, Clare's friend from their *Vanity Fair* days, once recalled, "I've known few men who could resist her spell, once she set her mind to it and had him face to face." Lawrenson further remembered, "Her eyes were not large, but there was a magical loveliness in her gaze, level, disquieting, spell-binding." Lawrenson witnessed one such takedown when her friend invited her on a double blind date. "Don't bother to dress," she assured. So while Lawrenson showed up in casual clothes, Clare arrived "in a long white satin evening dress, cut low in front, blazing with diamonds—bracelets galore, necklace, earrings, brooch, rings—an altogether breathtaking vision." They met the two men at Jim Moriarty's House of Lords, a plush New York speakeasy. Lawrenson saw that her date was mesmerized by the sight of her friend. "It was over coffee that she gave him the *coup de grace,*" she recalled. "'Let me read your palm,' [Clare] said, taking his hand, gently running her fingers over it, murmuring softly, and finally, when he was in a state fast approaching levitation, pressing his palm for a brief moment against the bare, pearly skin just above where her dress began. He was a gone goose."[5]

Clare Boothe later met and married Henry "Harry" Luce, founder of *Time* magazine, and thereafter she helped him create *Life* magazine. He gave her love and access to power; she gave him affection and glamour. In 1940, during a discussion on whether the United States should become involved in Europe's war, Harry supported her desire to see the war firsthand, even assigning her as a *Life* correspondent. With Harry later accompanying her on the trip, they stopped in to see Churchill, soon to be prime minister, and later visited with Gertrude Stein and Alice B. Toklas in Paris. Clare managed to witness Belgium's surrender and the Dunkirk evacuation. When the couple returned to the United States, they stayed overnight at the White House. At dinner Clare sat next to President Roosevelt.[6]

Although not a neglectful parent, when she traveled the world, Luce frequently left her daughter, Ann, in the care of a nanny. When Ann came of college age, she decided, with little guidance from her mother, to attend Stanford University. On her first day at college, her parents were off in China. There they met Chiang Kai-shek as well as his wife, perhaps the only woman who could stand toe to toe with Clare. On the same trip *Time* correspondent Teddy White was Clare's guide when she met with Chou En-lai, right-hand man to Mao Zedong. On a later trip she met General MacArthur and had an affair with one of his generals. Still later she interviewed General Joseph Stilwell. While riding with him in a Jeep on the road to Mandalay, she managed to inveigle enough information from "Vinegar Joe" to do a *Life* profile on him. Her meeting with Field Marshal Alexander sparked rumors of an affair.[7]

By 1942, having seen some of the war both east and west, Luce became the U.S. representative from Connecticut, the first woman so elected. In January 1944 she visited with daughter Ann in San Francisco, staying at the Mark Hopkins Hotel for five days and seeing the sights. She intended to drive her daughter, by then a senior, back to Stanford the next day, but Ann said a girlfriend could take her instead. Ann rode to Stanford the next morning in the friend's convertible. Two blocks from campus, another car rushed the light and sideswiped the convertible. The collision catapulted Ann from the car and killed her.[8]

In late 1944 the House Military Affairs Committee invited Luce to join them in taking part in a visit to better gauge the war effort in Europe. She hoped the trip would take her mind off her daughter's death, if only briefly. On a stop in France, she met Eisenhower and Patton and then went to Italy. There she reacquainted herself with Alexander and met Mark Clark; the latter reportedly surrendered his Jeep seat to her—almost unheard of. Thereafter, she met a dashing former horse cavalryman, Lucian Truscott. The Luces' marriage, always something of a question mark, suffered more after Ann's death. In March 1945 she decided to visit Italy once again, just two months since her previous visit, and took the opportunity to look in on Truscott. Still suffering the loss of her daughter, she found herself attracted to the tough but sensitive general.[9]

Now, in May 1945, Truscott's war was very near its end. The general had done his part to bring the Third Reich to its knees and had seen more death and destruction than anyone should ever have to see. Still, Truscott felt some uneasiness about his life. He likely suspected that the high point of his career, the Mediterranean war and Anzio in particular, was now history. World War II—his war—was essentially over. Truscott had committed every waking moment and more than a few nightmares to it for the past three years. His real family waited for him in the States, but now he had a second family, one he thought of as his "war family." Nevertheless, one by one, his closest staff began to leave, anxious to get on with their own lives. Truscott was fifty years old now, and the strong body that had raced on horseback through the various obstacles at the Cavalry School and had played hundreds of bumping and slamming games of polo had suffered during the war. Various ailments took up residence in his body and then refused eviction. Death, not on the battlefield but by some infiltrating illness, seemed to wait to ambush him. When one has been amid war for three years, in which missing even one detail of a complex and exacting operation might cost the lives of thousands of soldiers, the arrival of a midlife crisis could sneak in undetected.

Then, by accident or perhaps fate, a strong, vibrant woman came into his life. Just being in her presence sparked passions in him that had lain dormant for decades. What was especially pleasing was that she seemed to think so highly of him, making him feel younger than his years.

He was a gone goose.

It began innocently enough. In letters to Sarah, Lucian mentioned that in December 1944, Clare Boothe Luce and other members of Congress had visited his troops. In letters between Christmas and April, his adjectives for Luce migrated from "distinguished visitor" and "seeking . . . publicity" to one who is "keenly intelligent," "witty," "most attractive," and "a real beauty." They also became correspondents. An early letter to Luce dated January 7, 1945, not long after her first visit to Italy, greeted her as "Dear Mrs. Luce," but then parenthetically addressed her as "La Belle." Truscott confessed that it had been with trepidation that he and his staff had anticipated her visit. "Our fears were groundless! You gave us the nicest Christmas we have spent overseas!" Luce wrote that she would be making a second visit. His March 18 letter said he had arranged for one of his staff to meet her and provide her with a suggested itinerary for her three-day visit to the Fifth Army. He offered her the use of his villa—or his hotel suite if she preferred—and added: "If you return to Firenze [Florence] in time . . . perhaps you would have luncheon with me at the villa. Just the two of us. . . . Then we can talk—but not for a mere '1/2 hour'! I will devote myself to you for the remainder of the day—and as long as you and the war effort will permit." If lunch would not work, he suggested dinner instead.[10]

Since history has seen fit to save his letters but not hers, the evidence of an affair is one-sided but nonetheless sufficient. One of Luce's biographers, Ralph Martin, states directly, "The Truscott affair was more serious than most." In a March letter the general wrote that he hoped to show her the Anzio battlefield, adding, "Your note was beautiful—as you are—and I shall keep it always."[11]

His aides, Jack Bartash and James Wilson, found themselves serving as trusted go-betweens for two famous people, as did one of her assistants. While Luce's assistant was likely used to such duty, it was new for Bartash and Wilson, who shared the tasks of transporting the representative and shuttling letters marked "personal" back and forth.

Truscott's letter of April 10, 1945, reveals perhaps the high point of his passion. He references his "haunted trailer" twice, adding: "There will always be a glorious presence, a memory of golden hours, of warm red lips that smile on me, of heavenly blue eyes into the depths of which souls can disappear, of blond halos, and a companionship so perfect as to erase dull care, and pain, and time, and reality. Truly a dream world."[12]

By May 13, less than two months later, he realized that the affair was already waning. "It is perhaps just as well that we were both too old, too wise, too devoted to the task at hand, too conscious of duties to be done, and books and plays to be writ, and lives to be lived—to fall in love—or I might have written you a love letter indeed. I might have cried against fate that so arranged destiny." Truscott was learning what more than a few other men had learned. As Luce's official biographer, Sylvia Jukes Morris, writes: "To her, seduction was usually more satisfying than consummation. She tended to grow cold as lovers became hot."[13]

Thereafter, the correspondence continued, though with only occasional ardor. Truscott told her of returning to Anzio for a Memorial Day ceremony, of his arranging for almost one thousand representatives from divisions that had fought there, and of all the various governmental and diplomatic dignitaries who attended. "I spoke—briefly—to those who sleep," he understated. His letter to Sarah was similar: "My speech was very brief and addressed to the fallen comrades. People seemed to like it." His aide's journal entry of May 30, 1945, captures the spirit of the speech: "A beautiful Memorial Day ceremony and the Army Commander outdoes himself in his speech." Bill Mauldin later said he could not recall a gesture that had moved him more.[14]

In June 1945 Truscott returned temporarily to the United States to take part in various victory celebrations. He would have liked to see Sarah and his children first, but he had other stops to make before that could occur. Sarah, daughter Mary, and sons Doodie and Jamie would greet him in Charlottesville, Virginia. His visit with them would have to be short as his itinerary was tight and an immense amount of postwar work waited for him back in Italy. While in Washington, D.C., Truscott hoped to meet with General Marshall, but because Marshall was absent, he met instead with General Thomas T. Handy, deputy chief of staff. His message for Marshall was that he was available to serve in the Pacific if needed. On June 24 Truscott also met Luce at the Wardman Park Hotel for cocktails, dinner, and a long conversation; likely, it was one of goodbye. To what extent Sarah learned of her husband's infatuation is unknown, but it would be difficult for two famous people surrounded by journalists and others to keep a romantic affair secret.[15]

One of Truscott's early stops on this trip had been a special visit to Ellington Airfield near Houston, Texas. There, on June 13, he met a youngster, still not old enough to vote, who was about to receive a hero's welcome home. Eleven days earlier in Austria, General Patch had pinned onto the young officer's uniform the Medal of Honor and the Legion of Merit for his courageous actions in France. General O'Daniel was there too, immensely proud of the young man. Now Truscott and other generals would shake the hand of a celebrated

First Lieutenant Audie L. Murphy, 15th Infantry Regiment, 3rd Infantry Division, Medal of Honor recipient for heroic actions near Holtzwihr, France, January 1945. Courtesy of the U.S. Army and the National Archives.

hero from his beloved 3rd Infantry Division. The general was pleased to meet 1st Lieutenant Audie Murphy, who was happy enough just to be alive and back in Texas.[16]

In the spring of 1945, the war in Europe had slowly climbed to its apex and then slammed down into a contentious peace. It was like a rollercoaster that slowly "click-clicked" its way to the summit and then freefell amid screams of delight laced with breathtaking moments of fear. The up-and-down ride of war was over, but it had left a huge mess of sickness for someone to clean up. The Germans were disarmed, but the vacuum they left throughout the continent was implosive. It seemed every faction in Italy saw its chance to muscle into power. Truscott's troops were still cleaning out pockets of resistance and processing 250,000 prisoners when it became necessary to begin refereeing now-competing groups of partisans. Italy's infrastructure had collapsed, requiring U.S. Army Civil Affairs officers to establish and administer local governments and restore basic services. An understandable but frustrating complication was that American civilians wanted their citizen-soldiers to come home immediately. Of course, the men were more than anxious to leave and promised their loved ones that it would not be long. Soldiers with too little seniority to return stateside would have to stay in Europe on occupation duties or prepare for transfer to the Pacific theater. The army dislikes idle soldiers, who seem adept at finding trouble, and needed to keep them occupied. This prompted administrators to enlarge rest centers and develop an impressive educational program through Italian universities.[17]

On July 29 General Marshall informed Truscott that he would be sending him to China, where the general would command a group of Chinese armies fighting the Japanese. A citizen-soldier might have abhorred the notion of going off to yet another theater of operations, but as a professional soldier, Truscott was anxious to begin. He had come to realize that war was what he did best. On August 8 the general, along with Carleton, Conway, Harrell, O'Neill, Wilson, Bartash, Barna, and Hong, had already arrived in China when they received confirmation of Japan's surrender. They then returned to Italy, where in late September each packed his bags to return to the United States. Truscott, Carleton, Bartash, Wilson, and Barna would lift off from Paris for home in a week, leaving just enough time to drive over Brenner Pass and on to Germany to visit old friends George Patton, Geoffrey Keyes, and "Beetle" Smith.[18]

A drop-in call on Eisenhower in Frankfurt brought a surprise. "Lucian, you are just the man I need," the general blurted. "Unless you have some objections, I think I will send you down to relieve George Patton." It took Truscott only a moment to realize that his old cavalry friend had put his foot in his mouth again. Eisenhower well knew their friendship, but he also knew that Truscott's loyalty to him and the army was greater. "If General Patton had to depart," Truscott acknowledged, "I thought he would probably prefer being replaced by me than by someone who might be less sympathetic." That was precisely the case. In fact, when Eisenhower had asked

Patton who he preferred to command the Third Army, it took him only a second to say "Lucian Truscott." Truscott worked in visits to Berlin and Paris, then returned to Frankfurt. His friendship with Patton was still strong, but Patton insisted on a formal exchange of command in Frankfurt with "considerable fanfare and publicity." He assured Truscott, "I don't want Ike or anyone else to get the idea that I am leaving here with my tail between my legs." Having just given up the Fifth Army, Truscott now found himself commanding general of the Third Army and the Eastern Military District (Bavaria). He regarded Patton as a close friend and later wrote, "He was perhaps the most colorful, as he was certainly the most outstanding, battle leader of World War II."[19]

In October 1945 Truscott received a letter from his sister with an enclosed letter from one of his former school students from the frontier education days. Jewell, now known as Mrs. Lloyd Champeau of Norman, Oklahoma, had read Lang's story on the general in *Life* magazine. Her letter to his sister mentioned that thirty-five years ago Truscott had not only been her teacher but also had boarded in her family home. The general responded on October 29, noting in part, "My Dear Jewell, I do, indeed, remember my school-teaching days at Enterprise and all of your family." He surely paused and reflected—it was a lifetime ago.[20]

With the war won, the British, Soviets, French, and Americans would administer zones of occupation in Germany. In Truscott's portion of the American sector, Bavaria and part of Czechoslovakia, there was a full kettle of work to ladle out. The overall goal was to disarm, demilitarize, and eventually reconstruct Germany while holding its citizens responsible for their nation's aggression. The first major problem was to establish an interim military government until the general could reinstall civil administrations. An essential requirement for this, however, was the need to train democratic citizens to staff and operate local governments. In addition, no one who had been a member of the Nazi Party could hold a job in government or industry. The second immense problem was to resettle displaced persons (DPs), more than 1,000,000 of whom were in the American sector alone. Most wanted to return to their homeland or some other place of their choice. It frustrated Truscott that he had to do all this with a continually declining number of U.S. personnel, resulting from "the thoughtless demands of the American people and the Congress."[21]

On December 9 Patton's chauffeured Cadillac collided with a U.S. Army truck, seriously injuring the general. Paralyzed, he died in his sleep on December 21, his wife, Beatrice, at his bedside. Although Truscott and Patton had parried words on occasion, each had always liked and respected the other. Truscott attended George Patton's funeral and afterward felt the need to write to Luce. "We returned yesterday morning from Luxembourg where we buried George Patton Christmas Eve, with a show that would have delighted his heart. I'm sorry to lose him but if he had to go I'm glad that he could go in the fullness of his fame—a fortunate thing for a man." Truscott, no doubt, considered his own future death and wondered under what circumstances he would leave life.[22]

Amid all of this, the U.S. Army began to falter. Soldiers had already packed their saddlebags and could smell the barn, ready to ride long before they had finished mending the fences. Those who remained on occupation duty had little enthusiasm for the task. For Truscott, getting the job done had become harder. "What had been a magnificent fighting force," he lamented, "became little more than a rabble—an undisciplined mob." The general blamed Congress and the American population for these problems. Uncharacteristically, he held the highest commanders of the army and navy responsible for caving in to civilian demands to get the troops home immediately. The eventual report card for this national shortsightedness would arrive in about five years, when the army found itself seriously unprepared to fight in Korea. Truscott later wrote, "Evils engendered during these [postwar] months have continued to plague us."[23]

He was also perturbed that Congress and the other victorious nations were largely uninterested in dealing with the immense problem of repatriating nationals, primarily DPs, to their homelands, which the Allies had agreed to do. Truscott complained, "The Western nations, having few of their own nationals involved, except as prisoners of war, apparently did not comprehend the magnitude of this problem nor the complications which were to be encountered in carrying out this agreement." Hundreds of thousands of DPs still existed, and most of those from eastern European countries did not want to return to their homelands, which were now under Soviet control; they hated the Soviets and refused repatriation. The Russians, however, needed people to rebuild what had been destroyed and insisted that citizens of the countries they occupied be returned, whether they wanted to be or not. The Soviet

Union had paid the highest Allied death toll—20 million—and was intransigent. It and the other nations of eastern Europe needed rebuilding, they insisted. Eventually, most Poles returned home, most Jews found their way to Palestine or the United States, and many other eastern Europeans counted themselves lucky to receive one-way tickets to another part of the world. Yet as late as the early 1950s, refugee camps overflowed with more than 100,000 people awaiting resettlement.[24]

One of Truscott's many duties was "administration and maintenance" of war-crime prosecutions in Nuremberg and Dachau. Because of the immensity of the offenses associated with the death camps and with other crimes committed by major Nazi officials, he placed Brigadier General LeRoy H. Watson in charge of the Nuremberg venue and saw to it that he had all the resources he required. Truscott attended the first day of the Nuremberg trials, which he deemed a justified "conquerors' triumph." The army held other hearings in Dachau for those crimes committed within areas now under American control. Truscott also attended some of these trials, witnessing the impressive defense afforded the Nazi criminals by their defense attorneys—all American military officers. The courts found all but a few defendants guilty and gave them sentences ranging from a few years in prison to hanging. On their last day in court, as thirty-eight convicted Nazis were about to depart the courtroom, the Germans paused to thank their defense attorneys. The military lawyers were surprised. Lieutenant Colonel Douglas T. Bates, who oversaw the defense team, later told Truscott that the prisoners concurred that "no German lawyer would ever have made such a fight in their behalf even before a German court; they felt their trial had been fair and impartial."[25]

Truscott still thought of Clare Luce from time to time, but for the most part resignation replaced passion. His once hot embers had lost their glow, sparking only occasionally. By February 1946 she had become more of a sounding board as the general expressed bitter frustration at the prickly peace that had replaced war. "Life seemed so simple and honest when thousands of lives might depend upon a decision—and the measure of success was the annihilation of the enemies of one's country." In war everyone had worked together; in peace everyone worked on personal agenda.[26]

An army reorganization called for the deactivation of the Seventh Army. Now the Third Army would command all soldiers in the U.S. Zone of Occupation, a major portion of the Allied presence in Germany. Truscott began setting up a U.S. constabulary, something akin to a separate military-police occupying force, along the lines of a mechanized cavalry regiment but backed by a division of the regular army. He put in charge his old cavalry comrade Ernie Harmon, giving him a startup date of July 1946. Harmon was pleased to be of service, but when first told that he would lead a "constabulary," he asked, "What's that?"[27]

In April of that year, Lucian learned that Sarah had become seriously ill and was in Walter Reed General Hospital in Washington, D.C. He utilized a B-17 and its crew and flew home. Within two weeks she had improved. Lucian needed to get back, but he was pleased to know that Sarah would join him in Germany later in the summer. On his return flight, however, he became ill himself with a serious chest cold and was later admitted to a Heidelberg hospital. He cabled Sarah on April 27: "Entered hospital day of return Wednesday for penicillin treatment of infection. Cleared by Sunday but electrocardiograph shows spot on heart not normal, but not serious. Must stay in bed at rest for some time. Feel fine. Letter full explanation on way. Should be home by 1st June. Hope you are improving. Love, Lucian." Doctors treated the general for a chest infection and then gave him the startling news that his electrocardiograph showed that he had suffered a coronary occlusion. He was ordered to bed for six weeks. Truscott understood, but he was not happy. His disposition improved not at all when the doctor removed his cigarettes completely and cut his liquor consumption. Even at that, Truscott managed to imbibe a couple of highballs before lunch and a couple more before dinner.

After four very long weeks of looking out a hospital window, even though it presented a splendid view, something of a depression settled over him. Don Carleton, now acting more as very close friend than chief of staff, provided daily encouragement. Not knowing what his future would be was unsettling for Truscott. He had doubts about his future contribution to the army. He was not ready to write about the war, nor was he keen on Carleton's suggestion of a future for the general as the president of a college, perhaps the Virginia Military Institute, or maybe playing a key role in international relations. Truscott just cursed the electrocardiograph, "that damnable machine," the readings from which had so changed his life. It helped just a little when the doctor permitted the nurses to wheel his bed out onto the sunny terrace. In July his term of confinement over, he handed off the Third Army to Lieutenant General Keyes and flew to Washington, D.C. Six months of observation by doctors at Walter Reed followed. After that, for an additional six months, he served with the War Department while awaiting results of his final medical examination. Truscott, however, was not one to give up his general's stars easily, especially when it appeared that there might be a communist threat brewing. In May 1946, ever the optimist, he wrote a letter to Deputy Chief of Staff Thomas T. Handy: "You are no doubt familiar with all the medical aspects of my so-called illness, but I will relieve your mind by telling you there is not a damned thing wrong with me."[28]

Truscott's duty at the War Department was to oversee a personnel-screening board of seven members and eight alternates, initiated in October 1946, at Fort Monroe, Virginia. Their task was to review the military records of officers "referred to it by appropriate agencies" in order "to determine which of such officers should be required to show cause why they should be retained on the active list." Truscott recalled that the intent of the effort was to "vitalize the Army and to increase the standards for efficiency of military service." What it amounted to was recommending who could remain in the service and who had to go. Every identified officer's personnel file found its way onto one of three stacks: "outstanding war service," "satisfactory but not outstanding war service but [fills] a 'very useful niche in the Army,'" or "wisdom of retention doubtful." All of those in the third stack could begin looking for a new line of work.[29]

The latest medical news for Truscott was not good. On May 20, 1947, Lieutenant Colonel H. Bornstein, Medical Corps, reported on the general's condition: "Arteriosclerosis, generalized, mild, with coronary focalization, manifested by old myocardial infarction (April 1946) involving lateral and posterior well, left ventricle; unchanged. . . . This office is of the opinion that Gen Truscott may be incapacitated for active service." On May 23 a major inquired of the finance office as to when Truscott's next pay raise was due, for both his permanent rank (brigadier general) and his temporary rank (lieutenant general). The army factored in the general's leave time, and on September 30 his retirement commenced. Truscott was relieved of his duties at the personnel-screening board and given a reporting date for separation at Fort Myer, Virginia. He used some of his leave time to visit his daughter, Mary, now Mrs. Robert Wilbourn, in Chama, New Mexico, just south of the Colorado border. Although the army found him to be 60 percent disabled, his disability pay would be less than the amount of a full-service retirement, which Truscott elected to take. His monthly check would be $716.06.[30]

Truscott later reflected, "Since the cardiac condition had not improved I was retired from active duty on September 30, 1947, just six weeks after completing 30 years of service." All of the various advances in heart surgeries and medicines available today, which might have allowed him to remain in the army, were too distant in the future to help. His once clear complexion now showed the hard-earned wrinkles of the many roads he had traveled—most of which had been potholed and washboarded. Truscott returned to civilian life with a chest full of medals. These included a Legion of Merit for his early efforts as part of Lord Mountbatten's combined-operations effort; a Distinguished Service Medal for planning, landing, and leading his troops at Port Lyautey; and a Distinguished Service Cross for the Sicily landing and the capture of Agrigento. In addition to his Purple Heart from Anzio, he received a second Distinguished Service Medal for the Po Valley campaign and a third Distinguished Service Medal for his Third Army occupation efforts. The U.S. Navy gave him its own Navy Distinguished Service Medal for the amphibious operations at North Africa, Sicily, Anzio, and southern France. Finally, Brazil, Great Britain, Czechoslovakia, France, Italy, and Poland presented him with a total of thirteen medals. As Truscott summed it up: "So ended a career."[31]

Lieutenant General Lucian K. Truscott, Jr., circa 1945. Courtesy of Susan Truscott and James Truscott.

CHAPTER 29

Spying on the Spies and Retirement

Between October 1947 and February 1951, Lucian and Sarah lived on a country estate near Bluemont, Loudoun County, Virginia, about an hour's drive from Washington, D.C. The attraction of the beautiful countryside was understandable: rolling hills, woods with thick underbrush, and just five miles north of Upperville and five miles south of Bluemont. It was not far from the Appalachian Trail, the well-known hiking route that snakes up and down through thick woods from Georgia to Maine. The outer walls of most of the old homes in the area consisted of large stones as did the ubiquitous boundary walls. The smaller outer buildings looked even older than the houses, most of which had been built in the eighteenth and nineteenth centuries. Horses thrived in the green pastures, which must have pleased a middle-aged cavalryman. Roads leading through the fields and woods were narrow and seemed always to be climbing or descending, seldom level.

The seventy-acre estate included five acres that contained the outbuildings, kitchen garden, and apple orchard. The rest was mostly pasture with scattered trees and an inviting creek that crossed the property. The metal-roofed house, built in 1797, had three stories and a cellar, and its hilltop location provided an excellent all-around view. The couple would call the estate—previously known as Rock Hill—Bluemont, after the nearby community. Truscott was pleased that former owners had updated the old house at least once and that the estate included a barn, garage, smokehouse, corncrib, and various sheds. It offered something else that delighted Lucian—a shop in which he could once again practice woodworking. He and Sarah had no doubt that the estate was worth its $50,000 asking price.[1]

Still, Lucian found himself longing to be back doing what he did best—being a general. He also quickly discovered that maintaining an estate required not only a lot of work but also a good deal of money. In 1948 he borrowed against his veterans' insurance policy and from other sources to meet their expenses. It helped when General Devers recalled him to active duty for four months, beginning in November 1948. Truscott's assignment was to head a conference board establishing the army's position on doctrine, policies, and procedures relative to joint amphibious, airborne, and air-defense operations. Selecting the retired general to chair the board must have been an easy decision for Devers. Truscott had invaded North Africa, Sicily, Anzio, and southern France and had been associated with the invasions of Dieppe and Salerno. Following submission of his report, the old cavalryman returned to civilian life—still restless.

Truscott sent a note to Omar Bradley, who was now army chief of staff, inviting him to visit Bluemont. Bradley asked for a rain check, saying he would like to come but it would be a while before he could make it. Less than a year later, he wrote to Mark Clark, hoping the bubbling situation in Korea might require an experienced general. "In view of our long association during the last war," Truscott wrote, "this is just a note to say that if you find use for me I am ready." A similar note to Eisenhower read, "If I can be of service at any time, I am ready, willing and able, and would rather die in harness doing whatever I can than to live to a ripe old age sitting on the sidelines." Still later he sent a note to General Marshall: "I would like to assure you if whatever talents I may possess can be of use to you or to the country at any time, I am at your command." It was more than money that motivated him to reach out. A planned retirement after a long career can be difficult, but an unplanned retirement can be worse.

Clark replied, saying he would send a plane for Truscott so that he could come evaluate the action Clark proposed to take. Eisenhower responded as well, saying he hoped to resolve the current crisis soon but acknowledged that he might need Truscott for some yet unknown situation. Marshall also wrote, saying that he appreciated Truscott's offer and would certainly call if he could use his talents. As it turned out, the army did not recall Truscott for the Korean Conflict, likely because the other generals were well aware of his health limitations. Not having Truscott in Korea proved to be unfortunate, for early on the war could have used a good general. Those commanders in place were not to the satisfaction of General Matthew B. Ridgway, who relieved several of them. One general who was not relieved, much to the dismay of U.S. Marine major general Oliver P. Smith of Chosin Reservoir fame, was Edward Almond, likely because of the latter's close association with General MacArthur. Journalist Thomas E. Ricks has described Almond as being "overly aggressive while underestimating his enemy." General Smith, then temporarily assigned under Almond, would have agreed, as would have many World War II soldiers and officers of the 92nd Infantry Division.[2]

As it turned out, there was another job waiting for Truscott, this one in the fledgling Central Intelligence Agency (CIA).

With the war over, President Harry Truman disbanded the Office of Strategic Services (OSS). The military spy agency had provided valiant service by training, equipping, and directly assisting underground forces in France, Italy, and elsewhere. Now there was no need for it. Unfortunately, Truman was not quite sure what he wanted in its place. At any rate, most OSS agents had returned to civilian life. What had been a force of 13,000 agents dwindled to fewer than 2,000 in less than a year, and those remaining were uncertain as to what their new mission was.[3]

Truman finally acceded to arguments stressing the necessity for a central intelligence-collection unit, which eventually waxed into the CIA. What the president had in mind was an agency that would simply keep him informed as to what was going on elsewhere in the world, with agents who would also conduct espionage and report on what they learned. Some within the CIA agreed with him, but others had something else in mind—covert operations. They had less interest in reporting what happened than in making it happen. Truman later complained that all he had wanted was a center to keep him informed about world events, not a secret spy agency—a cloak-and-dagger outfit as he saw it.[4]

An early problem for the CIA was that it looked to some other federal offices like competition. The Pentagon, State Department, and FBI each saw the agency as a threat to its own intelligence-collection mission and funding. It would take quite an effort to get the various agencies to tolerate one another, much less cooperate. In addition, there were also shadowy forces working behind President Truman's back. Some in the military and Congress were determined that the correct focus should be on covert operations. Even within the CIA, there were ongoing discussions as to what its new role should be, with some advocating quiet but skillful information collection through invisible espionage, while others saw the need to engage the nation's enemies by launching undercover operations. By 1946, with little in the way of formal or statutory approval, the CIA began engaging in covert operations directed principally at the Soviet Union. Officials soon learned a harsh lesson when Soviet intelligence agents easily infiltrated an early CIA effort in Romania. The agency had hoped to promote underground resistance to Soviet power in that eastern European country. The Soviets subsequently killed or imprisoned those Romanians involved in the plot and later sent twenty-seven boxcars of German-Romanians to prison camps in the far east. The Russians had over two hundred years of espionage experience. The CIA had one.[5]

In July 1947 President Truman signed the National Security Act. Aside from launching the U.S. Air Force as a separate branch of service, it also created the Office of the Secretary of Defense, the National Security Council, and the CIA. The six paragraphs of rhetoric regarding the CIA did not address engaging in covert operations but included the fuzzy phrasing "other functions and duties related to intelligence affecting national security." This gave agency officials just enough room to drive through a locomotive. In December the National Security Council officially gave the CIA a top-secret order to undertake "covert psychological operations" relative to the Soviet Union.[6]

Before long the CIA had a solid funding source too. The Exchange Stabilization Fund, created during the Great Depression and subsequently used to impound seized assets of Germany, Italy, and Japan, had more recently been intended to help rebuild Europe. Instead of enabling that effort, however, the fund became a $200 million slush account to operate a spy agency. One of its first uses was to buy the Italian election so that the Christian Democrats could defeat the Italian Communists.[7]

By 1948 Berlin had become the epicenter of the emerging Cold War. For the CIA, it was the place to be. New agents received their basic training in the United States but undertook advanced training on the job, where the clandestine rubber met the Berlin roads. In 1950 President Truman appointed retired general Walter Bedell Smith, Eisenhower's former chief of staff and more recently ambassador to the Soviet Union, as head of the CIA—not a bad rise for someone without a college degree who had enlisted in the army as a private. What was problematic for Smith was that he was the fourth director in just four years, which was not a good sign. It did not take him long to recruit retired general Lucian Truscott, officially or unofficially, to oversee CIA activities in Berlin, with the understanding that he was to report any reckless operation that could embarrass the U.S. government. In February 1951 the CIA formally hired Truscott as a consultant, and by October his title was CIA senior representative for Frankfurt, Germany. Soon enough, Truscott uncovered and reported on the existence of three secret CIA prisons then operating in Germany, Japan, and the Panama Canal Zone. Their purpose was to imprison and interrogate suspected double agents. Whatever happened within those walls was likely to make for very nasty headlines. The agency shut down these centers immediately.[8]

When Dwight Eisenhower assumed the presidency in 1953, he decided to appoint a nonmilitary person as CIA director, knowing that Smith intended to resign for health reasons. Therefore, over Smith's objection, he selected Allen Dulles, a former OSS agent, as CIA director. Eisenhower also appointed Dulles's brother, John Foster Dulles, as secretary of state. The president chose to keep Truscott, whose loyalty to him was unquestioned, inside the agency.[9]

Eisenhower's hands were full. Aside from other presidential duties, he was winding down the war in Korea while trying to curb the bellicose Soviet Union—all without starting a nuclear war. Wanting no embarrassment from the CIA, he needed a trusted source on the inside to spy on the spies. Truscott, who had been Eisenhower's eyes and ears in North Africa, topped the list of candidates. Indeed, rumors at one time had surfaced that Truscott would succeed Smith as CIA director. Even though this did not happen, there was still a clear need for Truscott, who had already shown considerable experience in dealing with intelligence problems and seemed to have a better grasp of Cold War issues than most others. Of critical importance, he was a friend, a proven leader, and a man who had demonstrated his loyalty to Eisenhower repeatedly. Historian William R. Corson describes Truscott as one "who moved in quiet ways." Unlike Truman, Eisenhower did see some value in allowing the CIA to conduct covert missions. His appointment of Allen Dulles signaled a move away from mere Soviet containment, the previous U.S. policy, toward efforts to support liberation movements behind the Iron Curtain. Eisenhower was willing to take some risks, but he wanted Truscott on the inside reporting on what was happening before it was reported on the front pages of the *New York Times* or *Washington Post*.[10]

One of Truscott's early covert operations involved the 1954 digging of a tunnel from West Berlin to East Berlin, with the intent of tapping into East German and Soviet telephone lines. Insisting that the program be absolutely top secret and on a need-to-know basis, the result was a successful, yearlong eavesdropping operation through an 1,800-foot tunnel, part of which lay beneath Soviet-controlled East Berlin. Because the tunnel's existence was ultrasecret, the CIA could give Truscott little formal award or recognition for its success. Instead, the agency presented him with a small gift—a cylindrical, clear-glass paperweight, about an inch tall and four inches in diameter. Hollowed out within the solid glass was a "T," which had been filled with colored dirt from the Berlin excavation.[11]

In 1955 Truscott blew the whistle on a CIA operation that could have given the country a serious black eye. This was a *second* assassination attempt on Chou En-lai, the number-two leader in Communist China. Previously, an airplane thought to be carrying Chou mysteriously exploded in the air, but Chou had not been onboard. A second attempt on his life now anticipated poisoning his food while he attended a conference in Bandung, Indonesia. If all went well, Chou would be dead within forty-eight hours. Truscott got wind of the plot, finding it incredible that agency officials thought they could avoid suspicion in Chou's poisoning and demanded that they shut down the operation. That came as a relief to the hesitant leader of the operation, who had had a bad feeling about the mission from the beginning. The agency called it off "in the nick of time," he recalled.[12]

Truscott's primary job was to oversee and advise on day-to-day and covert operations in Germany, with special attention on refereeing disputes between military and civilian intelligence agencies. His secondary duty, written in invisible ink, was more global. He was to birddog the little known and occasionally duplicitous "Cold Warriors" that Eisenhower had within the CIA ranks. Sometimes his progress came from simply telling Allen Dulles about operations that the director thought Truscott knew nothing about. If he knew about an operation, Dulles feared, Eisenhower would soon know about it. Dulles quickly and quietly canceled some operations rather than have the president learn about them. Some other operations, however, he saw as too important to kill.[13]

One of these was a 1956 operation code-named Red Sox/Red Cap. Following Stalin's death, the Soviet Union had taken steps to "deStalinize" itself. The CIA concluded that the Soviet grip on its satellite countries was relaxed, at least momentarily. The Red Sox part of the operation would involve parachuting agents into countries to promote unrest; the Red Cap part would be assisting those who wished to defect. The Soviets had recently backed down in a confrontation with Poland. The Polish Communist Party had sought greater independence from the Soviet Union. When Russian troops began to muster, Polish students and factory workers dropped their books and tools and prepared to fight. Soviet premier Nikita Khrushchev softened; instead of sending troops, he sent congratulations. Hungarians studied what had happened in Poland and now demanded that Khrushchev remove his Stalinist puppet leader and replace him with Hungarian nationalist Imre Nagy. The premier acquiesced a second time. Hungarians next demanded that he remove all Soviet troops from their nation. CIA agents held their breath, hoping that Hungary might be the first satellite country to break from its Soviet orbit. Khrushchev this time decided to give the Hungarians a harsh lesson, sending in 2,500 tanks and armored cars and 200,000 troops. When the Soviets finally departed, somewhere between 6,500 and 32,000 Hungarians were dead and another 170,000 to 196,000 were in flight, more than 38,000 of whom sought asylum in the United States. The other satellite countries got Khrushchev's message.[14]

Truscott needed to get more information for Eisenhower on what had really happened in Hungary. He went to Camp Kilmer, New Jersey, where many of the refugees had arrived. His interviews with them resulted in a stinging report to the president. The CIA fingerprints on Operation Red Sox/Red Cap were easily detectable. According to William R. Corson, Truscott pointed out that the CIA did not seem to "recognize the differences between insurrectional violence, mass uprisings, and revolutionary action." He considered Operation Red Sox/Red Cap as a bad idea from the start, pointing out that if a satellite country's government was slow in responding to a crisis, the Soviets would simply rush in its own troops, increasing the likelihood of a full-blown war in Europe. Truscott's further digging unearthed a similar operation then afoot in Czechoslovakia. Eisenhower quickly shut it down.[15]

It is likely that Truscott was involved in many more CIA operations than is known. One observer during that time was his son,

James Truscott, who visited his parents in Germany during summer breaks from West Point. He later said of his father's CIA service in Germany, "He ran the whole show."[16]

When not spying on the spies, Truscott worked on two memoirs. In 1954 he published *Command Missions: A Personal Story*, an eloquent recollection of his World War II years. He later began the equally eloquent *The Twilight of the U.S. Cavalry: Life in the Old Army, 1917–1942*. In it Truscott seldom identifies himself, leaving the reader to infer that he was a participant in most of the events discussed. At the end of the preface to this book, he identifies himself merely as "L. K. Truscott, Jr., Cavalryman." He would pass away before the book could be finished, leaving his son, Lucian III, to complete it. The same year that Truscott published *Command Missions*, Congress gave him a special gift—a postretirement promotion to full general—four stars. On July 19, 1954, President Eisenhower signed an act of Congress that promoted certain generals on the retired list. The damper on the whole thing was the clause, "No additional retired pay accrues as a result of this advancement." Truscott must have wondered if giving a few generals a pay raise would have busted the budget. Of course, the government did give him a couple gifts: a three-foot by four-foot "General Officer" flag, and a six-inch by nine-inch metal automobile flag. On August 4 the army issued a special order correcting the wording on Truscott's four-star promotion, changing "Lucien" to "Lucian."[17]

The previous May Truscott had had something of a reunion with one of his primary enemies. Each was retired from the military now and had written a book about his war experiences. Neither had met the other before, and each was likely a little nervous about meeting the other. The event took place in Frankfurt, Germany, ten years after Anzio. The two former antagonists, Lieutenant General Lucian Truscott and Field Marshal Albert Kesselring, greeted each other warmly. Sarah was there as well, taking the arm of each former warrior, linking them in peace.[18]

In 1956 the CIA awarded Truscott the CIA Distinguished Intelligence Medal for his "outstanding service and meritorious performance." In 1957 it promoted him to deputy director for coordination, responsible for refereeing disputes between the CIA and those in the military who did separate covert operations. Truscott skillfully moved between the two groups, keeping his old friends in the military while maintaining respect within the agency. By May 1959, however, his health began to slip, and he found it necessary to resign from the CIA, stating, "Disabilities increasingly impair activities so essential in meeting properly the responsibilities of office." Director Dulles responded that he deeply regretted the departure of Deputy Director Truscott, adding, "We will miss your wise counsel and advice and the broad understanding you have brought to your work during these years."[19]

Truscott remained associated with the CIA as an on-call consultant, but the agency almost never called him. There seems little doubt that Dulles was relieved that he no longer had to worry about Truscott's eyes and ears and easy access to Eisenhower. As historian-biographer Wilson Heefner has observed, since Truscott was still a foremost authority on amphibious operations, Dulles should have consulted with him before launching the disastrous 1961 Bay of Pigs invasion. According to one of Truscott's closest associates at the time, the general would have warned Dulles that he was going about it all wrong and then explained how it might be achieved. Perhaps he might have even suggested that the operation not be attempted at all. Had Dulles considered him as a resource instead of a hindrance, the Bay of Pigs invasion might not have happened. A consultation between the two might have saved the CIA from getting a black eye and Dulles from public scrutiny. Instead, following an investigation, Allen Dulles retired from the CIA. The results of the Bay of Pigs investigation remained secret for forty years.[20]

CHAPTER 30

A Cavalryman's Last Parade

Truscott retired for the last time. The long war and harsh winters in the Italian and French mountains had taken their toll on his body, aided and abetted by continuous smoking. The Truscott home during the couple's elder years would be their "cottage on the Potomac"—as they liked to call it—in Waynewood, a sought-after community south of Alexandria, Virginia.[1]

By 1958 Lucian's health had become bad enough that Sarah began her daily journal with a summary of his condition. On January 2 she jotted, "Afflictions that beset Lucian recently," listing, "very puffy, several very bad stomach ulcers, a siege of boils, night sweats." Afflictions aside, Lucian, Sarah, and their good friends continued a tradition of celebrating January 22 as "Anzio Day." Usually there were a dozen or more, mostly former staff members from that operation. Sarah wrote about this year's gathering, "They all admired L. and are wonderful in their attitude about what he did for them." On February 10 she noted: "He is staying at home this week to get his strength back and is only getting worse. He stayed in bed most of the day." By February 26 she penned: "L. is utterly miserable, has to use the inhaler about every two hours. He stayed in bed most of the day." By March 5, though, he was better; she recalled how he came in with "shining eyes." They were excited to be the guests of the Italian government so that General Truscott could speak at Anzio for the 1958 Memorial Day celebration. She later recalled, "L. went off in uniform for the first time since the trip to France in '54; he looked very fine." They almost missed the event. "We reached the cemetery just in time for him to make his address," she wrote, "which he did in a clear and beautiful voice, standing erect with his beautiful grey hair shining in the sun." In June he spoke to the West Point graduates and presented their commissions. "L made a fine speech," Sarah remembered. Later that month doctors diagnosed Lucian with edema, a serious condition in which fluid accumulates in the body. By year's end his feet were so sore and swollen that he could hardly drive. "What misery will beset him next?"[2]

The Anzio Day celebration of 1959 was as enjoyable as the last, but by February Lucian had to spend time in Walter Reed Hospital. In April he and Sarah were pleased when Brazil appointed him an honorary general in that country's army. At the ceremony conducted at the Brazilian Embassy in Washington, D.C., the ambassador presented General Truscott with a ceremonial sword. By June his health seemed to improve, with Sarah noting that his doctors described him as being in "fine shape" and "almost perfectly normal." He returned to his hobbies and to doting on his grandchildren. He had been a strict father but was less so as a grandfather. Still, some correcting was necessary from time to time, which he delivered with a twinkling eye. One of his granddaughters, Mary Truscott, recalled many dinners at her grandparents' house, when she might hear Grandpa's raspy voice say, "Mary Truscott, strong and able, this is not a horse's stable, get your elbows off the table." Every grandchild present did an "elbow check" before the ditty ended.[3]

In December Sarah confessed, "I worry over him. He does not look well." She also noted, "L. is hanging on the brink of a real attack of his emphysema." In May 1960 he was pleased to lay a wreath at the Tomb of the Unknown Soldier. That same year Sarah's journal noted that there had been an air collision over New York in which 132 onboard had been killed as were several on the ground. She reflected, "I cannot help but think of L. ordering thousands out to meet their death for our country."[4]

An Austrian artist, Boleslaw Jan Czedekowski, had painted the general's portrait after the war while Truscott was still in Germany. The oil painting shows him in uniform wearing his leather bomber jacket, which displays three stars and a Fifth Army patch. He is also wearing army pinks—probably cavalry britches; a dark shirt, likely wool with open collar; white neck scarf; and leather gloves. Now, in January 1961, another artist, C. Gregory Stapko, arrived and painted his portrait.[5]

Between February and October, Walter Reed Hospital admitted and later released Lucian several times. A special honor arrived in October 1961 when his new portrait, along with those of other World War II generals, was mounted on the walls at West Point. In January 1962 *Movietone News* interviewed him and asked him about Anzio. That spring doctors diagnosed him with gout. Even so, he managed to build a library door, although he found it necessary to use his inhaler from time to time as he worked. Sarah could not help but conclude that she and Lucian had "jumped into old age with both feet."[6]

The year 1965 would be their last Anzio party. The usual gang showed, coming from every direction on that unusually warm, clear day. "We were lucky we did not have last week's snow," Sarah remembered. By now Lucian's walk was more of a shuffle. Everyone present had a good time, with much singing of the old cavalry songs. Sarah recalled that he "was generally gay but did sit down almost the entire time, which, within itself, tells a tale." By the next day Lucian's shuffle had become a limp. "He will not talk about it," Sarah complained to her journal. "He certainly does not look well." Older son Doodie, as Lucian and Sarah continued to call Lucian III, stopped by to cut the lawn. He also brought some good news about his own son, Lucian K. Truscott IV. Senator Patsy Mink of Hawaii had given Chick—the family nickname for Lucian IV—his appointment to West Point. Sarah and Lucian were very pleased. She lamented that the children grow so fast. The old general's health continued to slip throughout April—more gout attacks, coughing at night, and irregular heartbeats. He complained very little, though. She was deeply worried about his future.[7]

A fainting spell the previous November had been the first sign of serious trouble. Now, on April 27, a dark and overcast day, Truscott suffered a similar episode. He was admitted to Walter Reed Hospital, where he remained. On May 16 Doodie alerted his mother that Lucian had had a stroke while in the hospital. Doodie picked her up at the house and they sped to the hospital, finding Lucian paralyzed on his left side. Earlier he had had trouble breathing, necessitating that a doctor perform a tracheotomy. By evening, Lucian was well enough to quip, "I have never wanted my throat slit but since it had to be done, I certainly had a nice young man to do it."[8]

By late June, having been in the hospital seven weeks, he was recovered enough to sit at a desk. Even so, an orderly had to spoon-feed him. On Sunday, June 27, Lucian managed to write a letter to Chick, who was in the midst of packing to go off to West Point. He wanted the letter to be the first mail waiting for his grandson when he arrived at the academy. The next day Doodie and Chick stopped by to say goodbye before heading north to New York. Lucian was immensely proud of Chick, as he had been of sons Doodie and Jamie when they had departed for West Point. Throughout his career, the old cavalryman had had perhaps thousands of West Point graduates work under him, but he always revered anyone who had attended the academy.[9]

By early July the doctors thought Lucian could leave the hospital, and he was back at home on the tenth. By then, younger son Jamie had arrived. Knowing his father would be anxious to see the garden, Jamie had mowed the lawn and pulled any weeds the day before. It was a hot and clear day, and Lucian's garden was still full of color. He seemed pleased to gaze upon his flowers once again. Although limited in movement, he was feeling well enough to eat again, which had been an infrequent occurrence during his hospital stay. His spirits improved, but lung problems prompted severe coughing, especially at night.

Lucian's old friend and fellow polo player, Severance "Sev" A. Millikin, visited from Cleveland. While it was good to be home and among family and friends, he also felt fortunate that he could continue his physical therapy at Fort Belvoir, which was much closer than Walter Reed Hospital. Doodie and his wife, Anne, and Jamie and his wife, Helen, pitched in to maintain the lawn and garden. Jamie made some modifications to the two-story house to aid his father's mobility. Those grandchildren who were old enough to do so also helped where they could. Sarah's sisters—Mary Walker and Agnes—came to stay for a while, assisting her with Lucian's care.

The end of July brought two stressors for the old general. The first was that Jamie, having used his annual leave, needed to report to his piloting duties at Offutt Air Force Base in Omaha, Nebraska. Sarah jotted in her journal that she was sure that Lucian was grieving over Jamie's departure. The second was that it had become clear that their two-story house was not working well for Lucian. A level apartment would be better, so the couple put the house up for sale.[10]

By the beginning of August, Lucian felt stronger. Limping with a cane and with an arm carried in a Walter Reed sling, he managed to putter around his flower garden. He was able to pull a few weeds and pick some flowers for the dinner table. For Sarah, it was so good to see him improving. A minor irritation for Lucian was that real-estate agents, when showing the house, paid scant attention to his flower garden. Throughout the war, and especially at Anzio, whenever flowers were blooming, Sergeant Hong knew that the general

Retired general Lucian K. Truscott, Jr., at home following his release from Walter Reed Hospital with sling and cane, 1965. Courtesy of the George C. Marshall Foundation Research Library, Lexington, Virginia, and James Truscott.

expected a vase full of them on the dinner table. Doing his best to ignore his afflictions, Lucian sat outside in the late afternoons. He admired his mimosa and magnolia trees, enjoyed smelling the impressive variety of flowers, and looked forward to the daily visits of the birds. He, Sarah, Mary Walker, and any guests chatted as they sipped gin and tonics. Lucian could do no cooking now, so he left that in the good hands of Sarah and Mary Walker. They usually capped dinner with coffee, corrected with a splash of brandy. By late evening he was tired, even though he might have had a nap or two during the day. Going to bed was not something Lucian looked forward to, however, as it usually meant severe coughing, night sweats, and little real sleep.[11]

By mid-August Lucian was on oxygen, but even with its use, his hands and feet turned blue. In a week or so the house sold. Sarah and her sisters found an apartment that he would be able to navigate. For Lucian, losing the house was bad enough, but he could hardly watch when the time came to dismantle his workshop and remove his tools to Doodie's house. At his son's suggestion, Lucian donated his large desk, which he had built himself, to the Headquarters Building at Fort Myer. The only cheer that hot summer month was that Lucian's many friends, including Iron Mike O'Daniel and Eddie O'Neill, telephoned or stopped by from time to time to check on his welfare. By September it was necessary to summon an ambulance to transport Lucian to Walter Reed Hospital. The examining doctor told him that his lungs were failing, then added his name to the bottom of the serious list. On September 7 Lucian shared with Sarah: "We may as well be realistic about this thing. I do not expect to survive this."[12]

On September 11 Doodie stayed all night in Lucian's hospital room. Sarah and Agnes arrived the next day about 10:00 A.M. After visiting for a while, Agnes went home, planning to return at 6:00 P.M. Doodie needed to go home to rest but hesitated to leave his father, who could not speak but was quiet and peaceful. As Doodie said goodbye, Lucian said nothing but squeezed his son's hand. Sarah sat for some time with her husband of forty-six years. The doctor came in to check on the patient. In a few moments he turned to Sarah and suggested that she call Doodie to return. She reached him at the new apartment. When he arrived, he and Sarah sat with Lucian. In a few moments an alarm on Lucian's hospital equipment sounded. A nurse and an orderly rushed in to attend to him. Sarah later wrote: "L. gave a sigh, a little shiver, and stopped breathing. Both Doodie and I were right there. The stillness when a person stops breathing is awe-inspiring. I cried a little but was a little faint. It was ten minutes to one. We stayed with L. a little while. I hated so to leave him, kissed him on his Beloved Forehead, and we turned and walked out." Sarah's journal entry for Sunday, September 12, 1965, was brief: "Dark and dreary. Rain in the A.M. and hard later. Lucian died this day. May the Lord have mercy on us. Our pillar of strength is gone." Army doctors sent a more sterile notice to the Pentagon, saying of Truscott: "DIED 12 September 1965 at Walter Reed General Hospital, Washington, D.C., as the result of pulmonary emphysema, chronic lung disease, pulmonary insufficiency, and myocardial insufficiency."[13]

Sarah selected Lucian's burial plot, assisted by Doodie, Anne, and John T. Metzner, the Arlington Cemetery superintendent. She remembered, "We chose a beautiful spot that I know Lucian would love, on a gentle slope to the left just a few feet from the Fort Myer gate, one of the most beautiful parts of the cemetery, under some beautiful oaks."[14]

On Wednesday, September 15, General Lucian K. Truscott, Jr., was buried in full dress uniform. Sarah remembered: "This saddest of all days for us dawned somewhat overcast. . . . Some said it was hot, but I did not notice it if it was." Doodie and his army friends had arranged everything. Following the service in the cemetery chapel, those in attendance walked outside and stood in front, talking softly among themselves. The caisson awaited General Truscott's body. The honorary pallbearers were old friends Don Carleton, Dick Myer, Ted Conway, Ben Harrell, John Cassidy, and Eddie O'Neill—all having served with him during World War II. Doodie, Jamie, two of Lucian's grandsons, and a nephew would walk immediately behind them. Even some old horse soldiers from the 17th Cavalry Regiment came to see the general make his last parade. The flag-draped casket rumbled forth atop a horse-drawn caisson, its driver seated on the attached trammel. It was one of the same caissons Truscott had employed many years before, when he had served as a young cavalry captain overseeing funerals at Fort Myer. Now he was the guest of honor but would not have wanted it any other way. Six jet-black horses pulled the caisson. Impeccably dressed soldiers of the 3rd Infantry Regiment, the Old Guard, rode the three horses on the left side; the three horses on the right were saddled but carried no riders. A sergeant rode immediately to the left of the first mounted soldier. Another soldier on foot walked behind the caisson, leading by the reins a single, saddled horse. Mounted in reverse in the stirrups was a pair of boots, though not the ones typically used for such military funerals. Doodie had arranged to use his father's old cavalry boots, which Lucian had worn before and throughout World War II. His soldiers in Italy and France had considered them his lucky boots; as long as the general wore them, everything would be okay.[15]

Not far from the former home of General Robert E. Lee, seven soldiers aimed M-14 rifles into the sky. A funeral officer and bugler stood behind them as each soldier fired three shots. Each volley for him cracked as one shot. The bugler then played "Taps." In the background the entire 3rd Infantry Old Guard Regiment stood ramrod straight.[16]

"There were the usual three volleys . . . and Taps more beautifully blown that I have ever heard it," Sarah recounted. "I have

Sarah Truscott with sons James (*center-right*) and Lucian III (*right*) and two U.S. Army generals at the dedication of Truscott Hall, Carlisle Barracks, Pennsylvania, April 1966. Courtesy of the U.S. Army and the George C. Marshall Foundation Research Library, Lexington, Virginia, and James Truscott.

always been afraid I would break down if L. died before me and I had to receive the flag, but I had no inclination to break down during the whole service. I felt so proud for Lucian." The tears would flow later, every day, and would continue for months and months thereafter. "I cannot realize he has gone from us forever, cannot, cannot!"[17]

Sarah followed her husband in 1974. She had missed him every day since his death, but at least now would remain with him at Arlington National Cemetery. The dying words of one of Truscott's heroes, Lieutenant General Stonewall Jackson, might have served well as a way for Lucian to welcome Sarah: "Let us cross over the river and rest under the shade of the trees."[18]

Afterword

On January 8, 2012, about fifty people gathered in mild winter weather south of Dallas, Texas, at the small community of Chatfield, birthplace of Lucian K. Truscott, Jr. The sun, previously hiding behind high clouds, emerged for the event. The master of ceremonies, Robert N. Jones, Jr., welcomed those seated or standing before him. Jeff W. Hunt, director of the Texas Military Forces Museum in Austin, praised General Truscott's life. Lieutenant Colonel James J. Truscott, retired U.S. Air Force pilot, Vietnam veteran, and the last surviving offspring of the general, accepted the honor of unveiling a new highway marker erected in memory of Chatfield's most famous son. The Truscott family had come in numbers, not only the direct descendants but also members of distant branches of the family tree. Local residents were present as well, hoping to learn more about the famous Chatfield man born well over a century earlier. They had all come together to celebrate a man of humble origins who had risen to earn international fame.

If Truscott made any enemies during his life, they seem to have disappeared from history. Most everyone, from army privates to Pope Pius XII, seemed to hold him in high regard. The evidence is abundant that the most famous of World War II American generals—Marshall, Eisenhower, Bradley, and Patton—all thought highly of him. Even Mark Clark would have conceded that Truscott was the second-best general in the Mediterranean theater of operations—the first being Clark, of course. Some key war correspondents—Ernie Pyle, Bill Mauldin, and Mike Chinigo—also respected Truscott. Perhaps more important, his admirers not just respected him, they genuinely seemed to like him. They would have disagreed with the general's self-described "No sonofabitch, no commander" admonition given to his son Lucian Truscott III on the eve of his departure to fight in Korea.

Perhaps a close but yet atypical observer of Truscott was personal aide James M. Wilson, Jr. Born in China to missionary parents,

Wilson later earned a master's degree in law and diplomacy, then worked as a newspaper reporter. Called to duty for World War II, he found himself assigned to Truscott's staff. The position afforded him a keen perspective from which to gauge the many American, British, and French generals who passed through headquarters. After the war Wilson graduated from the Harvard School of Law and went on to become a career diplomat, retiring as assistant secretary of state for human rights and humanitarian affairs. He thereafter served on the board of the International Rescue Committee and in his spare time recorded books for the blind. During the war, Wilson had earned a Bronze Star and two Purple Hearts, even though by all appearances he was a reluctant warrior more interested in helping his fellow humans than harming them. When interviewed in 1999 and asked what he thought of Truscott, Wilson said, "I think he was the best general we had in the army—an opinion shared by quite a number of military experts—an exceptional individual."[1]

Another atypical observer was his one-time son-in-law, Graeme Bruce, an Englishman who worked in the postwar Rome film industry with Truscott's daughter, Mary. Bruce recalled: "LKT had a reputation in Italian aristocratic circles as an American gentleman; not bad for a commanding general who'd been obliged to requisition great houses and estates for his occupying army accommodation. I found in him great empathy, an unpretentious friend with an incisive sense of humor, which appealed to me and certainly to the distaff side of his family. It was easy to see why he was such a good leader and so popular with his men."[2]

British historians Dominick Graham and Shelford Bidwell, who fired from the hip with incredible accuracy, have described Truscott thusly: "He seems to have been as unflamboyant a leader as has appeared in the history of the US Army since Ulysses S. Grant. . . . We can only be sure of one thing: he was a first-class professional soldier. He had commanded the US 3rd Division . . . which had emerged unshaken from sixty-five continuous days of combat in the [Anzio] bridgehead. . . . An energizing current flowed from him down through the command hierarchy to the rank and file."[3]

Truscott surrounded himself with some of the best frontline combat commanders in the army—Bill Darby, Ernie Harmon, John O'Daniel, Robert Frederick, and George Hays. He demanded much, and they delivered. Like Truscott, they knew that the best battle plans were nothing without flexible implementation and that the only place to evaluate that was at the front, not fixated on a situation map at a rear headquarters. Truscott seemed at home at the front, continually encouraging his young soldiers and junior officers but not hesitating to correct a senior officer when he felt the need. Wearing his general's stars like a flak jacket, he crisscrossed the frontlines, convinced that the enemy could not touch him as long as he wore his lucky cavalry boots and britches and jingled the lucky coins and key in his pocket—despite a few narrow escapes.

What he regarded as luck was in actuality an impressive intellect and a willingness to work as hard as needed to succeed. His leadership ability simply boiled up, knocked off the lid, and overflowed. In truth, it would have happened the same way no matter what profession he had chosen. Certainly, he was fortunate to have received a commission in the cavalry and to have met Patton and Eisenhower early on, but those were merely career accelerators. Had he not enlisted in Officer Training Camp, the army would have drafted him soon anyway, and it is inconceivable that its leadership would not have recognized Truscott's talent and commissioned him. At the onset of World War I, the country needed strong leaders, and his leadership ability was too visible to go unnoticed.

Truscott's professional career had some exceptional high points. He was a standout polo player, competing at an international level. He did so well at the Cavalry School that its cadre recruited him to remain there as an instructor. The Command and General Staff School did precisely the same thing. While serving as an instructor in each school, he guided many officers in developing the skills they would need in the next war. Interestingly, at the time he had not experienced combat, as had many of them.

During the war, he elevated his 3rd Infantry Division to near-ranger/commando standards. He made it look easy, as though he were steering a speedboat instead of maneuvering a huge ship. Truscott went on to become a corps commander and later an army commander. He never considered for even a moment that he might not have the requisite ability for those positions. He was a general more at ease at the battlefront than in front of a group of reporters, and more at home riding in a Jeep across a just-built, untried wartime bridge than riding in a Jeep through the cheering crowd of a just-liberated city. Truscott orchestrated his part of winning World War II without fanfare.

A superb planner, he left no detail to chance. He engineered and led the breakout from the Anzio beachhead, synchronizing 150,000 soldiers and all their armored vehicles, specialized equipment, and variety of weapons in near silence until he released the catapult. Truscott next launched the highly successful invasion of southern France, in which he came close—once again—to trapping an entire German army.

While an obedient soldier, he did not hesitate to challenge an order when he disagreed with it, doing so with Generals Patton, Clark, Lucas, and Patch. If overruled, Truscott usually followed their instructions, though on a couple of occasions he went over the head of the commander who had given the order, confident that it was the right thing to do.

In truth, Truscott also had some low points; only generals who do little manage to avoid making mistakes. His handling of the 92nd Infantry Division was less than stellar. Admittedly, his sink-or-swim treatment of these African American servicemen was on par for 1945, yet he did little to improve their situation. He apparently never considered relieving Major General Edward Almond of his command, even though he had threatened to relieve another division commander for less. As a result, Truscott failed the soldiers of the 92nd Division because he left the wrong general in charge.

His affair with Clare Boothe Luce was likely a serious personal regret. It was his good fortune in life that Sarah, his wife of forty-six years, nursed him during his last years with the same love and dedication that she had given him—"a redneck from nowhere"—throughout their married life.

After the war President Dwight Eisenhower came close to appointing him as director of the spirited and unbridled CIA. There is no doubt that Truscott would have done a better job than the man ultimately placed in that position. Had his health not begun to slip away, he might have gone on to other key civilian positions, likely at the insistence of President Eisenhower or Secretary of State George Marshall. Sadly, Truscott was a constant smoker, back when society so accepted it that the army provided soldiers with small packs of cigarettes in their field rations. This addiction, coupled with immense, ongoing stress and probably a level of alcohol use no longer regarded as acceptable, eventually killed the warrior. He left his life not in battle but in his bed, and he left well before his time.

Lucian Truscott's journey through life was not an express ride but a local run with lots of stops: teenaged teacher, cavalry officer, polo champion, premier army instructor, founder of the U.S.

Army Rangers, battle commander, army commanding general, visitor to a pope, CIA insider, and confidante to a president. When the ride ended and life let him step down, those around him remembered him as a loving husband, a dedicated father and grandfather, a good friend, a talented leader, and an exceptionally bright star to his country.

Notes

Prologue

1. "Sicily-Rome American Cemetery," American Battle Monuments Commission, www.abmc.gov/cemeteries-memorials/europe/sicily-rome-american-cemetery, accessed 2014; author's visit to Sicily-Rome American Cemetery, Italy, May 11, 2009; Mauldin, *Brass Ring*, 272. The temporary cemetery located at Nettuno was formally established in 1956.
2. Truscott, *Command Missions*, 327–28; J. Eisenhower, *Intervention!*, 221–23, 234.
3. Lucian K. Truscott, Jr., Papers, George C. Marshall Foundation Research Library, Lexington, Va. (hereafter cited as LKT Papers), unsigned and undated document, probably written by Patsy Truscott, General Truscott's younger sister (hereafter cited as LKT Papers, unsigned and undated document); J. Eisenhower, *Intervention!*, xiv.
4. J. Eisenhower, *Intervention!*, xi, 192, 217–18, 224, 334; author's visit to Douglas, Ariz., Dec. 5, 2006.
5. J. Eisenhower, *Intervention!*, 210–11, 217.
6. Ibid., 191, 214, 220–22, 227.
7. Ibid., 218, 220, 223–24, 334.
8. Ibid., 221–24, 226, 334; author's visit to Columbus (N.M.) Historical Society Museum, Nov. 21, 2007; author's visit to Old Fort Bliss Museum, Fort Bliss, Tex., Nov. 20, 2007.
9. J. Eisenhower, *Intervention!*, 226–27, 232, 234, 324, 334–35.
10. Truscott, *Twilight of the U.S. Cavalry*, xi, 3–4; Coffman, *Regulars*, 199, 205–207; Gen. Lucian K. Truscott, Jr., U.S. Army Personnel File, National Personnel Records Center, St. Louis, Mo. (hereafter cited as LKT Army Personnel File).

Chapter 1

1. LKT Papers, unsigned and undated document; LKT Army Personnel File, letters of recommendation, affidavit regarding high school graduation.
2. LKT Army Personnel File, training forms and memoranda, Aug. 1917.
3. Ibid.; Lucian K. Truscott, Jr., professional résumé and biographical data, circa 1957, private collection of Susan Truscott (hereafter cited as LKT Résumé); author's visit to former site of Camp Jones and the Cochise County Historical Society, Douglas, Ariz., Dec. 5, 2006; "Camp Harry J. Jones, Douglas, Arizona," Cochise County, Arizona, Genealogy and History, last updated 2013, http://mycochise.com/history/campjones.php.

4. Truscott, *Twilight of the U.S. Cavalry*, xii.
5. James and Helen Truscott interview, Nov. 12, 2007; Lang, "Close-up—Lucian King Truscott," 98.
6. Truscott, *Twilight of the U.S. Cavalry*, 1–2, 5.
7. Ibid., 2, 49–50; Swafford Johnson, *History of the U.S. Cavalry*, 28. Information regarding Camp Jones derived from photographs courtesy of Cochise County Historical Society, Douglas, Ariz., Dec. 5, 2006.
8. Truscott, *Twilight of the U.S. Cavalry*, 2–5.
9. Ibid., 6.
10. Ibid., 20–22; Herr and Wallace, *Story of the U.S. Cavalry*, 78.
11. Truscott, *Twilight of the U.S. Cavalry*, 8.
12. Ibid., 8–9.
13. Ibid., 7; Essin, *Shavetails & Bell Sharps*, xvi, 95–96.
14. Truscott, *Twilight of the U.S. Cavalry*, 4, 16–17.
15. Ibid., 10; Ambrose, *Duty, Honor, Country*, 251.
16. Truscott, *Twilight of the U.S. Cavalry*, 11.
17. Ibid., 22; LKT Résumé.
18. Truscott, *Twilight of the U.S. Cavalry*, 22–24.

Chapter 2

1. Truscott Family Papers, private collections of Truscott family members (hereafter cited as Truscott Family Papers); author's visits to Chatfield, Nov. 13, 2007, Jan. 8, 2013; Truscott, Tex., Nov. 19, 2007; and to various locations in Oklahoma, Nov. 17–18, 2007; LKT, Central Intelligence Agency Personnel File, CIA Headquarters, Langley, Va. (hereafter cited as LKT CIA Personnel File), personal history statement, Feb. 14, 1951. In some instances of using items from the various collections of family papers, the author has changed wording or punctuation to clarify meaning. Also, some family information within these papers may have originated from Hill, *History of the State of Oklahoma*, 504–505.
2. LKT Papers, unsigned and undated document.
3. Patsy Truscott, Journal, circa 1942, 12–13, private collection of Susan Truscott. In her journal Patsy Truscott used pseudonyms for her siblings; the author has elected to use their real names instead (hereafter cited as Patsy Truscott, Journal).
4. Ibid., 33.
5. Ibid., 32.
6. Ibid., 27–28.
7. Ibid., 39.
8. Ibid., 36.
9. LKT Papers, unsigned and undated document.
10. Patsy Truscott, Journal, 42.
11. Ibid., 44.
12. Ibid., 47.
13. Ibid., 50; author's visit to Eufaula, Okla., Nov. 18, 2007.
14. LKT Papers, unsigned and undated document.
15. LKT Résumé.
16. Patsy Truscott, Journal, 56.

Chapter 3

1. Truscott, *Twilight of the U.S. Cavalry*, 24; Sarah Truscott, Journal, 1, private collections courtesy of Susan Truscott, Mary Truscott, Debbie Truscott, and James Truscott (hereafter cited as Sarah Truscott, Journal).
2. LKT Army Personnel File, telegrams, June 1918.
3. Truscott Family Papers, Debbie Truscott, e-mail to the author, Feb. 20, 2007; James and Helen Truscott interview, Nov. 12, 2007.
4. LKT Army Personnel File, "Board of Proceedings of a Board of Officers in the case of Lt. L. K. Truscott, 17th Cavalry, Douglas, Arizona, June 12, 1918." All quotations are from this transcript. The author has summarized other information.
5. Ibid.
6. LKT Army Personnel File, memoranda, July 1918.
7. Truscott, *Twilight of the U.S. Cavalry*, xvi; Truscott Family Papers, genealogy, private collections of Debbie Truscott and Patty McWilliams.
8. Truscott Family Papers, private collection of Debbie Truscott; e-mail to the author, Feb. 20, 2007.
9. Ibid.
10. Ibid.; Agnes Scott College, www.agnesscott.edu, accessed 2013.
11. Truscott, *Twilight of the U.S. Cavalry*, 25; LKT Résumé; LKT CIA Personnel File, personal history statement, Feb. 14, 1951.
12. Truscott, *Twilight of the U.S. Cavalry*, 24, 26.
13. Ibid., 26; Sarah Truscott, Journal, 1.
14. Truscott, *Twilight of the U.S. Cavalry*, 26–27; Coffman, *Regulars*, 364.
15. Truscott, *Twilight of the U.S. Cavalry*, 26–27.
16. Ibid., 29.
17. Sarah Truscott, Journal, 1–2.
18. Ibid., 1, 3.
19. Truscott, *Twilight of the U.S. Cavalry*, 30–31.
20. Ibid., 28–29.
21. Sarah Truscott, Journal, 4, 7.
22. Truscott, *Twilight of the U.S. Cavalry*, 31–32.
23. Ibid., 32–33.
24. LKT Army Personnel File, memorandum, July 19, 1919.
25. Sarah Truscott, Journal, 15–16.
26. Truscott, *Twilight of the U.S. Cavalry*, 34–35; Coffman, *Regulars*, 405; Herr and Wallace, *Story of the U.S. Cavalry*, 247.
27. Truscott Family Papers, Lucian Truscott III, tape recording, transcribed by Mary Truscott, 1999, private collection of Mary Truscott.
28. LKT Résumé; Truscott, *Twilight of the U.S. Cavalry*, 4, 37–38, 45.
29. Truscott, *Twilight of the U.S. Cavalry*, 45–46.
30. LKT Army Personnel File, correspondence, Hollins Randolph to Gen. P. C. Harris, Aug. 10, 1920; ibid., Gen. P. C. Harris to Hollins Randolph, Aug. 13, 1920.
31. LKT Army Personnel File; LKT Résumé; Sarah Truscott, Journal, 17; Truscott Family Papers, Lucian Truscott III, tape recording, 1999. Lucian Truscott III preferred the spelling of his nickname as "Dudie,"

which his aunt had used in letters to the family. Yet in letters quoted in this book, General Truscott spelled the name "Doodie," which Lucian III described as a shortened form of "Doodlebug."

32. Truscott, *Twilight of the U.S. Cavalry*, 46; M. R. Truscott, *Brats.*
33. Sarah Truscott, Journal, 5, 17; Truscott, *Twilight of the U.S. Cavalry*, 46.

Chapter 4

1. Truscott, *Twilight of the U.S. Cavalry*, 47–48; Sarah Truscott, Journal, 2.
2. Truscott, *Twilight of the U.S. Cavalry*, 47–48.
3. Sarah Truscott, Journal, 2.
4. Truscott, *Twilight of the U.S. Cavalry*, 48.
5. Ibid., 48–49; LKT Résumé; Sarah Truscott, Journal, 3.
6. Truscott, *Twilight of the U.S. Cavalry*, 49–50.
7. Ibid., 52.
8. Ibid., 53–56.
9. Davenport, *Soldiering at Marfa*, 24; author's visits to Marfa, Tex., Oct. 20, 2007, Mar. 25, 2011.
10. Truscott, *Twilight of the U.S. Cavalry*, 57–58.
11. Sarah Truscott, Journal, 6.
12. Davenport, *Soldiering at Marfa*, 24; Truscott, *Twilight of the U.S. Cavalry*, 63–64; Sarah Truscott, Journal, 5–6.
13. Truscott, *Twilight of the U.S. Cavalry*, 65; Sarah Truscott, Journal, 5.
14. Truscott, *Twilight of the U.S. Cavalry*, 72–73.
15. Ibid., 71.
16. Ibid., 71, 73–74; LKT Army Personnel File, correspondence, memorandum, Captain Truscott to Commanding General, Cavalry School, Aug. 17, 1925, endorsed by Major Chamberlin, approved by General Booth (quote); Debbie Truscott interview, Sept. 13, 2009.
17. Sarah Truscott, Journal, 19.
18. Sulzberger, *New York Times Page One*, Apr. 27, July 22, 1925.
19. Truscott, *Twilight of the U.S. Cavalry*, 52, 75–76.
20. Ibid., 80–84.
21. Ibid., 77–78, 87.
22. Truscott, *Twilight of the U.S. Cavalry*, 77–78, 87.
23. Ibid., 86.
24. Ibid., 97.
25. Ibid., 90–91.
26. Ibid., 101–102.
27. Ibid., 103–104.
28. Ibid., 157; Herr and Wallace, *Story of the U.S. Cavalry*, 261.
29. LKT Résumé; Sarah Truscott, Journal, 3.
30. Sarah Truscott, Journal, 17; James and Helen Truscott interview, Nov. 12, 2007.

Chapter 5

1. LKT Résumé; Truscott, *Twilight of the U.S. Cavalry*, 105.
2. Dickson and Allen, *Bonus Army*, 18; Truscott, *Twilight of the U.S. Cavalry*, 110; Arlington National Cemetery, www.arlingtoncemetery.mil, accessed May 2014.
3. Poole, *On Hallowed Ground*, 5, 10–11, 22, 24, 45–47, 58, 60–62, 92–93.
4. Ibid., 93–94; "Fort Myer History," last updated Sept. 5, 2013, Joint Base Myer-Henderson Hall, http://www.jbmhh.army.mil/WEB/JBMHH/AboutJBMHH/FortMyerHistory.html, accessed May 2014; Arlington National Cemetery, www.arlingtoncemetery/mil, accessed May 2014.
5. Truscott, *Twilight of the U.S. Cavalry*, 105–106.
6. Ibid., 106, 108.
7. Ibid., 109–10.
8. Ibid., 110–12.
9. Ibid., 113–14.
10. Ibid., 115.
11. Ibid., 116–17.
12. Ibid., 120–22.
13. Dickson and Allen, *Bonus Army*, 18, 20–21.
14. Ibid., 28–29.
15. Ibid., 60–61.
16. Ibid., 6, 31, 35–37; Truscott, *Twilight of the U.S. Cavalry*, 123; D'Este, *Patton*, 265.

Chapter 6

1. Dickson and Allen, *Bonus Army*, 56–58, 60–62, 73.
2. Ibid., 61–62.
3. Quoted in ibid., 63–64.
4. Ibid., 63, 65, 68–72.
5. Ibid., 72–73, 78–80.
6. Truscott, *Twilight of the U.S. Cavalry*, 120.
7. Ibid., 122; Dickson and Allen, *Bonus Army*, 2, 15, 43–44.
8. Dickson and Allen, *Bonus Army*, 43–44.
9. Truscott, *Twilight of the U.S. Cavalry*, 122; Glassford-Crosby verbal exchange quoted in Dickson and Allen, *Bonus Army*, 76–77.
10. Dickson and Allen, *Bonus Army*, 7, 73, 81–82, 94, 111, 121, 139, 161, 287–88.
11. Ibid., 76–77, 83–87, 97–99, 101, 136–37, 139; John D. Weaver, "Bonus March," *American Heritage* (June 1963), quoted in Watkins, *Hungry Years*, 134 (paraphrased by author). Glassford's personal expenditures, equivalent to about $12,000 in 2014, are calculated from Dickson and Allen, *Bonus Army*, 320; and Watkins, *Hungry Years*, 522.
12. Dickson and Allen, *Bonus Army*, 94–95, 110–11, 115, 155; Watkins, *Hungry Years*, 136–37.
13. Dickson and Allen, *Bonus Army*, 97, 117–18.
14. Truscott, *Twilight of the U.S. Cavalry*, 124.
15. Dickson and Allen, *Bonus Army*, 14–15, 139, 161; Blumenson, *Patton Papers: 1885–1940*, 975–76, 980–82.

16. Dickson and Allen, *Bonus Army*, 156–58; Truscott, *Twilight of the U.S. Cavalry*, 127.
17. Waters's recollection of conversation with Hurley and MacArthur quoted in Dickson and Allen, *Bonus Army*, 132.
18. Dickson and Allen, *Bonus Army*, 163–67; Watkins, *Hungry Years*, 137–38.
19. Dickson and Allen, *Bonus Army*, 167–70; Watkins, *Hungry Years*, 138.
20. Dickson and Allen, *Bonus Army*, 171; Truscott, *Twilight of the U.S. Cavalry*, 127; Blumenson, *Patton*, 124; D'Este, *Patton*, 352–53.
21. Truscott, *Twilight of the U.S. Cavalry*, 127; Dickson and Allen, *Bonus Army*, 171–72.
22. Dickson and Allen, *Bonus Army*, 171.
23. Ibid., 173–74, 182; Truscott, *Twilight of the U.S. Cavalry*, 127.
24. Dickson and Allen, *Bonus Army*, 173; Watkins, *Hungry Years*, 138.
25. Blumenson, *Patton*, 134; Dickson and Allen, *Bonus Army*, 172–74, 326; Bartlett quoted in Dickson and Allen, 173.
26. Dickson and Allen, *Bonus Army*, 174–75; Truscott, *Twilight of the U.S. Cavalry*, 128.
27. Truscott, *Twilight of the U.S. Cavalry*, 128; Patton quoted in D'Este, *Patton*, 354; Dickson and Allen, *Bonus Army*, 176.
28. Bartlett quoted in Watkins, *Hungry Years*, 139.
29. Dickson and Allen, *Bonus Army*, 177, 179; Watkins, *Hungry Years*, 139.
30. Watkins, *Hungry Years*, 139; Dickson and Allen, *Bonus Army*, 181; Truscott, *Twilight of the U.S. Cavalry*, 129.
31. Dickson and Allen, *Bonus Army*, 180–81, 188.
32. Ibid., 185.
33. Language based on Gen. George Van Horn Moseley, "Bonus March 1932," unpublished manuscript chapter, quoted in Dickson and Allen, *Bonus Army*, 179–80, 193.
34. MacArthur press conference, July 29, 1932, quoted in Dickson and Allen, *Bonus Army*, 181–82.
35. J. Prentice Murphy, "Report on Bonus Expeditionary Force Emergency Camp Johnstown, PA," quoted in Dickson and Allen, *Bonus Army*, 194–95; Manchester, *American Caesar*, 149.
36. Truscott, *Twilight of the U.S. Cavalry*, 129; R. H. Patton, *The Pattons*, 212–13.
37. Watkins, *Hungry Years*, 160–62; Dickson and Allen, *Bonus Army*, 207–208.
38. Roosevelt fireside chat, July 28, 1943, quoted in Dickson and Allen, *Bonus Army*, 269, 276.

Chapter 7

1. Truscott, *Twilight of the U.S. Cavalry*, 132–33.
2. Ibid., 133–34.
3. Coffman, *Regulars*, 242–43; LKT Résumé; LKT Army Personnel File, memoranda, General MacArthur to Truscott, May 1, 1934; ibid., index sheet listing members of Army Polo Team, Jan. 31, 1935.

4. LKT Résumé.
5. Lucian K. Truscott IV interview, Oct. 7, 2009.
6. Truscott, *Twilight of the U.S. Cavalry*, 136–39.
7. Ibid., 139, 142.
8. Ibid., 142; Truscott, *Command Missions*, 532.
9. Truscott, *Twilight of the U.S. Cavalry*, 142–43.
10. Ibid., 143.
11. Ibid., 137, 140.
12. Ibid., 150–51; LKT Papers, handwritten document by Sarah Truscott, n.d. [post 1944].
13. Truscott, *Twilight of the U.S. Cavalry*, 144.
14. Ibid., 77, 144; Coffman, *Regulars*, 410.
15. Truscott, *Twilight of the U.S. Cavalry*, 152.
16. LKT Résumé; Coffman, *Regulars*, 239–43.
17. LKT Résumé; LKT Papers, handwritten document by Sarah Truscott, n.d.
18. Truscott, *Twilight of the U.S. Cavalry*, 149.
19. Ibid., 153–54; LKT Papers, handwritten document by Sarah Truscott, n.d.
20. Blumenson, *Patton*, 123, 136; Truscott, *Twilight of the U.S. Cavalry*, xiv.
21. James and Helen Truscott interview, Nov. 12, 2007; Lucian Truscott III, tape recording, transcribed by Mary Truscott, 1999, private collection of Mary Truscott; Truscott, *Twilight of the U.S. Cavalry*, xiii.
22. Truscott, *Twilight of the U.S. Cavalry*, xv–xvi; Truscott Family Papers, Lucian Truscott III, tape recording, 1999.
23. Truscott, *Twilight of the U.S. Cavalry*, xv.
24. Ibid., xii, xvi; Susan Truscott interview, Sept. 24, 2006, and various conversations through July 2013.
25. Truscott, *Twilight of the U.S. Cavalry*, xvi; Susan Truscott interview, Sept. 24, 2006, and various conversations through July 2013.
26. Truscott Family Papers, Lucian Truscott III, tape recording, 1999.
27. Patsy Truscott, Journal, 119; Truscott, *Twilight of the U.S. Cavalry*, xiv.
28. Obituary, *Leavenworth Times*, Aug. 8, 1938, private collection of Patty McWilliams; author's visit to Hickory Grove Cemetery, Haywood, Okla., Nov. 17, 2007.
29. Truscott Family Papers, unknown relative to Lucian Truscott III and his wife, Anne Truscott, Aug. 22, 1984, private collection of Mary Truscott; LKT CIA Personnel File, personal history statement, Feb. 14, 1951.
30. Graeme Bruce, e-mail message to Mary Truscott, 1998, private collections of Mary Truscott and Graeme Bruce.
31. Truscott, *Twilight of the U.S. Cavalry*, xii; James and Helen Truscott interview, Nov. 12, 2007; James Truscott, "required" Fort Leavenworth Hunt Club journal entries for hunts in which he participated, Nov. 19 and Dec. 24, 1939, private collection of James Truscott.

Chapter 8

1. LKT Résumé; Truscott, *Twilight of the U.S. Cavalry*, 155, 157, 188; Herr quoted in Coffman, *Regulars*, 271.
2. Deighton, *Blitzkrieg*, 100, 155, 158, 160–61 (map notes).
3. Ibid., xix, xx, 118, 155–56, 159, 162.
4. Ibid., 82, 139, 157, 161–63, 192, 196, 201.
5. Ibid., 146–47, 156–58.
6. Ibid., 157, 192, 193 (map notes).
7. Truscott, *Twilight of the U.S. Cavalry*, 157–59; Blumenson, *Patton*, 141, 144, 147.
8. Truscott, *Twilight of the U.S. Cavalry*, 157–59.
9. Blumenson, *Patton Papers: 1940–1945*, 60.
10. LKT Résumé; Truscott, *Twilight of the U.S. Cavalry*, 159–61.
11. LKT Résumé; Truscott, *Twilight of the U.S. Cavalry*, 165, 169.
12. Truscott, *Twilight of the U.S. Cavalry*, 168.
13. Ibid., 169–70.
14. LKT Papers, telegram, Lucian Truscott III to LKT, June 4, 1941.
15. James and Helen Truscott interview, Nov. 12, 2007.
16. LKT Papers, correspondence, LKT to Sarah Truscott, May 20, June 9, 1941.
17. Truscott, *Twilight of the U.S. Cavalry*, 171–72.
18. Coffman, *Regulars*, 394–96.
19. Truscott, *Twilight of the U.S. Cavalry*, 179–81; LKT Résumé.

Chapter 9

1. Atkinson, *Army at Dawn*, 5.
2. Ibid., 8, 10; MacDonald, *Mighty Endeavor*, 21, 31–32; Coffman, *Regulars*, 396–98.
3. Mosley, *Marshall*, 129–30; MacDonald, *Mighty Endeavor*, 21–22, 33–37.
4. MacDonald, *Mighty Endeavor*, 30–31; Atkinson, *Army at Dawn*, 7.
5. Mosley, *Marshall*, 190–91.
6. D'Este, *Eisenhower*, 288–90.
7. Ibid.; Stalin quoted in Blumenson, *Mark Clark*, 70; Atkinson, *Army at Dawn*, 13–14.
8. MacDonald, *Mighty Endeavor*, 36–37.
9. Mosley, *Marshall*, 96, 188–89, 213–14, 300.
10. Truscott, *Command Missions*, 16; LKT Résumé.
11. Truscott, *Twilight of the U.S. Cavalry*, 172–73; Truscott, *Command Missions*, 18; Blumenson, *Mark Clark*, 49–50, 52; MacDonald, *Mighty Endeavor*, 46–47; Marshall tape recordings, Pinehurst, N.C., 1956–57, quoted in Mosley, *Marshall*, 188–89, 525–26; D'Este, *Eisenhower*, 277.
12. Smith quoted in D. Eisenhower, *Crusade in Europe*, 14; D'Este, *Eisenhower*, 283–85; Clark quoted in Blumenson, *Mark Clark*, 54.
13. Moseley, *Marshall*, 197, 200–201; MacDonald, *Mighty Endeavor*, 56–57; D'Este, *Eisenhower*, 296–97.
14. D'Este, *Eisenhower*, 299; MacDonald, *Mighty Endeavor*, 74–75.

15. Truscott, *Command Missions*, 200–201, 482–83; D'Este, *Bitter Victory*, 161–63, 167–75.
16. D'Este, *Eisenhower*, 289, 300; MacDonald, *Mighty Endeavor*, 73–74; Churchill, *Second World War*, 384–85, 387.
17. Coffman, *Regulars*, 289, 420 (Marshall quote).
18. Truscott, *Command Missions*, 17.
19. Ibid., 18.
20. Ibid., 18–19.
21. Ibid., 19.
22. Ibid., 20.
23. Ibid., 20.
24. LKT Army Personnel File, efficiency reports, 1919, 1921, 1925, 1929, 1932, 1940.
25. Truscott, *Command Missions*, 22–23.
26. LKT Papers; S. L. A. Marshall, review of *Command Missions.*
27. Truscott Family Papers, correspondence, LKT to Sarah Truscott, May 14, 1944; ibid., LKT to Gen. Thomas T. Handy, May 13, 1946; Truscott, *Command Missions*, 24–25.

Chapter 10

1. Truscott, *Command Missions*, 24–25; "Model 307 Stratoliner," Boeing, www.boeing.com/history/boeing/stratoliner.page, accessed 2014; Truscott Family Papers, undated notes written by Patsy Truscott, private collection of Debbie Truscott.
2. Truscott, *Command Missions*, 25–26.
3. Ibid., 25–26; LKT Papers, correspondence, LKT to Sarah Truscott, May 17, 1942.
4. Truscott, *Command Missions*, 21–22.
5. Ibid., 23–24.
6. Ibid., 26.
7. Ibid., 27.
8. Ibid., 21, 28; Mosley, *Marshall*, 183.
9. Truscott, *Command Missions*, 27–28.
10. Ibid., 29.
11. Ibid., 29–30.
12. Ibid., 32.
13. Ibid., 33–34.
14. Ibid., 36–37.
15. Ibid., 37–38.
16. Ibid., 37–38.
17. Ibid., 38–40.
18. Ibid., 39; Robert W. Black, *Rangers in World War II*, 11–12.
19. Truscott, *Command Missions*, 39; Black, *Rangers in World War II*, 12–13.
20. Black, *Rangers in World War II*, 13–14, 17; author's visit to Carrickfergus, Northern Ireland, June 20, 2004.
21. O'Donnell, *Beyond Valor*, 5; Black, *Rangers in World War II*, 21–22.

22. O'Donnell, *Beyond Valor*, 6; Black, *Rangers in World War II*, 23–24.
23. LKT Papers, memoranda, commando "ranger training" instructor comments to Truscott, n.d.
24. D'Este, *Eisenhower*, 303–304, 306–307; Truscott, *Command Missions*, 45.
25. Truscott, *Command Missions*, 41, 43, 46–47, 56.
26. LKT Papers, correspondence, LKT to Sarah Truscott, July 17, 1942.
27. Truscott, *Command Missions*, 48–50.
28. Ibid., 48–50; LKT Papers, correspondence, LKT to Sarah Truscott, July 22, 1942.
29. Truscott, *Command Missions*, 49–50.
30. Ibid., 51–53.
31. Ibid., 54–55.

Chapter 11

1. Truscott, *Command Missions*, 56–58.
2. Ibid., 58–59; D'Este, *Patton*, 415–16; Farago, *Patton*, 177–78; Truscott, *Twilight of the U.S. Cavalry*, 90.
3. Truscott, *Command Missions*, 59, 61.
4. Ibid., 59–60.
5. Ibid., 61–62.
6. Ibid., 62–63; Black, *Rangers in World War II*, 27–30; O'Donnell, *Beyond Valor*, 1–3.
7. LKT Papers, correspondence, Sarah Truscott to LKT, Aug. 5, 1942.
8. Truscott, *Command Missions*, 64, 71; O'Donnell, *Beyond Valor*, 1–2; Black, *Rangers in World War II*, 27–29.
9. Truscott, *Command Missions*, 63–65.
10. Black, *Rangers in World War II*, 27–29; O'Donnell, *Beyond Valor*, 2; Truscott, *Command Missions*, 64–65.
11. Truscott, *Command Missions*, 65; O'Donnell, *Beyond Valor*, 2–3; Black, *Rangers in World War II*, 27–29.
12. Truscott, *Command Missions*, 65; Black, *Rangers in World War II*, 29.
13. Black, *Rangers in World War II*, 33; Truscott, *Command Missions*, 67.
14. Black, *Rangers in World War II*, 35; O'Donnell, *Beyond Valor*, 2; Truscott, *Command Missions*, 67.
15. O'Donnell, *Beyond Valor*, 12–13.
16. Ibid., 4; Truscott, *Command Missions*, 68–70.
17. Black, *Rangers in World War II*, 34, 44–45.
18. Truscott, *Command Missions*, 69.
19. Ibid., 69–70
20. Ibid., 70.
21. Ibid., 70–71.
22. Ibid., 71.
23. Ibid.
24. Ibid., 72; O'Donnell, *Beyond Valor*, 4; D'Este, *Eisenhower*, 340.

Chapter 12

1. Bradley and Blair, *General's Life*, 118–19.
2. Truscott, *Command Missions*, 89; Bradley and Blair, *General's Life*, 118.
3. Truscott, *Command Missions*, 72; Bradley and Blair, *General's Life*, 120; Harmon, MacKaye, and MacKaye, *Combat Commander*, 76.
4. Truscott, *Command Missions*, 73–75; MacDonald, *Mighty Endeavor*, 83–84; Atkinson, *Army at Dawn*, 26–27.
5. D'Este, *World War II in the Mediterranean*, 5; MacDonald, *Mighty Endeavor*, 93; Atkinson, *Army at Dawn*, 42–43.
6. Truscott, *Command Missions*, 77; Atkinson, *Army at Dawn*, 145–46. Truscott identifies René Malvergne as "Jules Malavergne."
7. Truscott, *Command Missions*, 78.
8. Ibid., 79–80.
9. Ibid., 80–81; LKT Papers, military records, headquarters, Fifth Army, public-relations-section document regarding Brig. Gen. Don E Carleton.
10. Truscott, *Command Missions*, 81.
11. Ibid., 82–84.
12. Ibid., 84–85.
13. Ibid., 86–87.
14. Ibid., 87.
15. Blumenson, *Patton Papers: 1940–1945*, 89; Truscott, *Command Missions*, 87.
16. Truscott, *Command Missions*, 88.
17. Ibid., 88–89.
18. D'Este, *World War II in the Mediterranean*, 4–6; Atkinson, *Army at Dawn*, 30–31; D'Este, *Eisenhower*, 351–52; D'Este, *Patton*, 433.
19. Harmon, MacKaye, and MacKaye, *Combat Commander*, 77–79, 83; Truscott, *Command Missions*, 89–90; D'Este, *Patton*, 433; Atkinson, *Army at Dawn*, 22, 103.
20. Truscott, *Command Missions*, 91.
21. D'Este, *World War II in the Mediterranean*, 4; Harmon, MacKaye, and MacKaye, *Combat Commander*, 75.
22. D'Este, *World War II in the Mediterranean*, 2–4; Atkinson, *Army at Dawn*, 79; Flanagan, *Airborne*, 52; Black, *Rangers in World War II*, 11–12, 54; D'Este, *Eisenhower*, 351.
23. D'Este, *World War II in the Mediterranean*, 4–6; D'Este, *Eisenhower*, 351; D'Este, *Patton*, 426–27 (second and third quotes), 431; G. Patton, *War as I Knew It*, 5 (first quote).

Chapter 13

1. Truscott, *Command Missions*, 92–95.
2. Ibid., 91–93.
3. Ibid., 92, 97.
4. Ibid., 93–95; MacDonald, *Mighty Endeavor*, 106–107.
5. Truscott, *Command Missions*, 94–95; Atkinson, *Army at Dawn*, 142.
6. Truscott, *Command Missions*, 96–97, 270; Eisenhower quoted in Nixon, *Six Crises*, 235.

7. Truscott, *Command Missions*, 96.
8. Ibid., 97.
9. Ibid.; Atkinson, *Army at Dawn*, 143.
10. Truscott, *Command Missions*, 108–109, 112.
11. Ibid., 112–13.
12. Ibid., 113–15.
13. Ibid., 115.
14. Ibid., 117.
15. Ibid., 117–18.
16. Ibid., 118–19; Atkinson, *Army at Dawn*, 145–46.
17. Truscott, *Command Missions*, 118–19.
18. Ibid., 119–20.
19. Ibid., 121–22.
20. Ibid., 122–23.
21. Report, Patton to Stimson, Dec. 7, 1942, quoted in D'Este, *Patton*, 439.
22. LKT Army Personnel File, efficiency reports, 1943; Atkinson, *Army at Dawn*, 143; LKT Papers, correspondence, Victoria Craw to LKT, Jan. 9, 1943; Truscott, *Command Missions*, 77.
23. MacDonald, *Mighty Endeavor*, 112, 142; Atkinson, *Army at Dawn*, 147; D'Este, *World War II in the Mediterranean*, 6; D'Este, *Eisenhower*, 359.

Chapter 14

1. Buell et al., *World War II Album*, 284, 296; Anderson, *Guadalcanal*, 11–13, 22.
2. MacDonald, *Mighty Endeavor*, 141–43; Bradley and Blair, *General's Life*, 125–26.
3. Truscott, *Command Missions*, 124; Steinbeck, *Once There Was a War*, 141.
4. Truscott, *Command Missions*, 124–25, 127.
5. Ibid., 129–30; LKT Résumé.
6. Truscott, *Command Missions*, 151; Patton diary, Mar. 11, 1945, quoted in D'Este, *Patton*, 461.
7. D'Este, *World War II in the Mediterranean*, 6, 8–9, 15; Bradley and Blair, *General's Life*, 124–25; Truscott, *Command Missions*, 125–26.
8. D'Este, *World War II in the Mediterranean*, 10, 12–13, 15, 27; MacDonald, *Mighty Endeavor*, 127–28.
9. D'Este, *World War II in the Mediterranean*, 8, 10.
10. Truscott, *Command Missions*, 125, 127; D'Este, *World War II in the Mediterranean*, 11.
11. Truscott, *Command Missions*, 130; LKT Papers, correspondence, LKT to Sarah, Jan. 23, 1943.
12. Truscott, *Command Missions*, 81; LKT Papers, correspondence, LKT to Sarah Truscott, Feb. 2, 1943.
13. Truscott, *Command Missions*, 134; D'Este, *World War II in the Mediterranean*, 16–17.
14. Truscott, *Command Missions*, 146, 153–54; Bradley and Blair, *General's Life*, 128.

15. Truscott, *Command Missions*, 151.
16. D'Este, *World War II in the Mediterranean*, 18 (quote), 18–19.
17. Ibid., 16, 19–21.
18. Ibid., 23–24.
19. Truscott, *Command Missions*, 170, 173.
20. MacDonald, *Mighty Endeavor*, 138–39; Bradley and Blair, *General's Life*, 153, 159.
21. Whiting, *Hero*, 26, 32.

Chapter 15

1. Truscott, *Command Missions*, 175–76.
2. Ibid., 177.
3. Ibid., 176–77.
4. Ibid., 179, 186–87.
5. D'Este, *Fatal Decision*, 173.
6. Mitcham and von Stauffenberg, *Battle of Sicily*, 26, 29; Barzini, *Italians*, 257–60; Ratti et al., *Sicily*, 30.
7. Mitcham and von Stauffenberg, *Battle of Sicily*, 20–21, 30; D'Este, *World War II in the Mediterranean*, 42.
8. Barzini, *Italians*, 142–43, 190–92; Mitcham and von Stauffenberg, *Battle of Sicily*, 29–30.
9. Mitcham and von Stauffenberg, *Battle of Sicily*, 168; Deighton, *Blitzkrieg*, xix–xx; D'Este, *Bitter Victory*, 522; D'Este, *World War II in the Mediterranean*, 75.
10. D'Este, *Bitter Victory*, 181–91, 190 (Hitler quote), 191 (cable to Churchill). D'Este based his summary of the operation on Ewen Montagu, *The Man Who Never Was* (1953).
11. Truscott, *Command Missions*, 179.
12. Ibid., 177, 179–80.
13. Ibid., 180; Lang, "Close-up—Lucian King Truscott," 106.
14. LKT Papers, correspondence, LKT to Sarah Truscott, May 14, 23, 1943; Murphy, *To Hell and Back*, 12.
15. Truscott, *Command Missions*, 174–75, 178.
16. Ibid., 182–83, 185–87.
17. Ibid., 183, 199.
18. Ibid., 199–200.
19. D'Este, *World War II in the Mediterranean*, 39–46; Montgomery, *Memoirs*, 166.
20. Mitcham and von Stauffenberg, *Battle of Sicily*, 13; D'Este, *World War II in the Mediterranean*, 46–48; D'Este, *Bitter Victory*, 80–81, 114–22; Truscott, *Command Missions*, 193–95.
21. Kesselring, *Memoirs*, 159.
22. Truscott, *Command Missions*, 193, 195, 197–200.
23. Ibid., 200–201.
24. Ibid., 202–204.
25. Ibid., 204–205.
26. Ibid., 197, 204, 207.
27. LKT Papers, correspondence, LKT to Sarah Truscott, June 23, 25, 1943.

28. Truscott, *Command Missions,* 193–94; Mitcham and von Stauffenberg, *Battle of Sicily,* 356–57.
29. Mitcham and von Stauffenberg, *Battle of Sicily,* 69; Truscott, *Command Missions,* 196, 208–209.
30. LKT Papers, correspondence, LKT to Sarah Truscott, July 7, 1943.
31. Truscott, *Command Missions,* 209; Mitcham and von Stauffenberg, *Battle of Sicily,* 24–25, 78–79.
32. Bill Phillippi interview, Jan. 30, 2007.

Chapter 16

1. D'Este, *Eisenhower,* 433–34; MacDonald, *Mighty Endeavor,* 55; Bradley and Blair, *General's Life,* 105; Gavin, *On to Berlin,* 22; D'Este, *World War II in the Mediterranean,* 47.
2. D'Este, *World War II in the Mediterranean,* 51–52.
3. Ibid., 52.
4. Gavin, *On to Berlin,* 25–26.
5. Ibid., 25–28; Coffman, *Regulars,* 302, 311; D'Este, *World War II in the Mediterranean,* 52–53.
6. Truscott, *Command Missions,* 212–13.
7. Ibid., 213.
8. Ibid., 195, 209–10, 214, 229; MacDonald, *Mighty Endeavor,* 157; D'Este, *Bitter Victory,* 121, 264; D'Este, *Fatal Decision,* 502.
9. Bradley and Blair, *General's Life,* 179.
10. Truscott, *Command Missions,* 198, 211, 214.
11. Ibid., 198, 210–13.
12. Ibid., 214.
13. Ibid., 214–15; Montgomery, *Memoirs,* 166.
14. Truscott, *Command Missions,* 217, 378–79.
15. MacDonald, *Mighty Endeavor,* 175–77; Bradley and Blair, *General's Life,* 182–83.
16. Blumenson, *Patton Papers: 1940–1945,* 280; Flanagan, *Airborne,* 90–91; D'Este, *Bitter Victory,* 307–308.
17. Bill Phillippi interview, Jan. 30, 2007.
18. Flanagan, *Airborne,* 91–92.
19. O'Donnell, *Beyond Valor,* 53; D'Este, *Bitter Victory,* 307–308.
20. Mitcham and von Stauffenberg, *Battle of Sicily,* 129; MacDonald, *Mighty Endeavor,* 179.
21. Bill Phillippi interview, Jan. 30, 2007; Mitcham and von Stauffenberg, *Battle of Sicily,* 127.
22. MacDonald, *Mighty Endeavor,* 177, 180.
23. Truscott, *Command Missions,* 214–15; Bradley and Blair, *General's Life,* 186; D'Este, *World War II in the Mediterranean,* 61–62.
24. D'Este, *World War II in the Mediterranean,* 62–63; D'Este, *Bitter Victory,* 308–309; Bradley and Blair, *General's Life,* 188.
25. Bradley and Blair, *General's Life,* 187–89.
26. Truscott, *Command Missions,* 217–22.
27. Ibid., 222–24; D'Este, *World War II in the Mediterranean,* 67–68.

Chapter 17

1. Truscott, *Command Mission*, 222–24; D'Este, *Bitter Victory*, 418–19.
2. Bradley and Blair, *General's Life*, 191–93.
3. Kesselring, *Memoirs*, 163.
4. Truscott, *Command Missions*, 222–24; Murphy, *To Hell and Back*, 12; Lang, "Close-up—Lucian King Truscott," 106.
5. Truscott, *Command Missions*, 224–27; Bradley and Blair, *General's Life*, 193n.
6. Truscott, *Command Missions*, 226–27.
7. Ibid., 228–29; Blumenson, *Patton Papers: 1940–1945*, 306; D'Este, *Bitter Victory*, 452–53.
8. Truscott, *Command Missions*, 228–29, 231; Bradley and Blair, *General's Life*, 196; D'Este, *Bitter Victory*, 427, 445.
9. Truscott, *Command Missions*, 229–31.
10. Ibid., 230–31; D'Este, *Bitter Victory*, 478n.
11. Truscott, *Command Missions*, 231.
12. Ibid., 231–34; Murphy, *To Hell and Back*, 13.
13. Truscott, *Command Missions*, 233–34.
14. Ibid., 234–35; Blumenson, *Patton Papers: 1940–1945*, 318–19.
15. Bradley and Blair, *General's Life*, 196–97; LKT Papers, 3rd Division journal, Aug. 10, 1943.
16. Truscott, *Command Missions*, 235–40; Belden, *Still Time to Die*, 281; Morison, *United States Naval Operations in World War II: Volume 9, Sicily-Salerno-Anzio*, 204–205; Bradley and Blair, *General's Life*, 197.
17. Truscott, *Command Missions*, 241–42; Ernie Pyle, Scripps-Howard wire copy, Sept. 6, 1943, reprinted in Pyle, *Brave Men*, 69–70.
18. Truscott, *Command Missions*, 242; Pyle, *Brave Men*, 70–71.
19. Truscott, *Command Missions*, 242–43.
20. D'Este, *World War II in the Mediterranean*, 72, 75.
21. Truscott, *Command Missions*, 243–44; Lang, "Close-up—Lucian King Truscott," 106.
22. LKT Papers, correspondence, LKT to Sarah Truscott, Aug. 25, 1943; LKT Army Personnel File, efficiency reports, June 30, 1943, endorsed by Eisenhower, July 23, 1943.
23. D'Este, *World War II in the Mediterranean*, 62, 76–78; Bradley and Blair, *General's Life*, 200.
24. Mitcham and von Stauffenberg, *Battle of Sicily*, 30; Bradley and Blair, *General's Life*, 191; G. Patton, *War as I Knew It*, 72; Murphy, *To Hell and Back*, 15.
25. D'Este, *World War II in the Mediterranean*, 74–77.

Chapter 18

1. Blumenson, *Anzio*, 12–13; MacDonald, *Mighty Endeavor*, 192–94; D'Este, *World War II in the Mediterranean*, 79–80, 117.
2. Wallace et al., *World War II: The Italian Campaign*, 79–80, 101.
3. Ibid., 101, 154.

4. Blumenson, *Anzio*, 13; Blumenson, *Mark Clark*, 133; Wallace et al., *Italian Campaign*, 51–52; D'Este, *World War II in the Mediterranean*, 79, 81–84, 86–87; Montgomery, *Memoirs*, 173.
5. Blumenson, *Mark Clark*, 143; Blumenson, *Anzio*, 35; D'Este, *World War II in the Mediterranean*, 79; D'Este, *Fatal Decision*, 59; Wallace et al., *Italian Campaign*, 54.
6. Blumenson, *Anzio*, 36; Bradley and Blair, *General's Life*, 204–205.
7. Blumenson, *Mark Clark*, 20–22, 293–95; D'Este, *Fatal Decision*, 37, 43; D'Este, *World War II in the Mediterranean*, 99–100.
8. Blumenson, *Mark Clark*, 121–26; D'Este, *World War II in the Mediterranean*, 80, 86–87; Truscott, *Command Missions*, 247.
9. Wallace et al., *Italian Campaign*, 54–55; D'Este, *Fatal Decision*, 36–38, 40–41; D'Este, *World War II in the Mediterranean*, 82, 86–87, 90, 93, 97, 99 (quote).
10. D'Este, *World War II in the Mediterranean*, 90, 92–93; D'Este, *Fatal Decision*, 39–40; Wallace et al., *Italian Campaign*, 54–55.
11. Truscott, *Command Missions*, 246–47.
12. D'Este, *World War II in the Mediterranean*, 90–91, 116; D'Este, *Fatal Decision*, 46, 88; Wallace et al., *Italian Campaign*, 55, 100–101.
13. Blumenson, *Mark Clark*, 133–34; D'Este, *World War II in the Mediterranean*, 92–96; Wallace et al., *Italian Campaign*, 55–56; D'Este, *Fatal Decision*, 39–40.
14. D'Este, *World War II in the Mediterranean*, 100–104; Blumenson, *Mark Clark*, 134.
15. D'Este, *World War II in the Mediterranean*, 102–103, 107–108; Flanagan, *Airborne*, 129–36.
16. D'Este, *World War II in the Mediterranean*, 104–106; Wallace et al., *Italian Campaign*, 61–62; Blumenson, *Mark Clark*, 137–38; Sheehan, *Anzio*, 47.
17. Truscott, *Command Missions*, 249–53.
18. Ibid., 254; D'Este, *World War II in the Mediterranean*, 109–10.
19. D'Este, *World War II in the Mediterranean*, 110–12; MacDonald, *Mighty Endeavor*, 215–16; Blumenson, *Mark Clark*, 148.
20. D'Este, *Fatal Decision*, 104–105; D'Este, *World War II in the Mediterranean*, 110, 117; Truscott, *Command Missions*, 258.
21. Wallace et al., *Italian Campaign*, 76; Blumenson, *Mark Clark*, 145–48; D'Este, *World War II in the Mediterranean*, 110.

Chapter 19

1. D'Este, *World War II in the Mediterranean*, 118–19.
2. Ibid.; Truscott, *Command Missions*, 255–57.
3. Truscott, *Command Missions*, 257–58; Graham and Bidwell, *Tug of War*, 114.
4. Truscott, *Command Missions*, 259, 263; Wallace et al., *Italian Campaign*, 84–85.
5. Truscott, *Command Missions*, 263–65.
6. Ibid., 266–68; Wallace et al., *Italian Campaign*, 84.

7. Truscott, *Command Missions*, 268, 270.
8. Ibid., 270.
9. Ibid., 271–72.
10. Truscott, *Command Missions*, 272; Lang, "Close-up—Lucian King Truscott," 108.
11. Truscott, *Command Missions*, 272; Lang, "Close-up—Lucian King Truscott," 111.
12. Truscott, *Command Missions*, 272–74, 276; Wallace et al., *Italian Campaign*, 84–85.
13. Lucas diary quoted in D'Este, *World War II in the Mediterranean*, 118.
14. Truscott, *Command Missions*, 274, 276; Murphy, *To Hell and Back*, 80.
15. Truscott, *Command Missions*, 277–78, 282; Pyle, *Brave Men*, 252–53.
16. Truscott, *Command Missions*, 278–79.
17. Ibid., 280–81.
18. Ibid., 280–82; Murphy, *To Hell and Back*, 34.
19. Truscott, *Command Missions*, 284.
20. Ibid., 285; Murphy, *To Hell and Back*, 51.
21. D'Este, *World War II in the Mediterranean*, 123, 126.
22. LKT Papers, memoranda, Lucian Truscott to Dwight D. Eisenhower, Nov. 24, 1943; ibid., correspondence, Lucian Truscott to Bedell Smith, Dec. 1, 1943; ibid., Bedell Smith to Lucian Truscott, Dec. 15, 1943.
23. Blumenson, *Anzio*, 41–43; Sheehan, *Anzio*, 17–18; MacDonald, *Mighty Endeavor*, 218–19.
24. MacDonald, *Mighty Endeavor*, 220; Blumenson, *Anzio*, 43–44; D'Este, *Fatal Decision*, 69.
25. Blumenson, *Anzio*, 10, 43, 46–47, 49; MacDonald, *Mighty Endeavor*, 143; author's visit to Ljubljana, Slovenia, Sept. 4, 2013.
26. MacDonald, *Mighty Endeavor*, 217–20; Blumenson, *Anzio*, 34–35, 38–39; D'Este, *World War II in the Mediterranean*, 128.
27. Blumenson, *Anzio*, 40, 44–45; D'Este, *World War II in the Mediterranean*, 129.
28. Blumenson, *Anzio*, 43–46.
29. Ibid., 8, 46; D'Este, *Fatal Decision*, 75, 94, 102.
30. Blumenson, *Anzio*, 47–52; D'Este, *World War II in the Mediterranean*, 129–30.
31. Blumenson, *Anzio*, 49; D'Este, *Fatal Decision*, 97–102; Truscott, *Command Missions*, 298–301; D'Este, *Fatal Decision*, 98, 101–102.
32. Truscott, *Command Missions*, 303–304.
33. D'Este, *Fatal Decision*, 110–11.
34. Ibid., 110–13; Clark quoted in D'Este, *Fatal Decision*, 113; Morison, *United States Naval Operations in World War II: Volume 9, Sicily-Salerno-Anzio*, 336.
35. D'Este, *World War II in the Mediterranean*, 123–27; Blumenson, *Mark Clark*, 4.
36. Graham and Bidwell, *Tug of War*, 151.
37. Blumenson, *Anzio*, 56, 185; Truscott, *Command Missions*, 291–92, 298.

Chapter 20

1. Zaloga, *Anzio 1944*, 10; Blumenson, *Anzio*, 73–74, 79–81; D'Este, *World War II in the Mediterranean*, 125, 135; Truscott, *Command Missions*, 309–10.
2. Truscott, *Command Missions*, 308; Zaloga, *Anzio 1944*, 25–27; Adams et al., *World War II: Italy at War*, 11.
3. Truscott, *Command Missions*, 308; Zaloga, *Anzio 1944*, 6, 26, 27; Clark, *Anzio*, 156 (map); author's visit to Anzio and Nettuno, Italy, May 11, 2009.
4. Truscott, *Command Missions*, 308; D'Este, *World War II in the Mediterranean*, 138 (map); Zaloga, *Anzio 1944*, 26–28.
5. Zaloga, *Anzio 1944*, 32; Truscott, *Command Missions*, 371.
6. Truscott, *Command Missions*, 301, 307 (map), 308–309.
7. Blumenson, *Anzio*, 85–87; D'Este, *Fatal Decision*, 133–35; Clark (from Lucas diary) quoted in D'Este, *Fatal Decision*, 133.
8. Kesselring, *Memoirs*, 193–94; Kesselring quoted in D'Este, *Fatal Decision*, 405; Truscott, *Command Missions*, 306, 549–50. Truscott attributes Kesselring's comment to an interview with correspondent Daniel De Luce in January 1946.
9. Truscott, *Command Missions*, 113–14, 178, 310; Farago, *Patton*, 30.
10. Truscott, *Command Missions*, 312; LKT CIA personnel file, personal history statement, Feb. 14, 1951.
11. Truscott, *Command Missions*, 311; D'Este, *Fatal Decision*, 404–405, 405 (Kesselring quote); Harmon, MacKaye, and MacKaye, *Combat Commander*, 159.
12. Truscott, *Command Missions*, 311–12.
13. D'Este, *Fatal Decision*, 135; Truscott, *Command Missions*, 311–12.
14. Lucas diary quoted in D'Este, *Fatal Decision*, 142–43.
15. Alexander quoted in Blumenson, *Anzio*, 88; D'Este, *Fatal Decision*, 144, 147.
16. Truscott, *Command Missions*, 312–13.
17. Blumenson, *Anzio*, 97; Truscott, *Command Missions*, 315; D'Este, *Fatal Decision*, 160.
18. Harmon, MacKaye, and MacKaye, *Combat Commander*, 163–65.
19. Truscott, *Command Missions*, 313.
20. Murphy, *To Hell and Back*, 82, 84, 96; Whiting, *Hero*, 84.
21. Truscott, *Command Missions*, 313–14; Zaloga, *Anzio 1944*, 26 (map), 43–44; O'Donnell, *Beyond Valor*, 83.
22. O'Donnell, *Beyond Valor*, 83; D'Este, *Fatal Decision*, 162, 165, 168.
23. O'Donnell, *Beyond Valor*, 90, 92–94, 96.
24. Ibid., 83–84; Truscott, *Command Missions*, 313–14; D'Este, *Fatal Decision*, 167–69.

Chapter 21

1. Truscott, *Command Missions*, 314; Lucas diary quoted in D'Este, *Fatal Decision*, 171.
2. Truscott, *Command Missions*, 314–15; Blumenson, *Anzio*, 103–104, 108.

3. D'Este, *Fatal Decision*, 171, 181; Lucas diary quoted in Blumenson, *Anzio*, 104–105; Truscott, *Command Missions*, 316–17.
4. Truscott, *Command Missions*, 316–17.
5. Ibid., 317–18.
6. Zaloga, *Anzio 1944*, 57; Truscott, *Command Missions*, 317–19; D'Este, *Fatal Decision*, 5.
7. Truscott, *Command Missions*, 319.
8. Ibid., 319–20, 548; D'Este, *Fatal Decision*, 512n.
9. Truscott, *Command Missions*, 320–21.
10. Ibid., 321–23.
11. Ibid., 324–26; Harmon, MacKaye, and MacKaye, *Combat Commander*, 174; Zaloga, *Anzio 1944*, 10, 65–67.
12. Truscott, *Command Missions*, 327–28.
13. D'Este, *Fatal Decision*, 270 (quote), 420–21; Blumenson, *Anzio*, 167.
14. D'Este, *Fatal Decision*, 267–69; Truscott, *Command Missions*, 328.
15. Truscott, *Command Missions*, 328, 332–33.
16. Ibid., 328, 332–34. Truscott gives Eveleigh's first name as "Evelyn" rather than "Vivian."
17. Ibid., 330–31, 334.
18. Ibid., 335–37.
19. Ibid., 337; D'Este, *Fatal Decision*, 454–56.
20. Truscott, *Command Missions*, 337–40.
21. Ibid., 341, 344.
22. Ibid., 344–46; Zaloga, *Anzio 1944*, 68–69.
23. Zaloga, *Anzio 1944*, 68–72.
24. Ibid., 73–74; Truscott, *Command Missions*, 348–51.
25. LKT Papers, teletype, Lucian Truscott to Alfred M. Gruenther, Mar. 5, 1944.
26. D'Este, *World War II in the Mediterranean*, 158–59; Truscott, *Command Missions*, 351–53.
27. Truscott, *Command Missions*, 357–58.
28. Monahan and Neidel-Greenlee, *And If I Perish*, 270–71.
29. Carroll, *War Letters*, 249, 251.
30. Truscott, *Command Missions*, 358–59; Bellafaire, *Army Nurse Corps*, 20; Debbie Truscott, e-mail to the author, Feb. 20, 2007.
31. Pyle, *Brave Men*, 233, 237.
32. Ibid., 251–52.
33. Ibid.; Murphy, *To Hell and Back*, 115, 135–36.
34. Pyle, *Brave Men*, 237, 243, 257.
35. Mauldin, *Up Front*, 143–44.

Chapter 22

1. Truscott, *Command Missions*, 360.
2. Blumenson, *Anzio*, 185–86.
3. Truscott, *Command Missions*, 361–64; Mauldin, *Up Front*, 173–74.
4. Truscott, *Command Missions*, 364.
5. Graham and Bidwell, *Tug of War*, 241–42, 244–48.

6. Bill Hanrahan (pseud.) interview, Jan. 11, 2007.
7. Truscott, *Command Missions*, 366–67; Blumenson, *Anzio*, 178–79.
8. Truscott, *Command Missions*, 366.
9. Ibid., 366.
10. Ibid., 367–68.
11. LKT Papers, correspondence, LKT to Sarah Truscott, Apr. 7, 13, 16, 19, 1944.
12. Truscott, *Command Missions*, 368–69, 546–47; Blumenson, *Anzio*, 178.
13. Blumenson, *Anzio*, 179; Bill Hanrahan (pseud.) interview, Jan. 11, 2007.
14. Blumenson, *Anzio*, 179–80; Truscott, *Command Missions*, 370.
15. Truscott, *Command Missions*, 371.
16. Ibid., 366, 371–72; Blumenson, *Anzio*, 175.
17. Murphy, *To Hell and Back*, 150; Blumenson, *Anzio*, 186; Truscott, *Command Missions*, 374.
18. Truscott, *Command Missions*, 374.
19. Ibid., 374; D'Este, *Fatal Decision*, 360–61, 363–64.
20. Truscott, *Command Missions*, 375; Brann quoted in Clark, *Anzio*, 303.
21. Blumenson, *Anzio*, 191–92; D'Este, *Fatal Decision*, 367–68; Graham and Bidwell, *Tug of War*, 335.
22. Clausewitz, *On War*, 342.
23. Truscott, *Command Missions*, 375–76; Wilson quoted in D'Este, *Fatal Decision*, 368–69.
24. D'Este, *Fatal Decision*, 371–72.
25. Truscott, *Command Missions*, 375–77; D'Este, *Fatal Decision*, 388–89; Sevareid, *Not So Wild a Dream*, 405.
26. Truscott, *Command Missions*, 377–78; D'Este, *Fatal Decision*, 387–90.
27. Truscott, *Command Missions*, 378–79.
28. Ibid., 379–80.
29. Sevareid, *Not So Wild a Dream*, 414.
30. Truscott, *Command Missions*, 380.
31. Ibid., 550; Harmon, MacKaye, and MacKaye, *Combat Commander*, 191; Alexander quoted in D'Este, *Fatal Decision*, 409.
32. D'Este, *Fatal Decision*, 410–11.
33. Ibid., 380.
34. Blumenson, *Anzio*, 200–201.
35. Clark quoted in D'Este, *Eisenhower*, 531.
36. LKT Army Personnel File.
37. Mauldin, *Brass Ring*, 272; "Sicily-Rome American Cemetery," American Battle Monuments Commission, www.abmc.gov/cemeteries-memorials/europe/sicily-rome-american-cemetery, accessed 2014.

Chapter 23

1. Analogy based on a similar one presented in Murphy, *To Hell and Back*, 169.
2. Clarke, *Southern France*, 4–5; Truscott, *Command Missions*, 408.
3. Eisenhower, *Crusade in Europe*, 291–92; Murphy, *To Hell and Back*, 169; Clarke, *Southern France*, 5–6.

4. Truscott, *Command Missions*, 385; Mauldin, *Up Front*, 198; Murphy, *To Hell and Back*, 169.
5. Clarke, *Southern France*, 3; D'Este, *Eisenhower*, 503, 551–52; Butcher, *My Three Years with Eisenhower*, 453, 634–35.
6. Eisenhower, *Crusade in Europe*, 281–84; Churchill quoted in MacDonald, *Mighty Endeavor*, 351; D'Este, *Eisenhower*, 567.
7. MacDonald, *Mighty Endeavor*, 351; D'Este, *Eisenhower*, 565–67; Clarke, *Southern France*, 5, 10.
8. Truscott, *Command Missions*, 382; Asahina, *Just Americans*, 105–106.
9. LKT Papers correspondence, LKT to Sarah Truscott, June 15, 1944.
10. Clarke, *Southern France*, 6, 10–11.
11. Truscott, *Command Missions*, 382–83.
12. Ibid., 384–85.
13. Ibid., 385–86, 391, 393; Clarke, *Southern France*, 8.
14. Truscott, *Command Missions*, 393; Clarke, *Southern France*, 8.
15. Truscott, *Command Missions*, 385–86 (map), 392–94, 397, 399; Clarke, *Southern France*, 7–12.
16. Truscott, *Command Missions*, 394–95; Clarke, *Southern France*, 9–10; Mauldin, *Up Front*, 205.
17. Flanagan, *Airborne*, 225–28; Truscott, *Command Missions*, 396, 399–400.
18. Truscott, *Command Missions*, 400–402; Clarke and Smith, *Riviera to the Rhine*, 42.
19. Truscott, *Command Missions*, 403–404.
20. Ibid., 404–405.
21. Ibid., 405, 407; Lucian K. Truscott IV interview, Oct. 7, 2009; Clarke, *Southern France*, 17.

Chapter 24

1. Truscott, *Command Missions*, 408–10, 412; Clarke, *Southern France*, 11–12.
2. O'Donnell, *Beyond Valor*, 180, 183–85.
3. Flanagan, *Airborne*, 225–26, 229–31.
4. Ibid., 233; O'Donnell, *Beyond Valor*, 190.
5. Truscott, *Command Missions*, 412–13; D'Este, *Eisenhower*, 567; MacDonald, *Mighty Endeavor*, 351.
6. Murphy, *To Hell and Back*, 169.
7. Truscott, *Command Missions*, 405–406, 413–14.
8. Ibid., 414–15; author's visit to Côte d'Azur of France, May 10, 2009.
9. Truscott, *Command Missions*, 415, 417; Clarke, *Southern France*, 15.
10. Truscott, *Command Missions*, 415–18; author's visit to Montélimar, France, May 9, 2009.
11. Truscott, *Command Missions*, 400, 419–20.
12. Ibid., 420; MacDonald, *Mighty Endeavor*, 272–73; Lang, "Close-up—Lucian King Truscott," 102; Weiner, *Legacy of Ashes*, 4.
13. Truscott, *Command Missions*, 421.
14. Clarke, *Southern France*, 16.
15. Truscott, *Command Missions*, 421–22.

16. Ibid., 422; Clarke, *Southern France*, 17.
17. Truscott, *Command Missions*, 423–24.
18. Ibid., 424–25.
19. Ibid., 423–25.
20. Ibid., 426.
21. Ibid., 426–27.
22. Ibid.; Lang, "Close-up—Lucian King Truscott," 105.
23. Truscott, *Command Missions*, 428–29.
24. Clarke, *Southern France*, 19–20.
25. Truscott, *Command Missions*, 430–31.
26. Ibid., 432–33.
27. Murphy, *To Hell and Back*, 187.
28. Truscott, *Command Missions*, 433.
29. LKT Papers, correspondence, LKT to Sarah Truscott, Aug. 29, 1944.
30. Truscott, *Command Missions*, 434, 436–37; Clarke, *Southern France*, 29.
31. Clarke, *Southern France*, 7; Truscott, *Command Missions*, 437–38.
32. Truscott, *Command Missions*, 437–39; LKT Papers, Forrest C. Pogue, interview of Lucian K. Truscott, Jr., Mar. 21, 1959, 16.
33. Truscott, *Command Missions*, 439–40; Clarke, *Southern France*, 28–29; author's visit to Besançon, France, May 9, 2009.
34. Truscott, *Command Missions*, 441; author's visit to Belfort, France, May 8, 2009.
35. Truscott, *Command Missions*, 441.
36. Ibid., 442–44.
37. Ibid., 444.
38. Ibid., 444–45; Bradley and Blair, *General's Life*, 326–28; Ryan, *A Bridge Too Far*, 89.
39. Truscott, *Command Missions*, 445; Murphy, *To Hell and Back*, 196; author's visit to Bruyères, France, May 8, 2009.
40. Truscott, *Command Missions*, 445–46; Asahina, *Just Americans*, 8. Gen. Jacob L. Devers said on June 4, 1948, that the soldiers of the 442nd had "more than earned the right to be called just Americans, not Japanese Americans."
41. Murphy, *To Hell and Back*, 202, 220; Whiting, *Hero*, 136.
42. Truscott, *Command Missions*, 445–46; LKT Papers, correspondence, LKT to Sarah Truscott, Oct. 21, 1944; Lang, "Close-up—Lucian King Truscott," cover.
43. Truscott, *Command Missions*, 446.

Chapter 25

1. Truscott, *Command Missions*, 446–47.
2. Ibid., 447–48.
3. Ibid., 448.
4. Ibid.; D'Este, *Fatal Decision*, 428.
5. Truscott, *Command Missions*, 449; Shelton, *Climb to Conquer*, 171; D'Este, *World War II in the Mediterranean*, 182.

6. Asahina, *Just Americans*, 14, 18–19, 19 (quote), 22, 29, 212–13, 266; Matsuo, *Boyhood to War*, 14, 34–35; Shelton, *Climb to Conquer*, 31.
7. Matsuo, *Boyhood to War*, 28–29, 44–45, 55–57, 59–61.
8. Ibid., 45; Inouye, *Journey to Washington*, 85.
9. Matsuo, *Boyhood to War*, 61, 69–73; Asahina, *Just Americans*, 37, 57, 59, 61, 91.
10. Asahina, *Just Americans*, 19, 73–75, 106, 108–109; Matsuo, *Boyhood to War*, 80–82.
11. Asahina, *Just Americans*, 5, 98, 109, 121–22, 128, 132–35, 161–63, 195, 202, 225, 239.
12. Ibid., 197–98, 201. Asahina notes that the accuracy of Dahlquist's exact words cannot be confirmed, but as such they have achieved legendary status among 442nd veterans. This was also the author's conclusion while attending a JAVA (Japanese American Veterans Association) conference in Los Angeles in February 16–18, 2007.
13. Jenkins, *Last Ridge*, 15–16, 18, 21–22, 27, 31.
14. Ibid., 32–33.
15. Ibid., 14, 33, 35–36, 38; National Ski Patrol notice, May 5, 1942, quoted in ibid., 36; Bil Dunaway, conversation with the author, Arles, France, 1996.
16. Jenkins, *Last Ridge*, 49–51, 55, 70, 122; Shelton, *Climb to Conquer*, 107–109.
17. Shelton, *Climb to Conquer*, 107–10, 113–15; Jenkins, *Last Ridge*, 125–26, 128; Feuer, *Packs On!*, 31.
18. Jenkins, *Last Ridge*, 126–27; Shelton, *Climb to Conquer*, 113–16, 120; "Medal of Honor Recipients—World War I," Aug. 13, 2013, U.S. Army Center of Military History, www.history.army.mil/moh/worldwari.html#HAYS, accessed Mar. 2014.
19. Jenkins, *Last Ridge*, 122, 141; Burton, *Ski Troops*, 147.
20. Gibran, *92nd Division*, 12, 14–15, 17; Morehouse, *Jim Crow Army*, 70–71, 135.
21. Morehouse, *Jim Crow Army*, 26; Gibran, *92nd Division*, 355.
22. Hargrove, *Buffalo Soldiers in Italy*, 7–9; Gibran, *92nd Division*, 19.
23. LKT Papers, Brig. Gen. B. O. Davis and Truman K. Gibson, Jr., to Inspector General, "Report for War Department, Office of the Inspector General, Survey Relative Conditions Affecting Racial Attitudes at Fort Huachuca," Aug. 7, 1943, copy.
24. Gibran, *92nd Division*, 34–35, 41, 43–44, 46–48.
25. Ibid., 55–65.

Chapter 26

1. MacDonald, *Mighty Endeavor*, 548–50; D'Este, *World War II in the Mediterranean*, 180.
2. D'Este, *World War II in the Mediterranean*, 181, 185–89.
3. Bill Hanrahan (pseud.) interview, Jan. 11, 2007; D'Este, *World War II in the Mediterranean*, 186–87, 189.
4. Truscott, *Command Missions*, 457; Bill Hanrahan (pseud.) interview, Jan. 11, 2007.

5. MacDonald, *Mighty Endeavor*, 550; D'Este, *World War II in the Mediterranean*, 188–89.
6. Graham and Bidwell, *Tug of War*, 367–68, 386–87; Truscott, *Command Missions*, 448–51; Jenkins, *Last Ridge*, 137.
7. Jenkins, *Last Ridge*, 130–31; Truscott, *Command Missions*, 451–53; D'Este, *World War II in the Mediterranean*, 189.
8. Truscott, *Command Missions*, 453.
9. Ibid., 453–54.
10. Anne O'Hare McCormick, "The Italian Ordeal Surprises Members of Congress," *New York Times*, Dec. 23, 1944, quoted in Hynes et al., *Reporting World War II*, 571.
11. Truscott, *Command Missions*, 454–55; MacDonald, *Mighty Endeavor*, 551.
12. Truscott, *Command Missions*, 455–56.
13. Ibid., 457–59.
14. Ibid., 459–61; LKT Papers, memoranda, George C. Marshall to Lucian K. Truscott, Jr., [Dec. 20, 1944].
15. Truscott, *Command Missions*, 461–62. By war's end the 34th Division had served 500 combat days; only the 32nd, 37th, 45th, and the Americal Divisions had served more. Gawne, *Finding Your Father's War*, 236–48.
16. Truscott, *Command Missions*, 464.
17. Ibid., 464–65.
18. Ibid., 456, 465–66; Jenkins, *Last Ridge*, 135.
19. Shelton, *Climb to Conquer*, 121, 125–26.
20. Ibid., 126–28; Truscott, *Command Missions*, 466.
21. Shelton, *Climb to Conquer*, 129; Jenkins, *Last Ridge*, 164–65.
22. Truscott, *Command Missions*, 466–68; Shelton, *Climb to Conquer*, 129, 132–37, 141, 152–53; Jenkins, *Last Ridge*, 160–65, 177, 181, 185, 196.
23. Truscott, *Command Missions*, 470–71, 473; Gibran, *92nd Division*, 58–62.
24. Truscott, *Command Missions*, 117–18; D'Este, *World War II in the Mediterranean*, 18; Ambrose, *Citizen Soldiers*, 204–207.
25. Truscott, *Command Missions*, 468–69, 473–74; Buckley, *American Patriots*, 290.
26. Gibran, *92nd Division*, 18, 28, 34–35.
27. Truscott, *Command Missions*, 475.
28. Ibid., 473–75; Gibran, *92nd Division*, 64–67.
29. LKT Papers, Truman K. Gibson, Jr., "Report on Visit to 92nd Division (Negro Troops)," Mar. 12, 1945, report for Headquarters, Mediterranean Theater of Operations, APO 512; Gibran, *92nd Division*, 5.
30. Gibran, *92nd Division*, 35; Parker and unnamed battalion commander quoted in Ambrose, *Citizen Soldiers*, 349.
31. Pico quoted in Gibran, *92nd Division*, 133.
32. Morehouse, *Jim Crow Army*, 209–14; Gibran, *92nd Division*, 66; "African Americans in the U.S. Army," www.army.mil/africanamericans/timeline.html, accessed May 2014.

Chapter 27

1. Truscott, *Command Missions*, 477–79.
2. Shelton, *Climb to Conquer*, 169; Jenkins, *Last Ridge*, 210.
3. Truscott, *Command Missions*, 479–80.
4. Ibid., 480–82.
5. Ibid., 482–83.
6. Ibid., 484–86.
7. Ibid., 486.
8. Ibid., 486–87; Shelton, *Climb to Conquer*, 182.
9. Dole, *Soldier's Story*, 10, 16, 21–29, 27–28 (quote), 33, 139, 148–52, 152 (quote), 159–60, 180, 186, 204–205, 242–43, 253, 261.
10. Ibid., 214–16; Asahina, *Just Americans*, 223–24; Inouye, *Journey to Washington*, 85, 149–52; Shelton, *Climb to Conquer*, 182; Jenkins, *Last Ridge*, 220–23.
11. Vicky Phillippi (daughter of Paul Bennett) interviews, Dec. 3, 2011, Dec. 1, 2012; Paul M. Bennett, extracted page from undated, unpaginated document, entries 19–21, private collection of Vicky Phillippi.
12. Truscott, *Command Missions*, 487–89.
13. Ibid., 490.
14. Truscott, *Command Missions*, 491; LKT Papers, correspondence, LKT to Sarah Truscott, May 23, 24, 1945.
15. Truscott, *Command Missions*, 491.
16. Ibid., 492; author's visit to Bologna area, Italy, May 15, 2009.
17. Truscott, *Command Missions*, 492–93.
18. Shelton, *Climb to Conquer*, 188–89; Truscott, *Command Missions*, 493.
19. Truscott, *Command Missions*, 493.
20. Ibid., 493–95; Shelton, *Climb to Conquer*, 203–204; Jenkins, *Last Ridge*, 242–43; MacDonald, *Mighty Endeavor*, 553.
21. Truscott, *Command Missions*, 495.
22. Ibid., 495–96, 500.
23. Ibid., 500–501; LKT Papers, LKT photograph collection, German surrender, May 4, 1945; Blumenson, *Mark Clark*, 245.
24. D'Este, *World War II in the Mediterranean*, 196.
25. Eric Sevareid, "The Price We Pay in Italy," *The Nation*, Dec. 9, 1944, reprinted in Hynes et al., *Reporting World War II*, 569–70.
26. Westphal quoted in Feuer, *Packs On!*, 148.
27. Jenkins, *Last Ridge*, 243; Shelton, *Climb to Conquer*, 207–208; Truscott, *Command Missions*, 493.
28. Bill Hanrahan (pseud.) interview, Jan. 11, 2007.

Chapter 28

1. Martin, *Henry & Clare*, 13, 103. Martin attributes the "vamp" quotation to a "Time executive."
2. Ibid., 29, 35, 72, 75, 77, 79–81, 83.
3. Ibid., 101–104, 106–107, 110–11, 128–29.
4. Ibid., 124–27, 129–32.

5. Lawrenson, *Stranger at the Party*, 102, 104–105; Martin, *Henry & Clare*, 131–32; Morris, *Rage for Fame*, 216.
6. Martin, *Henry & Clare*, 138, 152, 154–57, 183, 197–99, 201–203.
7. Ibid., 77, 205–209, 213–14.
8. Ibid., 221, 231–32.
9. Ibid., 240–41, 243–44; Truscott, *Command Missions*, 453.
10. LKT Papers, correspondence, LKT to Sarah Truscott, Dec. 24, 28, 1944, Jan. 19, Mar. 20, 1945; Clare Boothe Luce Collected Papers, Library of Congress (hereafter cited as CBL Papers), correspondence, box 758, folder 9, LKT to Clare Boothe Luce (hereafter CBL), Jan. 7, 1945.
11. Martin, *Henry & Clare*, 248; CBL Papers, correspondence, box 758, folder 9, LKT to CBL, Mar. [?], 1945.
12. CBL Papers, correspondence, box 758, folder 9, LKT to CBL, Apr. 10, 1945.
13. Ibid., box 768, folder 9, LKT to CBL, May 13, 1945; Morris, *Rage for Fame*, 431.
14. CBL Papers, correspondence, box 768, folder 9, LKT to CBL, May 31, 1945; LKT Papers, correspondence, LKT to Sarah Truscott, May 31, 1945; ibid., general's aide's diary, May 30, 1945; Mauldin, *Brass Ring*, 272.
15. Mary Truscott interview, Aug. 11, 2008; Truscott, *Command Missions*, 504.
16. Whiting, *Hero*, 156–58.
17. Truscott, *Command Missions*, 496–97, 500, 502–503.
18. Ibid., 504–507; LKT Army Personnel File, assignments, "restricted" letter of orders assigning LKT and staff to temporary duty in China, Aug. 5, 1945.
19. Truscott, *Command Missions*, 507–509; Patton quoted in Farago, *Patton*, 819.
20. LKT Papers, correspondence, LKT to Mrs. Lloyd Champeau, Oct. 29, 1945.
21. Truscott, *Command Missions*, 510–15.
22. D'Este, *Patton*, 783–85, 795; CBL Papers, correspondence, box 758, folder 9, LKT to CBL, Dec. [?], 1945.
23. Truscott, *Command Missions*, 514.
24. Ibid., 514–15, 520–23; Weiner, *Legacy of Ashes*, 16.
25. Truscott, *Command Missions*, 524–25.
26. CBL Papers, correspondence, box 771, folder 21, LKT to CBL, Feb. 24, 1946.
27. Truscott, *Command Missions*, 528; Harmon, MacKaye, and MacKaye *Combat Commander*, 280–81.
28. Truscott, *Command Missions*, 530–31; LKT Papers, correspondence, cable, LKT to Sarah Truscott, Apr. 27, 1946; ibid., LKT to Thomas Handy, May 13, 1946; CBL Papers, correspondence, box 56, Don Carleton to CBL, [May–June?] 1946.
29. LKT Army Personnel File, assignments, appointment to screening board, Oct. 23, 1946, Apr. 11, 1947; LKT Papers, procedures for duties of screening board, Nov. 19, 1946.

30. LKT Army Personnel File, memoranda, Bornstein to Director of Personnel and Administration, May 20, 1947; ibid., Purdin to Chief of Finance, May 23, 1947; ibid., Maj. Gen. Edward Witsell to Truscott, Apr. 25, 1950.
31. Truscott, *Command Missions*, 531; LKT Résumé.

Chapter 29

1. LKT Papers, property description of Bluemont; author's visit to Bluemont, Va., Oct. 3, 2009; LKT Résumé.
2. LKT Papers, correspondence, LKT to Severance Millikin, Oct. 10, 1948; ibid., LKT to Clark, July 24, 1950; ibid., LKT to Eisenhower, July 24, 1950; ibid., LKT to Marshall, Sept. 20, 1950; ibid. Clark to LKT, July 29, 1950; ibid., Eisenhower to LKT, Aug. 1, 1950; ibid., Marshall to LKT, Oct. 3, 1950; ibid., "Report on Joint Amphibious Operation," Jan 9, 1948; LKT CIA Personnel File, undated letter of employment acceptance; Ricks, *The Generals*, 187–88.
3. Weiner, *Legacy of Ashes*, 4, 8, 13–15.
4. Ibid., 3, 11–12, 14–15.
5. Ibid., 10–15, 18–21.
6. Ibid., 27–29.
7. Ibid., 30–31.
8. Stockton, *Flawed Patriot*, 38–39; Weiner, *Legacy of Ashes*, 15–16, 55, 72–74; LKT CIA Personnel File, letter of acceptance for Truscott in position as senior representative, [Apr. 24, 1951].
9. Corson, *Armies of Ignorance*, 331–33; Weiner, *Legacy of Ashes*, 78; Trento, *Secret History of the CIA*, 86.
10. Weiner, *Legacy of Ashes*, 84, 86–87; Corson, *Armies of Ignorance*, 332–33, 359–60, 369.
11. Murphy, Kondrashev, and Bailey, *Battleground Berlin*, 213 (quote), 213–14, 219–20, 222, 227; Lucian K. Truscott IV interview, Oct. 7, 2009.
12. Trento, *Secret History of the CIA*, 194, 494n; Corson, *Armies of Ignorance*, 360, 365–66.
13. Corson, *Armies of Ignorance*, 359–60, 365–66.
14. Krebs, *Dueling Visions*, 64–65; Corson, *Armies of Ignorance*, 360, 365–70.
15. Krebs, *Dueling Visions*, 64–66; Corson, *Armies of Ignorance*, 360, 370–72.
16. James and Helen Truscott interview, Nov. 12, 2007.
17. LKT Army Personnel File, memoranda, John Klein to Lucian Truscott, Aug. 4, 1954.
18. *Corsicana (Tex.) Daily Sun*, June 4, 1954.
19. LKT CIA Personnel File, memoranda, [censored name] to Lucian Truscott, June 19, 1956; ibid., Dwight Eisenhower to National Security Council and Director of Central Intelligence, with copy to LKT, May 6, 1958; ibid., Truscott resignation from CIA, May 1, 1959.
20. Heefner, *Dogface Soldier*, 287–88; Weiner, *Legacy of Ashes*, 206–207; Stockton, *Flawed Patriot*, 39.

Chapter 30

1. Sarah Truscott, Journals, 1958–65, private collections of Mary and Debbie Truscott, courtesy of James Truscott (information not quoted summarized from daily entries); author's visit to Waynewood, Va., Sept. 15, 2009. Sarah Truscott, Journal, Aug. 18, 1965, references the Truscott "Cottage."
2. Sarah Truscott, Journal, Jan. 2, 22, Feb. 10, 26, Mar. 5, May 27, 30, June 7, 17, Nov. 24, 1958.
3. Ibid., Jan. 22, Feb. 16, Apr. 18, June 16, 17, 1959; Mary Truscott interview, Aug. 11, 2008.
4. Sarah Truscott, Journal, Dec. 23, 30, 1959, May 30, Dec. 16, 1960.
5. Ibid., Jan. 14, 1961; Gary Hood, curator of art, West Point Museum, U.S. Military Academy, New York, e-mail message to author, Dec. 14, 2007.
6. Sarah Truscott, Journal, Feb. 20, Apr. 8, 15, Aug. 27, Oct. 2, 6, 16, 1961, Jan. 5, Apr. 4, 5, May 2, 1962.
7. Ibid., Jan. 22, 23, 1965.
8. Ibid., Apr. 27, May 16, 1965.
9. Ibid., June 27, 28, 1965; James and Helen Truscott interview, Nov. 12, 2007.
10. Sarah Truscott, Journal, summary for July 1965.
11. Ibid., summary for Aug. 1965.
12. Ibid., summary for Aug., Sept. 1965, entry for Sept. 7, 1965.
13. Ibid., Sept. 11, 12, 1965; LKT Army Personnel File, C. H. Meade, adjutant general, "Report of Casualty," Sept. 14, 1965.
14. Sarah Truscott, Journal, Sept. 12, 13, 1965.
15. George C. Marshall Library and Museum, Truscott Photograph Collection, Truscott funeral procession, Sept. 15, 1965; Sarah Truscott, Journal, Sept. 15, 1965; Lang, "Close-up—Lucian King Truscott," 98; Lucian K. Truscott IV interview, Oct. 7, 2009.
16. Truscott Photograph Collection, Truscott funeral background, Sept. 15, 1965; Truscott, *Twilight of the U.S. Cavalry*, 111.
17. Sarah Truscott, Journal, Sept. 15, 1945.
18. Author's visit to Stonewall Jackson Monument, Fredericksburg and Spotsylvania County Battlefields Memorial National Military Park, Sept. 28, 2009; author's visit to General Truscott's grave, Arlington National Cemetery, Sept. 27, 2009.

Afterword

1. Author's attendance at ceremony in Chatfield, Tex., Jan. 12, 2012; Truscott, *Twilight of the Cavalry*, xv; transcript of James M. Wilson, Jr., interview by Charles Stuart Kennedy, Mar. 31, 1999, Foreign Affairs Oral History Collection, Association for Diplomatic Studies and Training, Library of Congress, (also available online, http://www.loc.gov/item/mfdipbib001275/); Wilson obituary, *Washington Post*, Nov. 21, 2009.
2. Graeme Bruce, e-mail message to author, Nov. 19, 2011.
3. Graham and Bidwell, *Tug of War*, 329.

Bibliography

Unpublished Sources

Luce, Clare Boothe. Collected Papers. Library of Congress, Washington, D.C.

Truscott, Lucian K. Jr. Central Intelligence Agency Personnel File. CIA Headquarters, Langley, Va.

———. Papers. George C. Marshall Foundation Research Library, Lexington, Va.

———. Professional résumé and biographical data. Private collection of Susan Truscott.

———. U.S. Army Personnel File. National Personnel Records Center, St. Louis, Mo.

Truscott, Patsy. Journal. Private collection of Susan Truscott. Courtesy of James Truscott.

Truscott, Sarah. Journal. Private collections of Susan, Mary, and Debbie Truscott. Courtesy of James Truscott.

Truscott Family Papers. Private collections of Susan, Mary, Debbie, and James Truscott, courtesy of James Truscott. Copies of some materials are in the author's possession.

Wilson, James M., Jr., interview by Charles Stuart Kennedy, March 31, 1999. Foreign Affairs Oral History Collection, Association for Diplomatic Studies and Training, Library of Congress. www.loc.gov/item/mfdipbib001275/, accessed December 4, 2008.

Interviews by Author

Hanrahan, Bill (pseudonym per his request), January 11, 2007, Oro Valley, Ariz.

Phillippi, Bill, January 30, 2007, Oro Valley, Ariz.

Phillippi, Vicky, December 1, 2010, and December 3, 2011, Oro Valley, Ariz.

Truscott, Debbie, September 14, 2009, Stafford, Va.

Truscott, Lt. Col. James J., USAF (Ret.), and Helen Truscott, November 12, 2007, San Antonio, Tex.

Truscott, Lucian K., IV, October 7, 2009, Franklin, Tenn.

Truscott, Mary, August 11, 2008, Bellevue, Wash.

Truscott, Susan, September 24, 2006, and ongoing conversations through July 2013, Mountlake Terrace, Wash.

Magazines and Newspapers

AP Wire Photo, *Bitter Wartime Foes in Warm Meeting. Corsicana (Tex.) Daily Sun*, June 4, 1954.

Lang, Will. "Close-up—Lucian King Truscott, Jr.: A Tough U.S. General, Once an Oklahoma Schoolmaster, Wants to be Provost Marshal of Berlin." *Life*, October 2, 1944.

Marshall, S. L. A. Review of *Command Missions*, by Lucian K. Truscott, Jr. *Saturday Review*, April 17, 1954.

McCormick, Anne O'Hare. "The Italian Ordeal Surprises Members of Congess." *New York Times*, December 22, 1944.

"Mother of Officer at Garrison Dies" (obituary for Dr. Lucian Truscott). *Leavenworth (Kans.) Times*, August 8, 1938.

Sevareid, Eric. "The Price We Pay in Italy." *The Nation*, December 9, 1944.

Sullivan, Patricia. "Diplomat Set up State's Human Rights Program" (obituary for James M. Wilson, Jr.). *Washington Post*, November 21, 2009.

Books

Adams, Henry, et al. *World War II: Italy at War*. Alexandria, Va.: Time-Life Books, 1982.

Ambrose, Stephen E. *Citizen Soldiers: The U.S. Army from the Normandy Beaches to the Bulge to the Surrender of Germany*. New York: Simon & Schuster, 1997.

———. *Duty, Honor, Country: A History of West Point*. Baltimore: Johns Hopkins University Press, 1966. Paperback edition, 1999.

Anderson, Charles R. *Guadalcanal: The U.S. Army Campaigns of World War II*. CMH Publication 72-8. Washington, D.C.: U.S. Army Center for Military History, 1972.

Asahina, Robert. *Just Americans: How Japanese Americans Won a War at Home and Abroad*. New York: Gotham, 2006.

Atkinson, Rick. *An Army at Dawn: The War in North Africa, 1942–1943*. New York: Henry Holt, 2002.

Barzini, Luigi. *The Italians*. New York: Simon and Schuster, 1964. New York: Touchstone, 1996.

Belden, Jack. *Still Time to Die*. New York: Harper and Brothers, 1975.

Bellafaire, Judith A. *The Army Nurse Corps*. CMH Publication 72-14. Washington, D.C.: U.S. Army Center for Military History, 1972.

Black, Robert W. *Rangers in World War II*. New York: Ballantine, 2002.

Blumenson, Martin. *Anzio: The Gamble That Failed*. New York: Cooper Square, 1963. Paperback edition, 2001.

———. *Mark Clark: The Last of the Great World War II Commanders*. New York: Congdon and Weed, 1984.

———. *Patton: The Man behind the Legend: 1885–1945*. New York: Morrow, 1985. New York: Berkeley, 1987.

———. *The Patton Papers: 1885–1940*. Boston: Houghton Mifflin, 1972.

———. *The Patton Papers: 1940–1945*. Boston: Houghton Mifflin, 1974.

Bradley, Omar, and Clay Blair. *A General's Life: An Autobiography by General of the Army Omar Bradley*. New York: Simon and Schuster, 1983.

Buckley, Gail, *American Patriots: The Story of Blacks in the Military from the Revolution to Desert Storm*. New York: Random House, 2001.

Buell, Hal, et al. *World War II Album: The Complete Chronicles of the World's Greatest Conflict*. New York: Black Dog and Leventhal, 2002.

Butcher, Harry C. *My Three Years with Eisenhower*. New York: Simon and Schuster, 1946.

Carroll, Andrew, ed. *War Letters: Extraordinary Correspondence from American Wars*. New York: Scribner, 2001.

Churchill, Winston S. *The Second World War: The Hinge of Fate*. Boston: Houghton Mifflin, 1950.

Clark, Lloyd. *Anzio: Italy and the Battle for Rome, 1944*. New York: Grove, 2006.

Clarke, Jeffrey J. *Southern France: The U.S. Army Campaigns of World War II*. CMH Publication 72-31. Washington, D.C.: U.S. Army Center of Military History, 1972.

Clarke, Jeffrey J., and Robert Ross Smith. *Riviera to the Rhine*. Washington D.C.: U.S. Army of Center of Military History, 1993.

Clausewitz, Carl von. *On War*. 1832. Translated, 1908. London: Pelican Classics, 1982.

Coffman, Edward M. *The Regulars: The American Army, 1898–1941*. Cambridge, Mass.: Belknap Press of Harvard University Press, 2004.

Corson, William R. *The Armies of Ignorance: The Rise of the American Intelligence Empire*. New York: Dial, 1977.

Davenport, B. T. *Soldiering at Marfa, Texas, 1911–1945*. Kearney, Neb.: Morris, 1997.

Deighton, Len. *Blitzkrieg: From the Rise of Hitler to the Fall of Dunkirk*. London: Jonathan Cape. 1979. New York: Ballantine, 1982.

D'Este, Carlo. *Bitter Victory: The Battle for Sicily, 1943*. New York: Dutton, 1988.

———. *Eisenhower: A Soldier's Life*. New York: Henry Holt, 2002.

———. *Fatal Decision: Anzio and the Battle for Rome*. New York: HarperPerennial, 1992.

———. *Patton: A Genius for War*. New York: HarperPerennial, 1996.

———. *World War II in the Mediterranean: 1942–1945*. Chapel Hill: Algonquin Books, 1990.

Dickson, Paul, and Thomas B. Allen. *The Bonus Army: An American Epic*. New York: Walker, 2004. Paperback edition, 2006.

Dole, Bob. *A Soldier's Story: A Memoir*. New York: HarperCollins, 2005.

Eisenhower, Dwight D. *Crusade in Europe: A Personal Account of World War II*. New York: Doubleday, 1948.

Eisenhower, John S. D. *Intervention! The United States and the Mexican Revolution: 1913–1917*. New York: Norton, 1995.

Essin, Emmett M. *Shavetails & Bell Sharps: The History of the U.S. Army Mule*. Lincoln: University of Nebraska Press, Bison Books, 2000.

Farago, Ladislas. *Patton: Ordeal and Triumph*. New York: Ivan Obolensky, 1963.

Feuer, A. B. *Packs On! Memoirs of the 10th Mountain Division in World War II*. Westport, Conn.: Praeger, 2004. Mechanicsburg, Penn.: Stackpole, 2006.

Flanagan, Edward M., Jr. *Airborne: A Combat History of the American Airborne Forces*. New York: Random House, 2003. New York: Ballantine, 2004.

Gavin, James M. *On to Berlin: A Fighting General's True Story of Airborne Combat in World War II*. New York: Viking, 1978. New York: Bantam, 1981.

Gawne, Jonathan, *Finding Your Father's War: A Practical Guide to Researching and Understanding Service in the World War II Army*. Philadelphia: Casemate, 2006.

Gibran, Daniel K. *The 92nd Division and the Italian Campaign in World War II*. Jefferson, N.C.: McFarland, 2001.

Graham, Dominick, and Shelford Bidwell. *Tug of War: The Battle for Italy, 1943–1945*. New York: St. Martin's, 1986.

Hargrove, Hondon B. *Buffalo Soldiers in Italy: Black Soldiers in World War II*. Jefferson, N.C.: McFarland, 1985.

Harmon, E. N., Milton MacKaye, and William Ross MacKaye. *Combat Commander: Autobiography of a Soldier*. Upper Saddle River, N.J.: Prentice Hall, 1970.

Heefner, Wilson A. *Dogface Soldier: The Life of General Lucian Truscott Jr.* Columbia: University of Missouri Press, 2010.

Herr, John K., and Edward S. Wallace. *The Story of the U.S. Cavalry: 1775–1942*. Boston: Little, Brown, 1953. New York: Bonanza Book, 1984.

Hynes, Samuel, et al. *Reporting World War II: Part Two: American Journalism, 1944–1946*. New York: Library of America, 1995.

Inouye, Daniel K., with Lawrence Elliott. *Journey to Washington*. Englewood Cliffs, N.J.: Prentice Hall, 1967.

Jenkins, McKay. *The Last Ridge: The Epic Story of America's First Mountain Soldiers and the Assault on Hitler's Europe*. New York: Random House, 2003. Paperback edition, 2004.

Johnson, Swafford. *History of the U.S. Cavalry*. Greenwich, Conn.: Brompton, 1985. New York: Smithmark, 1994.

Kesselring, Albert. *The Memoirs of Field-Marshal Kesselring*. Bonn: Athenaum, 1953. London: Greenhill, 2007.

Krebs, Ronald R. *Dueling Visions: U.S. Strategy toward Eastern Europe under Eisenhower*. College Station: Texas A&M University Press, 2001.

Lawrenson, Helen. *Stranger at the Party: A Memoir*. New York: Random House, 1972.

Manchester, William. *American Caesar: Douglas MacArthur, 1880–1964*. Boston: Little, Brown, 1978.

Martin, Ralph G. *Henry & Clare: An Intimate Portrait of the Luces*. New York: Putnam's Sons, 1991.

Matsuo, Dorothy. *Boyhood to War: History and Anecdotes of the 442nd RCT*. Honolulu: Mutual Publishing, 1992.
Mauldin, Bill. *The Brass Ring*. New York: W. W. Norton, 1971.
———. *Up Front*. New York: Henry Holt, 1944.
MacDonald, Charles B. *The Mighty Endeavor: The American War in Europe*. New York: Quill, 1986. New York: Da Capo, 1992.
Mitcham, Samuel W., Jr., and Friedrich von Stauffenberg. *The Battle of Sicily: How the Allies Lost Their Chance for Total Victory*. New York: Orion, 1991.
Monahan, Evelyn M., and Rosemary Neidel-Greenlee. *And If I Perish: Frontline U.S. Army Nurses in World War II*. New York: Knopf, 2003.
Montgomery, Sir Bernard Law. *The Memoirs of Field-Marshal The Viscount Montgomery of Alamein, K. G.* [New York]: New American Library, 1959.
Morehouse, Maggi M. *Fighting in the Jim Crow Army: Black Men and Women Remember World War II*. Lanham, Md.: Rowman and Littlefield, 2000.
Morison, Samuel Eliot. *History of United States Naval Operations in World War II, Volume 9, Sicily-Salerno-Anzio: January 1943–June 1944*. Boston: Little, Brown, 1984.
Morris, Sylvia Jukes. *Rage for Fame: The Ascent of Clare Boothe Luce*. New York: Random House, 1997.
Mosley, Leonard. *Marshall: Hero for Our Times*. New York: Hearst Books, 1982.
Murphy, Audie. *To Hell and Back*. New York: Holt, Rinehart, and Winston, 1949.
Murphy, David E., Sergei A. Kondrashev, and George Bailey. *Battleground Berlin: CIA vs. KGB in the Cold War*. New Haven, Conn.: Yale University Press, 1997.
Nixon, Richard. *Six Crises*. New York: Simon and Schuster, 1962. New York: Touchstone, 1990.
O'Donnell, Patrick K. *Beyond Valor: World War II's Rangers and Airborne Veterans Reveal the Heart of Combat*. New York: Simon and Schuster, 2001.
Patton, George S. *War As I Knew It*. Boston: Houghton Mifflin, 1947. Paperback edition, 1995.
Patton, Robert H. *The Pattons: A Personal History of an American Family*. New York: Crown, 1994. Washington, D.C.: Brassey's, 2004.
Poole, Robert M. *On Hallowed Ground: The Story of Arlington National Cemetery*. New York: Walker, 2009.
Pyle, Ernie. *Brave Men*. New York: Henry Holt, 1943, 1944.
Ratti, Fabio, et al. *Sicily: Eyewitness Travel Guides*. New York: DK Publishing, 2005.
Ricks, Thomas E. *The Generals: American Military Command from World War II to Today*. New York: Penguin Books, 2012.
Ryan, Cornelius. *A Bridge Too Far*. New York: Simon and Schuster, 1974.
Sevareid, Eric. *Not So Wild a Dream*. New York: Alfred A. Knopf, 1946.

Sheehan, Fred. *Anzio: Epic of Bravery*. Norman: University of Oklahoma Press, 1964. Paperback edition, 1994.

Shelton, Peter. *Climb to Conquer*. New York: Scribner, 2003.

Sulzberger, Arthur O., Jr. *The New York Times Page One: 1851–2001*. New York: Galahad Books, 2001.

Steinbeck, John. *Once There Was a War*. New York: Viking, 1958. New York: Bantam Books, 1960.

Stockton, Bayard. *Flawed Patriot: The Rise and Fall of CIA Legend Bill Harvey:* Washington, D.C.: Potomac Books, 2006.

Trento, Joseph J. *The Secret History of the CIA*. Roseville, Calif.: Forum, 2001.

Truscott, Lucian K., Jr. *Command Missions: A Personal Story*. New York: E. P. Dutton, 1954.

———. *The Twilight of the U.S. Cavalry: Life in the Old Army, 1917–1942*. Edited by Lucian K. Truscott III. Lawrence: University Press of Kansas, 1989.

Truscott, Mary R. *Brats: Children of the American Military Speak Out*. New York: Dutton, 1989.

Wallace, Robert, et al. *World War II: The Italian Campaign*. Chicago: Time-Life Books, 1981.

Watkins, T. H. *The Hungry Years: A Narrative History of the Great Depression in America*. New York: Holt, 1999. Paperback edition, 2000.

Weiner, Tim. *Legacy of Ashes: The History of the CIA*. New York: Anchor Books, 2008.

Whiting, Charles. *Hero: The Life and Death of Audie Murphy*. Chelsea, Mich.: Scarborough House, 1990. New York: Jove Books, 1991.

Zaloga, Steven J. *Anzio 1944: The Beleaguered Beachhead*. Oxford, U.K.: Osprey, 2005.

Index

Page numbers in *italics* refer to illustrations.